D1002467

Renegades

Studies in Canadian Military History

The Canadian War Museum, Canada's national museum of military history, has a threefold mandate: to remember, to preserve, and to educate. It does so through an interlocking and mutually supporting combination of exhibitions, public programs, and electronic outreach. Military history, military historical scholarship, and the ways in which Canadians see and understand themselves have always been closely intertwined. Studies in Canadian Military History builds on a record of success in forging those links by regular and innovative contributions based on the best contemporary scholarship. Published by UBC Press in association with the Museum, the series especially encourages the work of new generations of scholars and the investigation of important gaps in the existing historiography, pursuits not always well served by traditional sources of academic support. The results produced feed immediately into future exhibitions, programs, and outreach efforts by the Canadian War Museum. It is a modest goal that they feed into a deeper understanding of our nation's common past as well.

John Griffith Armstrong, *The Halifax Explosion and the Royal Canadian Navy: Inquiry and Intrigue*

Andrew Richter, *Avoiding Armageddon: Canadian Military Strategy and Nuclear Weapons, 1950-63*

William Johnston, *A War of Patrols: Canadian Army Operations in Korea*

Julian Gwyn, *Frigates and Foremasts: The North American Squadron in Nova Scotia Waters, 1745-1815*

Jeffrey A. Keshen, *Saints, Sinners, and Soldiers: Canada's Second World War*

Desmond Morton, *Fight or Pay: Soldiers' Families in the Great War*

Douglas E. Delaney, *The Soldiers' General: Bert Hoffmeister at War*

Michael Whitby, ed., *Commanding Canadians: The Second World War Diaries of A.F.C. Layard*

Martin Auger, *Prisoners of the Home Front: German POWs and "Enemy Aliens" in Southern Quebec, 1940-46*

Tim Cook, *Clio's Warriors: Canadian Historians and the Writing of the World Wars*

Serge Marc Durflinger, *Fighting from Home: The Second World War in Verdun, Quebec*

Richard O. Mayne, *Betrayed: Scandal, Politics, and Canadian Naval Leadership*

P. Whitney Lackenbauer, *Battle Grounds: The Canadian Military and Aboriginal Lands*

Cynthia Toman, *An Officer and a Lady: Canadian Military Nursing and the Second World War*

Michael Petrou

Renegades
Canadians in the Spanish Civil War

UBCPress · Vancouver · Toronto

17 16 15 14 13 12 11 10 09 08   5 4 3 2 1

Printed in Canada on ancient-forest-free paper (100% post-consumer recycled) that is processed chlorine- and acid-free, with vegetable-based inks.

Library and Archives Canada Cataloguing in Publication

Petrou, Michael, 1974-
   Renegades : Canadians in the Spanish Civil War / Michael Petrou.

(Studies in Canadian military history, ISSN 1499-6251)
Includes bibliographical references and index.
ISBN 978-0-7748-1417-1 (bound); ISBN 978-0-7748-1418-8 (pbk.)

   1. Spain – History – Civil War, 1936-1939 – Participation, Canadian. I. Title.
II. Series.

DP269.47.C2P48 2008   946.081   C2008-900086-2

Canadä

UBC Press gratefully acknowledges the financial support for our publishing program of the Government of Canada through the Book Publishing Industry Development Program (BPIDP), and of the Canada Council for the Arts, and the British Columbia Arts Council.

This book has been published with the help of a grant from the Canadian Federation for the Humanities and Social Sciences, through the Aid to Scholarly Publications Programme, using funds provided by the Social Sciences and Humanities Research Council of Canada.

Publication of this book has been financially supported by the Canadian War Museum. The author and publisher also acknowledge the financial assistance of the Faculty of Health Sciences, University of Ottawa.

Printed and bound in Canada by Friesens
Set in Fairfield and ITC Franklin Gothic by Blakeley
Copy editor: Judy Phillips
Proofreader: Jim Leahy
Cartographer: Eric Leinberger
Indexer: Patricia Buchanan

UBC Press
The University of British Columbia
2029 West Mall
Vancouver, BC V6T 1Z2
604.822.5959 / Fax 604.822.6083
www.ubcpress.ca

Spain

When the bare branch responds to leaf and light
Remember them: it is for this they fight.
It is for haze-swept hills and the green thrust
Of pine, that they lie choked with battle dust.

You who hold beauty at your finger-tips
Hold it because the splintering gunshot rips
Between your comrades' eyes; hold it across
Their bodies' barricade of blood and loss.

You who live quietly in sunlit space
Reading The Herald after morning grace
Can count peace dear, when it has driven
Your sons to struggle for this grim, new heaven.

Dorothy Livesay

Contents

Maps and Illustrations

Preface: Spanish Tinderbox

Spain, on the eve of its civil war of 1936 to 1939, was a country plagued by unsustainable divisions. The modernizing reforms that had swept much of Europe passed over Spain, leaving a country that was conservative, backward, and home to growing unrest among the poor and those who sought to break down the power of the military, the landed nobility, and the Catholic Church. In 1931, these tensions forced the abdication of King Alfonso XIII and the restoration of democracy in the form of the Second Republic. The new left-leaning government embarked on a series of ambitious measures to secularize the country and curb the power of wealthy landowners. This led to fury from conservatives, and also disillusionment from many rural peasants, who remained mired in poverty. A right-wing coalition therefore triumphed in the elections of 1933. Factions among the Spanish left tried to launch a nationwide revolutionary strike the following year. They were most successful in the northern coal-mining region of Asturias, where the strike morphed into a military uprising. Miners held out for two weeks before they were bombed and shelled into submission and overrun by government forces. The uprising led to accusations from the right that their opponents on the left respected the electoral process only when they were successful.

The left, however, did learn the lessons of democracy. It formed a broad coalition of socialists, liberals, Catalan nationalists, and anarchists who called themselves the Popular Front to contest the 1936 elections. The Popular Front defeated a right-wing coalition known as the National Front, and in May 1936 Manuel Azaña was elected president of the Republic. By this time, however, the divisions within Spain were irreconcilable and conflict was moving beyond the political arena. Churches were torched, and high-profile assassinations shook the country.

Spain's military elite began planning a coup to depose their country's elected government. It was launched, by Francisco Franco and other generals, on the night of 17 July 1936, with a revolt by the colonial army in Morocco. The rebellion spread to mainland Spain the following day. It was, however, not totally successful. Some military garrisons remained loyal to the Republic; others that rebelled were defeated by informal citizen militias. Almost immediately, Spain was divided into regions controlled by forces loyal to the insurgents and those that stood with the government. The rebels were victorious in much of northwestern Spain. Crucially, however, the Basque and Asturian regions remained loyal to the Republic. Although traditional and fiercely Catholic, the Basques – like the Catalans – sought greater autonomy and supported the government because it promised them exactly this. The Republic held most of eastern Spain, including its two greatest cities, Barcelona and the country's capital, Madrid. Both sides committed widespread atrocities against real and imagined political opponents. These acts hardened divisions within Spain.

Those who supported the coup feared the changes underway in their country and fought to preserve the old order and their privileged positions in it. Their coalition included monarchists, conservatives, outright fascists, and wealthy landowners.

Those who opposed the rebellion included socialists, anarchists, regional nationalists, liberal democrats, and communists. Their unlikely alliance would be strained – sometimes to the breaking point – during the course of the war. At issue was not their opposition to fascism or to Franco's rebellion but, rather, contrary ideas about how the war should be fought and the kind of country they wanted Spain to become. Some fought for regional autonomy and for their rights as Basques or Catalans. Some fought for communism, some fought for socialism, some fought for an anarchist revolution, and some fought for a traditional liberal democracy. These competing visions were reconciled – or at least accommodated – for much of the war. But tensions among those who fought together in Spain also erupted into episodes of violence.[1]

Some of those who fought for the rebels, or for the government, also did so because of an accident of geography. The tragic reality of a civil war is that many will find themselves trapped in what they consider to be enemy territory.

Facing a probable defeat in the early days of the war, the Spanish rebels requested and received assistance from Adolf Hitler to transport the crack Army of Africa, including Spain's foreign legion, across the Strait of Gibraltar to southern Spain, from where their columns began a seemingly unstoppable offensive north.

Hitler and his fellow dictator Benito Mussolini in Italy would later provide Franco with tanks, artillery, planes, pilots, instructors, and tens of thousands of troops. Germany's contribution amounted to some six hundred planes, two hundred tanks, highly effective artillery pieces, and sixteen thousand men, including civilian instructors.[2] Spain functioned as a testing ground for Hitler's incipient war machine and was also something of a secret playground for the young pilots of Germany's Condor Legion. Adolf Galand, a German pilot, recalled that between 1936 and 1939 a colleague who had disappeared for six months might suddenly show up again in Germany "in high spirits, with a suntan and having bought himself a new car" and confide to his friends about his Spanish adventures.[3]

Benito Mussolini, motivated by ideological affinity with Franco as well as grandiose national vanity, sent 75,000 soldiers and airmen, 800 artillery pieces, 660 aircraft, 150 tanks, as well as aircraft motors, bombs, ammunition, rifles, and almost 7,660 motor vehicles. Italian airmen were extremely active in bombing raids and in aerial combat; Italian warships and submarines were also engaged in the war. But Italy's intervention was not as pleasing for those who took part as it was for the Germans. Italian troops were mauled on the battlefield, with more than 4,000 killed over the course of the war. Italy also lost perhaps as much as 25 percent of the effective military equipment that it had sent to Spain.[4]

Franco's soldiers included some seventy-five thousand Moroccan Moors from Spain's colony in North Africa. These capable troops were used to great effect during Franco's advance north from the Strait of Gibraltar and, along with his German and Italian allies, would prove crucial to his ultimate success in the war. Smaller contingents, notably soldiers from Portugal and private volunteers from Ireland, also fought for the rebels, though their support was not decisive. Two Canadians are known to have fought with Franco. Warde Harry Phalen volunteered as a pilot but was soon back in Canada and charged with assaulting a taxi driver.[5] The second man, "Tug" Wilson, deserted a British navy vessel to join the Spanish Foreign Legion and subsequently deserted again, surreptitiously leaving the country with the Irish volunteers for Franco.[6]

The Spanish government also sought help from abroad. The Republic, however, was barred from buying weapons on the open market by an arms embargo imposed by the great powers. Nominally designed to prevent Spain's civil war from spreading, the Non-Intervention Agreement placed Spain's elected government on equal footing with the rebels leading a coup d'état. The agreement itself was a chimera designed to give the international community the veneer of neutrality. But the blockade still severely restricted the Spanish government's ability to defend itself. Mexico flouted the agreement and sold Spain rifles, ammunition, and trucks, though much of the equipment was of poor quality.[7] France also supplied equipment and planes, and the Republic was able to obtain weapons from international arms dealers. Spain's biggest and most reliable supplier was the Soviet Union, which sold Spain a thousand aircraft and nine hundred tanks, as well as ammunition, fuel, artillery, and trucks.[8] Soviet personnel in Spain included pilots, tank drivers, and instructors – and also military advisors and intelligence agents who were able to pressure and influence the Spanish government and military because of the aid they brought with them. The size and strength of the Spanish Communist Party would grow substantially during the course of the war.

Soviet leaders might have sympathized with the left-leaning Spanish government, but their support for Spain was also motivated by Russian security concerns. When the Spanish Civil War began, the Soviet Union was following a policy of rapprochement with the Western democracies against the growing powers of Nazi Germany and Fascist Italy. Fearing an attack from Germany, the Soviet Union entered the League of Nations in 1934, and in 1935 concluded a pact with France. Moscow instructed foreign communist parties to pursue a popular front strategy, seeking alliances with "progressive" or anti-fascist movements in their own countries, even those composed of the so-called liberal bourgeoisie. The only anti-fascists whom communists were instructed to shun were Trotskyists – a term that referred to followers of Stalin's former rival and nemesis Leon Trotsky, but which was a label communists affixed to almost anyone suspected of opposition to their party.

After hoping for more than a decade to export socialist revolution, the Communist International, or Comintern, now postponed this goal and concentrated on protecting the Soviet Union. Soviet dictator Joseph Stalin feared that a nationalist victory in Spain would surround the Soviet Union's ally France on three sides with potentially hostile neighbours, making it easier for an emboldened Germany to attack Russia without worrying about a French strike from the west.[9] These concerns were articulated at a 3 November 1936 meeting between Ivan Maisky, the Soviet ambassador to London, and British foreign secretary Anthony Eden. Eden reported that Maisky told him that the Soviet government was convinced that if General Franco were to win, "the encouragement given to Germany and Italy would be such as to bring nearer the day when another active aggression would be committed – this time perhaps in central or eastern Europe. That was a state of affairs that Russia wished at all costs to avoid and that was her main reason for wishing the Spanish government to win in this civil strife."[10] Laurence Collier, head of the Northern Department at the Foreign Office, accepted Maisky's account as "substantially accurate."[11]

The Soviets, however, did not commit sufficient troops and materiel to guarantee a quick victory. They were concerned that a victorious Spanish Republic, especially one explicitly committed to socialist revolution, might lead to a wider European conflict, with France and Britain neutral or possibly even aligned against Russia. Stalin wanted to avoid altering the international balance of power and alienating France and Britain while his armies were unprepared for war. Instead, he hoped to prolong the war in Spain, bog down Hitler far from Russia's borders, and keep the Spanish Republic alive for as long as possible while the Soviet Union rearmed and prepared for an inevitable confrontation with Nazi Germany.[12]

The Soviet Union, through the Communist International and national communist parties around the world, was also responsible for the recruitment and organization of forty thousand international volunteers, who fought in

Spain on the side of the Spanish government. These volunteers, known as the International Brigades, included the vast majority of the Canadians who took part in the Spanish Civil War. Shortly after hostilities began in Spain, it became clear that there was a desire among sufficient numbers of leftists and democrats around the world to physically confront fascism. Unorganized volunteers intent on fighting had been arriving in Spain since the war began. The Soviet Union saw an opportunity to capitalize on popular sentiment and seized it. The International Brigades epitomized the Soviet ideal of a broad, anti-fascist popular front. Built on a communist foundation, but with wider leftist and even mainstream support, the brigades were a stirring and tangible symbol of global support for an anti-fascist cause that was not explicitly linked to the Soviet Union. The Spanish government, though initially reluctant, accepted its formation in October 1936, recognizing both the military and propaganda value of the international volunteers, and the benefits of Soviet military aid, which would not have been so forthcoming had the Republic rejected the brigades.

The International Brigades made their first appearance as a fighting force in November 1936, as rebel columns began their assault on Madrid. The Spanish capital took on enormous symbolic importance around the world for those who believed that Spain was the centre of a global showdown between fascism and freedom. The city was expected to fall quickly. But pro-government militias and civilians, poorly armed and desperate, kept the attacking rebels at bay under banners that read *No Pasarán* – "They shall not pass." Madrid's defenders were joined by mostly German and Italian volunteers, plus some British, French, and Polish. No Canadians were yet in their ranks; they would arrive within months. But already the Canadian doctor Norman Bethune was at work in the besieged city, bringing blood to wounded soldiers and civilians. Together, the city's defenders stopped the nationalist advance on Madrid.

The Spanish capital would remain beyond the reach of Franco until the final days of the war, in March 1939. By then the Spanish Republic was defeated and in ruins. Hundreds of thousands of refugees were streaming toward France or to Spanish ports, hoping – usually in vain – that they would be evacuated before Franco's troops caught up with them.

Their fear was justified; tens of thousands of suspected republican supporters and soldiers were imprisoned, sentenced to forced labour, and executed in bloody purges after Franco's victory. The international volunteers who had survived the previous three years had all left Spain by this time. Thousands of Germans, Italians, and Hungarians, who knew they would face prison or worse in their home countries, stayed in France, where many were interned in concentration camps. Volunteers from Canada, the United States, and Britain, those with homes to which they could safely return, did so.

War, however, would soon find these men, as it would engulf the world.

The Second World War, a conflict many internationals in Spain said they had foreseen and fought to prevent, broke out within months of Franco's victory. The Western democracies, which had turned a blind eye to fascism's rise in Europe, and which had sacrificed Spain in a vain attempt to appease it, belatedly took up arms in their own defence.

Acknowledgments

This book began as a doctoral thesis, which was completed at the University of Oxford in 2006. I wish to acknowledge and thank my supervisor, Tom Buchanan, who was a steady source of insight and guidance. I would like to thank my internal and external thesis examiners, Frances Lannon and Tim Rees. Oxford is a dynamic place to live and study, and this book is no doubt better because of my time spent there. Completing a doctorate at Oxford is also an expensive undertaking. I received financial assistance from the Social Sciences and Humanities Research Council, the British High Commission through the Chevening scholarship program, and Saint Antony's College. I am grateful for it.

I have benefited from the helpfulness, efficiency, and depth of knowledge of archivists and librarians at institutions in Canada, the United States, and Britain. I must thank especially Myron Momryk, an accomplished scholar now retired from Library and Archives Canada, who shared the results of his research on the Canadians who fought in the Spanish Civil War and was always available with advice and expertise. Momryk's not yet published list of the Canadians who fought in Spain, "The Fighting Canucks: Biographical Dictionary of the Canadian Volunteers, Spanish Civil War, 1936-1939," contains information on most of the volunteers and provided the foundation of my own biographical database.

I interviewed – in person, by phone, by email, and by letter – the following Spanish Civil War veterans: Maurice Constant, John Dunlop, Carl Geiser, Joe Juk, Arne Knudson, Fred Kostyk, William Krehm, Jules Paivio, Bob Peters, David Smith, and Jack Vanderlught. All touched me with their kindness and willingness to share their experiences and insights. I am deeply grateful to all of them but must thank especially Maurice Constant (deceased), Fred Kostyk (deceased), William Krehm, Jules Paivio, and their families. I visited all these men. In some cases, they or their families provided me with a meal or a place to stay. Maurice Constant agreed to meet me in the palliative-care wing of a Kitchener-Waterloo hospital. I am also particularly grateful to Joe

Juk, who shared with me his unpublished memoirs.

Another veteran invited me into his home and sat down for a long interview during the course of my doctoral research. However, he later asked not to be identified and so is quoted only anonymously. I thank him also.

Large portions of the archival material I consulted were written in Spanish or French. Much of this, including almost all documents written in French, I translated myself. The more complicated documents, particularly those written in Spanish, were translated by Jacqueline Behrend. Behrend also translated important documents from German to English and from Italian to English. She did professional work, and I owe her my thanks. Christian Claesson, Emma Eckered, and Richard Eklow all translated articles from Swedish to English, which were extremely useful as I researched Kajsa Rothman's relationship with Norman Bethune.

Glenn Wright, in the RCMP's historical section, kindly verified many details pertaining to the RCMP, such as the ranks, divisions, and assignments of RCMP members discussed in the text.

In the course of researching and writing this book, I have been helped in unexpected ways by scores of scholars, historians, researchers, archivists, and others who simply shared an interest in my topic. Some sent files from archives I could not visit; others shared the results of their own research or critiqued my own. Some provided me with a place to present my work. Inevitably, I will inadvertently omit some, but I would like to thank the following people by name: Richard Baxell, Phil Buckner, Stephen Burgess-Whiting, Jim Carmody, Peter Carroll, Erika Gottfried, Larry Hannant, John E. Haynes, James Hopkins, Samuel Karlsson, Judith Keen, John Kraljic, Gail Malmgreen, Paul Philipou, Paul Preston, Sharon Skup, Robert Stradling, and Mark Zuehlke.

UBC Press and the Canadian War Museum, publishers of this book, were wonderful partners, especially for a first-time author. A special thank you is owed to Emily Andrew and Camilla Blakeley at UBC Press, who guided this book through to completion with patience and good advice.

I am grateful to the estate of Dorothy Livesay for permission to reproduce her poem "Spain" as the epigraph to this work.

Finally, I should acknowledge *Maclean's* magazine, in which portions of the chapter on Norman Bethune have previously been published.

This book is dedicated with love and thanks to Janyce McGregor, my wife.

Chronology

April 1931	Second Spanish Republic proclaimed following abdication of King Alfonso XIII
November 1933	Right-wing coalition wins general election
October 1934	Attempted uprising in Asturias
February 1936	Popular Front wins general election
July 1936	Spanish Civil War begins Bill Williamson arrives in Spain
September 1936	William Krehm arrives in Spain
November 1936	Norman Bethune arrives in Madrid International Brigades join defence of the Spanish capital
January 1937	First volunteers from Canada enlist in the International Brigades
February-June 1937	Battle of Jarama
May 1937	Violent clashes in Barcelona between republican advocates and opponents of revolution Norman Bethune leaves Spain

July 1937	Formation of Mackenzie-Papineau Battalion Battle of Brunete
August-October 1937	Battles at Quinto, Belchite, Fuentes de Ebro
December 1937-February 1938	Battles at Teruel and Segura de los Baños
March-April 1938	Retreats
July-November 1938	Battle of the Ebro
September 1938	International Brigades withdrawn from lines
January 1939	Barcelona falls to the nationalists Canadians begin leaving Spain in large numbers
March 1939	Nationalists enter Madrid
April 1939	General Francisco Franco announces that the war is over

Renegades

Spain, July 1936

Introduction

Canadians in the 1930s had little obvious reason to feel as if their own lives and fates were entwined with those of Spaniards. Spain was, after all, far away. Its inhabitants spoke a different language. Few Canadians could trace their origins to Spain or had any relatives there. The two nations might as well have belonged to different worlds. And yet, between 1936 and 1939, almost seventeen hundred Canadians chose to fight in the Spanish Civil War, of whom more than four hundred were killed. Why?

This book is an attempt to answer that question – to establish who were the Canadian men and handful of women who risked their lives in Spain, why they volunteered, and what happened to them during the course of the war and in the years that followed. The focus is on the majority of the Canadians who served in the International Brigades, and several chapters are devoted to the major campaigns in which they fought. But this book also includes chapters on three Canadians – Bill Williamson, William Krehm, and Norman Bethune – who spent significant amounts of time in other units. Their stories are unique and have been given a detailed examination here. Two chapters are devoted to the issues of discipline, morale, and punishments in the International Brigades – a topic on which much of the current historiographical debate on internationals in Spain is centred. The book concludes by examining the reaction of the Canadian government and security services to Canadians fighting in Spain, and to the return of the volunteers in the years, and decades, after the war.

Writing history, especially the history of a war, is always contentious and political. But rarely has a war evoked such passion and produced such intense debate as has the Spanish Civil War. It was a conflict that divided much of the world as it occurred, and today, seven decades later, old and new divisions are fought out in history books, movies, novels, and academic journals.

The battle over how the civil war should be described and remembered began as soon as the guns fell silent. During the almost forty years of Franco's dictatorship, Spanish historians were not permitted to write accounts of the

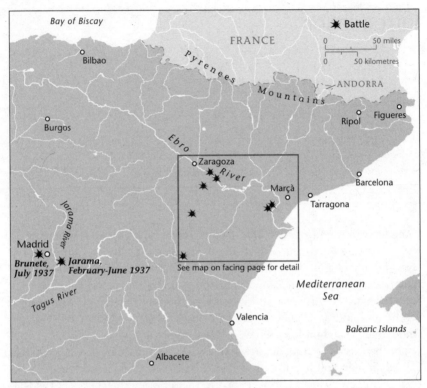

Spanish Civil War military actions involving Canadians

civil war in a way that cast shame on the nationalist cause and on Franco's regime. Francoist historians blamed the war on left wing, usually communist, extremists who drove moderate men in the Spanish military to fight in defence of Spain. Atrocities committed by republicans, especially crimes against the Catholic Church and clergy, were recounted in detail; nationalist crimes were brushed over.[1]

Franco had good reasons to portray his military rebellion as a necessary, glorious, and defensive war beyond a need to legitimize his regime. The Second World War concluded with many observers believing that Franco's fate would soon follow that of his erstwhile comrades Adolf Hitler and Benito Mussolini. But as Berlin fell to the Allies, a new conflict – the Cold War – divided Europe. Franco's regime now found itself on the right side of the Iron Curtain, and it sought to exploit its position as sentinel of the West against communism. Francoist historians played up the dictator's supposed clairvoyance in recognizing the dangers of communism and fighting against it. Franco was rehabilitated in the eyes of the West, and his regime persisted unmolested for decades.

Of course, not all Spaniards who survived the Spanish Civil War were nationalists, and many republicans were equally anxious to write about the

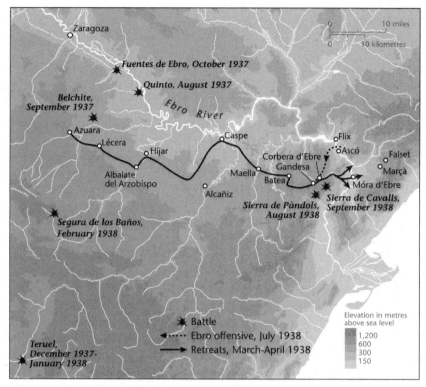

Spanish Civil War military actions involving Canadians, detail

conflict. Those in Spain, for obvious reasons, could not. But thousands of republicans found exile outside the country. They were hampered by their lack of access to Spanish archives. For some, the wounds of war were also too fresh. Unable to agree on the reason for their defeat, exiled republicans continued wartime debates about how the war should have been fought in the first place.

The inevitable result of all this turmoil within Spanish historiography was that many of the most important histories written about the conflict in the decades following the war were published outside Spain.[2] Non-Spanish historians have been criticized for exaggerating the international dimension of the civil war. This criticism is valid – to a point. The Spanish Civil War was deeply rooted in Spain's class and regional divides. However, the conflict was also played out on the international stage. Tens of thousands of foreigners fought on both sides of the civil war, and international diplomacy and intervention played a significant role. The nationalist uprising might have failed at its inception without the assistance of Hitler's air force, which carried Franco's Army of Africa to mainland Spain.

The International Brigades also sharply reflected the Spanish Civil War's global dimensions. For nationalists, the brigades represented the threat of international communism made real. The existence of foreigners fighting on behalf of the Republic provided them with tangible proof that they were fighting to liberate Spain from outsiders and traitors. For their supporters, the brigades were the purest example of international solidarity. Foreigners have always been especially inspired by the International Brigades and have written most of the books about them.[3]

The Canadians, however, have attracted little attention. This is only the fourth book to be written about Canadians in the Spanish Civil War. The first, *The Mackenzie-Papineau Battalion*, by Victor Hoar, was not published until 1969.[4] Hoar's study was hampered by his inability to access key archives in the Soviet Union. But he assembled an impressive collection of material and recollections from surviving veterans; his book is still essential reading for anyone interested in the topic. *Canadian Volunteers: Spain 1936-1939*, by veteran William Beeching, is a celebratory account of Canadians in Spain that lacks much in the way of objective analysis but contains valuable recollections from veterans who were still living in the 1980s.[5] *The Gallant Cause: Canadians in the Spanish Civil War 1936-1939*, by Mark Zuehlke, is written in a style the author describes as literary non-fiction.[6] It is a vivid description of the war from the perspective of those who took part. It lacks footnotes or endnotes. In addition to these books about the entire Canadian contingent in Spain, there is one published memoir, by Douglas Padrig (Pat) Stephens, which is an engaging account of the author's experiences. Greg Lewis recently wrote a short and lively biography of Bob Peters, who emigrated to Canada in 1931 and later fought in Spain. A biography of volunteer Jack Brent, who was born in Cobourg, Ontario, and moved to Scotland as a child, was also published over fifty years ago.[7]

This book builds on the work of previous authors but also breaks significant new ground, in part because of its extensive use of recently declassified documents from the archives of the Communist International in Moscow. These documents reveal tantalizing details about the makeup of the volunteers, how they lived in Spain, the battles they fought, and the influence of the Communist Party among them.[8] The party carefully evaluated the Canadian volunteers on their attitudes and political commitment and kept detailed notes. Many, while described as brave men and good soldiers, were accused of insufficient loyalty to the Communist Party. These evaluations help us to understand what demands were made by the party in Spain and how Canadians responded. Most did so with solid, if irreverent, resolve to continue their fight against fascism. Others rebelled against the party. Faced with high casualty rates and extremely punishing conditions, scores of Canadians tried to flee the war. Documents in the Comintern archives show how these men were treated.

The archives also include sensational material about two Canadians – one famous, one virtually unknown – who were both unjustly accused of espionage in Spain. The first, Dr. Norman Bethune, became romantically embroiled with a woman whom Spanish authorities believed was a spy or a fascist. Bethune left Spain with his life and reputation intact. The second, William Krehm, a young student at the University of Toronto, was accused of spying by the Republican secret police but had no fame to protect him. He spent three months in various Barcelona jails and was lucky to escape Spain alive. I interviewed Krehm at his Toronto home in 2004.

Library and Archives Canada in Ottawa contains several collections pertaining to Canadians in the Spanish Civil War, including extensive files from the RCMP, which closely watched the volunteers during and after the war. I have obtained additional material from the RCMP through government access-to-information requests.[9]

The Canadian Broadcasting Corporation's Radio Archives in Toronto holds dozens of interviews with Canadian veterans of the Spanish Civil War that were recorded in the 1960s but never broadcast. They are an excellent resource.[10]

The Thomas Fisher Rare Books Library at the University of Toronto contains material relating to Methodist minister and communist Albert E. Smith, including a notebook he kept with him while visiting Canadians in Spain. The library has a small amount of good material on radical anti-Stalinist leftist organizations in Toronto during the 1930s, including the League for a Revolutionary Workers' Party, to which William Krehm belonged. William Krehm's personal archives are also an excellent resource. They are located at his home, and it is, of course, necessary to obtain Krehm's permission to consult them.

The Sound Archive of the Imperial War Museum in London contains recordings of interviews with several Canadian veterans who lived in Britain after the war. The museum's Department of Documents holds letters and recollections from Canadian veteran Joseph Turnbull, and its Photograph Archive includes good unpublished material on the Dr. Norman Bethune. The Marx Memorial Library in London, an excellent repository of material on the British in the Spanish Civil War, has useful material on Canadians in the conflict.

Twelve veterans shared their memories and recollections with me as I researched this book. Their insights were invaluable. I have also visited the battlefields where Canadians fought and died, and the villages where they prepared for attacks and recuperated afterward. International Brigades veterans and Spaniards, civilians and former fighters, were there and recalled what they had seen and experienced all those years before. The civil war is never very deep beneath the surface in Spain, and this becomes clear when one walks on the ground where it was fought.

Part 1
Origins of the Volunteers

Who Were the Canadian Volunteers?

On 17 January 1937, Thomas Beckett, a twenty-two-year-old from Moose Jaw, Saskatchewan, wrote a letter from the International Brigades base at Albacete, where he had just arrived, to a girl in Canada named Audrey. Beckett told Audrey that the Spanish girls reminded him of her, and he asked her to try to explain to others back in Canada why he had come to Spain. "You no doubt know why I am here," he wrote. "It is because I am what you do not want me to be, a Communist. Even if I had no political beliefs and was not a Communist, my abhorrence of cruelty, of unnecessary suffering, brutality, greed, and tyranny would lead me to do the same thing ... I feel as though I was talking to you, and would like to go on. I could write pages, but it is necessary for me to close now, for reasons I might tell you some day, if all goes well. As I said in the postcard – 'Wish me luck?'"[1]

All did not go well for young Beckett. In February he joined the predominantly American Abraham Lincoln Battalion, along with up to forty other Canadians.[2] On 15 February, battalion members climbed onto trucks and began a long, cold, and crowded night journey to the village of Morata de Tajuña, just behind the front lines in the Jarama Valley, where republican forces were trying to prevent a nationalist encirclement of Madrid. Around dawn the convoy stopped and the new recruits were told to fire five shots at a nearby hill. The next evening, when the battalion drove toward the front, the drivers of two trucks, including one carrying Thomas Beckett, got lost and veered toward enemy lines. More than twenty men disappeared and were not heard from again.

Beckett's mother, Jessie, and his father, Reid, spent the remainder of the war seeking information about the fate of their lost son. They wrote the Canadian and British governments, asking them to intervene on his behalf. British diplomats accredited to Franco's government made inquiries but were told that Beckett was not in nationalist custody.[3] A friend of a friend even wrote to Franco asking for information about Beckett and received a similar reply saying that the nationalist government had no record of the Canadian in any of its prison camps.[4] Beckett's former comrades corresponded with Beckett's parents as well. "The world would look much brighter to me too, if I knew Tommy to be alive," wrote Larry Ryan from a Hamilton sanatorium. Ryan had been at Jarama the day Beckett disappeared. "But I tried to be honest in my talk to you," Ryan continued, "and I cannot allow my hopes to rise for in my heart I still feel as I told you."[5]

It was not until nearly five decades after the war that Beckett's fate was confirmed. The American veteran Carl Geiser returned to Spain and talked with a former nationalist sergeant who witnessed the two American trucks drive through his army's lines. The first truck rolled onto its side, and the second, following close behind, crashed into it. The uninjured international volunteers took up rifles and remained with the trucks or made a run for it. All were killed but one, who was taken prisoner and presumably shot later, as he does not appear to have survived the war.[6] Thomas Beckett, in the country for barely two weeks, perhaps without ever firing a shot at the fascists he had come to fight, became the first Canadian to die in the Spanish Civil War.

Over the next nineteen months, more than four hundred Canadians in the International Brigades would follow Beckett to their graves in Spain. Of these men, and of those who survived, little was known for decades. The Friends of the Mackenzie-Papineau Battalion, a Communist Party of Canada-affiliated support group, kept file-card records on almost seven hundred volunteers. However, these often amounted to little more than a name, possibly a photograph or listed hometown, and a note about the volunteer's ultimate fate. After the war, the organization recorded that 1,239 Canadians volunteered to fight in Spain, but it did not have detailed biographical information for most of them.

Efforts were made – by veterans and researchers – in the postwar years to compile an accurate roster of the Canadians who fought in Spain, but this was not an easy task. In Spain, volunteers might have anglicized their names or altered them to sound more Spanish. As well, often volunteers fought in a variety of units, sometimes with foreigners from other countries, almost always with Spaniards, making it difficult to immediately identify them. This was especially the case with the Canadians. Most were immigrants and often joined battalions made up of volunteers from their countries of origin. It was not until the international volunteers were pulled from the lines in the autumn of 1938 that all the Canadians were gathered in one place and collectively became known as the Mac-Paps, after the nominally Canadian Mackenzie-Papineau Battalion. But by this time, hundreds had already died and disappeared.

The opening of the Moscow archives made it more feasible to reconstruct the identities of these Canadians. International Brigades officials and party leaders kept meticulous notes, recording biographical details on individual volunteers and reporting on their actions and fates in Spain. Numerous lists were compiled, evaluations were made, letters to and from home were seized and filed. However, the real identities of some volunteers remain obscure even in party and brigade records that were meant to be clear and accurate. In addition to numerous aliases, party names, and nicknames, some volunteers came to Spain having appropriated someone else's identity. American Eugene Cullen, for example, noted that he was in the country on the passport of another comrade.[7] Another American, Israel Goldenberg, was known in Spain as José and travelled with the documents of an American named Joseph Budish.[8] Some American volunteers were listed as Canadians because they served in the Mackenzie-Papineau Battalion, and several Canadian-born volunteers were listed as Poles or Hungarian because they fought in units made up of volunteers from these countries.

Sometimes files on volunteers simply got lost or were misplaced in the normal course of trying to run a bureaucracy in the midst of war. In October 1937, a brigade official paid a visit to Canadian Bob Kerr, who, as head of the Canadian cadre service, was assigned the task of keeping track of all the Canadians in Spain. Most Canadians belonged to the 15th International Brigade. Kerr knew that Canadians were fighting in other units – with the Hungarian Rakosi Battalion, for example, or with the mostly Slavic Dombrowsky. But he did not have accurate records on men who were so widely scattered. Kerry told the official that of the eight hundred Canadians then in Spain, he had no idea where two hundred of them were.[9] Many volunteers were killed or captured before anything could be recorded about them.

Record keeping had improved somewhat by the end of the war. A majority of the Canadian volunteers had a personnel file that has survived in the Comintern archives – although some contain only a scrap of paper with a name scrawled on it. Other files are more detailed and contain evaluations made by party officials and notes about promotions, demotions, hospitalizations, attempts to desert, and punishments. Many Canadians also completed questionnaires during their time in Spain. Questionnaires from the Historical Commission of the International Brigades were given to members of the Mackenzie-Papineau Battalion in August 1937, before most of them had been in action. Other questionnaires, from the International Brigades War Commissariat and from the Communist Party of Spain, were distributed in the spring of 1938, and again in October and December 1938, when the Canadians were awaiting repatriation at Ripoll, in northern Spain. They were asked about their political affiliations, their roles in the labour movement in Canada, why they volunteered, if they had been unemployed or jailed, their impressions of Spain and of their comrades, and what they wanted to do after the war.

Volunteers were not always open and truthful on these questionnaires. Few who deserted and were subsequently jailed recalled the event when asked if they had been punished. Others appear to have been wearily fed up with the lengthy paperwork. Asked to write, "even using a separate sheet if necessary," what they thought of the popular front policy, the International Brigades, or Spanish prime minister Juan Negrín's government, scores of volunteers gave one-word answers: "good," "okay." Some filled their forms with phrases that might have come from a propaganda pamphlet, while others were less verbose but perhaps more honest. One American in the Mackenzie-Papineau Battalion said he had come to Spain for the sunshine. Another, asked what was the most outstanding thing he had noticed since leaving North America, described a recent bowel movement.[10]

I have sifted through these reports, lists, and questionnaires from the Comintern archives and from other sources to construct a database of all the Canadians who fought or served in Spain.[11] An abbreviated version is included as an appendix to this book. The information in the database is not perfect, but it forms the most accurate and complete biographical profile in existence of the Canadians in Spain. It contains the names of 1,681 volunteers, including nine women.[12]

Age

The Canadians who fought in Spain were on average older than their comrades in other countries.[13] In 1937, the year most enlisted, their average age was thirty-two, and their most common ages were thirty-three and thirty-four. More than half were between the ages of thirty and forty, and those aged thirty and over totalled almost two-thirds. The youngest volunteers were sixteen and the eldest fifty-seven.[14]

The Canadian volunteers entered the world at an unlucky time and came of age in the midst of social upheaval. Most were born between 1895 and 1910. Those in Europe and Scandinavia had their youth interrupted by the First World War and the disorder that followed, including civil wars, the Russian Revolution, and other attempted socialist revolutions. Unable to find peace and prosperity in Europe, they emigrated to Canada. The Canadian-born volunteers, though typically younger than those born abroad, also grew up in a time of uncertainty. A few fought in the First World War. Others were born too late to establish themselves in the relative prosperity of the 1920s. They entered adulthood as Canada plunged into the Great Depression of the 1930s.

Marital Status

Choosing to risk one's life in a war is an easier decision for a single man to make than it is for a married man, and the Canadians who fought in Spain were no exception. The Communist Party preferred volunteers without families so that it would not be responsible for widowed wives and orphaned children should its recruits die. Information is available on the marital status of 611 of the Canadian volunteers. Of these, 492 were single when they volunteered to join the war; 103 were married before going to Spain; and a further 6 married during the war. Three were divorced or separated; 6 were widowed, including female nurse Florence Pike; and another was in a common-law marriage.

Fifty-seven Canadian volunteers, including those who were widowed or divorced, had children.

Employment

Volunteers were asked in several questionnaires about the jobs they held before the war. These details emerge in letters, memoirs, and postwar interviews also. Employment data are available for 815 volunteers. Many listed more than one profession, and some might have been trained or had experience in a certain job but were unemployed.

Manual and skilled labourers

Miners	136
Lumberjacks	111
Factory and mill workers (including machinists, steelworkers, etc.)	74
Drivers	59
Mechanics	57
Construction workers (including carpenters, roofers, crane operators, etc.)	56
Farmers and farm workers (including ranchers and cowboys)	42
Sailors	28
Painters	26
Cooks	20
Road and railway workers	20
Hotel, bar, and restaurant workers	17
Blacksmiths	15
Electricians	12
Bakers	7
Barbers	7
Dockworkers	6
Furriers and tanners	5
Plumbers	4
Trappers	4
Fishermen	3
Butchers	2
Firefighters	2
Gardeners	2
Masseurs	2
Prospectors	2
Sports instructors	2
Surveyors	2
Telegraphers and telephone operators	2
Amateur boxer	1
Grocer	1

Horse trainer I
Jockey I
Letter carrier I
Photographer I
Radio technician I
Warehouse worker I
Workers .... IIO

Craftsmen

Shoemakers 13
Tailors and textile workers 13
Upholsterers 2
Cigar maker I
Glassworker I
Gunsmith I
Harness maker I
Jeweller I
Leather cutter I
Locksmith I

Professionals and students

Accountants, bookkeepers, and clerks 23
Writers and journalists 19
Salesmen 15
Nurses, medics, orderlies, and other hospital staff 13
Students 13
Teachers 8
Engineers 6
Doctors (including one likely fraud) 4
Pilots 4
Chemists 3
Musicians 3
Pharmacists 3
Social workers 2
Architect I
Artist I
Businessman I
Laboratory assistant I
Lawyer I
Office worker I
Public servant I
Secretary I

The majority of Canadian volunteers were workers, and many listed themselves simply as such. More than two hundred held punishing jobs in mines and lumber camps. The rest were manual and semi-skilled workers whose work was mostly seasonal or temporary. Few volunteers held steady jobs, and hundreds found work only in relief camps, where they laboured on road crews or make-work projects deep in the woods. Some men optimistically listed themselves as skilled workers even though it appears that their most recent jobs were more manual. Danilo Gabrylyk, for example, said he was a blacksmith but most often worked in lumber camps or on railway crews.

Several volunteers held jobs that are usually associated with higher education or an elevated social status, but these were a notable minority. They included accountants, students, pilots, teachers, chemists, a businessman, and at least one public servant. Seven nurses, including five women, volunteered, as did four doctors – though one of the four was almost certainly a fraud, only posing as a doctor.[15]

The jobs held by volunteers often divide roughly along ethnic lines. All but two Croatian Canadians worked as workers or miners, most often in northern Ontario or Quebec mining towns such as Val d'Or, Timmins, Schumacher, and Kirkland Lake. A disproportionate number of Finns worked as lumberjacks, frequently in Silver Mountain and the lakehead cities of Port Arthur and Fort William. More Jews had skilled jobs, often requiring some training or education, than did volunteers from other ethnic groups. Almost half of all the cooks were Macedonians, usually from Toronto.

Volunteers from other countries were, like those from Canada, predominantly workers. But there were notable differences. The British contingent included a minority of middle- and upper-class volunteers, often writers and intellectuals who at times struggled to fit in with their working-class countrymen.[16] As many as five hundred American volunteers were students or recent graduates.[17] Many were attending or had recently graduated from the City College of New York, a major centre of communist activity. A large number were also Jewish. They made up a close-knit group with comparatively high levels of political training. One Canadian volunteer would later complain that the 15th International Brigade was run by a "clique of New York [Young Communist League] Jews."[18]

Even for an army of workers, the Canadians had led difficult lives. The work they carried out was gruelling and often dangerous. Safety standards in mines were minimal. Cave-ins were frequent and deadly. Few would willingly choose to cut trees during a Canadian winter if alternative work was available. Many of the jobs Canadian volunteers held were seasonal or temporary, forcing the men to continually move in search of employment, travelling on the tops of trains and sleeping on the ground. In the eyes of some of the Canadian volunteers, this set them apart from the Americans with whom they most often served. "Let's put it this way," Louis Tellier later recalled of his

American comrades, "I don't think any of them ever slept out under the stars. I think most of them would starve to death in a grocery store."[19]

One hundred and thirteen Canadian volunteers said in various question-naires, interviews, or letters that they had been unemployed before the war, but the actual number was probably much higher. In December 1938, Edward Cecil-Smith, the top Canadian commander in Spain, addressed the Foreign Cadres Commission of the Spanish Communist Party to discuss alleged problems the party was having with the Canadian volunteers. He said that the Canadians were quite different from their comrades in the 15th International Brigade: "Most of these boys have never had any but the most casual transient kind of a job in their lives ... Neither do they have any homes, having been on the tramp since leaving the school."[20]

Education

The Canadian volunteers by and large lacked the education or professional training that might have helped stave off the worst effects of the Great Depression. Only thirty-two Canadian volunteers are known to have received some form of higher education – either from a university, medical school, or college.[21] This figure includes six volunteers who attended community colleges, one who attended a college of pharmacy, and four who enrolled in medical school. Not all of these men and women graduated. Volunteers with higher education were almost all born in Canada and were often Jewish.

The majority of volunteers, however, received only a rudimentary formal education – attending elementary or, if they were lucky, secondary school. Half the volunteers who did attend secondary school did not finish; many dropped out in their early or mid-teens. Even this basic education was often more than that attained by immigrant volunteers, whose education might have been interrupted by war and revolution. One Finnish Canadian noted that he had been working since he was eight years old.[22]

Criminal Activity

Questionnaires given to Canadian volunteers asked if they had been arrested, faced trial, or had been detained by police before coming Spain. Although the surveys did not reach all the Canadians who volunteered, they nevertheless reveal that a minimum of 105 Canadians had a criminal record of some sort in Canada – or had at least been held in custody by police.

The nature of the offences for which they were charged tell us as much about the official Canadian attitude toward transient unemployed men and political militants in the 1920s and 1930s as they do about the volunteers themselves. Most were charged during protests and confrontations with the police, or for flexibly defined offences such as vagrancy, illegal assembly, soliciting funds without a permit, or hitching a ride on railway wagons – a common means of transport during the 1930s for unemployed men looking for work. A few men were charged with more serious offences. Bert "Yank" Levy was jailed for six years for armed robbery.[23] Frank Whitfield, a Canadian army veteran of the First World War, said he spent three years in the infamous Alcatraz prison, though his name does not appear in prison records.[24] Harry Rushton said he was framed for kidnapping a municipal official during a strike.[25]

There is little to indicate that serious criminals were attracted to joining the International Brigades or were welcomed by its leadership. An unsigned 22 June 1937 report on Fred Walker describes an unrepentant drunkard who was arrested for brawling in the streets with local Spaniards. "This element has a troubled past," the note reads. "He spent three years in prison for burglary and was condemned under the name of Wilson Dan and investigated by the police. He says that to live in Canada it is necessary to take dollars where they are, but he refuses to indicate the crimes that he has committed."[26] Walker was recommended for expulsion and left Spain in January 1938.

Social Organizations and Activities

Communist officials, who wanted to discern the depth of the volunteers' political commitment, asked Canadians about their involvement in unions and community organizations. From surviving questionnaires and reports on several hundred Canadians, it is clear that the majority were involved in unions, ethnic community groups, or labour and unemployment organizations, which were occasionally fronts for or affiliated with the Communist Party.

One of the most important organizations in Canada for future volunteers was the Relief Camp Workers' Union, later called the Relief Project Workers' Union. About 20 percent of all Canadian volunteers had belonged to this group, which organized and agitated on behalf of the hundreds of relief-camp workers who eventually made their way to Spain. Communist Party members easily infiltrated the camps, which were established in the Canadian wilderness during the 1930s to house and provide menial labour for unemployed young men. The camps became hotbeds of militant radicalism. Thomas Aucoin, when asked on a questionnaire how he got involved in the labour movement, responded, "While in relief camps in [British Columbia], Canada."[27] Many other volunteers would have said the same thing.

Future volunteers who were lucky enough to have real jobs joined trade unions in large numbers. The most popular included the Lumber and Sawmill Workers' Union, whose leaders were affiliated with the Communist Party. Miners' unions also attracted numerous future volunteers. The most prominent of these was the Mine, Mill and Smelter Workers' Union. Other volunteers typically joined trade unions relevant to their own profession. More than sixty said they had been involved in strikes and demonstrations.

Ethnic community organizations, many of which were explicitly political, played an important role in organizing immigrants and ethnic minorities, from whose ranks so many future volunteers were drawn. Left-wing Ukrainians became active in the Ukrainian Labour Farmer Temple Association and the Association to Aid the Liberation Movement in Western Ukraine. Konstantin "Mike" Olynyk, a future volunteer, was one of the founding members of the Association for the Defence of Bukovina and Bessarabia.[28] Other eastern European emigrants joined organizations such as the Federation of Russian Canadians, the Maxim Gorky Club, and various left-wing Polish, Hungarian, and Russian clubs. Left-wing Finns established the Finnish Organization of Canada and numerous Finnish sports clubs.

Many of these organizations had their own ethnic-language newspapers and community halls, with networks stretching across the country. The Association to Aid the Liberation Movement in Western Ukraine made contacts with communists in Europe, and its board of directors included known communists such as Peter Arsen (Krawchuk), who had worked in the communist underground in eastern Europe before coming to Canada. By 1932, the organization had seventy-eight branches across Canada and 6,675 members. In 1937, it sponsored a speaking event by Dr. Norman Bethune, who had just returned from Spain to promote the republican cause.[29] The left-wing Ukrainian newspaper *Narodna hazeta* also carried regular reports about the conflict in Spain and Ukrainian volunteers who were arriving there from Europe and North America.[30]

The Communist Party of Canada recruited heavily through these organizations. Some, including the Croatian Fraternal Union and the Ukrainian Labour Farmer Temple Association, they were able to control. Even when the party did not infiltrate the leadership of an ethnic community group, they were often popular places for politically radical immigrants to gather. Joe Juk, a Canadian volunteer from Hungary, first made contact with the Young Communist League through Hungarian organizations in Winnipeg.[31]

Future volunteers also joined organizations that campaigned on behalf of the unemployed, such as the Single Men's Unemployed Association, and the Canadian Labour Defence League – a Communist Party front. Other party fronts included the Friends of the Soviet Union, the Workers' Ex-Servicemen's League, and the League against War and Fascism. They played an important role in the Communist Party's attempts to reach out beyond its traditional radical base. Party official Zack McEwen was candid about the strategy: "We've never made any bones about it that the Communist Party is vitally interested in the promotion of such organizations, because we know that among the social circles in Canada and in other countries there are people ... who are sympathetic to many things, who are devoted advocates of peace, but who wouldn't come near so-called communists with a ten-foot pole. So what are you going to do with those people? You've got to play around and help to create those organizational channels through which they feel they can work."[32]

Hometown

Few Canadian future volunteers lived in the same place for long.[33] They moved frequently in search of work in mining and lumber towns or on prairie farms. Some said they were familiar with dozens of Canadian cities, from Halifax to Vancouver. They usually lived among their working-class compatriots; many also sought homes in towns and cities that contained large numbers of immigrants or established ethnic communities.

Hundreds of volunteers drifted to British Columbia, where winters are mild, the Communist Party was strong, and the labour movement was active. Vancouver held a status among Canadians similar to New York's among Americans as a centre for the politically radicalized, and the surrounding wilderness contained scores of company towns and relief camps full of unemployed and disaffected young men. At least 350 volunteers lived in the province. The majority, almost 300, lived in Vancouver. The remaining volunteers from British Columbia generally lived and worked in interior lumber and mining towns such as Fernie, Kamloops, and Prince George. At least two men lived for a while in Yukon.

Ontario was home to more volunteers than any other province. At least 780 lived there at some point before going to Spain. Toronto, a popular destination for new immigrants, housed more than 300 future volunteers, including almost all the Macedonians and Bulgarians.[34] Ontario's industrial towns in the southwest of the province also attracted future volunteers. At least 47 lived in Hamilton and 42 in Windsor. Outside the heavily populated areas around Lake Ontario, many future volunteers lived in or near northern mining and forestry centres, such as Sudbury and Timmins, which were home to 37 and 32 volunteers respectively. Scores more lived in smaller northern outposts such as Kapuskasing, South Porcupine, and Kirkland Lake. Many of these men were Croatian emigrants. The Ontario settlements that sent the most volunteers besides Toronto, however, were the twin cities of Port Arthur and Fort William, home to at least 119 future volunteers – predominantly Finnish-Canadian lumberjacks.

In Quebec, at least 150 volunteers lived in Montreal, including many of the Jewish volunteers. Outside Montreal, few of the French-Canadian towns or cities in the province sent many men to Spain, though 6 did come from Quebec City. The northern mining towns of Val d'Or, Rouyn, and Noranda, home to many Slavic miners, sent at least 22 volunteers. All told, the province sent approximately 200 volunteers.

About another 200 volunteers came from Manitoba, of whom more than 150 lived in Winnipeg. Many of these men were Ukrainian emigrants or their descendents who settled the Canadian Prairies earlier in the twentieth century. Alberta sent approximately 180 volunteers. Sixty-two came from Edmonton, 41 from Calgary, 26 from Lethbridge, and 16 from Drumheller. These numbers included several Ukrainian Canadians, though many Hungarian volunteers who had not settled in Toronto, Windsor, or Montreal also had found homes in Alberta cities and towns, including Lethbridge, Drumheller, and Edmonton.

Relatively few volunteers came from the Atlantic provinces: 31 in total from Prince Edward Island, Nova Scotia, and New Brunswick. Newfoundland, which had not yet joined Confederation, sent at least one of its sons to Spain. At least 19 volunteers came from Nova Scotia. Five of these men came from Halifax; most of the others lived in Cape Breton mining towns such as New Waterford or Glace Bay, which itself sent 6 volunteers. Given the generally poor economic climate in Atlantic Canada, few immigrants tried to settle there. Almost all the volunteers from the region were born in Canada, and most travelled to other parts of the country in search of work before deciding to fight in Spain.

Military Experience

At least 215 Canadian volunteers had previous military experience. Of those who lived through actual combat, most had fought in the First World War and in the European civil conflicts that followed. One Canadian volunteer, Bert "Yank" Levy, reportedly trained soldiers in Mexico and then fought with Augusto César Sandíno in Nicaragua.[35] Future Canadian commander Edward Cecil-Smith was also rumoured to have fought in Central and South America. These men were the exception, however; the Canadian contingent did not comprise professional soldiers or mercenaries.

Thirty-five volunteers had served in the Canadian army, navy, and air force, at least twenty-three of whom fought in the First World War. Another twenty-nine had been in the Canadian militia or reserve forces. Three men had been members of the Canadian Officers Training Corps at college or university. Twenty-five British-born volunteers were veterans of the British army, navy, or air force, of whom at least seventeen fought in the First World War. Nine Canadian volunteers were members of armed groups in Ireland, usually the Irish Republican Army; another nine had served in the American army, navy, coast guard, and the Reserve Officers Training Corps university cadets. The remaining Canadian volunteers with military experience usually acquired it in a European army or revolutionary group.

The Canadian volunteers on average had less military experience than did volunteers from many countries in Europe, where military conscription was common.[36] But they were more battle-tested than their American partners in the 15th International Brigade, many of whom had formal military training but had not experienced combat.[37] Not all the Canadians were prepared for what they would face in Spain, however. Asked if they had previous military experience, several responded with a mixture of bravado and bewildering naïveté, claiming, yes, in street fights and riots against the police.

Ethnicity

The vast majority of the Canadian volunteers, 78 percent, were born in another country. It is the one thing – along with poverty – that almost all the volunteers shared: they were immigrants. More than 80 percent of the immigrant volunteers arrived in Canada between 1925 and 1930.[38] Many came as single men, some with families. Others left a wife and children behind, believing they would earn enough to send for them in six months or a few years. Some never did. They uprooted their lives and gambled on a new start in Canada only a year or two before the country's economy collapsed, hitting the poor and those with shallow roots in Canada the hardest.

The exact breakdown of Canadian volunteers' ethnicity, excluding those whose birthplace is unknown, is as follows:[39]

Canadian (25 Jewish) 245
Ukrainian (4 Jewish; at least 80 lived in areas under Polish control
    before emigrating to Canada)...239
Hungarian (2 Jewish) 135
Finnish (1 Jewish)..116
English 100
Scottish 69
Croatian 63
Polish (3 Jewish)..59
French Canadian 56
Irish..42
Slovak 35
Czech (3 Czechoslovakian) 23
Bulgarian..20
Macedonian 19
American (4 Jewish)...18
German 16
Danish (1 Jewish) 12
Swedish 12
Lithuanian (2 Jewish)..11
Belarusian (1 Jewish)..9
Russian (2 Jewish)..9
Yugoslav (more specific identity unknown) 9
Jewish (birthplace unknown)...7
Serbian 7
Swiss..6
Welsh 6
Greek (at least 1 Greek Cypriot) 5
Slovenian 5
Australian...4

Norwegian..4
Romanian..3
"Slavic"...3
Spanish...3
Aboriginal (1 from Canada; 1 from Alaska) 2
Belgian 2
Dutch 2
Estonian 2
Armenian 1
Austrian..1
Icelandic...1
Newfoundlander 1
New Zealander..1
Ruthenian...1

Certain ethnic groups were disproportionately represented among the Canadian volunteers, especially Finns, Hungarians, Ukrainians, and Poles. Large numbers of southern European Slavs also volunteered. If Croatians, Macedonians, Bulgarians, Slovenians, Serbs, and Yugoslavs are counted together, the total is 123 volunteers – this from a group of immigrants that made up a relatively small percentage of Canada's overall population. Many Scottish and English-born Canadians volunteered. However, given the high percentage of ethnic Britons in Canada at the time, this group does not stand out.

Volunteers from no other country included as high a percentage of immigrants as did those from Canada. France had its exiles from failed revolutions. Britain sent a large contingent of Jews, mostly from London's East End, making them a sizable ethnic minority of sorts. At least one-third of the American volunteers were also Jewish.[40] And a survey in the 1980s of two hundred surviving American volunteers revealed that one-third had been born in Europe, and 80 percent had at least one parent born outside the United States.[41] But more than three-quarters of the Canadian volunteers were born abroad and emigrated to Canada. This presented some problems for Communist Party recruiters who, according to RCMP investigations, sought to recruit volunteers who would be more appealing to mainstream Canada, especially those of United Empire Loyalist ancestry.[42]

Party Affiliation

National communist parties downplayed the number of their members who volunteered to fight in Spain because they wanted to bolster the image of a popular front uniting communists, socialists, and liberals against fascism. North American propaganda in support of the International Brigades invoked not communism but patriotism and democracy. Battalions were named after national figures such as Abraham Lincoln, George Washington, and, for the Canadians, 1837 rebellion leaders Louis-Joseph Papineau and William Lyon Mackenzie. "In Defending Spain – They Defend Canada" read a typical banner from a wartime rally.

Party officials, however, considered it of vital importance to know exactly who among the volunteers were communists – and how well they were keeping up their party obligations. The resulting lists and evaluations have survived in Moscow archives and are the source for most of our information about the political affiliations of Canadian volunteers.

Approximately 76 percent of the Canadians in Spain were communists – either full-fledged party members or members of the Young Communist League.[43] More than 90 percent of these men and women became communists during the 1930s, and enrolment was highest in 1935 and 1936 – years of heightened militancy on the part of unemployed Canadians, and of the Communist Party's strategy of a popular front.[44] It is unclear if some future volunteers joined the party specifically as a result of the Spanish Civil War but, given the spike in enlistment in 1936, it is reasonable to assume this might have been the case.

Communist recruiters usually welcomed non-communist volunteers as proof of anti-fascism's growing appeal. But potential volunteers without knowledge of the party would have moved in different circles and might not have known how or where to enlist. Nevertheless, 176 Canadian volunteers – or about 25 percent of those for whom information is available – are identified in Comintern files or elsewhere as non-communists. (At least ten of these men later joined the Communist Party for the first time in Spain.) Seven belonged to the Co-operative Commonwealth Federation or its youth wing; four belonged to the Industrial Workers of the World, or Wobblies, a radical union movement; two belonged to the Liberal Party; one was an anarchist. At least one volunteer was a member of the Conservative Party; another belonged to the League for a Revolutionary Workers' Party, a radical Marxist organization.

Other documents from the Moscow archives support an estimate of 65 to 80 percent for the number of communists in the Canadian contingent. Near the end of the war, Helge Meyer, a Danish emigrant to Canada and trusted party member in Spain, wrote to party officials to ask what his fellow Canadians should do about their party cards. "Chances are that we will be frisked thoroughly by the Canadian immigration officials at our arrival to Canada," he wrote. "On one hand it [would] be politically bad if they [find out] that 65% of the Mac-Pap Battalion was 'red,' and on the other hand we would hate to lose our cards."[45] Sandor Voros, an American communist, kept a notebook during his time in Spain in which he lamented the high percentage of volunteers who were communists. He put the figure at 70 percent, and as high as 80 percent in some units. Despite its popular front strategy, the party in Canada still had a difficult time attracting non-communist volunteers for Spain. The "aim was to bring 3-4 times as many non-communists as communists," he wrote.[46]

The number of communists among the Canadian volunteers is roughly in line with contingents from other countries. More than 70 percent of American volunteers were members of the Communist Party or its youth wing.[47] Some 64 percent of French volunteers belonged to the party or one of its front organizations.[48] Three-quarters of the British volunteers were communists, including those who belonged to the Young Communist League.[49] The Irish were an exception. The atheistic nature of communism repelled most people in Catholic Ireland, and comparatively few Irish volunteers were party members.[50]

Asked thirty years after the war what set the Canadian volunteers apart, Irving Weissman, an American commissar in the Mackenzie-Papineau Battalion, said they were on average five to seven years older than their American comrades and were much graver in their demeanour. "I consider them to be far more proletarian," he said. "They were very, very working class. The overwhelming majority – it was stamped on them."[51] Carl Geiser, another American commissar who served with Canadians in the Mackenzie-Papineau Battalion, recalled that many were lumberjacks.[52] Both these men were right, figuratively and literally. The Canadians in Spain were a rough-hewn group. Their ranks contained few urban aesthetes and undergraduate poets. They had come to Canada in the 1920s from a Europe ravaged by war and revolution, with little money or formal education, and they faced a hard life when they arrived. Hundreds worked as lumberjacks or as miners or farm and road-crew workers. They were unemployed for months and years at a time. Looking for work scattered them across the country, most often into the west, riding in boxcars and sleeping in flophouses or in the woods near rail yards.

Unemployment drove many into relief camps, make-work projects that isolated the poor and angry far from the eyes of polite society. In these camps, and in ethnic community halls where they sought kin and comfort, hundreds of future volunteers encountered and often joined the Communist Party of Canada and groups such as the Single Men's Unemployed Association or the Relief Camp Workers' Union. They became more political and more radicalized, striking, rioting, and fighting with police. The Canadians, for the most part, were neither adolescent naïfs nor militant revolutionaries – though their numbers contained a few of each. Most lacked a formal education. They were poor and in many cases desperate. But they were not ignorant. They read, attended meetings and classes, listened to speeches. And although most were members of the Communist Party of Canada, they were not ordered to fight by the party. They made a choice.

Why Did They Fight?

There were guys who were running away from their wives. There were guys
who were sick of living on relief. There were guys who were hotshot Communist Party members. That's what the International Brigades were. It
wasn't a bunch of guys all shouting, "Hooray for Stalin!" and "Over the top!"
That's ridiculous. It was just you and me and him and fifteen other guys with
all sorts of reasons for joining an army.

Hugh Garner, interview with Mac Reynolds, CBC Radio Archives and Library
Archives Canada, c. 1965

Jules Paivio approached the cabin belonging to his mother and father with
trepidation. It was the winter of 1937. Snow blanketed the woods surrounding
the log structure on the outskirts of Sudbury. In Spain, on the other side
of the Atlantic Ocean, the first Canadians were already enlisting in the
International Brigades. Paivio, still a teenager, had decided to join them and
wanted to see his parents one last time before he left. But when Paivio stood
before his mother, he simply could not bring himself to admit that he was
going to war. Instead, he told his parents only that he was going away for a
while, that he would be taking a bit of a holiday.

As he left the cabin, however, Paivio motioned for his father, Aku, to follow
him outside. The two men stood facing each other in the bitter cold, their
shoulders hunched and chins tucked into their chests to protect their faces
from the wind. Paivio told his father, an editor at the leftist Finnish language
newspaper *Vapaus*, that he was leaving for Spain. They embraced, and then
Paivio turned and disappeared into the woods. Aku was proud of his son,
but his heart ached. He described the moment in a poem, "To My Son in
Spain."

A son's loss, a life so young
Perhaps forever
That presses down on me, in gloom[1]

We may not be able to fully understand why Paivio and almost seventeen hundred other Canadians chose to fight in Spain without looking at each volunteer individually. Hugh Garner, quoted above, is correct. The decision a man makes to go to war is a personal one, and every volunteer arrived at this decision in his own way. But there are enough similarities among the Canadian volunteers that distinct patterns emerge – characteristics and life experiences are shared among a sufficient number of volunteers that we can make accurate generalizations.

We know that the vast majority were immigrants. They came from eastern and central Europe, the Balkans, and Finland – the countries most affected by the Russian Revolution and the European civil conflicts that followed. Large contingents also immigrated from Ireland, Scotland, and England. At least two-thirds were members of the Communist Party or Young Communist League, and almost all were leftists of one degree or another. Most suffered grievously during the Great Depression. They were overwhelmingly single and frequently unemployed. Hundreds were transient, with no homes other than temporary ones in lumber and mining shanties or, more often, relief camps.

These factors combined to push many future volunteers into political activism. A desperate and unemployed man naturally sought to fight against the political system he felt was crushing him; a recent immigrant in an unfamiliar country with few prospects looked for community and support in ethnic-language and cultural organizations, many of which were affiliated with the Communist Party. Even Canadians with jobs and promising futures were politicized by the times in which they lived. Workers' and ethnic-language newspapers flourished; communists clashed with fascists on the streets of Montreal; newsreels in movie theatres beamed footage of what appeared to be an emerging global conflict half a world away, in Abyssinia and Spain. The political and economic upheavals of the 1920s and 1930s pushed Canadians to look beyond their own borders in ways that were unprecedented since the First World War. When Norman Bethune, French author and Spanish republican air force commander André Malraux, and delegates from the Spanish government toured Canada, they spoke to overflowing halls and theatres. It seemed as if the world were barrelling toward a crisis point.

"As I saw it in 1936, my view was very simple about what the situation was," said volunteer Maurice Constant, who spent almost two years in Spain. "What was going on was a tremendous battle, almost like Armageddon ... I saw this as the first armed resistance of the left against the forces of the right. In Spain, that was where it was taking place. Armageddon was taking place right there."[2]

Constant was not a communist when he volunteered to join the International Brigades in early 1937, but he clearly identified himself as an anti-fascist. Most Canadians in Spain saw themselves the same way. Anti-fascism, however, meant different things to different people. Some volunteers equated anti-fascism with real democracy; for others it was a euphemism for Soviet communism. And fascism itself took on many forms in the minds of the Canadian volunteers – from Franco's rebels in Spain, to Hitler's Nazis, to the Poles occupying areas of eastern Europe inhabited by ethnic Ukrainians, to the British in Ireland, and even to the Canadian government of the day.

A few volunteers fit no pattern at all. There were a couple of Canadian pilots, Frank Parker and Allan Felton, who said that they could not have cared less about the politics of the war and came to Spain only because they were promised a chance to fly. In an 18 June 1938 letter to a Communist Party official, Parker complained that he and Felton were repeatedly assured they would get the chance to pilot planes in Spain, "but the moment we reached Spain we found it was a joke ... Somehow they got hold of Felton and he landed in the infantry. I raised as much hell as I could, but [William] Lawrence and [Bob] Kerr realized it was a good joke ... and it's been quite a joke for us to try to get back home." Parker said that he was not even vaguely interested in fighting and dying for democracy and demanded that the party in Canada, whom he and Felton presumably had first approached about going to Spain, help bring them back. He said other volunteers had suggested he skip for the border, and he noted that some volunteers who had applied for repatriation were jailed or sent to the front. "Nobody said the Communist Party of Canada is running Spain. But both Felton and I consider it the duty of your party to damn well correct their mistake instead of leaving us here to rot."[3] Neither Felton nor Parker was permitted to leave Spain ahead of their compatriots, in January 1939.

One Montreal man got too involved in the underworld of New York criminal gangs and joined the International Brigades because he feared his life was in danger if he stayed in North America.[4] Arne Knudsen, although a leftist, said his primary motivation to volunteer for the International Brigades was a desire to get out of Denmark, where he had been forcefully conscripted into the navy, and back to his adopted Canadian home of Vancouver.[5] Frank Woods allegedly claimed he volunteered for Spain only to get someone else to pay the cost of his passage from Canada to Britain.[6]

Adventurers and drunks also volunteered – though the extreme difficulties involved in simply getting to Spain from Canada kept this number relatively low. Ron Liversedge later estimated that about 20 percent of the Canadians in Spain were adventurers who volunteered so that they could go to war and see the world. Liversedge, however, was a dedicated communist who had long worked with the masses of unemployed relief-camp workers in British Columbia, and he might have been harshly judging those volunteers who did not live up to the standards of political activism he set for himself. According to Liversedge, some of these adventurers deserted, some became politicized in Spain, and some who remained apolitical throughout the war had nevertheless come to love the Spanish people and stayed to fight for them.[7]

Other volunteers were irredeemable. Early in the war, American Steve Nelson wrote to leading Canadian communist Jack Taylor (Muni Erlick), who would later come to Spain as a liaison representative from the Friends of the Mackenzie-Papineau Battalion. Nelson complained about the quality of the first American volunteers. He urged Taylor to tell the Canadian recruiters not to make the same mistakes the Americans had by sending only unemployed men "because they can be 'spared.'" A "more serious approach to the question of sacrifice to obtain better material must be made," he wrote, and

> our comrades at home must not let any fellow on ... with the impression once they reach Spain they can go on a drunken or whoring spree. Rather we should impress on them that they cannot become any more loose about this matter than a Communist should anyplace. This is important, as the general impression of backward people is that they can do what the U.S. expeditionary force did in 1917 – drink until they are paralyzed and rape every woman in sight. By the way, our boys at the base acted as a model example for others on the above problems. This must be continued.

Nelson noted that two volunteers had recently been sent back. The first had heart trouble, and the second, a Canadian, was a degenerate drunkard. "Incidentally," Nelson said, "this drunkard did not know anything about the situation and only left Canada because he was tired of the place."[8]

Soldiers of the Great Depression

It is impossible to understand why so many Canadians chose to fight in Spain without understanding the world in which they lived during the 1930s. The Great Depression devastated Canada. The country's prosperity had been tied to the export of primary products and semi-processed goods, such as fish and lumber. Wheat prices, which accounted for 25 percent of Canada's total export trade, is a good example of a trend that hit all sections of Canada's resource-based economy. In 1928, Number 1 Northern, Canada's highest grade of spring wheat, sold for $1.03 a bushel. Four years later the price per bushel had dropped to 29¢.[9] The shock waves reverberated across the Canadian economy and gained momentum as drought hit the Prairies.

By the fall of 1932, following the failure of another harvest, an estimated 100,000 Canadians were homeless, traversing the country on the tops of freight trains or on the backs of trucks. Approximately one million Canadians survived on government assistance, and the unemployment rate continued its climb, peaking in early 1933 at 30 percent.[10] Hobo shanties, known as "jungles," sprouted outside communities across the country, usually close to rail yards. Men who drifted into the cities crammed into the overcrowded rooming houses of urban slums, but few stayed anywhere long.

Canadian prime minister Richard Bennett introduced relief camps during the fall of 1932. The program began on a small scale, with 2,000 men, but eventually more than 170,000 passed through them. They were designed to give men food, board, and some financial reward in exchange for manual labour on public works projects – often in national parks or on road crews. But the camps functioned in effect as jails. Although supposedly voluntary, those who wanted relief had to stay in them, working for pennies – usually twenty cents a day – and disconnected from the outside world. The alternative was begging or looking for work in a jobless economy.

The camps were supposed to have a fringe benefit as well. Bennett was extremely concerned by communism – a movement he saw as a foreign plague threatening Canadian society. He believed that the camps would isolate and subdue the subversives. The opposite occurred. The Communist Party sent agitators into the camps, often using assumed names, to encourage unrest, hoping to discredit the relief-camp system and capitalism itself. These agitators organized the relief-camp workers into the Relief Camp Workers' Union, or Relief Project Workers' Union, and they pushed the men to strike. The party's message was well received. Strikes and demonstrations were frequent, and during the four years in which the camps were open, over 17,000 men were expelled for disciplinary reasons.[11] The Communist Party of Canada had already taken advantage of mass layoffs and unemployment to launch aggressive campaigns to win over the workers and the unemployed. The camps only helped their cause. The party's power and influence soared during the Depression as thousands of unemployed Canadians came to believe that there was no one else who spoke on their behalf.

"We couldn't see anything but blackness in front of us," volunteer Frank Roden remembered; "all we saw were these camps." Roden said the men who lived and worked in the relief camps were "practically forced" to become involved in trade unionism and militant politics by their dire circumstance. "We didn't know what the governments were going to do for us. Everything looked so black. And so therefore we took this stance. And that's how most of the young people, well, they became workers. That's all there was to it."[12]

Unrest in the camps peaked in the summer of 1935, when nearly two thousand men from western relief camps went on strike, filling the streets of Vancouver with noisy protests. They were joined by unemployed men from the city's skid row. They climbed aboard freight trains heading east, hoping to take their grievances all the way to the prime minister in Ottawa. But the On to Ottawa Trek was stopped in Regina by the RCMP, which broke up the trekkers' peaceful outdoor meeting by charging into them with clubs. In the riot that ensued, police fired into the crowd, injuring dozens. The trekkers threw up barricades against the mounted policemen and hurled rocks and other missiles. One plainclothes police officer, Detective Charles Millar, was clubbed to death with a shovel and a stick of wood. Protester Nick Schaack, beaten by mounted policeman who charged and overran his makeshift barrier, died three months later, apparently of injuries sustained in the attack.[13] Ron Liversedge, who helped organize the trek and later went to Spain, estimated that five hundred of these men fought in Spain.[14]

The On to Ottawa Trek and the riots in Regina were the most visible demonstrations of the widening chasm between the Canadian state and its unemployed citizens, but they were hardly isolated incidents. Almost half of a sample of 115 Canadian volunteers who completed questionnaires in the summer of 1937 had been arrested or jailed, usually for riding in boxcars, distributing flyers, fighting with police, or rioting – a reflection of both their militancy and, in the case of those arrested for vagrancy and handing out flyers, the eagerness of police to harass the politically subversive and the down-and-out.[15] "We were very bitter people," Harvey Hall remembered.[16]

For many of these men, Spain was a chance to fight back against the police and government in Canada. Most knew that there were no real links between Canadian security forces and Franco's rebellion in Spain. But the future volunteers saw the two as part of a larger, global system of oppression. The poor and unemployed in Canada wanted to go to Spain, Ron Liversedge said, "because it would give them an opportunity to actually fight against the people, against the same kind of people, whom they thought were responsible for their condition, and who were oppressing them here in Canada."[17]

Nick Elendiuk, who before the war found occasional work breaking horses on Prairie ranches, believed his struggle as a frequently unemployed man in Canada connected him to Spaniards fighting fascism in Europe. He had taken part in the On to Ottawa Trek and various protest actions in Canada, but he thought these efforts were half-hearted. "I was pretty darn disgusted with everything here. The whole thing was so namby-pamby," he said, "and when I heard and read that the people of Spain had taken a stand and were fighting back against Franco and the fascists, I immediately became very much interested. I figured any people that had the courage to do that deserved any help that I could give them."[18]

The Great Depression did more than simply radicalize young Canadian men. Without jobs, and by and large without wives or children, packing up to fight in a foreign war seemed like a much better idea than it would have if prospective volunteers faced leaving loved ones and prosperous lives. The Depression severed their ties to Canada even before they left the country.

Frank Hadesbeck said he went to Spain simply because he was fed up with being unemployed. "I didn't know what the word 'anti-fascist' meant at that particular time," he said. But he had heard there was a war on in Spain, and that "the pay was supposed to be good, and conditions fairly good, and one thing led to another ... I blame most of it on the conditions here in Canada for me going over. I wanted to better myself, and these people offered a way out."[19] Hadesbeck spent more than a year in Spain. Despite his lack of political conviction when he volunteered, and the difficult conditions he encountered, there is no evidence in the archival records to suggest he was anything other than a good soldier.

It is unlikely that many Canadians volunteered primarily for money, though a handful no doubt did. (The RCMP reported in January 1937 that Canadian volunteers were told their salary in Spain would be similar to that of a soldier in the United States Army, a lucrative income during the Depression. But this claim is not supported elsewhere, and volunteers in Spain were paid much less.)[20] Once in Spain, few complaints made by Canadian soldiers were about their pay. Poverty and unemployment exacerbated and intensified other factors propelling a man to volunteer.

Some thirty years after the war ended, two veterans, Ed Shirley and John "Paddy" McElligott, got together to reminisce over a few drinks. Shirley tried to explain to a researcher who was present why he had volunteered:

> This thing comes up, the Spanish Civil War. I was down on my luck. I had nothing. I had ideas in my head. I had idealistic ideas ... Now if someone asked me: Why did you go to Spain? Was it because of ideals, or was it became of money? Truthfully, I couldn't answer. It was a mixture of both. I had nothing. And I had nothing to look forward to. I had ideals ... It was a crazy mixed up thing.[21]

The notion that Shirley might have volunteered for the money seemed to offend or annoy McElligott. "I don't believe that," he said. He pressed Shirley to explain his choice to fight in Spain, asking, "What are your ideals?"

"An equal chance to live for everybody," Shirley replied.

"Exactly," McElligott said, satisfied.[22]

Both McElligott and Shirley were answering honestly. Spain was a way out for a suitably desperate man, and during the Great Depression many were desperate. The Depression also made these men receptive to the Communist Party's message that capitalism was a broken system, because for these men the system simply was not working. It had left many of them trapped in what were effectively wilderness prisons, or homeless and wandering, never able to find permanent work. Those few who had jobs knew they could not count on keeping them. It was a time of immense social and political upheaval. Asked sixty-five years later why he volunteered for Spain, Fred Kostyk was unsentimental:

> Those were hard times in them days. After that I looked around for something to do. Work was hard to get. I figured, well – they were advertising in the papers, wanted volunteers for the Spanish Civil War. My brother said, "Well, why don't you go? It will be an experience. You'll be helping the Spanish people" ... Well, there was nothing else to do around Winnipeg. No jobs. So like I said, it was hard times. I figured I might as well do something useful. So that's why I volunteered to go.[23]

Kostyk did feel sympathy for the Spanish Republic and, according to questionnaires he completed in Spain, for the idea of a revolution. But he also simply felt there was not enough in Canada to keep him at home.

Jules Paivio had similar memories. "It was partly dissatisfaction with a lack of real purpose and this being an opportunity for a real purpose in life," he said in 1965.[24] Paivio was an intelligent and idealistic young man, but he knew his family could not afford to send him to university. He belonged to the Young Communist League and was a committed anti-fascist. The hopelessness of the Depression pushed him toward Spain, too.

Immigrant Army

In 1928, Walter Gawrycki was lured to Canada from his home in Poland by promises of good pay and readily available work. He planned to emigrate, work a few years in Canada, and then, with his bags and pockets full of money, he would return to Europe, buy some land, and live like a rich man. "They promised me that I will make sixteen dollars a day, and I will [spend] fifty cents a day for room and board, and you will eat better than you do at Easter."[25]

Gawrycki's life in the New World did not unfold as he had planned. Some work was available during the harvest, but wages were a fraction of the sixteen dollars a day he had hoped for. He drifted back and forth across the country, often living in Vancouver alongside the thousands of transient unemployed men who gravitated there. The work he did find was usually in lumber camps, with Ukrainian and Finnish emigrants. A few years after arriving, Gawrycki could barely afford to feed himself, let alone buy a plot of land in Europe. "I thought I was fooled worse than ever," he said.[26]

Gawrycki was not alone. The Great Depression was a particularly difficult time for new immigrants. It forced them to compete for scarce jobs with native-born Canadians who had better language skills, contacts, and work experience. This left many immigrants unemployed and rootless, herded into wilderness relief camps or left trying to eke out a living in urban flophouses. Men in these conditions sought out ethnic workers' clubs and other left-wing organizations, which were often affiliated with the Communist Party.

However, many of the Canadian immigrant volunteers had already been politically radicalized in Europe. Although the conflicts and tensions they had left behind had their own unique characteristics, what tied many of them together was a division between supporters and opponents of the Soviet Union and socialist revolution. In the interwar period it was difficult to remain neutral. Europe at times seemed to be lurching toward a civil war, and many of the immigrant Canadians who would later fight in Spain had been caught in its epicentre.

Ukrainians in eastern Europe suffered through several wars following the Russian Revolution and the messy dissolution of the Austro-Hungarian Empire at the end of the First World War. By 1922, much of their territory was divided between Poland and the Soviet Union, of which Ukraine was a constituent republic. Ukrainians living under Polish rule suffered a certain amount of ethnic discrimination, and many covertly embraced communism and looked to the Soviet Union for liberation. Others, living under either Polish or Soviet control, yearned for independence. These divisions flourished among Ukrainian immigrants in Canada. It is noteworthy that many of the ethnic Ukrainian volunteers from Canada were born in or near cities that came under Polish control after the First World War, such as Stanislawow, Tarnopol, and Lwow. Ethnic Ukrainians in Bukovina also chafed under Romanian rule during the 1920s and 1930s, when the Ukrainian language and culture were marginalized. Some believed that relief might come from the Soviets. Thousands of Ukrainians from Bukovina emigrated to Canada.

Finns at the time were similarly divided in the wake of a 1918 civil war between "reds," supported by Soviet Russia, and "whites," supported by the German empire. A fragile peace following a "white" victory did little to quell heated political divisions inside Finland, or among Finnish emigrants and their descendants in Canada. Jules Paivio grew up hearing about the defeat of the Finnish left during Finland's civil war and feared the same result in Spain. "You're emotionally affected by all this," he said. "And it just never left me."[27]

In the Balkans, the defeat and break-up of the Ottoman and Austro-Hungarian empires brought neither peace nor security. The region's ethnic groups were pulled in different directions by emerging nationalisms, which often took on overtones of political ideology. The Communist International recognized the potential presented by this instability, though its leaders were slow to understand and appreciate its complexities. The Comintern originally supported a united Yugoslavia and consequently had no separate parties for the various South Slav ethnic groups. This changed in 1934, when the Comintern created parties for Macedonia, Slovenia, and Croatia, all of which were affiliated with the Communist Party of Yugoslavia.[28] The new policy allowed the party to draw on ethnic nationalism as a means of furthering its reach.

The party had a strong base on which to build. Many Croats and other Slavs in the Balkans already resented Italy, which had annexed the ethnically mixed but largely Slavic peninsula of Istria following the First World War and had subjected its Slavic residents to cultural suppression and forced Italianization. The resulting anger found expression in fierce anti-fascism and support for the Soviet Union among some Croats and other Southern Slavs in the region.[29] They supported the Spanish Republic for the practical reason that it was in the midst of an armed struggle against their common enemy, Italy, which was supporting Franco with soldiers, planes, and other weapons.

Croatian emigrants in North America were very much engaged in these political conflicts. They totalled 500,000 people, many of whom were single men or men with families still in Europe. This number represented about 12 percent of all ethnic Croats worldwide. The Croats in North America were well organized. They were early supporters of trade unions, and they also founded the Croatian Fraternal Union, which had more than eighty thousand members by mid-1937.[30]

Many were in favour of the creation of an independent Croatian homeland, and they linked this cause to that of the Spanish Republic. The US-based Croatian-language newspaper *Radnicki glasnik* declared in January 1937 that the Basques and Catalans, like the Croats themselves, "had also long been enslaved by a monarchical dictatorship." The battles in Spain are fought, it continued, "not only for the freedom of Catalonia and Euskadi within Spain" but also for "Croatian national liberation … If fascism wins in Spain, it will be strengthened in Yugoslavia, and that means even greater slavery for the Croatian people."[31] The Communist Party-controlled Croatian language newspaper *Slobodna misao* went further on 18 May 1937, claiming in an article headlined "Croats and the war in Spain" that the outcome of the war in Spain would determine whether "the international situation will favour the liberation struggle of the Croatian people." The *Radnicki glasnik* declared on 21 July 1937 that Croatian volunteers in Spain in fact represented the defence of Zagreb against the fascists.[32]

Support for the republican side in the Spanish Civil War among Croats in Canada was far from universal. Some Croatian emigrants were concerned about the treatment of Catholics in republican Spain, and some simply felt it was none of their business. The Canadian newspaper of the Croatian Peasant Party, *Hrvatski glas,* said that Croats in Canada should be more concerned about what was happening in Croatia than in Spain.[33]

At least forty-two Canadian volunteers who fought in Spain were Irish emigrants. It is tempting to assume that among the Irish-Canadian volunteers, as was arguably the case with Canadian volunteers from the United Kingdom, ethnicity played a much smaller role than did class and political affiliation. Ireland, however, went through its own divisive revolution and civil war in the decades before the Spanish Civil War, and these divisions persisted until the time of the war in Spain. The majority of Irish volunteers in the International Brigades had at some point been involved with the Irish Republican Army.[34] The Spanish Civil War offered Irish republicans the symbolic chance to revisit their own war of independence and to strike a blow against what they wanted to believe was an enemy similar to British imperialism. Irish volunteer Bob Doyle explained in 1976 that he hoped "every bullet I fired would be a bullet against the Dublin landlord and capitalist."[35]

The existence of Eoin O'Duffy's unit of Irish volunteers for the nationalist side introduced another uniquely Irish element to the decision of some Irish to volunteer for the republicans (though their experience was perhaps echoed by German anti-fascists who reacted viscerally against Nazis in their own country). Frank Ryan, leader of the Irish contingent in the International Brigades, told the press upon leaving with his men for Spain that their departure represented "a reply to the intervention of Irish fascism in the war against the Spanish Republic which, if unchallenged, would remain a disgrace on our people."[36] In Spain, the Irish volunteers for Franco and Irish members of the International Brigades continued to draw on their own civil war as a rallying cry in battle. Eoin O'Duffy had been a general in the Free State army during the Irish Civil War. Frank Ryan recalled a time in Spain when a rumour reached his men that O'Duffy's troops faced them across no man's land. "You should have seen our lads charge," he said. "'Up the Republic' ... rang out all along the line."[37]

It appears that these sentiments remained just as intense among Irish emigrants. Thomas William O'Malley, an Irish American who fought in the Mackenzie-Papineau Battalion, cited his anger at Eoin O'Duffy's contingent of volunteers as a reason for his decision to fight on the side of the Spanish republicans.[38] Several Canadian volunteers fought in the Irish Republican Army before emigrating to Canada. John McElligott said that when he was thirteen years old, the Black and Tans, a pro-British paramilitary unit, murdered his father and baby brother. McElligott and his older brother joined the IRA and were eventually captured and imprisoned. McElligott escaped and made his way to Canada in 1929, where he organized in relief camps and unions before volunteering to fight in Spain. Paddy O'Daire brought his repertoire of Irish rebel songs and ballads with him to Canada, where he used them to entertain workers involved in labour disputes in western Canada.[39] He surely did the same in Spain.

It was generally believed during the war that comparatively few French Canadians volunteered to fight in Spain, an allegation that was often explained by citing the influence of the Catholic Church, which was hostile toward the republican side.[40] *The Book of the XV Brigade,* published by brigade officials during the war, specifically blamed the "powerful Catholic Church of French Canada" for spreading disinformation about the republican cause.[41] Québécois media and the province's political and cultural elites – especially those who wanted Quebec to separate from Canada – were generally more Catholic, conservative, and sympathetic to Spanish nationalists than were Canadians elsewhere in the country during the 1930s, and an initial glance at the ethnic breakdown of Canadian volunteers appears to bear out the theory that French Canadians were underrepresented. Only fifty-six volunteers are known to have been French Canadian, mostly Québécois. However, if one considers that 302 out of 1,383 volunteers were born in Canada, the French-Canadian contribution does not appear so unbalanced. Many of these French-Canadian volunteers had left their original homes to look for work in Ontario and western Canada, where the influence of the Catholic Church was not as strong and where prevailing social attitudes were not as hostile toward the Spanish Republic as they were in much of Quebec.

The cause of the Spanish Republic resonated with so many immigrant Canadians because it sounded familiar. Art Siven, a Finnish Jew who emigrated to Canada in 1929, said he knew what fascism was "because we had it in Finland."[42] These men believed that they recognized the suffering inflicted on the Spanish people by Franco's rebellion from their own experiences in Europe, and they thought that all those who lived unwillingly under fascist or authoritarian regimes, no matter where, shared a common cause. A blow against fascism in Spain would be a blow against the Nazis in Germany, the Poles in "West Ukraine," or the "whites" in Finland. Numerous anecdotes related by Canadian immigrant volunteers reflect the prevalence of these perceived connections.

Konstantin "Mike" Olynyk said Franco's policies in Spain reminded him of the way Romanian officials and gendarmes oppressed Ukrainians in his homeland of Bukovina. The similarity became clear to him upon hearing descriptions of the conflict at meetings and fundraising events in Canada, before he volunteered for Spain: "When they started talking about fascism, then I realized how we had been treated in Romania. This caused me to jump." Walter Gawrycki said many of the Ukrainian-Canadian volunteers had served with the Red Army during the Russian Civil War and had subsequently emigrated to Canada. They believed that the fascists in Spain were the same kind of people they had fought in Europe.[43]

William Krysa, another Ukrainian emigrant, drew a direct connection between the republican cause in Spain and the struggle of ethnic Ukrainians in Poland. Krysa wrote letters from Spain to Ukrainian-language newspapers in Canada. In one, he wrote of a visit by a Ukrainian from Europe who described the harsh treatment of Ukrainians living under Polish rule: "His speech was greeted by loud applause, and at the end we swore to carry on the struggle against the fascists 'til they were conquered. When we have defeated the fascists in Spain we promised to go to Poland and help the Ukrainians in their struggle against the fascist regime."[44]

Hugo Lehtovirta, a Finnish Canadian, explained on a form he completed in Albacete that he volunteered because "I made up my mind in the revolution in Finland back in 1918 that at the first opportunity I would fight to avenge the murder of my sister and others."[45]

One veteran, a German emigrant, said his decision to go to Spain was influenced by his impressions of Nazism in Germany. The man had moved to Canada in part because of his family's persecution in Germany. "I went to Spain because I believed in the cause," he said. "I knew the fascists from Germany. When I lived in Germany and went to school, there was the Hitler Youth. And they were loud, quarrelsome, fighting, beating up people all the time. My hatred of them grew from then."[46] Another volunteer said he decided to fight in Spain to avenge his father, who had been killed by Germans during the First World War. Ironically, the only Germans he met in Spain were his comrades in the International Brigades.[47]

Volunteer Isaac Schatz cited his Jewish faith as the primary reason he volunteered. "Being of Jewish origin, my hatred of fascism was so great as to compel me to leave a good home and fight the bastards," he wrote on his Albacete questionnaire.[48] Ethel Magid, the wife of Canadian doctor Aaron Magid, said Germany's persecution of Jews also drove her husband to Spain: "Well, we were hearing all these things from Germany about what was happening to the Jews, and we wanted to fight the fascists, so that is what we did."[49] Jewish Canadians did volunteer in disproportionate numbers, though not nearly to the extent as their American counterparts. Given that Jewish volunteers from Canada had on average higher levels of education and better jobs than the other Canadian volunteers, it is reasonable to suppose that faith and ethnicity played a greater role in their decision to volunteer than did class.[50] Jews were also heavily represented in the Communist Party, and so it follows that large numbers of Canadian volunteers were Jewish.

Clearly, Lehtovirta had no chance of avenging his sister in Spain, and Franco's forces were not the Romanian soldiers who occupied Olynyk's native Bukovina, or the Polish authorities who ruled Ukrainians in eastern Europe. Anti-fascist Germans at least faced the possibility of confronting Nazis on the battlefield in Spain, or in the skies above them, and anti-Semitism was an attractive tenet for some Spanish nationalists. But the personal reasons cited by these men were rooted in conflicts far from Spain. This made little difference to these volunteers and to many of their fellow immigrants. The seeds of their political radicalization were sown by revolution in Europe and nurtured in Canadian relief camps and in ethnic workers' clubs, where new Canadians struggled to establish themselves in the midst of a punishing economic depression. In Spain, the immigrant volunteers saw the roots and the reflections of their own unique injustices, and a way to reverse them. They were battered and desperately looking for a chance to fight back. The Spanish Civil War offered one.

Communist Army

The Communist Party of Canada organized and funded almost every Canadian volunteer who served in Spain; Canadians were too far removed from Spain to get there on their own, and the cost and planning involved were prohibitive. The party made fighting in Spain a possibility for Canadians, and without the party, regardless of their will and commitment, most potential Canadian volunteers would have been stranded in Canada, on the wrong side of the Atlantic Ocean.

This does not mean that the Communist Party of Canada drafted its members to fight in Spain the way governments dispatch their soldiers to overseas wars. The party in Canada was able to exert less pressure on its members than was possible in Wales, for example, where, according to Hywel Francis, "there was a thin line between recruiting and volunteering."[51] Canadian communists were much more loosely organized. It appears that only a few leading members were sent to Spain because the party decided they should go.[52] Some members were no doubt pressured, but most made their own decision to fight.

Before the Communist International's approval of the International Brigades, however, the Communist Party of Canada rejected any suggestion of its members fighting in Spain. Ed Jardas, a Croatian Canadian, said that he approached leading Canadian communist Sam Carr in August 1936 and asked him how he felt about allowing a group of South Slav emigrants to fight in Spain. Sam Carr, according to Jardas, rejected the proposal as "abstract and adventuristic" and "anarcho-syndicalist in substance."[53] But the Communist International in Moscow soon changed its mind, and the Canadian party followed Moscow's lead. In September 1936, Tim Buck, general secretary of the Communist Party of Canada, attended a conference in Brussels with a large communist presence, where he claimed Canada could send and maintain 250 volunteers.[54] He then travelled to Paris, Moscow, and Spain itself, before returning to Canada on 10 November.[55] It is not clear at what date the party began to formally recruit volunteers. The first Canadian volunteers sent by the party left Canada before the year's end and sailed from New York for Spain in early 1937.

The Communist Party of Canada had goals of its own it hoped to fulfill by sending Canadians to Spain. Some of these were similar to those held by Moscow: the protection of the Soviet Union and the strengthening of the global anti-fascist popular front. But the Canadian party had ambitions to expand and strengthen its reach and influence and to train its members for work in Canada. Spain gave the party this opportunity but also presented a dilemma. The party was torn between developing future cadres and protecting its most promising members. Thus we have Steve Nelson's above-quoted admission that the party began the war sending mostly unemployed and presumably down-and-out men because they were less valuable to the party and could be spared. This policy appears to have changed. A Communist Party report on Canadian Francis Harold Parsons noted that Parsons was a newcomer to the revolutionary movement in Calgary but "was sent to Spain to be hardened and matured."[56] This suggests that Spain also functioned as a sort of testing ground for marginal comrades.

On the other hand, French Canadian Robert Martineau joined the Communist Party and desperately wanted to go to Spain. The party would not let him go because, as a rare French-Canadian communist, he was too valuable to risk losing in the war. Martineau was eventually allowed to leave, but the party soon changed its mind and called him back to Canada, once he was already in New York and on his way to Spain. Martineau was furious: "I told them even if they would do everything to hold me I would go just the same."[57] The party relented. Martineau went to Spain and survived the war.

Party leaders in Spain carefully evaluated volunteers for work back in

Canada. Volunteers were asked if they were known in Canada as communists, and it was noted if they had experience or the capacity to work in journalism, teaching, organization, or illegal activities.[58] Party leaders prepared their own independent evaluations on volunteers, whether they were party members or not, to be forwarded to Communist Party district committees in the regions to which the volunteers were returning. Similar evaluations were sent to the Central Committee of the Communist Party of Canada. Many evaluation lists began with this introduction:

> While we can fully expect that the Party will derive a tremendous benefit from the major-ity of the comrades returning, it is to be expected that we will have some trouble with the bad, demoralized elements. They must be dealt with very coolly and without any methods which would push them into the arms of our enemies. They must be allowed if possible to find their place without taking them into the Party or trusting [them] with any positions of confidence or trust in the Labour Movement. It is to be expected that the Trotskyite enemies of the Party will endeavor to pick some of them up for their own purposes. This as far as possible must be prevented.[59]

Typically, the volunteers were then assigned a ranking: cadre, requires political instruction, good, fair, weak, or bad.

Newly arrived Canadian volunteers were also asked in several questionnaires what they planned to do when the war was over.[60] Many were asked specifi-cally what military and political skills they had learned in Spain to take back to anti-fascist organizations in their own countries. Most answered with general comments about the need for working-class unity, for example. But the Finnish-Canadian volunteer Untamo Makela noted his ability to operate various kinds of weapons and make explosives.[61] Hryhori Vasylchyshyn and David Watchman said skills they learned in Spain that could be put to use in Canada included musketry and proficiency in the use of mortars and machine guns.[62]

There is no evidence that the Communist Party of Canada had active plans to put any of the military skills the Canadian volunteers learned to use in Canada, but this was the fear of the RCMP. The RCMP spent a lot of effort during the 1930s spying on and working to infiltrate the Canadian party. Every week or two it summarized its findings in security bulletins for cabinet and senior civil servants. In the 6 January 1938 security bulletin, the RCMP reported details of a mass meeting held on 8 December 1937 in Moose Jaw, Saskatchewan. At this meeting, party functionary Albert E. Smith spoke about the Canadians in Spain:

> These boys who are now serving in Spain are undergoing training, so to say, which will be very useful to these men when the Spanish struggle is over ... The Canadians who are now over there will upon their return home become a great factor in this country's social and political set-up ... There are political commissars attached to every fighting

unit who belong to a very strong organization whose ramifications are world wide. The Spanish people are being correctly led by these commissars, and the people of Canada will also sooner or later have to fight for their freedom; they, too, will be correctly led by our organization; they, too, will receive galvanic education which has been working miracles in Spain and will do the same over here when the proper time arrives.[63]

Smith was not articulating a formal party policy of preparing for armed revolution in Canada. But even allowing for rhetorical exaggeration, his remarks demonstrate that the Canadian party had plans for the volunteers that extended beyond fighting in Spain.

Volunteers in Spain also provided the Soviet Union with assets in its efforts at global espionage and intrigue. All international volunteers in Spain were required to relinquish their passports, which in many – perhaps most – cases were not returned. They were taken by International Brigades officials and used for various purposes, without the passport holders' knowledge or consent. Ramón Mercader, Leon Trotsky's assassin, reportedly travelled to North America on the altered passport of a Canadian volunteer who was killed on the Aragón front.[64] We also know, thanks to the 1945 defection to Canada of Igor Gouzenko, a cipher clerk in the Soviet embassy in Ottawa, that the Soviets planted a long-term agent in the United States using the stolen identity of a Polish emigrant and Spanish Civil War veteran named Ignacy Witczak. The Soviets thought the real Witczak had been killed during the war and appropriated his identity for one of their agents, but Witczak had survived and returned to Canada. When the spy's stolen passport expired in 1945, the Soviets risked blowing his cover by trying to renew it. Soviet military intelligence directed Sam Carr to bribe a Canadian official $3,000. The bribe was passed successfully, but Gouzenko's defection alerted Canadian authorities to the scheme. The fake Witczak, whose real identity is not known for certain, eluded American authorities and disappeared.[65]

The Soviet Union, through its NKVD secret service, recruited spies and potential agents from among the international volunteers. The Venona transcripts, consisting of decrypted messages sent by Soviet intelligence agencies and recently declassified by the American government, reveal that up to ten American veterans of the Spanish Civil War later spied on the United States for the Soviets.[66] Soviet agents in Spain also targeted Canadian volunteers. Canadian Jules Paivio said he was interviewed by a man, possibly an American, about going to the Soviet Union for "special work," which Paivio understood to mean eventual espionage activities in Canada or the United States. To Paivio's relief, he was not selected. "Fortunately I didn't have to make this decision ... I wasn't a true-blue Communist. Never have been," he said.[67]

It is unclear if other Canadian members of the International Brigades were successfully recruited. Ron Liversedge, who worked for a time at the Canadian cadre service in Albacete, said he and fellow Canadian Jack Lawson were assigned the task of compiling an index-card file of all the Canadians in various units throughout Spain. "We would receive requests from time to time from the Brigade Estado Mayor [Headquarters], asking if we had a man or men of certain types for special work," he recalled. "Description of requirements would be added, physical, linguistic, willingness to volunteer to travel in Europe, etc. ... I never knew if any of these men were used, as there were six hundred Canadians who never came back."[68]

According to Elizabeth Bentley, an American spy for the Soviet Union and later an informer for the FBI, Hazen Sise, a Canadian who worked with Norman Bethune's blood transfusion unit in Spain, told her he was approached by Soviet agents in Spain and instructed to meet a contact in Paris. Sise allegedly did as he was told, but the contact never showed up.[69] Bentley also alleged that in 1943 and 1944 Sise passed on political gossip that he obtained from his friend Lester Pearson, a diplomat at the Canadian embassy in Washington and future prime minister of Canada. Bentley said she was almost certain that Sise knew the information he was giving her was forwarded to the Soviets. She did not know if Pearson was also aware, though the FBI later concluded that it had no information to indicate that Pearson was involved in espionage or any related activities.[70] When Bentley's allegations against Sise were made public, he denied ever knowing her.[71]

The Communist Party of Canada and the Comintern had much to gain by organizing the International Brigades, but this does not explain why so many Canadians, even those who were members of the Communist Party, volunteered. To understand this, we need to know how devoted the Canadian volunteers were to the party. Fortunately, hundreds of volunteer evaluations made by party officials in Spain dwell sometimes exclusively on the political makeup or discipline of the volunteers. They reveal high levels of dissatisfaction about the political commitment and party loyalty of the Canadians, even among those considered by party functionaries to be selfless and courageous in battle.

A typical evaluation, in this case of Harry Fenton, says he is a good comrade "but doesn't seem to carry much interest in political questions."[72] John McElligott was described as "courageous at the front" but undisciplined. The "district secretary should have [a] serious talk with him before being re-admitted to the Party." Frank Tierney was a "good soldier" but "did not show much interest in political work." Harvey Hall was singled out as a clean-cut volunteer who was never "even near" the Communist Party before Spain and who had served in the Canadian army. "He ... can be developed as one of our leading elements," his evaluation concluded.[73]

Edward Cecil-Smith's description of the Canadians, delivered to party officials disturbed by his countrymen's undisciplined behaviour, is also revealing. "Quite different from the makeup of the United States volunteers is that of the Canadians," he said, then continued:

> Whereas the large group of the Americans are the New York YCL [Young Communist League] comrades who have been brought up in the discipline of a city industrial unit, on the other hand the largest single group of Canadians is that from the British Columbia slave camps ...
>
> Due to their circumstances and also the form their struggles have taken back home in Canada they retain very many traditions which the west has inherited from the Wobblies.
>
> In the army those showed themselves particularly in a combination of rank and filism and a sort of theory of spontaneity. Many of them even now have not entirely got over the belief that leaders will appear when needed and at other times are not necessary.
>
> This also shows itself in a refusal to accept permanent authority. There are cases where some of them have been good leaders in battle but have lain down on the job when in reserve. Others have been given many chances to take over leadership, but have resisted it, even till today.
>
> Unfortunately, the political delegates and party organizers in the Mac-Paps, who have been mostly appointed from comrades from industrial cities in the United States, have found it very difficult to work with these comrades on account of mutual misunderstanding.[74]

Another description by Cecil-Smith, this time sent to the Vancouver Committee of the Communist Party of Canada, expanded on the same theme. "In reference to most of the Vancouver boys one must particularly remember that so many of them have come from the Relief Camps," he wrote, "and that their previous history has in many cases resulted in anarchistic tendencies, lack of discipline and so on. However, most of the men who went from Vancouver will undoubtedly be an asset."[75]

American party officials appear to have been struck by the Canadian volunteers' lack of political conformity and reflexive obedience. Irving Weissman, an American and secretary of the Communist Party of Spain in the Mackenzie-Papineau Battalion, wrote of the Canadian volunteers. "The Canadian cadres, without exception, must all be characterized as needing a great deal of political education; and now especially on the heels of their experience in Spain is the time to give them some basic Marxism Leninism. With training some of them will undoubtedly develop into important leaders." Weissman continued to focus on Canadian volunteers from Vancouver:

> These comrades, who were all good fighters at the front and self-sacrificing and devoted, especially showed the harm that results from a lack of political education. It was hard for them to understand that the authority of the People's Front was an authority which was their own and which they had to build up, and that it was utterly different from the authority of the capitalist state which they had been fighting to break down in Canada.

> This is what accounts for their apparent "anarchism." But when they were given correct political leadership by the party this was to a great extent overcome. But this is what accounts for a "mutiny" that these otherwise good soldiers had, when they refused to go out on a maneuver because the food was bad.[76]

Weissman's evaluations of individual Canadians were similar. Canadian James Lucas was "excellent at the front" but politically backward. "He has anarchist tendencies," Weissman said, and blamed Lucas' lack of good political guides.[77] An unsigned note scrawled on the bottom of another report on James Lucas reveals the attitude of much of the brigade leadership toward the Canadian volunteers: "The key to this comrade's trouble and to the trouble of so many of the Canadians, was the poor political leader[ship] they had and the lack of political education back in Canada."[78]

The alleged political weakness and anti-party attitudes of the Canadian volunteers were not universal. There were Canadians in Spain who were completely committed to the party. Volunteer Maurice Constant referred to the most dogmatic as Stalinists:

> I detested them. They were most of them stupid. Ideologically stupid in terms of Marxist theory is what I'm talking about. The good thing about them – and this is like the Jesuits – they had their discipline. And that's why they're effective. They're soldiers. They do as they're bloody well told. And that's why an intellectual can't stand them. I never could abide them.

According to Constant, these men were some of the best fighters in the International Brigades: "I'll tell you this. They were the effective ones. When it came to conducting a strike, I'd rather be with a Stalinist group, a Stalinist unit, than with a socialist unit. They had guts. They would fight. And they were organized."[79]

Even beyond the so-called Stalinists, however, there were many Canadian party members who remained dedicated communists throughout the war, and this is reflected in dozens of positive individual evaluations made by party and brigade leadership. Some volunteers came to Spain at least in part because they felt it their duty as communists. Asked on an August 1937 questionnaire what he planned to do after the war, Oleksander Melnychenko said, "I will take orders from the party and they will decide my future actions."[80] On the same questionnaire, Joseph Bélanger said that after the war he hoped to build a Soviet Canada.[81] Percy Hilton said he had come to Spain "to fight on party lines."[82] His opinions seem to have changed by the end of the war, however. He was captured by the nationalists and, in a report on the political commitment of Canadians taken prisoner by Franco forces, was described as anti-party, "not the vicious type but absolutely unreliable."[83]

Whatever the political affiliation that might have influenced their decision to volunteer, once the volunteers got to Spain, their letters home and to their commissars and commanding officers suggest they were much more concerned with missing mail, food, and cigarettes than with politics. "Well, shit, we were in the trenches most of the time," Fred Kostyk said when asked about the political commitment of the volunteers. "We were always in battle."[84]

The Canadian volunteers, as Cecil-Smith noted, rejected authority and structure, even when it came from the Communist Party. The vast majority of Canadian communists in Spain joined the party in the 1930s, usually only one to three years before volunteering to fight in Spain – they were not long-time party members. A report on volunteer Louis Tellier, dated 3 June 1938, is typical: "Joined the CP during a strike of single unemployed men in Canada in 1935. He was a transient single unemployed man and had no association with the Party until that time. As a transient unemployed man, has never stayed for any length of period in one city or at one place."[85] It is hard to imagine how Tellier, leading such a life, might have absorbed more than the rudiments of Communist Party dogma.

Before going to Spain, the Canadians led lives that were often harsh, yet they involved a degree of independence alien to American communists in organized New York City party cells. Even the jobs many Canadians took – seasonal work clearing bush and logging – cultivated a sense of independence from organized authority. At least four Canadian volunteers were trappers. One, Earl Rose, spent so much time in the wilderness of northern Alberta that he learned to speak Cree. While other volunteers, when writing about their plans after demobilization, said they wanted to continue the struggle back in Canada, or even in China or the Soviet Union, Rose said his only goal was to get back to Cold Lake, near Edmonton, to trap and fish.[86]

Those who belonged to the Communist Party were comrades, not cadres; and party membership on its own was not enough to propel the majority of Canadians to volunteer. Many Canadian volunteers had become communists because of the party's stance on their behalf in Canada and against fascism worldwide. The Communist Party seemed to encapsulate their own anti-fascism. When the party demanded something more or something different of the volunteers in Spain, their commitment to the party waned.

Anti-Fascist Army

Maurice Constant was a student at the University of Toronto when the Spanish Civil War broke out. An intense and intelligent man, Constant had read much of the Western literary canon by the time he was fourteen. With what he later described as the arrogance of youth, Constant decided that a liberal arts program at university could not teach him anything new and so enrolled in science. However, he still spent all his free time in the library, reading and studying political philosophy and gradually coming to believe in socialism. "I myself belonged to no party. I'm not a joiner. I'm not that type," he said. "But I was on the left, very much so on the left, really, because I was anti-fascist."[87]

Constant was captivated by the writing of French author André Malraux, then a commander in the Spanish republican air force. In April 1937, Malraux came to Toronto to speak on behalf of the Spanish Republic at the University of Toronto's Hart House Theatre. Constant remembered that the university was sharply divided between supporters and opponents of the Spanish Republic. Even some staff members were rumoured to be supporters of either Fascist Italy or Nazi Germany.

Constant arrived at Hart House in the early afternoon to wait for Malraux. The atmosphere in the theatre, with its low, vaulted ceiling and no windows, was cramped, claustrophobic, and electric. Tension between opposing students was near the breaking point. "When I arrived there to get a seat, the place was full of smoke," Constant said. "Banners flying. People sort of looking askance at each other. You wouldn't know if there was going to be a riot." There was no riot. Malraux, accompanied by a stunning French blond, described the siege of Madrid and its heroic defence by the Spanish people. Spain, he said simply, needed help. Then Malraux paused for an intermission and stepped outside with the beautiful woman to smoke a cigarette.[88]

Constant followed him. They stood on the porch near the black antique cannons that guard Hart House and talked about Spain, Malraux smoking the entire time. Constant was smitten almost as much by Malraux as by the woman beside him. He was, to Constant, anti-fascism personified. "The reason I admired this guy, that he was my idea of a model, was that he was an intellectual and a man of action," Constant said. "I went out and I told him I was going to go. That decided it. Something had to be done. This was a period when intellectuals, writers, across North America, had to stand up and be counted."[89]

Constant volunteered to fight in Spain that summer, though his decision to do so was not quite the epiphany it initially seems. Constant was inspired by Malraux, but he was already committed to fighting fascism. He had even started to prepare for war, joining the Canadian Officers Training Corps at the University of Toronto. "I knew damn well there was going to be a war and I wanted to be prepared for it," he said.[90] Many Canadians shared Constant's belief that a global confrontation with fascism was inevitable, and the sooner it happened, the less bloody it would be. "We were trying to head off the Second World War. We actually believed that we could," Ron Liversedge explained years later. "And we believed by opposing the fascist invasion of Spain at the time – which, by the way, it was – that we could rally support in our own home countries to the extent that they would move politically and influence their own governments to stop the fascist trend and the fascist expansion and the fascist invasion of Spain."[91]

Liversedge was a long-time organizer among the Canadian unemployed and a member of the Communist Party of Canada. Maurice Constant was neither, but he also believed that Spain was a chance to stop fascism before it spread like a malignant cancer even farther across Europe. He came to this belief independent of any political party or organization.[92] He was a student who, although he no doubt absorbed the atmosphere of the Depression, had the luxury of spending his youth studying, not wasting away in relief camps. But he felt strong enough about his convictions to fight for them.

Constant was not unique. Although almost all the Canadian volunteers were working class and usually communists, Canadians from a wider spectrum of society shared Constant's opinions on Spain, even if they were unprepared to fight there. Non-communist labour unions pledged financial donations or advocated the boycott of goods from Italy, Germany, and nationalist Spain. Clothing workers in Toronto agreed to make suits on their own time and donate the profits to the Spanish Republic, something the RCMP apparently considered a security threat and duly reported.[93] The Republic was vilified in much of the Canadian media, especially in Quebec, but several mainstream Canadian newspapers, including the *Toronto Daily Star* and the *Winnipeg Free Press,* supported it.

André Malraux's speeches were well attended by radical students, but he also spoke to capacity crowds at the Presbyterian Church in Montreal and at Massey Hall in Toronto, where the RCMP noted audience members donated a total of $600, a sizable sum.[94] Indeed, the RCMP reported that the Spanish Civil War allowed Communist Party front organizations and affiliated Aid Spain committees to reach an audience of middle-class liberals who had hitherto been untouchable. Former judge Lewis St. George Stubbs, for example, told an audience at a Winnipeg rally on 2 September 1937, "If anybody had told me one year ago that I would now be on the platform of a communist convention, advocating war, I would have said they were crazy, but that is just what I am doing."[95]

Norman Bethune, after returning to Canada from Spain in 1937, toured the country and spoke to large audiences wherever he went. Audience members packed into overflow rooms or onto the streets to listen to him speak. The RCMP reported that "as a direct result of Bethune's meeting in the Orpheum Theatre at Vancouver on 1 August, there has been a rush of relief camp workers to enlist for Spain."[96] The RCMP noted that these speeches attracted much attention from middle-class Canadians, including intellectuals and medical workers.[97] Support for the Spanish Republic, and by extension opposition to fascism in Spain and around the world, extended beyond poor relief-camp workers and the extreme left of Canadian society.

Most Canadians who opposed fascism did not volunteer to fight in Spain, but almost all Canadians who volunteered were anti-fascists. "To fight fascism" was the most common response given by volunteers on questionnaires asking why they had joined the war. Fascism meant different things to different volunteers, but all these definitions converged on Spain, where Canadian volunteers – whatever their background and histories – believed they would have a chance to confront it.

Like soldiers in all wars, the Canadians in Spain probably ended up fighting more for the men beside them than for nuanced political reasons. "We were just like a bunch of brothers in the end – because we knew we had to be," said volunteer Frank Hadesbeck.[98] Hugh Garner felt the same:

> The one thing that keeps a fighting force together, and makes them fight as a unit, and makes them brave as a unit, is a crazy mixed up thing that they call esprit de corps. Esprit de corps is being afraid of the guy next to you, is being afraid that he will know that you are a coward … That's what a fighting force is. It's people who are all scared but are striving to show the guys next to them that they're not scared. And because of this they become a very good fighting force.[99]

Garner said that soldiers come to love each other, and this is reason enough to fight. But long before they stepped into a shallow trench cut through the Spanish hills, those who volunteered made a decision while they were still safe and far away to risk their lives in Spain. All these decisions were made during the Great Depression, which hung like a dark cloud over Canada throughout the 1930s. "Because of the times, the ways things were, everybody was sort of fed up with the system," one veteran said. "You know, it was the Great Depression. People felt kind of hopeless."[100]

That so many Canadian volunteers – about 80 percent – were immigrants suggests this was a crucial factor in their decision to volunteer. Coming of age in a time of political upheaval and revolution in Europe radicalized many of the immigrant volunteers. The poverty they suffered in Canada did little to subdue their anger and frustration. In Spain these men saw a chance to revisit conflicts they had physically left behind in Europe but still held close to their hearts.

The majority of Canadian volunteers in Spain were also members of the Communist Party. For a few militant Communist volunteers, their opposition to fascism in Spain and around the world might have arisen out of loyalty to the party, but for many it seems the reverse is true. They gravitated to the Communist Party because no other organization campaigned so aggressively on behalf of the down-and-out or appeared to be willing to stand up to fascism.

Eventually all these factors coalesced in Canada as Spain slipped toward war. Immigrants wanting revenge for recent European wars and conflicts found common cause with dedicated Communists, a few professionals and intellectuals, and the angry unemployed who felt their lives would be better spent in battle than in relief camps. All shared a common opposition to fascism, in the many ways fascism itself was defined. Spain was most simply a chance to put these convictions into action. "I thought in my mind it was something I should do," one veteran later recalled. "It wasn't good enough to just talk."[101]

Part 2
International Brigades

Going to War

Art Siven's journey to Spain began one cold January day in 1937 on a train leaving the northern Ontario city of Port Arthur, a transport hub for loggers and miners carved out of the rust-coloured rock on the north shore of Lake Superior. Siven, a twenty-nine-year-old Finnish Jew, had been in Canada less than ten years. Unlike a lot of men during the Great Depression, he found steady employment as a truck driver and had a lot to lose by going to war. However, the Spanish Civil War resonated with Siven. He was a communist, but he also saw in Spain a reflection of the Finnish Civil War of 1918, which resulted in defeat for the Finnish reds and the death through malnutrition and neglect of many red prisoners of war, even after hostilities had ended. "I was scared that the same thing would happen there to the working people as happened in Finland after the war," he said.[1]

And so Siven found himself sitting next to one of his closest friends on a rattling train bound for Toronto, and from there a port city and on to Spain. As the train skirted Lake Superior's shoreline, they looked out over its frozen and snowy expanse, which disappeared beyond the horizon like the inland sea the great lake really is. Just east of Port Arthur a narrow peninsula jutted into the lake, dubbed the "Sleeping Giant" because from a distance the land mass looks like a great Indian chief reclining on his back.

The two watched all this slip by their train window, and Siven told his friend this would be the last time they would ever see it.

His friend said nothing for a moment and then scolded him softly: "Listen, Art, there's never been a war where everyone dies."[2]

Across Canada, other volunteers were making similar journeys. Almost everyone travelled with financial and organizational support from the Communist Party or front organizations. The party arranged transportation and helped with visa and passport applications, instructing those born in Europe to say they were visiting family there; others were told to claim they were going to Paris to see the World Fair. According to Peter Hunter, a leading

Canadian communist who handled the recruitment of volunteers, the party tried to screen out adventurers as well as RCMP spies and that old communist bugbear, the Trotskyists. "I don't know which we hated most," he said.[3]

The volunteers were usually sent by train to Toronto, and from there to New York, Montreal, or Quebec City. They were given cheap second-hand suits and cardboard suitcases. Whenever possible, a trusted party member was assigned to each group of men to shepherd them across the country and keep them sober and out of trouble. Peter Hunter recalled that it was difficult to keep secret the ultimate destination of the departing volunteers. Typically, they would leave Toronto's Union Station bound for New York or port cities in eastern Canada in groups of up to ten or fifteen, with one or two hundred people coming to the station to see them off. The volunteers often had a couple of drinks before they left, and when the train pulled out of the station in a cloud of steam, the young men would hang out the windows, full of hope and energy, waving clenched fists and shouting the rallying cry of the Spanish Republic: *No Pasarán!* They shall not pass.

Others had a more melancholy departure. Walter Gawrycki left Vancouver for Spain on New Year's Eve. He was told to say his goodbyes, but by the time he found his friends, they were already drunk and emotional. He left them in tears.[4] William Hamilton, who was only seventeen or eighteen years old in February 1937, told his mother and father in Moose Jaw that he was going to Spain. When he disappeared from home, his distraught parents stopped and searched trains leaving from Moose Jaw and Regina, but their son eluded them. He wrote from Spain in March.[5] Then, much to the relief of his parents, he was sent home in July 1937, probably because of his age. A note in Hamilton's personnel file says he suffered from *maladie de cœur,* "heart sickness."[6]

For those Canadians with connections to the Communist Party or to party-affiliated unions and ethnic organizations, initiating a trip to Spain was a fairly straightforward matter of contacting the party and letting it take over. For others, the process was more difficult. Hugh Garner, a tough young man from the Cabbagetown neighbourhood of Toronto who would eventually become a successful author, desperately wanted to join the war in Spain. He could not even locate the country on a map but was still drawn to its civil war. "Coming from a poverty-stricken background, I felt a great love for the poor people of Spain," he said. "That's about the best way I can put it, I guess."[7]

With no idea how to get to Spain, Garner took out a personal advertisement in the *Toronto Daily Star* asking for help, without success.[8] Garner had a decent-paying job as a salesman and could afford regular haircuts. He patronized a barber on Danforth Avenue in Toronto who displayed a large photograph of the Soviet dictator Joseph Stalin in his store window. One day, as the barber traced a hot and soapy razor across his throat, Garner told him he wanted to go to Spain.

"Are you sure?" the barber asked, wiping the soap suds and newly removed stubble off on a towel draped over Garner's shoulder.

Garner said he was. "This is the one big thing that I want to do."

The barber told Garner that someone would be in touch with him. Sure enough, one day at work he got a phone call. The caller told him to meet a contact on Wellington Street. Garner arrived and was taken to an unidentified office, where he was interviewed by a man with a foreign accent who wanted to know about Garner's background and trade union connections (he had none). The man told Garner he'd be in touch in a few days. He was, and soon Garner had a passport, a bus ticket to New York City, five dollars, and an introductory note to an Italian working men's club in New York. It was January 1937 and he was on his way to Spain.[9]

The recruiting effort going on across Canada did not escape the attention of the RCMP. The police force had a network of informers who hung around in meeting halls and bars frequented by the unemployed and suspected subversives with the aim of penetrating the recruiting network. A typical dispatch from the RCMP in Winnipeg, dated 15 January 1937, records in detail a conversation between two prospective volunteers the previous night in Manor Hall, a sort of assembly room for men on relief.

"I should hear about going tomorrow night. I'll be glad to get on that old boat," the RCMP informer recalled one man saying. His companion replied, "You'll probably get a bullet anyway, what's the odds. You'll get one in this country before long." According to this dispatch, Manor Hall functioned as an unofficial recruiting office in Winnipeg: "Both toilets are used for this purpose. The doors are closed and no sound may be heard outside. Conversation is carried on in subdued tones."[10]

The RCMP were able to unravel details of the recruitment process. However, without instructions from the government, they could not prosecute or arrest those involved in recruiting men for Spain. This frustrated the force and led to numerous memoranda from the RCMP to the government, hoping to highlight the threat and prod the government into taking action. When the RCMP took up the matter with the Department of External Affairs in January 1937, it was told that the government's policy on Canadians fighting in Spain was still undecided.[11]

It would remain undecided for months, even after Parliament passed the Foreign Enlistment Act, banning participation in foreign wars, including the Spanish Civil War. On 1 September 1937, RCMP commissioner James Howden MacBrien wrote to Ernest Lapointe, the minister of justice, asking for direction:

It would be appreciated if we could be advised as to whether you desire that the provisions of the Foreign Enlistment Act should be strictly enforced ... It is pointed out that the whole question of recruitment of volunteers for the Spanish Civil War is one which is cloaked with secrecy and unless secret informers are employed who can be used to give evidence in Court it will undoubtedly be a very difficult – if not impossible – matter to secure convictions in respect to the Foreign Enlistment act ... The whole question regarding the action to be taken in connection with the Foreign Enlistment Act appears to be entirely dependent upon the wishes of the Government in this connection.[12]

Two weeks later, on 15 September 1937, MacBrien got his answer. "This matter has been the subject of discussion by officers of the Department of External Affairs and the Department of Justice, but so far no conclusion has been reached as to the machinery which should be set up to enforce the provisions of the Act," Lapointe wrote. "As soon as some decision is arrived at on this question, I will give considerations to the suggestions for prosecuting violators of the Act contained in your letter of September 1."[13]

The RCMP had no choice but to bide its time, gather information, and wait for instructions. Sooner or later, it hoped, legal proceedings against those fighting in Spain and those sending them could begin. When this happened, it would be ready. "There appears to be no action which can be taken at present," wrote RCMP assistant commissioner Stuart Taylor Wood in a 2 September 1937 letter to the officer commanding at F division in Regina. "It is, therefore, considered desirable at present to allow such persons as those mentioned to proceed to their destination, until an opportunity arises whereby a prosecution or prosecutions can be instituted."[14]

MacBrien's request to use "secret informers" probably referred to under-cover officers and represented an escalation in the force's surveillance of the Communist Party's recruitment efforts. Previously, the RCMP had engaged civilians to penetrate the recruitment network. Recall the detailed reports on overheard conversations in Winnipeg's Manor Hall. It is not clear if these informers were formally hired or simply questioned when convenient. However, the force had not yet employed undercover officers, and efforts were made to change this. In an August 1937 memorandum, Charles Rivett-Carnac in the RCMP's Liaison and Intelligence Section wrote: "Best idea would be to detail a number of constables who would pose as transients and offer selves for recruitment."[15] Wood's response, enclosed in a note he attached to Rivett-Carnac's memorandum, which he forwarded to MacBrien, indicated that he did not like the idea but admitted that it was unlikely the RCMP could secure a conviction otherwise. And without a conviction, he said, "there does not appear to be any way of exposing the fact that the Communist Party is the only agency recruiting volunteers for Spain."[16]

The RCMP stepped up its surveillance activities several weeks later. On 22 October 1937, the police force approved a plan to a plant an informer among the volunteers by having him pretend to enlist. "It would appear that the best method to make use of the co-operation offered by [Joseph] R. Berubé would be to suggest to him that he enlist as an ostensible volunteer for Spain," a memorandum to the RCMP's Montreal branch explained, "and after making complete notes of the procedure adopted by the Communist Party in regard to enlistment of volunteers express himself as wishing to cancel his enlistment." The note concluded that such a plot would secure evidence that could later be used to prosecute volunteers and their recruiters.[17]

What remains unclear, however, is the exact status of Joseph Berubé. There is no evidence indicating that a man named Joseph Berubé served in the RCMP in 1938.[18] Subsequent proposals to infiltrate RCMP agents into the recruitment network by posing as prospective volunteers were turned down by Wood as a technical breach of the Foreign Enlistment Act that might invite criticism of the police force.[19] This strongly suggests that Berubé was a civilian who offered to work on behalf of the RCMP.

Meanwhile, on the transatlantic voyage, volunteers were told to keep to themselves and not talk to strangers. But their clandestine routine fooled no one, least of all the other volunteers, who were wearing similar clothes and carrying identical cardboard suitcases. Ron Liversedge kept up the charade for the first few days on board. Then one afternoon while playing table tennis with an Italian-American man, his opponent stopped briefly before serving and whispered, "No Pasarán!" The phrase, first used as slogan by the republican defenders of Madrid, became a crude code in the midst of the Atlantic crossing. Liversedge grinned, and the two men began to openly discuss their voyage to Spain.[20]

Some volunteers later said that an official from the American embassy met them as they disembarked at Le Havre, France, and offered to pay their way back to the United States, insisting that the border with Spain was sealed. None accepted his offer, and the volunteers continued on to Paris, where French party-linked organizations looked after their accommodation and food. Some men were given physical examinations, but these were not too rigorous. "If you can see lightning and hear thunder, you know you're home free," Hugh Garner said.[21]

Paris overwhelmed a few of the Canadian volunteers who had spent most of their lives in small farming towns on the Canadian Prairies. Nick Elendiuk grew up in Winnipeg and later worked on an Alberta ranch breaking horses. His first experience in a Paris hotel was bewildering, but he caught on quickly.

The twenty-six-year-old returned to his room after a walk around Paris to find a woman lounging in his bed. Flabbergasted and angry at the thought that someone had taken the suitcase and extra pair of socks he had left in his room, Elendiuk rushed downstairs and confronted the proprietress.

"Did you rent my room out?" he demanded.

"Oh, no," she said.

"Well, there is a lady in my bed."

"If you don't want her there, tell her to get out," the proprietress said calmly. "She is a *fille de joie*."

"What the hell is a *fille de joie*?"

"Let's say she is a professional companion," the woman explained patiently. "If you don't want her there, tell her to leave. Or I will. Do you want her to leave?"

Elendiuk said nothing for a few moments. Perhaps he considered the very real possibility that he would be dead in a few weeks, or maybe he just thought again about the possibilities involving a friendly woman in his bed.

"Maybe I'll go tell her myself," he said.[22]

Elsewhere in the city, William Beeching, Alex Forbes, and Alex Chambers returned to their hotel after sampling their first cognac and coffee to find that their respective roommates were passed out drunk and unable to open the door. The hotel owner heard the commotion and, furious, kicked the trio out onto the streets. They decided to visit the Montmartre neighbourhood, drawn by rumours of exotic and raunchy cabaret shows, but somewhere along the way they got lost or distracted. The three ended up in a dingy café, where they met two émigré Russians from the Czarist White Guards. Forbes spoke Russian, both he and Beeching were communists, and all three of them were stoked with cognac and visions of revolution. They stayed in the café until dawn, drinking and arguing with their two ideological opponents.[23]

From Paris the volunteers travelled to southern France and the Spanish frontier. Some men reported elaborate cloak-and-dagger routines involving secret contacts and child guides with colour-coded ribbons in their hair.[24] Others simply boarded a train and sang revolutionary songs all the way to the border. In the early months of the war, the frontier remained open and volunteers crossed into Spain with few problems. Facing international pressure, France officially closed the frontier in early 1937. Some volunteers attempting to cross were temporarily arrested; others were forced to seek alternative ways across the border.

A few attempts were made to bring volunteers into Spain by boat. The night of 29 May 1937 the *Ciudad de Barcelona* sailed from Marseille with 250 internationals on board. The following morning, two Canadians, Joe Schoen and Ivor "Tiny" Anderson, stood on deck and watched the Catalan coast slip past them on the boat's starboard side. Anderson earned his nickname because he stood an imposing six foot three. He and Schoen had met in Toronto after they had separately travelled to the city from western Canada; they had vowed to stick together all the way to Spain. This morning the two were enjoying the sun and the warm Spanish breeze. A large collie was on deck, and Schoen joked to Anderson that if they were torpedoed, he'd have to hang on to the dog and hope the animal towed him to shore. Schoen could barely swim.

Minutes later, the *Ciudad de Barcelona* was torpedoed. The ship erupted in confusion as passengers from below deck rushed upward and the boat pitched and heaved. Anderson, Schoen, and the boat's first mate made it to a lifeboat, but it was tangled in ropes and water rushed over them. Fearing that he might be sucked under with the boat, Schoen bid "so long" to Anderson and jumped overboard. He dog-paddled toward shore. Around him other passengers were already slipping beneath the waves. Schoen himself was weakening quickly as the tide, a current, or the suction of the sinking boat swept him away from shore. "I kept swimming until I got so tired I figured well, heck, what's the difference? A minute more or less, I might as well go now. I was just about to give up and Anderson hollers for me to hang on."[25]

Anderson, a much stronger swimmer, was now in the water and kicked toward Schoen with a life preserver. He supported his friend until a pontoon plane landed near them after dropping depth charges, which buffeted all those in the water, and ferried the two to shore.[26] Others managed to swim to safety or kick their way to the coast hanging on to bits of floating debris. About fifty volunteers, including at least seven Canadians, were killed in the attack. One of the last men to go down with the ship, a Canadian from Winnipeg named Karl Francis, was frozen with fear and wrapped himself around the mast. People in the water yelled at him to jump, but he refused and clung to the mast as it sank beneath the waves.[27]

After this disaster, almost all volunteers entered Spain by climbing the Pyrenees, setting off in the middle of the night guided by smugglers who had been hired for the job. The task was a gruelling one – especially for the softer city-bred volunteers. Most were woefully unprepared. Some were given *alpargatas* – rope-soled sandals – by their guides, but many struggled and slipped up mountain trails wearing dress shoes that were cut to ribbons. Some men were given a bit of food; others were not. Volunteers collapsed and were carried or left behind. Members of the Non-Intervention Committee claimed after the war that they found the bodies of two hundred men who had fallen down crevices or collapsed and died of exhaustion during the climb.[28]

The suffering on the ascent became an initiation of sorts that bound the men who completed it to each other. Many described the experience of at last cresting the ridge of the Pyrenees and looking down on Spain as an almost spiritual moment. Spain was, literally, a new dawn. "We finally reached the top. I'll never forget that, because you look at Spain, on the opposite side of the Pyrenees, you see the daylight. You look back on France and it was all night," Louis Tellier said. "It was a sight, and it is a sight, one does not forget."

Lionel Edwards remembered his thoughts when he saw Spain for the first time from the mountaintop: "To paraphrase the poet, God was in his heaven and all was right in the world."[29]

Once in Spain, the volunteers typically collapsed in a shepherd's hut, where they were usually given coffee before trucks arrived to take them to the fortress town of Figueras. The fortress, dating from the eighteenth century, failed to make much of an impression on the newly arrived volunteers. "Everyone that had been there for the last four thousand years must have been using it for a toilet," Percy Hilton remembered.[30] From Figueras the volunteers travelled by train through coastal orange groves, where peasants sometimes watched them pass with their fists raised in solidarity or pushed armloads of fruit through the train's open windows.

Eventually they arrived in Albacete, the headquarters and main depot of the International Brigades, where the new arrivals were formally inducted. They were also required to give up their passports. "That's where I started to get in trouble, right off the bat," said Frank Hadesbeck, who initially refused to hand over his documents until convinced to do so by one of his fellow volunteers. "Oh, they didn't like it the way I talked right then and there. I possibly would have been branded a fascist immediately ... It wasn't hard to be branded a fascist if you didn't say the right thing the minute you got on Spanish soil, because apparently nobody trusted anybody there."[31]

In the town's bullring, the volunteers were divided according to nationality and skill and deployed to surrounding villages and towns. The many Canadian immigrant volunteers faced a dilemma at this point. Most had been in Canada less than twenty years. Some felt they belonged with their new countrymen; others felt more comfortable with men from the countries they had left. To complicate matters further, commanders from European battalions, naturally eager for more men, pressured the new arrivals to join their units. Sandor Voros, a Hungarian-born American who had worked in Canada as a Communist Party organizer, said that in Albacete a Hungarian commander ordered him to enlist with the Hungarians. When Voros insisted he serve with his fellow Americans, the Hungarian tried, unsuccessfully, to have him arrested.[32] Canadian Konstantin Olynyk, an ethnic Ukrainian from Romania, ultimately decided he would be better off with other Ukrainians. He joined a Ukrainian company in the 13th International Brigade. "The problem was really the language," he said. "My English wasn't very good at the time, and I thought with my Ukrainian I could manage better."[33]

Although the nominally Canadian Mackenzie-Papineau Battalion accommodated hundreds of immigrant Canadians, and even had units composed almost entirely of ethnic Finns and Ukrainians, scores of Canadians made the same decision as Olynyk and served in European battalions, most often the Hungarian Rakosi Battalion; the Polish, Hungarian, and Yugoslav Dombrowsky Battalion; or the Balkan Dimitrov Battalion. By October 1937, Bob Kerr, a Canadian commissar at the Albacete base, said that Canadians formed their own company in the Dombrowsky Battalion, and that forty-five Canadians in the Dimitrov Battalion might also have formed a section of their own.[34] Others served in ethnically mixed artillery, transportation, communication, and artillery units. Several Finnish Canadians fought behind enemy lines in units of partisans. One French Canadian, Narcisse St. Louis, was originally assigned to a French unit but staged a sit-down strike to demand that he be allowed to fight with his fellow Canadians in the Mackenzie-Papineau Battalion. He was jailed as a result.[35]

Immigrant volunteers occasionally found that they now had less in common with their former countrymen than they might have expected. Writing in April 1937, Gustav Regler in the commissariat of the 12th International Brigade reported: "Chatting with the Polish Comrades, I heard of the tension that exists between the Communists who come from that country and the émigré Communists."[36] In total, at least half the Canadian volunteers served in the 15th International Brigade, the majority of these with the Mackenzie-Papineau Battalion.

In the first year of the war, however, there was no Canadian battalion for Canadian volunteers to join. The first Canadians were sent with their American counterparts to the nearby town of Villanueva de la Jara to be organized and equipped. Within days of arriving, these men, barely trained and poorly led, were called upon to defend Madrid. They were thrown into action in a valley that flanked the Jarama River. It was a place that few who survived would ever forget.

4

Protecting Madrid, February–July 1937

Madrid was seen by both nationalists and republicans as the key to winning the civil war – as much for its symbolic as for its strategic importance. Emilio Mola, one of the generals who planned the coup d'état, promised an easy conquest of the capital. He went so far as to predict that he would shortly take his coffee in a café on the Gran Vía, the main avenue in Madrid. When his initial assault of November 1936 was repulsed, with the help of the first units of the International Brigades, cocky residents of the capital placed a card reading "Reserved for General Mola" at an empty table, where it remained for much of the war. The fight for Madrid soon settled into a stalemated battle of attrition, as both sides established lines facing each other on the outskirts of the city. Franco, however, had invested too much in taking Madrid to abandon the offensive. He changed tactics and planned an assault to cut off and isolate Madrid by flanking the city and severing the highway to Valencia.

The nationalist forces, consisting primarily of Moors and Foreign Legionnaires, launched their assault at dawn on 6 February 1937. They advanced rapidly, surging to the banks of the Jarama River, where they were held up for days by rain, which made the river impassable. Just before dawn on 11 February, Moroccan troops, already feared for their lethal knife work, silently dispatched French International Brigades sentries on the Pindoque railway bridge, which spanned the river, and seized a foothold on the far shore. The bridge had been prepared for demolition, but the explosion proved insufficient to wreck the structure. Moors captured the bridge at San Martin de la Vega in a similar dawn attack, and the nationalists were across the river in force.

A savage and desperate battle now took place across the Jarama Valley. The newly formed 15th International Brigade, consisting of the British Battalion, the Balkan Dimitrov Battalion, and the Franco-Belgian Sixth of February Battalion, was thrown into the breach on the road from San Martin de la Vega to Morata de Tajuña. The British lost half their number attacking and then holding Pingarron Hill, which was soon dubbed "Suicide Hill" by the men who fought there. The British were eventually overrun. Their machine-gun company was captured when the Sixth of February Battalion withdrew suddenly, leaving the unit defenceless on its flank. Among the prisoners was Canadian Bert "Yank" Levy. Short and wiry, with dark eyes and the flattened hook nose of a boxer, Levy survived captivity and eventually taught guerrilla tactics to British Home Guard troops in the Second World War.[1]

Similar scenarios unfolded across the front. Violent attacks took a punishing toll on Spanish and international defenders. The lines teetered on the verge of disintegration, but they ultimately held. The front stabilized, with both sides exhausted.

Meanwhile the American Lincoln Battalion, including about forty Canadians, was rushed through its training at Villanueva de la Jara. On the afternoon of 15 February, the battalion formed up in the Villanueva bullring, where it received rifles – still packed in grease – and helmets. André Marty, the French communist commander of the Albacete base and the de facto head of the International Brigades, addressed the new soldiers and hugged the few French Canadians in the battalion.[2] The men ripped strips of cloth off their shirts and tried to clean their rifles, then climbed aboard trucks for the long, cramped drive to the front. They were bombed once on the way, but all survived. In the morning the trucks stopped and the volunteers were told to fire five shots at a nearby hillside. For many, about to join one of the most intense battles of the civil war, this was the first time they had fired a gun. But at least they had weapons that worked; volunteers in the International Brigades fought the war with a haphazard collection of often antiquated rifles and machine guns that frequently jammed and broke down – when the correct calibre ammunition could be found at all.[3] At least one Canadian arrived in the Jarama trenches with no rifle. "I had a knife," Hugh Garner remembered. "I said the first Moor that comes in here I'm going to cut his nuts off."[4]

That evening, the men stopped for a brief hot meal at Morata de Tajuña but were soon ordered back onto the trucks and driven the final few kilometres to the front. Here, two truckloads of volunteers, including the ill-fated Canadian Thomas Beckett, inadvertently veered into nationalist lines and were slaughtered. The rest of the battalion disembarked from the trucks and were told to dig in. The men had no shovels. Worse, no one had taught them how and where to dig trenches. With helmets and bare hands, they scraped shallow ditches clearly visible against the skyline and were promptly cut to pieces by sniper fire and shells in the morning.[5]

The Lincolns moved into new trenches on 23 February and were ordered over the top in a pointless attack in which twenty were killed and nearly sixty wounded. The battalion now fielded fewer than three hundred men. More volunteers were killed over the next few days by enemy snipers who preyed on the internationals in their too-shallow trenches. The Lincolns, however, had no time to lick their wounds before being ordered to attack again, on 27 February 1937.

Seventy reinforcements had arrived the day before, including the Canadian Walter Dent, who had come to Spain the previous week, on 18 February. He said that on 26 February the new reinforcements were given rifles and ten rounds of ammunition and were taken just behind the lines, where someone had placed a rag on a hillside. The reinforcements were told to shoot at it. They were then given a few minutes of instruction on how to use a bayonet before being sent into the trenches. Dent happened to be working as a runner that day and missed even these rudimentary instructions. "I learned to fire my rifle in the front lines five minutes prior to the attack," he said. "Those of us who lived became better soldiers."[6]

The assault was conceived by the commander of the 11th and 15th International Brigades, Colonel "Gal" (Janos Galicz), a central European communist who was living in exile in the Soviet Union before being dispatched to Spain. This was a time when foreigners in the Soviet Union were viewed with suspicion, and perhaps Gal hoped to redeem himself in Spain. But Gal was bad-tempered and an incompetent commander, and his efforts to achieve glory on the battlefield would prove costly.[7] Gal faced a well-entrenched enemy on a stabilized front that bristled with machine guns. Dislodging men from such a position would require more than bravery from attacking troops, and so Gal promised the necessary supporting firepower. On the eve of the battle he called the Lincoln Battalion's commander Robert Merriman to his headquarters and explained that the Lincolns would have infantry support on their flanks and a preliminary bombardment by artillery, planes, tanks, and armoured cars.

The next morning dawned wet, cold, and foggy. There was no sign of the promised support, though a few planes flew over, dropped their bombs far behind enemy lines, and thereby alerted the nationalists that an assault was imminent. The morning mist lifted and there was still no barrage, save some scattered shells that landed wide of their mark. Merriman telephoned brigade headquarters to protest the futility of the attack. He reached the Yugoslav commander of the 15th Brigade, Colonel Vladimir Copic, a veteran of the Red Army and another European exile in the Soviet Union before the Spanish Civil War. Copic came to be resented by many of the Canadian, American, and British volunteers, who believed that he was an archetypal "Albacete general" – a commander who avoided the front and did not value the lives of his men. That morning, Copic ordered Merriman to attack "at all costs" and insisted that the troops on the Lincolns' flanks had already advanced. Merriman protested but eventually accepted the order and bravely resolved to lead the attack himself.[8]

The assault was a massacre. The new international volunteers did not know enough even to leave their heavy packs behind but trudged toward enemy machine guns with all their equipment on their backs. The nationalists waited until the majority of the attacking Americans and Canadians had climbed out of their trenches before mowing them down. Within minutes the assault had been stopped, and dozens of men were dead and dying in no man's land. Incompetent commanders compounded the tragedy by ordering those in the trenches to rush forward ammunition to their already dead comrades. At nightfall, the few survivors struggled back to their muddy trenches, where the badly wounded died for lack of medical attention. More than one hundred men had been killed or wounded.[9] Several survivors slipped away hoping to desert, but most were caught and forced back into lines. The wounded included Merriman himself. Furious, he demanded to be carried on his stretcher to speak with Copic but was rebuffed.

The battered Lincoln Battalion stayed in the lines, at first exhausted, then bitter and cynical about their commanders and political leaders. "We were expecting that at any time some idiot would send us over again," Hugh Garner said.[10] A month after the attacks, the battalion totalled only 260 men, of whom only 130 were Americans and Canadians; the rest were Spanish.[11] They were reinforced on 17 April by 40 men, including several Canadians, and they received one day's rest on 1 May. But the battalion did not leave the lines until 17 June, after 120 days in the trenches.

The front was relatively quiet following the 27 February assault, with the exception of an attack by Franco's Moors in mid-March, which was repelled. The trench-bound soldiers were even able to set up an informal recreation area in a protected depression just behind their lines. Here they could play table tennis as stray bullets whizzed and snapped six metres above their heads. But this did little to ease the resentment of members of the Lincoln Battalion and of other internationals on the Jarama front. A June report on "political work in the brigade" noted that the English volunteers had been hit by a "wave of desertions." The French were abusing alcohol, fleeing to Madrid and begging their consulate to help them get back to France, and defecting "en masse" to the anarchists. The Americans showed "violent criticism" toward their military commanders.[12]

Of the Canadians who took part in the Jarama fighting, at least eighteen were killed, including Thomas Beckett and another Canadian who died fighting with the Dimitrov Battalion. At least four were wounded, and another man, listed as missing, presumably died there as well. Despite the unnecessary slaughter of 23 and 27 February, Jarama was not a failure for the Republic and for the International Brigades: they stopped the nationalist flanking assault on Madrid.

The lethal incompetence demonstrated by brigade high command was a bitter pill to swallow, however. The men knew that those who led them were too often given leading positions because of their party connections rather than military skill and experience. "In the XV Brigade there have been too many politicians and too few professional soldiers," Harry Rayfield wrote in October 1938.[13] There were few real soldiers available to place in positions of leadership, and some non-party members, including Hugh McGregor, also were sent to officers' training school.[14] But Rayfield was correct: volunteers who were trusted members of the Communist Party were more likely to be given command positions than those who were not.

The Lincolns were withdrawn for rest to Albares, a village thirty kilometres to the east. Some veterans said they spent their happiest days in Spain there. They rested their aching bodies, ate real food, and flirted with local women. Jules Paivio enlisted the help of a Cuban volunteer to help him communicate with a Spanish girl named Juliana at a village dance. The Cuban revised Jules' comments about the weather and the grass, instead conveying the Canadian's undying love and affection. It worked, though, and the twenty-year-old spent the remainder of his time in Albares going on long walks with Juliana. "I had a splendid time while it lasted," he said.[15]

The Lincolns' stay in town did not start out this well. Walter Dent recalled that when they marched in, haggard, unshaven, and stinking after four months in the trenches, only a few curious children came out to greet them. That night most of the men got drunk and "whooped it up." One man ended up at the front door of a house where a funeral was taking place and pestered the mourners for food and alcohol. A few others made similar nuisances of themselves. The next day the worst offenders were tried and sentenced to be jailed for the entire length of their leave. This built up trust with local people. The volunteers also took a collection to buy gifts for the children, organized a baseball game, and helped out in the fields. A much larger crowd turned out to see them leave than had come to greet them.[16]

Volunteers continued to arrive from Canada throughout the spring. During this rest period another forty Canadians were incorporated into the Lincolns; by July, one of the Lincoln companies had more Canadians than Americans.[17] About forty other Canadians were assigned to the newly formed George Washington Battalion, which had not yet seen action.[18] There is some confusion over how exactly the Canadians were organized in these two battalions. Walter Dent said there was a loosely formed company of Canadians at Jarama.[19] Reports refer to Canadian sections in both battalions by July, and even to a Canadian company in one of the battalions, though these appellations might have been informal.[20] Volunteers in Spain were not organized into sections and companies as rigidly as they would have been in a conventional army. We do know that several Canadians commanded companies in the George Washington Battalion. Alec Miller was appointed commander of the first company on 25 June 1937.[21] Ed Jardas and future Mac-Pap commander Edward Cecil-Smith also led companies.[22] These appointments would prove short-lived. The George Washington Battalion, along with any Canadian units it contained, was disbanded after its baptism of fire on a dusty and stifling plain before the Castilian town of Brunete.

The spring of 1937 saw nationalist forces closing in on the few remaining republican positions in the north of Spain. German bombers razed Guernica, the spiritual capital of the Basque people, and Franco's soldiers were marching on Bilbao. Prime Minister Francisco Largo Caballero's general staff drew up plans for an offensive in Extremadura in southwestern Spain, where national-ist troops were poorly trained and thin on the ground. They hoped that an attack here would force Franco to divert his forces and thereby ease pressure on Spain's beleaguered north. But communist ambition centred on Madrid, whose defence was vital if the Spanish republican government was to retain legitimacy on the international stage. Soviet advisors and communist leaders therefore refused to commit tank and air support to the planned Extremadura offensive.[23] Largo Caballero was forced to resign in May, replaced by Juan Negrín, who had Soviet support, and whose minister of defence, Indalecio Prieto, was prepared to cooperate with the communists.[24] The Extremadura offensive was cancelled. Instead, the Republic launched two attacks in May and June, in the Sierra de Guadarrama, and against Huesca in Aragón. Both failed. Bilbao fell to the nationalists, but the Basques, Asturians, and other republican soldiers holding out in the north refused to surrender. They were now engaged in a fighting retreat into the mountains and along the coast toward Santander.

The Republic, however, had not yet launched its largest operation designed to relieve the north. This offensive called for a massive and concentrated attack on the front lines opposite Brunete, some twenty-five kilometres west of Madrid. The attacking force, which included all five International Brigades, comprised the largest collection of men and materiel yet assembled in the war. The hope was that the main offensive would see republican troops drive south across hot and dusty plains and then swing east to link up with a complementary attack probing west and north from the suburbs of Madrid, thereby freeing the Spanish capital from its siege.[25]

The 15th Brigade arrived at Valdemorillo just behind the Brunete front lines on 5 July, exhausted after a three-day march. The Canadians collapsed in olive groves on high ground above the valley through which they would soon be attacking. They spread their bedrolls among the discarded clothes, blankets, and canteens that other soldiers had elected to jettison during the long march. Steve Nelson, a commissar in the Lincoln Battalion, recalled that the Finnish Canadians stood apart because they kept all their equipment with them:

> These guys were workers from the woods. They knew what the hell it meant to have a shovel, what the hell it meant to have blanket, what it meant to have a mess kit for water, a bucket for water ... They lived in the bushes, in the mountains, in the woods. Students from Columbia University – what the hell did they know about these things? ... Of course the next night, it's cold in the mountains and the only ones who weren't bitching and moaning for blankets were these Finnish Canadians.

One of the shivering Americans approached Steve Nelson and demanded blankets. Nelson recalled, "I said, 'Boys, you know where you left them.'"[26]

On the eve of the attack, Copic and Brigade Commissar George S. Aitken issued a written statement intended to encourage their men:

> Now our turn has come. Today we are about to participate in a mighty drive which will prove a decisive operation in this war for the liberty of the people of Spain – and indeed, of the whole human race ... FORWARD TO THE ATTACK! FORWARD TO SMASH FASCISM, TO SAVE SPAIN AND TO ENSURE THE TRIUMPH OF DEMOCRACY! PASAREMOS! WE SHALL PASS![27]

Dawn began with a deafening republican artillery barrage. The nationalists responded in kind, albeit with fewer guns. The republicans had successfully assembled their attacking forces at Brunete in secret. With a yell, their soldiers rushed into the valley and the battle was joined.

Problems began almost immediately. The 15th International Brigade was not supposed to march down from the hills above the valley floor until the town of Villanueva de la Cañada had fallen. The plan called for the 15th Brigade to bypass the town and proceed to the nationalist strongpoint of Mosquito Ridge – easily defended high ground that threatened the entire offensive. From their elevated vantage point, the Americans, Canadians, British, and Balkan Slavs in the 15th Brigade's Dimitrov Battalion watched as republican troops and tanks were pinned down outside the town. The 15th Brigade was diverted to aid in the assault. It advanced into the now scorching valley and encircled Villanueva de la Cañada, but it too was immobilized by machine-gun fire from the church steeple. The heat took its toll. There was no water, no shade, and little cover. Those who had replaced the water in their canteens with local red wine suffered most.[28] Men began collapsing with heatstroke; others, without proper entrenching equipment, made futile efforts to dig into the dry earth.

Bryce Coleman, a towering man from the Prairies, was shot and killed while carrying canteens full of water back to his parched comrades. His younger brother, Macdonald, later described Bryce as an intense and serious man but also a bit of a loner. During the Great Depression he had wandered across western North America, herding sheep in Montana, working on an Alberta ranch, and picking fruit in the Okanagan Valley. From time to time he'd gone back home to stay with his family and take his younger brother swimming in a nearby river. Before leaving for Spain, Bryce gave his brother a speech about facing down Hitler and fighting for mankind, and then he added, "And anyway, kid, there isn't much of a future for me in Canada when I can't even get a job." A few months after his death, Bryce's mother received a parcel in the mail with some of his personal belongings, including a bible. Bryce had signed his name inside the front cover, and in the space reserved for the owner's address he had written: "The World."[29]

The exhausted survivors of the initial attack on Villanueva de la Cañada were ordered to storm the town, which was now far behind the main line of advance. They did so, finally breaching nationalist defences at nightfall and clearing out machine gunners in the church by setting the building on fire. At least thirty men from the Lincoln and George Washington battalions were killed in the assault, including the Canadian section leader Paddy O'Neil (whose real name was Stewart Homer). O'Neil was an Irish emigrant to Canada and a former organizer in wilderness logging camps. He took command of the unit when its original leader, Canadian Joe Armitage, was killed.[30] At least six other Canadians also died taking the town, and several more were wounded. Tom Bailey recalled that of the forty Canadians in his section, only twenty-one were later still on their feet and able to respond at roll call.[31]

The battalions of the 15th Brigade spent the morning of 7 July resting, eating captured provisions, and waiting for new orders, which were a long time coming. Captured nationalist prisoners were marched past the dozing internationals. Two Belgian members of Franco's foreign legion yelled out, "Hello, Ruskies!" Hugh Garner, somewhat irritated, shouted back in Spanish: "We're North Americans!" But the Belgians just laughed and did not believe them. "We were all Russians to them."[32] Their rest was interrupted by shelling from Mosquito Ridge. Finally, in early afternoon, the brigade was ordered to take these heights.

The 15th Brigade marched across a landscape snarled with dry riverbeds and small stands of forest. It was terrain perfectly suited to ambushes sprung by retreating infantry, but it provided the advancing internationals with little cover from aerial bombardment. German planes now ranged above the valley floor, bombing and scattering the soldiers below them. On 8 July, the men of the 15th International Brigade followed Soviet tanks across the Guadarrama River, flitted through the poplar stands on the opposite shore, and began their direct assault on Mosquito Ridge, whose crest loomed above them one and a half kilometres away. They would spend five days attacking the ridge. Many died in the attempt, victims of snipers, artillery, and the relentless sun. During the nights, Moors climbed trees, sniping at the internationals below when the sun came up. The attacking volunteers learned to begin each day by raking the treetops with machine-gun fire, but this did little to stop the steady attrition.[33]

Eventually, brigade command ordered them to stop advancing and hold their ground. After seven days of action, they were withdrawn from the front lines. The two American and Canadian battalions had lost half their number and now totalled about 300.[34] The British Battalion had dwindled to eighty men.[35] Around this time, Colonel Hans Klaus, a former Prussian officer and the brigade chief of staff, and George S. Aitken, the brigade's political commissar, issued a memorandum to all battalion and unit commanders informing them that Colonel Copic had been "slightly wounded" in an aerial bombardment and that Klaus was taking over leadership of the 15th Brigade.[36] Copic apparently recovered and soon resumed command.

The surviving Canadians had no time to rest. News of nationalist attacks elsewhere on the front led to immediate redeployment and all-night forced marches. The Lincoln and Washington battalions spent almost two more weeks shifting from sector to sector before finally being relieved on 25 July. The entire offensive ground to a halt and, after the nationalists retook some of the ground that had initially been overrun, the front stabilized again. On 11 August 1937, Luigi Longo (known in Spain as Gallo), the Italian communist inspector general of the International Brigades, reported that the 15th Brigade, which had begun the Brunete offensive with more than 2,000 men, now totalled 885. Almost 300 men were dead, 735 were wounded, and another 167 were missing. The Lincoln and Washington battalions, which included scores of Canadians, had been reduced from 524 to 286 effectives.[37]

The nationalists had been forced to ease their attacks in the north because of the Brunete attacks, but the reprieve was temporary. With the threat at Brunete neutralized, Franco redoubled his efforts to crush the Republic's Army of the North. Aided by Italian soldiers and German planes, nationalist soldiers advanced on Santander and Santoña, where large republican formations surrendered. About half of the republican soldiers pulled back into the Asturian mountains. Desperately brave, they would not be dislodged until the end of October, and even then holdouts waged a fierce guerrilla campaign until the following spring, when resistance in the north was finally extinguished.[38]

The Canadians and Americans who could still walk and potentially fight were removed to Albares, the scene of many happy days only a few weeks previous. Few were in the mood to chat up local girls, but they took frequent trips to Madrid, where the Americans and some of the Canadian volunteers liked to visit Ernest Hemingway in his well-stocked hotel room. The Abraham Lincoln and the George Washington battalions had suffered such heavy losses that they were now combined into one battalion – the Lincoln-Washington Battalion, though it was usually simply called the Lincolns.

Meanwhile, recruits from Canada and the United States arriving in Albacete were organized into a new and still unnamed battalion. Canadian volunteers in Spain had long been agitating for formal recognition of Canada's contribution to the war effort. Communist Party of Canada propaganda had been touting the existence of a Canadian battalion in Spain – dubbed the "Mackenzie-Papineau Battalion," or the Mac-Paps – for months. That this battalion did not exist was a potential publicity disaster. Several leading Canadians, including Ron Liversedge and John "Paddy" O'Shea, pleaded with the American Robert Merriman to name the new battalion the Mac-Paps. The existence of a formally named Canadian battalion would be vital for continued fundraising efforts in Canada, they told him, and it was hard to justify naming yet another battalion after an American hero when several hundred Canadians had already arrived in Spain but had received little official acknowledgment.

Merriman and the Americans who dominated brigade staff initially would not be swayed, agreeing only to designate a "Mackenzie-Papineau Company" within the American battalion, which was to be named after Patrick Henry or some other American historical figure. The tide finally turned when Albert A. MacLeod, a prominent Canadian communist, came to Spain and addressed the new trainees in an impassioned speech sometime around 1 July, Dominion Day in Canada. The men and brigade leadership were won over by MacLeod's oratory, and the new battalion was named the Mackenzie-Papineau Battalion, after two Canadians – one anglophone, one francophone – who led short-lived rebellions against colonial rule in Canada in 1837.[39] One of the two, William Lyon Mackenzie, was the grandfather of the Canadian prime minister William Lyon Mackenzie King, which only added to the new battalion's propaganda potential. At least half those who served in the battalion at its inception were American, and many of the Canadians serving with the Lincolns stayed in that battalion.[40] However, new Canadian recruits arriving in Spain now had a designated battalion, and supporters in Canada had a name around which to rally. "The Americans took it fine, and voted unanimously for it," Joe Dallet, the battalion's first commissar, wrote in a letter to his wife. "The Canadian comrades, who are a fine lot, are blissfully happy at having won their objectives."[41]

Aragón Battles, August 1937-February 1938

When the Brunete offensive failed to achieve a breakthrough or decisive victory, republican command considered other options. Republican soldiers were still holding out in Spain's north, and it was hoped that another offensive elsewhere would draw off some of Franco's troops. The rocky hills of Spain's northeast beckoned for a different reason. Catalonia and Aragón were strongholds of Spain's anarchist movement, and of POUM, the Partido Obrero de Unificación Marxista, a radical Marxist party that fiercely opposed the brand of communism espoused by Joseph Stalin and the Soviet Union. Sending eighty thousand government troops into areas where anarchist and POUMist troops were stationed on a relatively quiet front would allow Prime Minister Juan Negrín's new government to assert its control.[1] The ultimate goal of the planned offensive was Zaragoza, an important transport hub and a city with a supposedly anti-fascist population. The route to Zaragoza ran through the much smaller towns of Quinto, Belchite, and Fuentes de Ebro.

Quinto fell during the last week of August 1937, following two days of hard street fighting. The British Battalion led an assault on the town's garrison on nearby Pulburrel Hill, where Paddy O'Daire, who lived in Canada between 1929 and 1934, temporarily took command of the battalion. As at Villanueva de la Cañada and countless other besieged towns, Quinto's strongpoint was its church. The building's defenders did not submit easily, despite intensive point-blank bombardment from the brigade's anti-tank battery. The defenders were finally burned out and several of the captured nationalist prisoners were shot. Some reports claim Spaniards in the battalion shot the prisoners, allegedly after the prisoners had insulted their captors. But Marvin Penn, a Canadian who was there, said that after those who were barricaded in the church refused repeated requests to surrender, members of the International Brigades were in little mood to show them mercy. "We were too mad. We were too angry. It was ten minutes and they were gone, finished," he said in an interview thirty years later. The ten to twelve nationalists still alive in the church did not surrender until they were flushed out with fire and smoke: "We asked them. We explained to them. We had good propaganda in Spanish: 'Isn't life precious? You are surrounded. What are you fighting for?' After all that they'd always answer with a burst of fire. Well then, we weren't going to treat them like human beings." As Penn related it, the nationalists emerged from the church, gave the fascist salute, and shouted, "Arriba España," which enraged the internationals. Copic reportedly wanted to take the men prisoner but was refused. "All the boys, we all felt that way ... We had lost a lot of comrades, you see, because of those twelve guys ... We just grabbed those guys, lined them up and shot them right there ... They didn't march more than two hundred yards from where they came out," Penn said, adding that this was the only time of which he was aware when internationals shot prisoners.[2]

Louis Tellier, who took part in the battle, confirmed that captured Spanish officers were shot out of hand. "They were shot, period," he said. "Some of our guys got mixed up in that. They weren't doing what they were supposed to. They had no business doing that. They were out of control ... You could almost say anything: 'Well, he was going to shoot me. He had a revolver by him.' It wasn't many. It was maybe two or three characters I know done that."[3]

According to Carl Geiser, two civilians who had been sheltering in the church were also shot by American volunteers at the request of young Spanish soldiers, who identified them as fascist officials. The executions did not stop there. After the prisoners taken from the church were shot, Geiser reports that General "Walter" (Karol Swierczewski) shot several nationalist officers, saying "for Dubois" each time he killed a man, in memory of his friend Dubois, a doctor who had been shot by a nationalist sniper. Walter then ordered the murder of a small group of non-commissioned officers. Spanish and international troops opened fire on them, but many of the victims were still living after the initial volley. Most were given a *coup de grâce,* but one had only a leg wound and was very much alive. At the sight of his suffering, some of the Americans revolted and demanded to call over a commissar to see if the man could be hospitalized. An international nicknamed Crazy O'Leary ended the dispute when he put a bullet in the Spaniard's head.[4]

Quinto was a bloody and horrific battle, but the outcome was a military success for the International Brigades. They had been deployed as shock troops in a situation requiring courage and the ability to improvise, and they rose to the challenge. The next town to fall was Belchite, though this assault was more costly. Once again, sniper and machine-gun fire from the town's church pinned down the attacking troops. Advancing and even retreating over open ground courted death; many of the Lincolns were stuck in shallow trenches several hundred metres outside the town. Merriman, now at brigade headquarters, ordered Captain Hans Amlie to charge the church. One squad of twenty-two men made for the town. All were cut down.[5] Merriman ordered another attack and threatened Amlie with court martial when Amlie refused. Fortunately for Amlie, the American Steve Nelson discovered an empty culvert leading to a disused olive factory on the edge of town. He was able to lead a diversionary assault that permitted the attacking internationals to breach Belchite's defences.[6]

Even so, nearly two weeks of bloody house-to-house fighting followed. The mostly British anti-tank battery peppered snipers' nests with accurate shelling, but actually rooting out the defenders was a close-combat affair. Each house had to be cleared by dropping grenades down the chimneys or through open windows and then, after the explosions had blown off the doors, rushing inside to spray the interior with machine-gun fire. The nationalists once again made their last stand in the church. This time, however, the American commissar Dave Doran (born Dave Dransky) was able to persuade the defenders to surrender with a spur-of-the-moment speech, which he wrote and a Spanish Lincoln read over a loudspeaker, after the broadcast of the Spanish national anthem, "Himno de Riego." The town now belonged to the Republic.

Some veterans remembered that Vladimir Copic ordered the execution by firing squad of captured nationalist prisoners at Belchite.[7] This may well have taken place, though Canadians interviewed years later did not mention it. The American Carl Geiser said the only prisoner shot at Belchite was the head of a local Falange unit, who was executed at the insistence of locals. One of Geiser's friends carried out the order and was greatly disturbed by the prisoner crying and begging with his arms wrapped around his executioner's knees before he was shot.[8] Marvin Penn, who openly described the execution of captured nationalists at Quinto, said prisoners were treated well at Belchite. Belchite itself was a blackened ruin and would never be lived in again. In the 1940s, a new town was built a kilometre or so down the road. Today, the original town of Belchite is still rubble.

The Mackenzie-Papineau Battalion had meanwhile completed its three-month training, the longest any battalion in the International Brigades received. It joined the 15th Brigade in mid-September, replacing the crack Dimitrovs, who now left the brigade. After so long in Spain without action, the Mac-Paps were earnest and eager to meet the enemy in battle. Their fellow volunteers in the 15th International Brigade, transformed from similarly fresh-faced recruits to hardened veterans in only a few short months, regarded the Mac-Paps, when they acknowledged them at all, with scorn and bemused contempt.

The Mac-Pap tradition of beginning each day with an early morning bugle call was quickly ended when one of the veteran soldiers in another battalion placed the offending instrument beneath the wheels of a truck, where it was soon run over and crushed – an incident that allowed everyone to sleep longer but also broke the ice between the Mac-Paps and the more experienced soldiers. The new battalion's shooting drills were similarly discontinued, as they annoyed the veterans of Jarama, Brunete, Quinto, and Belchite, who had heard enough gunshots since arriving in Spain.[9]

The Mac-Paps were led by Robert Thompson, an American communist who, according to the American volunteer George Watt, had come to Spain directly from Moscow's Lenin School, a training facility for international communists.[10] Another American named Joe Dallet was commissar. Most of the company commanders were also American, though the Canadian Finn Niilo Makela led the machine-gun company, which was primarily composed of fellow Finns from Canadian lumber camps.

Makela, a tall, quiet man with broad shoulders, piercing blue eyes, and a ruddy complexion, became one of the most respected military leaders in the Mac-Paps – in part because he lacked completely the hectoring political airs that afflicted so many commanders in Spain. Canadian John McGrandle remembered that Makela never raised his voice yet commanded respect. He was impossible to shake. When German planes strafed the Mac-Paps' positions, he ignored the airborne threat and focused on the enemy facing them on the ground. "I don't think I saw a braver man in my life," McGrandle said. Lawrence Cane, an American who served in the Mackenzie-Papineau Battalion, said Makela tried to encourage and look after his men instead of ingratiating himself with them. The men in the battalion looked up to him for it.[11]

The battalion's commissar, on the other hand, was disliked even before the men went into action. Joe Dallet tried to cloak his privileged past with affected working-class mannerisms. This was not uncommon among middle-class volunteers, and tensions existed within the American contingent between the majority of working-class Americans and the few intellectual volunteers, who struggled to fit in with an army of workers.[12] "People like Joe Dallet, people like myself, perhaps, who came from the student movement, we were always trying to prove that we were workers," George Watt remembered.[13] But Dallet was also a cold and petty authoritarian. So severe was the discontent about Dallet among the men in the Mac-Paps that leading American communists summoned Dallet to an all-night meeting, where he was castigated. Dallet offered to resign, but as the Mac-Paps were due to go into battle the next day, his offer was refused. Instead, he was told to prove himself on the battlefield.[14]

The Mackenzie-Papineau Battalion's inaugural action was to be an attack on the town of Fuentes de Ebro, the next stop in line on the road to Zaragoza. General Walter revealed the plan to the 15th Brigade late in the afternoon of 12 October, explaining that they were to take the heavily fortified town the next day. This left no time for proper reconnaissance or even to work out details of the impending assault, but General Walter had a plan that was designed to trump these inconveniences. Soviet tanks carrying Spaniards from the brigade's 24th Battalion would rush the machine-gun-infested defences of Fuentes de Ebro and deposit these troops behind nationalist lines. Meanwhile, the British, Canadian, and American battalions would attack from the front. Caught between the two attacking forces, the nationalist defenders would

1 Alex Forbes and Walter Hellund were two of many Canadian veterans who returned home wounded.

2 A wide variety of Canadians supported the Spanish Republic, but most fundraising was organized by the Communist Party of Canada. Here American nurses and Spanish aides pose in front of an ambulance donated by the CPC.

3 International volunteers man a Soviet-made Maxim heavy machine-gun.

4 Niilo Makela, a miner and lumberjack from northern Ontario, was one of the most loved and respected Canadian commanders of the war. He was fatally wounded during the battle for Caspe in March 1938. "I don't think I ever saw a braver man in my life," a fellow volunteer remembered.

5 Belchite's main square shows evidence of the fierce, close-quarters fighting that took place during its capture by republican forces in September 1937. Several Canadians died in the battle.

6 Norman Bethune stands before a vehicle attached to his Canadian Blood Transfusion Service.

7 Despite large numbers of Canadians fighting in Spain since February 1937, there was no designated Canadian battalion until July of that year. "The Canadian comrades, who are a fine lot, are blissfully happy at having won their objectives" the American Joe Dallet wrote to his wife after the Mackenzie-Papineau Battalion was officially formed.

8 American Joseph Dallet, the Mackenzie-Papineau Battalion's first commissar, struggled to win the respect of his men. He led from the front during the battalion's first action, perhaps in an effort to prove himself, and was shot dead.

9 William Skinner from Winnipeg asked that his wife be allowed to join him in Spain. He led a section of the Mackenzie-Papineau Battalion but later clashed with party leaders.

Fifteenth International Brigade Photographic Unit Photographs Collection, Abraham Lincoln Brigade Archives, Tamiment Library, New York University

10 International volunteers relax between actions.

Fifteenth International Brigade Photographic Unit Photographs Collection, Abraham Lincoln Brigade Archives, Tamiment Library, New York University

11 New Yorker John Gates rose to the rank of commissar of the 15th International Brigade. Commissars formed a parallel political command structure in the brigades.

Fifteenth International Brigade Photographic Unit Photographs Collection, Abraham Lincoln Brigade Archives, Tamiment Library, New York University

12 Wilfred Cowan, a twenty-year-old volunteer from Toronto, was wounded but survived and served with the Canadian army during the Second World War.

13 After weeks of bitter fighting in the frozen city of Teruel, volunteers in the 15th International Brigade assaulted several hilltop positions near the village of Segura de los Baños.

14 Following the disastrous retreats of March and April 1938, the Mackenzie-Papineau Battalion needed to be rebuilt, and its members needed to recuperate. Numerous fiestas were held in Marçà, where the Canadians were stationed before the Ebro offensive in July.

15 The Ebro offensive of July 1938 was the Republic's last hope for victory. Lightly armed attackers crossed the river in boats and on floating bridges, hoping to advance quickly and push deep into nationalist territory before their opponents could react.

16 A floating bridge is built across the Ebro River on the first day of the offensive.

17 Granollers, a city near Barcelona of no military significance, after a nationalist air raid in late May or early June 1938. About a hundred people, mainly women and children, were killed.

18 A captured German airman.

19 Lionel Edwards commanded a company of the Mackenzie-Papineau Battalion during the battle of Teruel in January 1938. Dug in on a hilltop position, his men stood against a ferocious nationalist assault for two days before the last four surviving defenders finally retreated. "I knew now what a lamb feels like awaiting the slaughter," Edwards later recalled.

20 Canadians gather for lunch. Many never got used to a diet of chickpeas and olive oil, occasionally fortified with donkey meat.

21 An international volunteer fires at his pursuers during the retreats of April 1938.

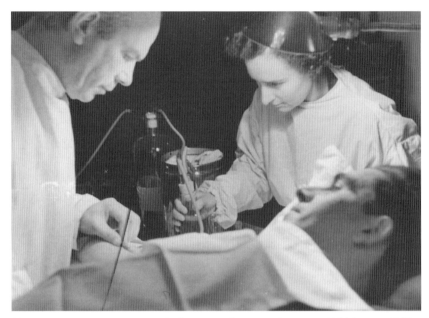

22 Norman Bethune collects blood for future transfusions, c. December 1936-January 1937.

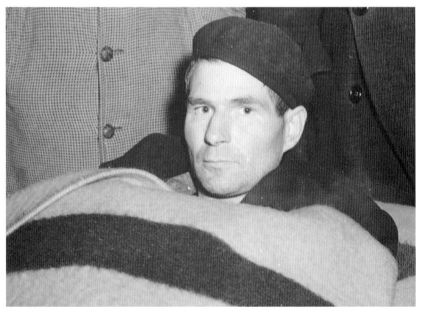

23 Ed Potvin returns from Spain after being wounded in August 1938.

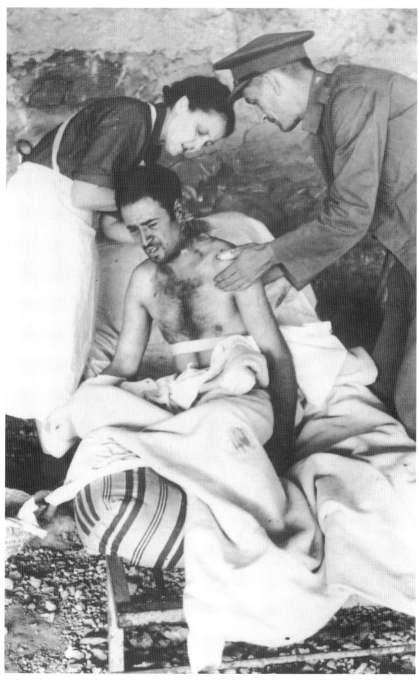

24 A wounded nationalist prisoner is treated by republican medical staff.

25 The Mackenzie-Papineau Battalion's soccer team, spring or summer 1938.

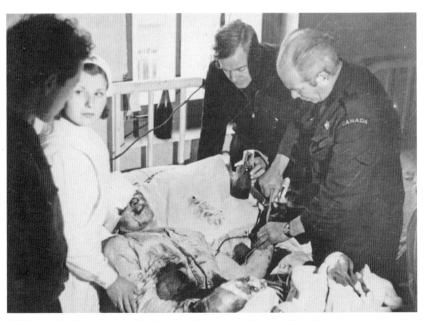

26 Norman Bethune, assisted by Henning Sorensen, performs a blood transfusion.

LAC C-067451, Geza Karpathi photographer

crumble. Rumours at the time had it that this plan mimicked a battle scene from a Soviet propaganda film.[15] As usual, a preparatory aerial and artillery bombardment to soften up the defences was also promised.

The men were scheduled to enter the trenches under the cover of darkness, but transporting the battalions from Quinto to republican positions outside Fuentes de Ebro lasted most of the night. Already dysentery was so bad that members of the battalion took turns holding each other as they hung their backsides over the edge of the trucks during the bumpy ride.[16] The Mac-Paps arrived at the trenches with the sun already up and suffered their first casualties running across open ground into the too-shallow communication trenches that led to the foremost lines. With the element of surprise now gone, the Mac-Paps waited for the promised bombers and artillery. The artillery barrage, when it came after a forty-minute delay, missed its intended target.[17] Eventually, a line of planes appeared and dropped their bombs on nationalist lines. The international troops prepared to go over the top behind the tanks, which they expected at any moment. But no tanks arrived. Nationalists in Fuentes de Ebro had ample time to repair their defences and train their machine guns on the empty expanse in front of them.

One or two hours later, Soviet tanks rumbled across the republican trenches, crushing some. A few of the Spaniards riding the tanks thought the International Brigades trenches they were crossing belonged to the nationalists and fired at the bewildered Canadians and Americans below, some of whom shot back.[18] At least one Spaniard elected to jump off his tank and stay in International Brigades trenches, a decision that probably saved his life. The tanks meanwhile raced ahead, outpacing the international volunteers, who now jumped out of their trenches and sought cover behind the advancing machines. Those Spaniards who did not fall to the ground as the Soviet tanks tried to navigate a terrain criss-crossed with ditches and dry *barrancas* were shot off the tanks they were riding by machine-gun fire. Canadians following on foot were similarly cut down or sprawled on the earth, trying to dig themselves cover with dinner plates. Most of the tanks were stopped and many were soon burning.

The attack had turned into another massacre. Lionel Edwards, destined to become one of the best Canadian commanders in Spain, was terrified. "I was shocked almost immediately by hearing the cry of a Spanish recruit, lying on the ground, hugging his stomach and calling for his mother, '*Madre! Madre!*'"[19]

Joe Dallet, determined to redeem himself, proved wrong all those who had bet he would reveal himself as a coward under fire. He led from the front, still with his much-ridiculed Joseph Stalin pipe clenched between his teeth, and was shot and killed. No one advanced more than several hundred metres, though the Mackenzie-Papineau Battalion showed the most courage and advanced farthest before they too were pinned down.[20] Those Canadians and

Americans who had not been killed sought cover or played dead and waited for nightfall, when they could creep back to their own lines. Lionel Edwards said that when the sun finally set and it was obvious the attack had ended in failure, the nationalists defending Fuentes de Ebro whooped and cheered in the darkness.

One of the tanks attacking nationalist lines at Fuentes de Ebro was commanded by William Kardash, a Canadian communist from Winnipeg and one of the few non-Soviet *tanquistas,* or tank crew members, in Spain.[21] Kardash came to Spain after attending the Lenin School in Moscow, from where at least four more Canadians joined the war.[22] He took a three-month training course on tanks in Archena, where he was trained by Soviet instructors.[23] The training was rudimentary and they had little ammunition with which to practise shooting. But Kardash said the Soviet tanks worked like the tractors he drove on Canadian farms and felt familiar. Besides, he was a skilled mechanic and he learned quickly. By the time of the Fuentes de Ebro attack, Kardash was considered a veteran *tanquista*. He had fought at Brunete and then served as a tank instructor. The assault on Fuentes de Ebro was his first action in two months.

"Things did not go as planned," Kardash recalled years later. They received orders to attack late in the morning and knew nothing about the terrain the tanks were expected to cross. Some got stuck in gullies on the approach to Fuentes de Ebro. Kardash's tank rolled toward the nationalist trenches very slowly. Any Spaniards still clinging to the sides of his tank were shot and fell to the ground. They crossed the first line of nationalist trenches and almost immediately Kardash and his crew were hit by a Molotov cocktail. "The first thing, the motor stopped. The wires burnt ... So we couldn't move. So long as we had ammunition, we kept firing," Kardash said. "I gave orders for the driver to get out because the fire began to get closer to the turret."[24]

Kardash watched as his driver and gunner fled the burning tank and were gunned down. Kardash looked certain to meet the same fate if he ran, but flames inside the tank were spreading and left him with little choice. He bolted from the tank while shots rang out all around him. As he ran toward a highway that linked Quinto and Fuentes de Ebro, a grenade knocked him down and filled his legs with shrapnel. He looked up and saw that another tank had broken through the nationalist defences and was still operational. Kardash waved the tank over to where he lay and climbed on top. Somehow he managed to cling to the tank while it sped back over nationalist lines to the safety of republican positions.

Kardash would spend until May 1938 in a Madrid hospital with gangrene in both legs. One was amputated right away. The thigh of his other leg was almost blown off and the pain was so bad that Kardash begged doctors to remove it as well. His remaining limb was saved, however, and Kardash eventually made it safely back home to Canada.[25]

At least 46 and perhaps as many as 150 men in the 15th International Brigade were not as lucky. Copic, in a letter to General Walter, said that 46 men in the brigade died on the first day at Fuentes de Ebro and 200 were wounded. The Spanish Battalion reported another 126 missing. Most of these men must have been killed, though a lucky few might have been taken prisoner.[26] Another official report on Mac-Pap casualties listed 16 dead, 63 wounded, and 4 missing.[27] Other sources reported much higher casualty rates, listing dead in the Mac-Paps alone at 60, with 200 wounded.[28] My research revealed the names of 9 Canadians who were killed at Fuentes de Ebro and 11 who were wounded; however, given that the date and place of death or wounding for scores of Canadians is not known, the true figure is certainly much higher.[29]

Several Canadians were praised for bravery shown during the attack. The Mac-Pap commander Robert Thompson singled out Ivor "Tiny" Anderson as the first man over the top and said he was cool and collected throughout the battle. Thompson also praised the medic and former masseur James Black, from Kingston, Ontario. A biography of Black, written in jest for the amusement of the battalion's men, contains nothing about Black's political convictions. Instead, it reports that Black was raised a Roman Catholic but left the church because "confessions began to interfere with his sex life." His chief complaint about Spain was its lack of "cat houses," and his ambition was to turn Toledo's cathedral into a massage parlour.[30] According to Thompson, however, at Fuentes de Ebro Black "time and again gave first aid to wounded comrades under intense fire, not taking time to rest or sleep."[31] Neither Black nor Anderson would survive the war. Black was captured and shot when he elected to stay behind with wounded comrades during the chaotic retreats across Aragón the following spring.[32] Anderson died under a nationalist artillery barrage on a barren mountaintop a month before the Canadians were pulled from the lines.

Among the Canadian dead at Fuentes de Ebro was the Scottish-Canadian miner and labour activist Roderick Gillis, who before coming to Spain had frequent clashes with Canadian authorities because of his agitation on behalf of Canada's unemployed. He was sentenced in 1933 to twelve months' hard labour for "rioting" in Saskatoon, thirty days' imprisonment in 1930 for stealing a coat, and another thirty days' imprisonment in 1930 for "vagrancy" – a criminal offence that gave police the means to lock up unemployed troublemakers. Gillis died barely two months after arriving in Spain.

Casualties declined sharply after 13 October but did not end, as sniping, scouting, and skirmishes to retrieve tanks and spare parts in no man's land continued to take a toll. Fifty-one replacements were brought in on 20 October; the Canadians were withdrawn from the lines less than a week later.[33] The Mackenzie-Papineau Battalion's first battle was a disaster, but they had acquitted themselves well, earning praise even from Copic in a memorandum he wrote to General Walter. But the bravery the Canadians showed in no way compensated for the poor judgment of those who planned the attack. Copic's report, probably written near the end of October, is instructive as a catalogue of everything that went wrong.

Copic claimed that he was not informed of the attack he was to launch in the morning until after midnight on 13 October. "I did not receive *any information on enemy positions, forces, firing objectives; also no detailed instructions on the attack itself*," he wrote. Lacking even the rudimentary information necessary to launch an attack, Copic moved the men of the 15th Brigade into the trenches facing the well-fortified town. The artillery bombardment was late and missed its target anyway. The tanks likewise arrived late, with the result that "*the enemy was given time* to prepare the defence against attack." Copic said that the Mac-Paps advanced 800 to 900 metres before being stopped, compared with the British Battalion's 600 metres and the Lincolns' 250 to 300 metres.[34]

Copic noted that one brigade was not enough to send against a heavily defended position and added, "*The preparation of the operation was very superficial and insufficient*." The brigade and the tanks corps had only a few hours to coordinate their plans, but during reconnaissance of the terrain at Fuentes de Ebro – limited given that it took place at night – no member of the tank corps was present. Sending tanks against enemy positions with infantry clinging to the vehicles was, in Copic's words, "an adventure and a crime." Furthermore, the brigades flanking the 15th at Fuentes de Ebro received no instructions to advance or support the attack with firepower. The 15th Brigade attacked on its own and was cut to pieces. The only positive aspect to the whole operation was the gallantry shown by the Mac-Paps: "We could not ask more of the Battalion than what it gave."[35]

Copic finished his report by noting that already attempts had been made to blame the 15th Brigade for the failure of this "absurd operation."[36] Following the attack, officers and commissars of the 5th Army Corps were summoned to meetings in the town of Lécera before Crescenciano Bilbao, chief of the War Commissariat of the Army of the East. Ominously, the officers and commissars were stripped of their weapons before entering the hall and then asked to explain why Fuentes de Ebro had not been taken.[37] It's not known what conclusions were reached at the meeting. However, Edwin Rolfe, an American communist who fought in Spain, said it was later discovered that the failure of the artillery and barrage was caused by "sabotage" by the tank corps commander.[38]

With the advance on Zaragoza now irrevocably halted, the battalions of the 15th Brigade were pulled out of the trenches at Fuentes de Ebro. Before leaving the region, the Mac-Paps stopped briefly to rest and recuperate in Belchite. The battalion was quartered near the cemetery. Shelling had churned up the graves and opened up ossuaries where bones had once filled the shelves. "The place was full of bones and skulls, and it stank of the dead," remembered Irving

Weissman.[39] It was a fitting postscript to the debacle at Fuentes de Ebro.

The Mac-Paps returned to central Spain and were deployed in small villages to the east of Madrid. From there they got occasional leave to visit the capital city, with its cafés and brothels. Several Canadian volunteers again visited Ernest Hemingway, who always welcomed volunteers to his hotel room with cigarettes, alcohol, and a hot bath. Around this time, the International Brigades were formally integrated into the Spanish army. This meant that soldiers in the brigades were now expected to conform to regular military standards of discipline and deference to authority. Most notably, they were now obligated to salute their superiors – a particularly meaningful gesture, as the international volunteers had previously considered saluting something that was practised only in bourgeois armies. More and more Spanish soldiers were also integrated into the International Brigades; this process would be accelerated throughout the remainder of the war as fewer replacements arrived from outside Spain. Men in Canada were still volunteering, and would do so as long as recruits were accepted, but their numbers were declining.

The Mac-Paps were now led by their first Canadian commander, Edward Cecil-Smith, who replaced Robert Thompson after Thompson fell ill at Fuentes de Ebro. Cecil-Smith, an Englishman born in China who subsequently emigrated to Canada, was a competent military leader – a rare quality in Spain – but also strict and aloof. He was respected by some of his men but loved by few. "Officers don't have to engage in popularity contests and should be judged by their accomplishments," the American Lawrence Cane said of Cecil-Smith after the war. "Smith had to make some mighty tough decisions, and a lot of guys bought it carrying them out, but that's what combat command is like."[40]

Canadians in the Mac-Paps had been badly bloodied. Around them, however, the tide appeared to be turning in favour of the republicans. Just before Christmas, the international volunteers learned that republican troops had captured Teruel. A week later, the mountain city was on the verge of being recaptured, and the internationals were called to bolster its defences.

Teruel is a windy city situated on a knoll above the intersection of the Turia and Alfambra rivers. It is surrounded by jagged peaks, ridges, and twisted gorges. In the wintertime it is cold and desolate. Government forces attacked here as a pre-emptive strike after republican spies intercepted plans that General Franco planned to attack at Guadalajara, where his Italian allies had suffered a humiliating defeat at the hands of the International Brigades that spring. The republican offensive, launched on 15 December, was carried out by Hernández Saravia's Army of the Levant, backed by soldiers from the Republic's Army of Maneuver. Altogether, some 100,000 troops were committed to the assault, and initially they achieved almost total success.

Moving quickly under heavy snow, with no artillery or aerial bombardment that would have alerted the enemy, republican troops surrounded Teruel and breached the old city walls by Christmas. A stalwart group of nationalist soldiers, including the bishop of Teruel, bravely held out without food or water in ruined government buildings, cellars, a hospital, and a convent. Finally they surrendered, civilians were evacuated, and the Republic took control of the now deserted city.

General Franco, however, refused to lose a provincial capital and launched a counter-offensive. Franco's armies attacked on a narrow front, led by two divisions of Navarrese, famed for their ferocity and strong Catholic faith. His troops were protected by Nazi Germany's Condor Legion air force, and the ground for their attack was prepared by the heaviest artillery barrage yet unleashed in the war. The Navarrese advanced and pushed back the republicans defending the outskirts of Teruel. Their lines buckled but held.

Meanwhile, troops from the International Brigades were struggling over windswept and snowy mountain roads, where trucks more than once slid across the frozen ground and plunged into yawning valleys below. The 15th International Brigade arrived at Argente, about forty kilometres north of Teruel, on the evening of 1 January 1938. The battalions of the brigade spread out in nearby villages; the Mac-Paps stayed in the ruins of Argente itself. For ten days they saw no action save a few night patrols, but they watched as battles unfolded far below their positions. The weather took a steady toll as the battalions were moved up and down the Sierra Palomera, from where they could see the overwhelming numbers of artillery and planes that Franco's forces now brought to bear against them. The Canadians in the Mac-Paps slept outside in the snow. Those with the Lincolns found shelter in a disused railway tunnel, but this was no better, as wind shrieked through and attempts to light fires filled the tunnel with smoke and turned the ground to a wet and dangerous slush.[41]

The international volunteers at Teruel suffered greatly from exposure and lack of food. In a 10 January letter to Crescenciano Bilbao, now commissar general of war, Luigi Gallo said that in some units 100 percent of the men had lice. Skin infections were rampant. "According to the doctors' declarations," he wrote, "food is inferior to the needs of the men ... There is a danger of scurvy."[42] One volunteer remembered that the cold was so severe, and their clothing so thin, that lice stopped crawling on their skin, rousing themselves to torment their human hosts only during brief moments of warmth.[43] The men of the 15th International Brigade appeared to be in no condition to fight. But on the night of 14 January, the brigade moved down from the heights above Teruel and joined the direct defence of the city.

The Mac-Paps deployed in a valley that ran north from Teruel, between a twenty-metre-high ridge called La Muela, or The Molar, to the west, and another hill three kilometres to the northeast called El Muletón – The Big

Mule. The valley floor was not flat but consisted of smaller hills, where the Mac-Paps set up defensive positions. The Americans established themselves in the ruined outskirts of Teruel. Here they dressed in furs and outlandish costumes looted from the empty city. The British defended a long hill called Santa Barbara jut north of the city, from where they could look out on the valley floor and across at the nationalists facing them.[44]

For two days the nationalists and internationals sniped at each other and dispatched furtive patrols across a frozen no man's land. One night, Lionel Edwards found himself crawling through the darkness with a "whimsical" American named Pete who wore earrings as if he were a pirate. The pair had slithered to within nine metres of the enemy's barbed wire when they were confronted by a large dog that threatened to give them away – a calamity potentially fatal so close to nationalist lines. Pete reached into his pocket and pulled out scraps of food, which he tossed to the dog before scratching it behind the ears. The dog stayed quiet, and Edwards and Pete were able to safely return to their positions.[45]

Dogs were not the only animal residents of Teruel's broken landscape. A small collection of hogs, perhaps released from their enclosure by bombs or shell explosions, or simply abandoned when Teruel's civilian residents fled, also inhabited the city. The pigs shuffled among shattered buildings. One night, Percy Hilton, one of the Mac-Pap Battalion's cooks and a first-class scrounger, went on a mission with several other men to collect the potential windfall.

The group crept to within a few dozen metres of the animals, and Hilton's companion, a sniper, took aim. Then, in one of the ironies of war, the marksman froze. The man who had no doubt coolly taken aim and fired at his human enemy refused to shoot the pigs.

"Give me your rifle," another member of the group snapped in frustration. He grabbed the weapon, took aim, fired, and missed.

The pigs barely moved when the bullet slammed into the concrete above them. They were so stunned or cold that Hilton realized he could approach the animals himself and simply cut their throats. He butchered the pigs in the darkness, and that night members of the battalion gorged themselves on pork.[46]

The growing tension between the two opposing armies finally broke on 17 January, when the nationalists launched a devastating attack down the valley toward Teruel. The mostly German 11th Brigade on El Muletón was hit first by the onslaught; they suffered many casualties but held their line. The Canadians then felt the brunt of the attack, trapped with their backs against broken cliffs. They were saved by the British anti-tank unit, which fired over their heads to drive off the nationalist attackers.

Two squadrons of Moorish cavalry then raced between the Canadian lines and the shattered remnants of the German Thaelman Battalion toward the Mackenzie-Papineau Battalion's headquarters. Cecil-Smith, the new Mac-Pap leader, was put to the test, and he reacted well. He rallied his staff of clerks and cartographers and set up a defensive line consisting of three heavy machine guns. The charging Moors were stopped dead in their tracks by the concentrated fire; those not cut down immediately wheeled on their horses and raced back up the valley, through a gauntlet of fire from the British and Canadians on their flanks.[47]

The nationalists were not turned back for long. On 18 January, they took El Muletón; the surviving German defenders retreated to join the British. The nationalists then decided to revert to a full frontal assault down the valley. Blocking their path were Lionel Edwards and the third company he commanded, dug in among small knolls on the valley floor. They were surrounded by the ruins of a stone wall that had once been a dam, and by a tiny chapel. For a few days they shivered in the cold and passed around bottles of cognac. Then one evening Edwards and his men heard artillery being dragged into place in front of them. In the morning a reconnaissance plane dropped smoke on their position. "I knew now what a lamb feels like awaiting the slaughter," Edwards said.[48]

The ensuing artillery barrage pummelled the hills the Canadians were occupying. A section of young Spaniards in the Mac-Paps broke in terror and ran over to the nationalist side. Edwards and his company, together with British reinforcements, bore the brunt of repeated assaults the next two days. The Navarrese, banners flying, charged with such determination, Edwards said they appeared "bewitched." In the first Navarrese assaults, the attackers suffered heavy losses. But Edwards and his defenders were pulverized by artillery; finally, the last four survivors from his position retreated and ceded the outer defences of Teruel. Even so, the Navarrese had been so impressed by the ferocity of the Mac-Paps' defence that they declined to occupy the now abandoned position immediately, lest one or two defenders remained alive.[49]

Inevitably, however, the superior firepower and now especially the aircraft that the nationalists had at their disposal meant that even dogged holding actions could not stop their advance for long. In a freezing lookout post, Maurice Constant, who had been a student at the University of Toronto only months before, watched the seemingly endless waves of nationalist planes bombarding his comrades in surrounding hills and in the valley below him. He wrote everything down in a minute-by-minute log for his commanders. "Airplanes coming out of the clouds circling north of Teruel," reads a typical entry. "12:18. They begin to fire on Teruel; our anti-aircraft [guns] fire against them, but without consequence."[50]

After two weeks in the wind and cold of Teruel, the 15th Brigade was pulled from the lines and began an exhausted march south. Nineteen kilometres outside town, a new draft joined the brigade's battalions. From here, the

Lincolns caught a train to Valencia; the remaining battalions were told to wait a day. However, even before their leave began, the brigade was called back to carry out a series of diversionary attacks with the 11th International Brigade. The Lincolns and Mac-Paps were told to assault two hilltop perimeters near Segura de los Baños, across a snowy ravine.

The battalions reached their new positions and hid out, hungry and cold, in village huts, with little to eat for two days. They crept into the valley the bitterly cold evening of 16 February, the night sky full of stars, which were occasionally obscured by drifting clouds. The Mac-Paps were assigned Mount Atalaya, the Lincolns a smaller hill to the south. The Mac-Paps successfully reached the base of Atalaya undetected, cut the wire, and stormed the heights, blasting their way up the hillside with grenades. Their assault alerted nearby nationalist garrisons that further attacks were imminent, thus creating stiffer resistance for the Lincolns. But they too were ultimately successful.

The Mac-Paps were immediately dispatched to attack another hill. But by now, the element of surprise was long gone. Canadians James Cochrane and Michael Szlapek died in these two attacks, the former when clouds slipped away from the moon while he was cutting wire to illuminate the hillside. He was bathed in light and shot dead. The battalion captured approximately one hundred prisoners. A rough line was established, and the battalion was withdrawn, though its effective strength was now about half what it had been when the battle for Teruel began.[51] The nationalists, meanwhile, had retaken the city.

Retreats, March-April 1938

On 9 March 1938, republican Spain's Aragón region bore the brunt of a massive combined ground and air assault that foreshadowed the blitzkrieg attacks Germany would launch against Poland, Holland, Belgium, and France in the coming Second World War. The offensive began with devastating artillery barrages, which softened the ground for Spanish and Italian troops and German tanks. The Republic's exhausted and underarmed soldiers reeled in retreat and were bombed and strafed by German and Italian planes as they fled. Franco's goal was to cut off the human and industrial resources of Catalonia from the rest of the Republic and, eventually, once Catalonia was completely overrun, seal the border with France. At first his success was almost total. Republican defenders who survived the barrage of artillery shells and bombs were so disoriented that Franco's foreign legion simply walked through republican trenches and bayoneted the dazed survivors.[1]

Those who did survive now flowed east. Confusion prevailed and desertions plagued all units, Spanish and international. When the lines first broke, Canadians in the International Brigades were in reserve, recuperating after the battles of Teruel and Segura de los Baños, which had ended only a few weeks before. Bill Matthews (Vasyl Matvenko) and other commanders in the Mac-Paps were sent forward with orders to arrest any retreating soldiers and shoot any retreating officers.[2] At Letux, Edward Cecil-Smith tried to stop at gunpoint the hordes of fleeing men, but they swarmed past him. Some claimed they had been told to establish a new line at Belchite, but Lincolns stationed there knew nothing of this.[3] The Lincolns were ordered to hold what they thought were reserve positions just west of the town, only to wake up under fire and virtually overrun. Soon they too were in a full-scale retreat.

Meanwhile, the Mac-Paps were also taking heavy fire at their positions in the hills west of Azuara. On 10 March, all republican units, with the exception of the Mackenzie-Papineau Battalion, were withdrawn east of the Cámaras River, and the bridge at Azuara was blown. No one tried, or managed, to tell the Mac-Paps that they were now cut off, and so Cecil-Smith held his position until nightfall, when he finally pulled the surviving Mac-Paps back across the broken bridge. They briefly took up positions on cliffs east of the river before retreating in the direction of Lécera. A machine-gun crew and several riflemen on a high cliff were not informed of the withdrawal. Cut off and doomed, its members covered the retreat of their comrades.[4]

Among those left behind were Frank Whitfield, Arthur Rose, several Finnish Canadians, at least one American, and Percy Hilton, who had been transferred from the battalion's kitchen staff to the machine gunners. When dawn broke, Hilton implored the Finns manning the machine gun to pull back, but they would not flinch from their position without orders. The Finnish Canadians in the Mac-Pap Battalion had come by their reputation for bravery honestly.   *Henry Baska*

Hilton realized they were probably trapped. With Whitfield, Rose, and the American, he scrambled up the hills behind their position in the direction from which their dinner had been brought the night before, hoping that the battalion would still be there, or that they might be able to find food that had been left behind. The American was shot by an unseen sniper. Rose, a first-aid man, rushed to help; he too was shot dead. Whitfield and Hilton clawed their way higher into the hills. They saw several hundred nationalist soldiers approaching from both directions on the road below. In the hills they saw another unit. Mistaking it for their missing battalion, they ran toward it. Whitfield was shot and killed. Hilton threw himself on the ground and was captured. He did not see any of his Finnish comrades as prisoners of the nationalists and expected that he too would shortly be executed.

By a quirk of fate, however, the tall Hilton was spared. One of his Spanish captors, a short man, found it amusing to stand next to Hilton to demonstrate their height difference. "The other Spaniards were having quite a show of seeing me beside him. It was a big joke to him, so they forget to shoot me," Hilton said. Perhaps the horseplay humanized Hilton to his captors, or maybe they simply lost their rage. Either way, Hilton became the first Canadian prisoner taken during the retreats. There would be many more.

A nationalist officer later confirmed that the Finnish Canadians who stayed behind with their machine gun were captured, lined up, and shot. The officer told Hilton that this was a mistake, as the nationalists now had orders to take internationals prisoner when captured. Apparently, this latest order was also news to many nationalists. As Hilton was marched toward the rear, scores of Spanish soldiers he passed looked him in the eyes and drew a finger across their throats.[5]

A combined force of internationals and Spaniards rallied and made a half-day stand at Lécera – but a brief stand was all that was necessary to stem the panic and permit an orderly retreat to Albalate del Arzobispo. The weary Mac-Paps acted as rearguard protection during the fifteen-kilometre march to the town, where a motley collection of internationals and Spaniards again turned to face their pursuers. But the nationalist advance was impossible to break, and even the most resolute were beginning to despair. Men dropped their weapons and ran on a road now clogged with machines, refugees, and panicked soldiers. They fled north toward Híjar, only to find that the road had been cut by nationalist cavalry. They swung east overland until they intercepted the highway leading to Alcañiz, where the Mac-Paps met up with other units of retreating republicans, including the Lincolns.

At this point, John "Paddy" McElligott, a former relief-camp organizer in Canada, was ordered to set up a defensive position to cover the Mac-Paps' retreat. He dug in with four light machine guns and two heavier ones, then walked to a farmhouse behind his position, where a Spanish runner asked him if he wanted some meat.

"You're kidding? Meat?" McElligott said. He had not tasted meat for weeks.

"Sure," the Spaniard replied, handing him a dish of what McElligott assumed was chicken. It was cat, and McElligott soon spotted his meal's skin still steaming in the corner. The food tasted wonderful. "I wished we had another cat," he later remembered.[6]

The nationalists, also exhausted by their rapid gains, paused in pursuit. The tattered remains of the 15th Brigade did not take advantage of this lull to put more distance between them and their advancing enemy. Showing remarkable courage, they threw up defensive positions in the hills on either side of a hairpin road on the way to Alcañiz. Then, pointing their guns in the direction from which they expected the attack, most dropped off to sleep. The attack, however, did not materialize the next day, 13 March, and the depleted remains of the 15th Brigade were ordered to fall back to Alcañiz.

Once again, the Mac-Paps acted as rearguard force, but the soldiers were so fatigued that units soon lost sight of each other. Men warily eyed the hills above them, which offered cover for flanking attacks. Cecil-Smith ranged up and down his column of men in an ambulance, urging them on. The ambulance rounded a corner; there, fifty metres down the road was an Italian tank. The driver slammed his foot down on the accelerator and drove frantically off road, shells exploding behind. The rest of the column scattered. Some groups pressed eastward overland to Maella and Batea. Most Canadians converged on Caspe, where the five hundred remaining men in the 15th International Brigade, reinforced with men from other units who had also fled to the city, prepared to stand and fight. They did not have long to wait. Hours after the last stragglers stumbled into Caspe, nationalist troops advanced on the city's outskirts.

The battle for Caspe was desperate. The brigade first defended a cemetery on heights approaching the city. They ceded this ground reluctantly and at great cost. The much-loved Canadian Finn Niilo Makela died here. His death hit his fellow Finnish Canadians especially hard. He was close to many of them before Spain and had stayed that way as their commander. "There was a time in Sudbury when we shared the same bed for a while, and one night, after the loss of Teruel, we shared the same snow bank," Sulo Huhtala later recalled.[7] Makela's comrades later named a square after him in the village of Capçanes and erected a plaque to honour his memory. "When a man's death breaks through this protective shell, he must really have been something," the American Lawrence Cane said.[8]

A force mostly of Mac-Paps rallied and briefly retook the cemetery hill, capturing about thirty prisoners. But soon they too retreated into the city proper. Inside the smoking rubble of Caspe, the International Brigades held off a much larger and stronger force. They fought house to house and street to street. The battle was like that of Belchite, only this time it was the Canadians and Americans who were the city's hunted defenders. After two days, the survivors – at least those who received the order in time – were evacuated from the city across a broken railway trestle.

The Canadians trudged to Batea, where they were able to rest at last. Here, the Mac-Paps were reinforced with the final sizable draft of volunteers from home – approximately 160 new volunteers from Canada and the United States who had been rushed through their training and sent to the front. Mike Storgoff, one of the new arrivals, said that he and the other Canadian recruits were in the middle of a baseball game with Cuban volunteers when they received word that the front lines had broken and they were to plug the gap. Like so many other recruits in the International Brigades, their "training" consisted of firing three bullets at a nearby hill.[9] Added to this new draft were bloodied veterans taken from hospitals and training schools to join the fight.

The Canadians got little rest or food at Batea, but at least they were no longer on the move. They were still in little condition to fight, however. Carl Geiser, in a letter to Dave Doran, reported that twenty men in the battalion had diarrhea and another sixty-one were on sick call with feet and stomach problems. Half the men were without footwear; 75 percent needed blankets; the whole battalion needed new equipment of one sort or the other.[10]

On 31 March, the battered men of the 15th International Brigade were sent into action to meet the renewed nationalist thrust to the Mediterranean. The Lincolns were deployed near Batea; the British, followed by the Mac-Paps, marched west along the highway from Gandesa to Calaceite.[11] Walking in darkness, the British ran into an advancing nationalist column and were scattered, leaving many dead. The Canadians, only a few kilometres back, knew nothing of this. Still thinking the British stood between them and the enemy, the Mac-Paps set up positions on either side of the highway and waited for the sun to rise.

At dawn, Copic ordered the Mac-Paps to take control of two prominent hills a few kilometres away, though it now appeared that nationalist troops were flooding into the area. A patrol was dispatched and, cresting a hill, it saw a group of soldiers boiling kettles of water and preparing breakfast. The Mac-Pap patrol, led by their commissar, Carl Geiser, and followed by another group that included Jules Paivio, couldn't make out if the soldiers were friend or foe. They approached cautiously, trying to stay out of sight, but were spotted. "Don't worry! We're friends!" called out one of the breakfasting soldiers in a heavy Brooklyn accent. Relieved, most members of the patrol walked forward to join their comrades for breakfast. Before they reached the cooking fires, however, they noticed the men were wearing Italian uniforms and had several machine guns trained on them. The Mac-Pap patrol had walked into a trap.

They were stripped of their weapons, and Geiser was ordered at gunpoint to call the remaining members of the patrol, still hiding on a nearby hill, to join him. But they had by now realized what was going on and opened fire. Geiser and the others were rushed to the rear, where Geiser learned that his captor with the New York accent had spent a few years in the United States and several more of the Italians had relatives there. The prisoners chatted quite amiably with the Italian soldiers, and Geiser even joined their captain for breakfast. Within a couple of hours, however, they were all lined up to be shot. Geiser and the young Jules Paivio, who was captured later that morning, stood beside each other against a wall, so close their fingers could touch. "It's interesting the thoughts that go through your mind. Jeez, I'm too young. I have so much to live for," Paivio later recalled. "But fear – at that moment you don't know what fear is. You're expecting the worse. You're steeling yourself to go down standing up, without whimpering or crying, and you do it."[12]

Paivio and the others tried to keep themselves composed. They could see a medic standing nearby to verify their deaths. The firing squad milled about waiting for final orders. Just then, a motorcade pulled up. A man in the back seat of one of the cars rolled down his window and called over the officer in charge of the firing squad, asking what was going on. "Well, we're going to shoot the reds," Paivio heard the officer say. The two men talked, gesturing toward them. Then the motorcade drove off, and the officer dismissed the firing squad. With shock, the condemned prisoners realized they were not going to be executed after all. They were loaded into trucks and driven away.[13]

More than forty Canadians were taken prisoner during the retreats of March and April 1938. They were fortunate, because Franco had temporarily suspended his policy of shooting international prisoners of war. But even during the retreats this decision was not universally applied. Jack Thomas was captured, along with Nick Elendiuk, who witnessed the former being taken away, never to be seen again. Thomas had blond hair, and Elendiuk guessed that he was shot because he was suspected of being Russian, as many nationalists believed the majority of the International Brigades were. "This is one thing you couldn't drive out of their stupid heads," Elendiuk said.[14]

Carl Geiser, who completed a detailed study of American prisoners of war, writes that of 287 Americans captured by Spanish nationalists, Italians, and Moors in Spain, 173 were killed on capture without trial. (The figure may not be exact since some of the men Geiser lists as captured might have died fighting or of wounds, but it reflects the harsh fate international volunteers could expect if captured.)[15]

Members of the International Brigades also shot prisoners, though this does not appear to have been a common occurrence. The hatred roused by civil war was often felt more intensely by the Spaniards involved – especially when they faced foreigners fighting alongside their opponents. Spanish republicans particularly feared and detested Franco's Moors. Canadian Jack Lawson recalled crossing paths with a line of Moorish prisoners, wired together and escorted by Spanish cavalry. One of the prisoners, battered and bleeding, pleaded for water, rasping *"Agua! Agua!"* As Lawson reached for his water bottle, one of the cavalry men swung his rifle around until it was pointing at Lawson's chest and backed him away from the Moor. The cavalry escort watered their horses but gave none to their prisoners. When their animals were sated, they marched the Moors behind a nearby grove of trees and shot them.[16]

Spanish nationalists treated internationals on the republican side with equal contempt. Peter Kemp, an Englishman who served with Franco's foreign legion, described being ordered to shoot a captured international volunteer, an Irishman claiming to be a sailor who had missed his departing ship and was forced to join the International Brigades. It was an unlikely story, but the man was clearly desperate. He pleaded with Kemp to spare his life – something that was not in Kemp's power to do. The prisoner was shot and killed by a firing squad. Kemp gave the order to fire.[17] "The Spaniards' attitude was that if they took Spanish prisoners, they treated them well and sent them back to rear areas," Kemp said in an interview. "But foreigners in the International Brigades – they were very bitter about that, and they did shoot a lot of them. There is no question about that at all because I saw it happen."[18]

Compared with the scores of internationals who were shot on capture, Paivio and his fellow Canadian prisoners were fortunate. They spent a year in nationalist prison camps. They were fed poorly and beaten, even for offences as petty as sitting down to eat. Those implicated in escape attempts were beaten near to death – although after two prisoners complained to the camp commandant about particularly brutal beating that took place after five Germans escaped, the commandant said he was unaware of such mistreatment and ordered it stopped. It was, but only in the commandant's presence.[19] Scurvy was rampant. Many of the prisoners had running sores, and Paivio ate grass in a vain attempt to get vitamin C into his body.[20] Spanish republican prisoners were executed, but all Canadians survived their captivity with the exception of Frank Papp, a Hungarian emigrant to Windsor, Ontario, who died of pneumonia in prison in June 1938, and Isaac Matson, who succumbed to cancer.

One of the guards, dubbed "Tanky" because he was serving in a tank when an encounter with the British Battalion rendered him useless for front-line duty, liked to beat the prisoners as they ran past him into the courtyard for roll call or mealtime. Percy Hilton learned that if he swerved to run past Tanky as close to him as possible, the latter could not land a particularly powerful blow from his whip or swagger stick. The guard soon caught on and would step back when he saw Hilton coming to deliver a proper smack.

At one point, the prisoners were ordered to strip and were then subjected to a series of tests and measurements. They were quizzed about their sex lives, and their skulls and noses were carefully measured and examined, as were their skin colour and the distance between their eyes. The German Gestapo had previously been to the camp to interrogate the German and Austrian prisoners.[21] Most prisoners believed that the Gestapo had come back to oversee these "medical" tests. This is entirely possible; it would fit with prevailing Nazi attitudes about eugenics. Franco's chief psychologist, Dr. Antonio Vallejo Nagera, certainly took part in the experiments at the camp. He concluded that almost one-third of the English prisoners were "mental retards." "A priori, it seems probable that psychopaths of all types would join the Marxist ranks," he wrote in a military medical journal.[22]

To keep their spirits up, the prisoners constructed chess pieces out of bread and organized classes on everything from languages to math. On Christmas Eve 1938, the prisoners put on a concert of skits, folksongs, Christmas carols, and a rendition of the opera *The Barber of Seville,* which had been subtly altered to mock fascism. The prisoners invited the commander of the prison camp and his officers and soldiers, who all accepted the invitation and uproariously applauded at its conclusion. Geiser said that even Tanky stopped beating the prisoners for several weeks afterward.[23]

Meanwhile, the remaining members of the Mackenzie-Papineau Battalion were being pursued over hills and through high brush as they retreated toward the sea. Small squads of men set up machine guns to cover the retreat of their comrades, and then they too made a run for it. Any semblance of a front line had disintegrated. By nightfall, the battalion consisted of eighty or so men who gathered where the roads from Batea and Calaceite intersected, just west of Gandesa, plus whoever else might have been struggling unseen through the darkness.[24] Stragglers were cut down by roving bands of Moorish cavalry. Exhausted and suffering from blisters, Mike Hyduk crawled under shrubs to sleep. He was awakened by the screams of retreating volunteers being chased down and hacked to death by Moors on horseback. "It was something like the pig-sticking contest," he said.[25]

"Many men retreated and just kept on going," William Beeching recalled. "When you feel you're expendable, that already creates a problem for you … When you're retreating and you feel you're being beaten and beaten and beaten, and there's no anchor to hold on to ... you don't know where you're at."[26] A group of Mac-Paps stumbled into brigade headquarters and were immediately confronted by Copic, who berated them for retreating. According to Lawrence Cane, when two Italian tanks appeared fifty metres away, Copic cut short his tirade and bolted.[27]

The Mac-Paps marched in a file east to Gandesa, scattered on at least one occasion by machine-gun fire from flanking nationalist forces. They set up positions outside town and turned once more to face their attackers. The Mac-Paps forced back a nationalist tank attack before they slipped into the darkness and headed east, hoping to find safety somewhere on the other side of the Ebro River. Members of the battalion lost contact with each other. Hungry and exhausted, they wandered though the hills and tried to evade the enemy.

A small group of volunteers, including Bill Matthews, Henry Mack, and John "Paddy" McElligott, struggled throughout a day and night carrying one of their wounded comrades. He asked to be left behind, and finally they laid him down beside a farmhouse, clutching a couple of hand grenades. Matthews and the others stumbled off into the darkness. When dawn broke, they heard a familiar voice yelling. They had walked in one big circle, ending up back at the farmhouse, where their wounded comrade still lay. "He called to us: "Paddy! Mack!" And we had to ignore it," McElligott said. "We had to keep going. That was hard. He was a guy that we respected and loved ... in our quiet way. And we had to leave him."[28]

Another group of internationals encountered an enemy patrol in the half-light before dawn. A Spaniard in their group advanced to converse with the enemy unit, bluffing and stalling for time before surrendering, while his comrades slipped away into the hills.[29]

James Cameron, a Scottish-born Canadian, eluded capture longer than most. He had been shot in the ankle on 1 April. The wound was dressed, but Cameron was left behind the following morning. Waking up to find himself stranded and alone, Cameron limped and crawled to a deserted farmhouse, where a French volunteer had barricaded himself with a supply of hand grenades and wine. They were joined by an Argentine volunteer, and the three stayed there, awaiting their fate. The Frenchman had a bad habit of getting drunk and throwing grenades every time he heard a bump in the night. Cameron and the Argentine left him; eventually, they were separated by a nationalist night patrol that fired on them. Cameron hid out and foraged for almost ten weeks before he was turned in by a farmer and taken prisoner.[30]

Some who made it to the Ebro River in time crossed the bridge at Móra d'Ebre before it was blown. A group of Mac-Paps protected the retreat as nationalist patrols advanced on the outskirts of town. Most of the volunteers, however, reached a swollen river that could not be waded. Those who were able swam or crossed on makeshift rafts. The rest drowned or stayed on the west side of the river and were taken prisoner or shot.

What was left of the Mackenzie-Papineau Battalion congregated on the other side of the Ebro River. It is doubtful that more than sixty men had made it across. Luigi Gallo reported on 6 April that the entire 15th Brigade now consisted of three hundred men.[31] Surviving internationals set up rough defensive lines on the banks of the Ebro and tried to catch their breath. A few Finnish Canadians found an abandoned kitchen, complete with tile walls and floor, and transformed it into a Scandinavian-style sauna. They sweated months' worth of dirt out of their bodies and roasted their flea-ridden clothes on hot rocks dragged inside.[32]

Brigade leadership surveyed the broken and devastated remains of their fighting units and decided that someone needed to be blamed. On 21 April, Gallo ordered that the 15th Brigade establish "personal responsibilities" for the nationalist breakthrough. He demanded that each commander and commissar write a "detailed report in the least possible time," which, among other requirements, indicated the "exact place and hour of the operations," the "behaviour of the political and military cadres, as well as of the men in each Unit" and "for every abandoned position, indicate the reasons as well as the orders received or given for the retreat movement carried out."[33]

For weeks, the Canadians and other internationals had been under attack, often in isolated groups, half-starving and lost. Few had a clear idea of where they were or even what day it was. Now commanders behind the lines were demanding, in threatening tones, to know why their plans had not developed as they had envisioned them. This order was followed immediately by a notice from General Gal instructing the surviving volunteers to give up their wages for a day, ostensibly to benefit the Republic's medical work. This evidently led to dissent from many of the volunteers, so Lieutenant-Colonel Klaus, the brigade chief of staff, issued a memorandum attempting to clarify Gal's request:

> General Gal has in no way given an order but, rather, a call to all the comrades, in memory of the sixth anniversary of the Republic, to voluntarily give one day's wages. As an imposition does not correspond with the ideals of a Republican Army, we hereby order that the quartermaster reimburse the withheld wages; we are sure that all the units will contribute voluntary donations and will hand them in to the political commissar.[34]

Franco's forces had in the meantime reached the Mediterranean, on 15 April. Their offensive had driven a wedge between republican armies and split the Spanish Republic in two. Madrid and Barcelona, Spain's greatest cities, still eluded Franco's grasp. But the tide of the war had shifted irrevocably against the Spanish Republic and the Canadians who fought on its behalf.

7

Back to the Ebro, May-September 1938

The spring of 1938 saw the Spanish Republic in desperate shape. Franco's successful drive to the Mediterranean Sea had decimated republican ranks. Barcelona lay vulnerable and poorly defended. However, instead of attacking the Catalan capital, Franco ordered his armies to push southwest along the coast toward Valencia, where the Republic had moved its capital before the nationalist assault on Madrid in the fall of 1936. His decision is puzzling; a swift march on Barcelona would almost certainly have shortened the war. But the general was no longer interested in a quick and clean victory. He wanted to punish his opponents and methodically grind out resistance to his rule.[1] The march against Valencia was much more difficult than Franco had envisioned. Republican defenders dug in and inflicted punishing losses on the advancing nationalists, who were shocked that those they had rolled over in March and April were now resisting so stubbornly and so well. The nationalists lost the momentum they had built up during their blitz through Aragón; they were still grinding forward, but at great cost. Valencia was safe for the moment, and republican soldiers had time to catch their breath, regroup, and reorganize.

For the Canadians and Americans in the Mackenzie-Papineau and Lincoln battalions, this meant repairing to Marçà and Falset, two picturesque Catalan villages surrounded by grape vines and olive groves, ringed by hills covered in pine trees and wild rosemary. This could be no two-week break such as the Lincolns were given after Jarama; the International Brigades needed to be rebuilt almost from the ground up, and even brigade high command understood that this would take time. They built, in the adjoining valley, rough lean-to shelters out of fallen trees to sleep in. One volunteer described them in a letter home as "little ramshackle huts made of branches and what-have-you, and the result is everyone is soaked."[2] Understandably, the men spent as much time as possible in town.

The first order of business was to replenish the Mackenzie-Papineau Battalion's depleted numbers. One or two internationals joined the battalion at this time, but recruiting had been stopped in Canada. The ranks were therefore filled mostly with young Catalan conscripts. The brigade tried to bind these boys to the internationals by instituting a policy of Spaniards "adopting" an international "brother" and vice versa. For the most part, though, the conscripts were too young, inexperienced, and scared to be much good on that front. "To us, they looked like children," George Watt later remembered.[3]

The Mac-Paps were still remarkably underequipped. Walter Gawrycki spent most of the war barefoot. He had large feet, so shoes were hard to come by at the best of times. His feet built up calluses, but even then the skin was too thick to heal properly and old wounds continually cracked open. He tied rags around his feet or took worn-out, discarded shoes and tried to wrap the material around his own feet. It was most difficult during the winter.[4]

"The clothing and shoes problem is very bad – I am surprised there has not been more sickness and actual injuries to feet," Frank Rogers wrote on 11 May to the War Commissariat of the 15th Brigade. "Is there any hope of some sort of issue of clothing?"[5] A report for the week of 9 July noted that the soldiers of the 15th Brigade still badly needed footwear.[6] In fact, $5,000 had been sent to Spain from supporters in the United States to buy sandals and water bottles. Jim Bourne, the party's representative in the brigade, appealed at the War Commissariat to find out what had happened to this money and to numerous parcels that had been addressed to the men in Spain but never arrived, without success.[7]

In June, brigade leadership warned of a violent campaign on the part of the North American and English volunteers against the leaders of the International Brigades and especially against André Marty.[8] This violent campaign apparently consisted of nothing more than gripes and insults, but it was deemed serious enough for party hierarchy in Spain to be informed.

Even so, morale in the battalion slowly climbed. Soccer matches and celebrations marked the two years of resistance to the nationalist uprising. The men sneaked out into the vineyards, drank from barrels of new, barely fermented wine, and got "roaring drunk."[9] The battalion also put on numerous fiestas for local children and residents and held sports matches against both Spaniards and other international units.

Despite these festivities, many volunteers were agitating for leave. The lack of cigarettes angered them. (Spanish tobacco tasted so bad to North Americans that Walter Dent, back home in Canada on a publicity tour, handed out Spanish cigarettes to his Canadian audience and encouraged them to have a smoke, knowing this would effectively inspire them to send Canadian tobacco to their countrymen in Spain.)[10] Desertion levels remained high, even away from the horrors of everyday battle. By July, Gallo suggested granting foreign leave to international volunteers as a way to combat the problem, which suggests that many of the deserters did not want to quit the war so much as they needed a break.[11]

In between the fiestas, the football games, and wondering what happened to their missing care packages, the men at Marçà and Falset resumed their military training. Much of this training consisted of pretending to row across a dry patch of ground representing a river and assaulting another patch of dry ground representing the opposite bank. Most of the volunteers could guess what their next assignment would be, and few were surprised when the brigade marched out of town in the third week of July. After a two-day hike, they arrived on the banks of the Ebro, the same river they had crossed in terror and defeat only three months before.

The Ebro offensive in the summer of 1938 was a last-ditch attempt to reverse what now appeared to be an inevitable nationalist victory. The campaign was designed to smash through Franco's corridor to the sea and reunite the divided Republic. It was hoped that such an assault might reverse the nationalists' momentum and allow the Republic to survive until the expected wider European war against fascism broke out. With republican war capabilities already weakened, it was a large risk. But the Republic had its back against the wall, and its leaders felt compelled to gamble. The Ebro offensive was its final hand.

The attack began on a hundred-kilometre front around midnight on the night of 24 July 1938. Thousands of republican troops slipped into wooden and inflatable boats and silently rowed to the far banks of the Ebro River. Floating cork footbridges were also positioned to allow soldiers to race across, in single file. Crucially, republican tanks and heavy artillery would be stranded until stronger bridges could be built. The plan was to bypass heavily defended areas, instead infiltrating deep into nationalist territory as quickly as possible.

Soldiers from the Mackenzie-Papineau Battalion crossed the river between the villages of Ascó and Flix. They quickly overran the defences on the far bank, though already nationalist artillery was causing casualties. Lionel Edwards was badly wounded but would survive. The Mac-Paps advanced rapidly but warily through a landscape they had previously fled. They lost contact with their flanks and with the other battalions in the brigade, which were making similarly successful but cautious progress.

Nationalist resistance stiffened, just as the attacking internationals began to feel the effects of advancing without proper support. They had crossed the Ebro travelling light, hoping to overrun nationalist territory before Franco's forces could regroup. Now the element of surprise was gone, and the Canadians west of the Ebro River found themselves behind nationalist lines with dwindling rations and no support or reinforcements. Gallo assessed the early days of the offensive a week later:

> On the 27 and 28 of July, there were difficulties in the supply of ammunition, an almost complete absence of means of transport (the division counted three trucks). Due to this we could not transport supplies and had troops who had spent more than a day without

eating. As a result of this lack of nourishment, the troops were in a state of weakness, aggravated by their having walked many kilometres through mountains several times. On the third day, the state of the medical service was alarming. The evacuation could not be carried out, as there were two ambulances for two brigades. The intense strong combats on the 27 and 28 produced a great number of casualties. (The report by the 15th Brigade's commissar signals 120 casualties in the 58th Battalion, "Lincoln," and 170 casualties in the 57th.)[12]

The Lincolns were initially stopped by a strong defence outside Vilalba dels Arcs, while the Mac-Paps' advance took them to the unoccupied town of Corbera d'Ebre. One of the first Canadians into Corbera was Jim Higgins. As he was walking through the town's stony streets, a nationalist bomber flew overhead and unloaded its bombs on Corbera's water reservoir. The resulting flash flood almost swept a young Spanish boy to his death, but Higgins waded into the water and carried the bleeding child to the safety of a makeshift first-aid post. Higgins repeated the only words of Spanish he knew in an effort to calm the boy down. "Soy canadiense," he said, I am Canadian, and, "Me llamo Jim."[13] The rest of the Canadians moved into the city, where they found an overflowing nationalist food depot and feasted on tinned octopus. They then moved on as part of a much larger offensive involving all the battalions of the 15th International Brigade against the stronghold of Gandesa. Here, in numerous assaults on the rocky hills surrounding the town, the Ebro offensive was stopped. The men of the 15th International Brigade were subjected to murderous fire in positions that offered little shelter. After ten days, the survivors were pulled back to a reserve position. According to a 10 August report by Gallo, they had lost 878 casualties in the campaign thus far, including 92 dead.[14]

The International Brigades tried to regroup in rear positions, but they knew that any respite would be temporary. On 15 August, the battalions of the 15th International Brigade were sent into the soaring, hot, and barren Sierra de Pàndols in an attempt to hold advances made in the recent offensive. Brigade battalions took up positions on adjoining hilltops – the Canadians on Hill 609, the Americans to their right on Hill 666, the 24th Battalion to their left, and the British in immediate reserve.[15] There was no water, and many of the men still had no blankets or shoes.[16] Relentless shelling burned off what little vegetation had clung to the heights, leaving hillsides with no cover and no protection from the oppressive sun. Digging in was also impossible. All they could do was fill sandbags with pebbles and loose rocks and use these for protection, but even sandbags were in short supply. Shells sent rock splinters careening across the Mac-Pap positions, augmenting the explosions' deadly effects. The dead, which could not be properly buried, bloated and stank in the sun. Requests for disinfectant to keep down the smell went unanswered.[17] At night the wounded were carried down the mountain and water was brought up.

Among the Canadians still holding on Hill 609 were Ivor "Tiny" Anderson and Joe Schoen, the two men who had stuck together since setting off for Spain from Toronto more than a year earlier. Anderson was supposed to stay behind the lines because his eyes were bad, but he had hitched a ride to the front after dropping off casualties at a hospital and attached himself to a unit on Hill 609. Schoen was happy to see the friend who had saved his life when the *Ciudad de Barcelona* was torpedoed, and the two joked about what they'd do after the war. Anderson believed that neither of them would leave Spain alive.

"Yeah, we will," Schoen told him. "I'll see you on Hastings Street, crippled and selling shoelaces."

"I'd rather die," Anderson said.[18]

The next day a mortar blew off both of Anderson's legs. A runner was sent to find Schoen. Anderson meanwhile begged Henry Mack, a Finnish Canadian with the unit, to finish him off. Mack refused and sent for a stretcher. Anderson then asked Fred Kostyk, who was standing beside him in the trench, for his rifle: "He asks me: 'Give me my rifle.' I said, 'Come on, you're not going to …' But he says, 'Give me my rifle!' So I figure, all right. So I gave him his rifle. So he pulls the trigger, and he almost hit another guy. You know, he missed himself and nearly hit another guy. But the next one he really put it up."[19] Schoen arrived to find his friend. It was impossible to bury Anderson properly. They could only cover him with rocks.[20]

The only redeeming feature of the Sierra de Pàndols was that its barren and empty landscape offered no protection for attacking soldiers either. Moors who tried to push the internationals off the hills were beaten back with heavy losses. Their bodies littered the sierra slopes and rotted in the sun. After eleven days, the Mac-Paps were ordered to withdraw from the Sierra de Pàndols. They passed their Spanish replacements climbing the mountains as they descended, and the two groups gave each other a cheer in the darkness.

Back in reserve, members of the 15th Brigade heard new rumours that all internationals were to be sent home. With the end of the war seemingly in sight, some men talked openly of desertion. As more and more volunteers slipped away, a night patrol was established to intercept would-be deserters before they could flee.[21] Spaniards in the battalions heard all this talk about repatriation, realized they might soon be left on their own, and grew resentful. "They are also under the impression that the internationals consider desertions a normal thing and that within a short time they will all leave," said John Gates, the 15th Brigade commissar, in a 6 September meeting with other commissars in the brigade.[22]

However, the 15th Brigade would be sent to the front twice more in the following weeks – both times in the Sierra de Cavalls east of Gandesa. The Mac-Paps were deployed for about a week in early September before being pulled back once again to reserve positions. During a skirmish, members of the battalion broke and ran for the rear. "The commander of the 1st Company … shot one of them and they went back to their positions," Gates noted in a terse report on the action.[23]

Among the dead was twenty-one-year-old Charles Bartolotta, a student from Hamilton. Bartolotta had spent much of the previous few months writing earnest and shyly heartfelt letters to a girl in Canada named Florence. "It all amounts to a beautiful sight, which I can't explain on paper," he wrote in a June letter from Marçà, describing the surrounding mountains and pine forests. "All this the fascists will have to pass through if they try again to get to Barcelona."[24] Bartolotta was killed when an anti-tank shell took off his head. Florence kept his letter for more than forty years.

Earlier that year, Bartolotta's brother, William, had written to Friends of the Mackenzie-Papineau Battalion's representative in Spain, Jack Taylor, begging him to send Charles home. "My mother's health has not been too good and she has been very worried all along. She is now getting to the point where she can hardly sleep at nights, or get him out of her mind," he wrote. "She is very upset and I know that if he stays in Spain much longer my mother will come to a breakdown."[25]

Charles Bartolotta came within weeks of seeing both Florence and his mother again. On 21 September, Spanish prime minister Juan Negrín stood before the League of Nations in Geneva and confirmed the rumour that had been circulating with increasing urgency for weeks among the Canadians and other foreigners in Spain. He pledged that all international volunteers in the Republic would be withdrawn from the front immediately. Negrín hoped his gesture would force Franco to likewise send home his German and Italian allies – or at least expose that the nationalist forces were dependent on foreigners. The International Brigades were also no longer the effective fighting force they once had been. They had suffered appalling casualties over the past two years, and their ranks were now filled with Spaniards. Sending them home was a gesture Negrín could afford to make, but it did not make a difference. The Germans and Italians remained in Spain.

Despite the best efforts of brigade command, word leaked back to the Canadians, Britons, and Americans in Spain, who had just been ordered to the front. "So every man knew that whatever he was going to be doing in the next few days, if he got through it, he would live – probably," the American Gerald Cook recalled years later. "An awful lot of guys got killed in those last few days."[26]

The Mac-Paps were told to hold the lines for one more day. Then reinforcements would arrive, and they could go home. The morning began with a nationalist artillery barrage, followed by an attack against the entire section of front held by the International Brigades. The units flanking the Mac-Paps were forced back, leaving them exposed. They held their ground for a while but were the focus of a ferocious assault as squads of nationalists stormed their forward trenches under a volley of grenades.

Mac-Paps in the first line of trenches and foxholes struggled against their attackers and were overwhelmed by sheer numbers. Expecting capture or death, Henry Mack bellowed at his men to destroy their personal documents and retreat. In such close quarters, slow-loading rifles were almost useless; anyone with a sidearm was now firing madly and scrambling toward the battalion's second line as nationalists poured into their trenches. Those who reached this line alive found comparative safety. The soldiers here managed to defend their positions for the rest of the day – though they too lost men to nationalist planes, which flew over and bombed them. At one o'clock in the morning, the surviving members of the Mac-Paps who were still able to walk filed down from the hills. There were thirty-five of them on their feet.[27]

Leaving Spain

Goodbye to many a happy day,
It is a farewell cup, I must say,
You, my dear Spanish fate,
From memory will not fade.

Song popular with Finnish-Canadian volunteers, recollection of volunteer
Sulo Huhtala

The war was over for the Canadians in Spain, but it would still be a long time before they could go home. A few Canadians in artillery batteries and other units were stranded in the southern zone of the divided Republic and kept fishing for up to another month.[1] They would be evacuated to the north by boat. Those not in hospitals and rest homes returned to Marçà and Falset. More fiestas and dances with the local civil population were held. The internationals pledged pacts of brotherhood to their Spanish comrades. But all outward attempts to celebrate were dampened by a pervasive sadness and sense of loss. Even those who had dreamed about escaping the war for months regretted leaving Spain to almost certain defeat.

There was also a burial service for a local favourite, John Cookson, who was killed in the September fighting. He was interred in a secluded spot by a tiny stream outside town. His grave was kept hidden from authorities throughout the subsequent decades of the Franco dictatorship and still stands today.

The Canadians formed ranks one last time, and then command of the battalions of the 15th International Brigade was formally handed over to Spanish soldiers. At goodbye parades in Marçà and Falset, and again in Barcelona, hundreds of thousands of Spaniards bade them farewell. Dolores Ibárruri, the Spanish communist political leader always known as La Pasionaria, delivered a speech that many veterans would remember for years. "You can go with pride," she said. "You are history. You are legend. You are the heroic example of democracy's solidarity and universality. We shall not forget you. And when the olive tree of peace puts forth its leaves, entwined with the laurels of the Spanish Republic's victory – come back!"[2]

But there would be no victory for the Spanish Republic. And as nationalist troops converged on Barcelona and prepared to take the city, which symbolized Spanish resistance perhaps as much as did Madrid, the Canadians now awaiting repatriation in the northern Catalan town of Ripoll were asked to make a last stand in the threatened city. This was more than a simple request; the volunteers were given the choice of turning in their party cards and thereby giving up membership in the Communist Party, or fighting to the death in Barcelona.[3]

"I figured, Christ, we're almost finished and here they are asking for volunteers," Fred Kostyk recalled. Kostyk estimated that of about three hundred Canadians still in Spain, maybe thirty-five volunteered.[4] Another veteran, speaking in 1948 to an RCMP officer in Toronto, said that the only volunteers who agreed to fight for Barcelona were Edward Cecil-Smith, two or three Ukrainians, and the battalion's commissar.[5]

Fortunately for the Canadians, Negrín or someone else high up in the Spanish political leadership forbade any of the volunteers to return to Barcelona. Those who had survived thus far would not face any more battles in Spain. Nevertheless, volunteers who refused to return to Barcelona had this fact noted on evaluations sent back to district Communist Party committees in Canada.[6]

The Canadians therefore lingered in the town of Ripoll and grew more and more restless. Thousands of ragged Spanish republican refugees streamed past them on their way to France. The Canadians stayed where they were and became haggard and hungry. According to Canadian veteran Ron Liversedge, they were visited one night by André Marty, the overall commander of the International Brigades in Spain. Marty, a large and overweening man with a walrus moustache and bulbous eyes, stood on a platform beside a man with a submachine gun and berated the skinny, hollow-cheeked internationals before him. "Why did you come to Spain if you're such cowards?" he demanded. A few of the volunteers had married Spanish women, whom they now had with them. Marty yelled at these men directly. "If you rabbits want to run out of the country with your *putas,* your whores, go ahead and run."[7]

The Canadians had heard all this from Marty before, and few were in any mood to hear it again. They began talking among themselves as Marty ranted and raved on the podium. One man lit a cigarette, which triggered a new outburst from the Frenchman: Marty declared the man a spy and said he was signalling the fascists. Bring him up here, Marty demanded, and we'll "finish him." But after nearly two years of war, the Canadians could see that the emperor had no clothes. They laughed at Marty. He backed down and slunk away.[8]

Officials from the League of Nations came to supervise the Canadians' evacuation. One of the officials, a Finn who spoke Russian, tried to trip up the volunteers when interviewing them by slipping in a question in Russian. He evidently believed there were Soviet plants among the internationals.[9]

The volunteers were already predisposed to scoff at these bureaucrats. "We were such a bedraggled gang," Irving Weissman said. "Such bums. Such hobos. Such ragamuffins. And in come these people with their spic and span numbers ... How could we even look on them with respect?"[10]

But Weissman, an American, was allowed to leave Spain before most of his Canadian Mac-Pap comrades. The Canadians watched in frustration as the British and American volunteers were repatriated while they remained in Spain. Their exit was delayed because of a lack of funds to pay for their passage home. Tim Buck, general secretary of the Communist Party of Canada, later said the party had never planned how they might evacuate the Canadian volunteers from a collapsing country because they believed the Republic would win the war.[11] Now the party was forced to confront its oversight and scrambled to raise money from the volunteers' families and from the public at large.

Albert A. MacLeod, acting on behalf of the Friends of the Mackenzie-Papineau Battalion, secured a deal that ensured cooperation from Canadian Pacific Steamships to bring volunteers home. He then travelled to London, where he reportedly obtained 500 dollars from the unlikely source of former Canadian prime minister Richard Bennett.[12] Business tycoon Garfield Weston is also said to have donated 5,000 dollars after being approached by Canadian journalist Matthew Halton.[13]

In Spain, MacLeod liaised with Canadian government and Canadian Pacific officials and frantically toured the country looking for missing Canadians and trying to come to an arrangement with the shattered remnants of the Spanish government, whose members knew they probably had only weeks before they were defeated. MacLeod achieved a breakthrough in the final stages of the war, as this report, signed by A.M. Elliott in Barcelona on 19 January 1939, makes clear: "McLeod has been officially informed by Quero Morales and Colonel Sirón (the latter from the War Ministry) that the issue of travel expenses for the Canadian comrades has been arranged. For this purpose, the Spanish consul in Perpignan has 100,000 francs and the Spanish Embassy in Paris 48,000 dollars. This information is definitive."[14] This money was received by Canadian Pacific's representative in Paris on 25 January 1939, ensuring safe passage across the Atlantic for the first shipload of returning volunteers.[15]

More money was to come with the help of the Friends of the Abraham Lincoln Brigade. On 1 February 1939, Corliss Lamont, a prominent professor of philosophy, sent a letter to Jack Taylor at the party's headquarters in New York that read:

Dear Sir:

I am enclosing a check for $5,000 and have forwarded you $15,000 in cash for the transportation and care of the returning Canadian veterans of the International Brigade. I do so in accordance with the instructions of the Paris Committee which transferred the money to me and asked me to place it at your disposal.

Very truly yours,
Corliss Lamont.[16]

Unfortunately for the Canadian volunteers, money did not solve all their problems. The Canadian government wanted to screen those who wished to return to Canada to ensure that no one who had never lived in Canada before tried to slip in and cause trouble. They dispatched Colonel Andrew O'Kelly, assistant commissioner of Canadian immigration services in London, and a Canadian Pacific agent named Coakley to do the job.[17] O'Kelly and Coakley circulated among the survivors in Spain, checking the few papers any of them could produce and interviewing the rest in an attempt to establish their legal status. As many of the volunteers were recent immigrants, this was a difficult process. Frank Hadesbeck was saved because he could describe the Calgary Stampede to a suspicious O'Kelly.[18] A few were rejected outright.

A small number of Canadians remained scattered across Spain, separated from the main contingent at Ripoll. Most were trapped in the southern zone of the country, and others were still in hospitals and rest homes. Maurice Constant, the former University of Toronto student, was working with the Spanish government on its international propaganda. He spent Christmas in Barcelona, where he was asked to read the introduction to Spanish prime minister Juan Negrín's Christmas Eve broadcast to the world. In the same hotel was the Hungarian photographer Robert Capa, whom Constant remembered rushing into the streets to photograph air raids on the city. The Canadian volunteer was effectively trapped in Barcelona, no longer officially attached to the International Brigades but still a foreigner working on behalf of the Republic. On the morning of 26 January 1939, with Franco's troops marching down the Gran Vía, Constant fled to a smuggler's wharf, where a contact arranged for a boat to take him to the British destroyer HMS *Greyhound,* which was anchored offshore and later carried him to Marseille and safety.[19]

The bulk of the Canadians in Spain left the country in January 1939 under less dramatic circumstances, taking a slow train north from Ripoll to France. It was a much different journey from the one many of the Canadians took when they first arrived in Spain. This time no peasants stopped working in their fields to raise a clenched-fist salute as the train passed, and no one flocked onto station platforms to pass fresh oranges through the windows. None of the volunteers leaned out the train and shouted, "No Pasarán!" Volunteer William Beeching said the only time he cried in Spain was when this departing train passed into the yawning mountain tunnel that marked the frontier with France.[20]

The first group of approximately 270 returning Canadians arrived at the port of Halifax on 3 February 1939. They marched off the gangplank, carrying the Canadian Red Ensign and the flag of the Spanish Republic. They were welcomed by supporters and carefully watched by plainclothes RCMP officers. The report filed by the force's Nova Scotia branch on the arrival of the war veterans read: "The latter party was met before disembarking by [Constables] Fitzsimmons, Hanson, Collins, and myself. We kept a sharp watch for members of this unit who might have been injured in such a way as to become public charges. All were without funds, one had lost his left leg, and another was paralyzed from the hips down."[21]

Smaller batches of men crossed the ocean throughout February and into the spring. Ron Liversedge, who had been trapped in southern Spain and was one of the last Canadians to leave the country, came over with a group of forty. He was emaciated and his head was shaved because of a skin infection, which had left his scalp covered in scabs. Earlier, on their way to Liverpool by train, the returning volunteers had exasperated a British waiter by demanding more and stronger coffee. "Four hundred bleedin' cups of coffee for forty fuckin' Canadians," the waiter fumed.

In the ship's restaurant, however, staff members were eager to please. "What would you like, sir?" one waiter asked.

"Listen, we've been starving for two years," Liversedge told him. "One, don't call us 'Sir.' 'Mac' is fine. Two, keep bringing the food, and we'll tell you when to stop." The waiter brought porridge, kippers, and bacon. Liversedge and the other volunteers ate themselves sick.[22]

Arriving in Saint John, New Brunswick, they were met by a government official, who wasn't quite sure what to make of the ragged men before him or how he should describe them in his paperwork. He asked if the Canadians were Foreign Legionnaires – a question that angered some of the veterans, who associated all foreign legions with the Spanish one, which many of them had spent the last two years fighting. Finally, one of the veterans told the official: "You can call us anti-fascists."[23]

A handful of Canadians who had been separated from the main body of volunteers, or who could not prove that they had lived in Canada before the war, languished for weeks and months in French concentration camps hastily erected on Mediterranean beaches. Conditions were so bad that one detainee, Alexander Forbes (Kabatoff), wondered if the French government intended to starve them to death. The detainees slept in the sand, and Senegalese troops fed them by throwing bread over the barbed-wire fence.

Konstantin Olynyk, born in Romania, was initially rejected by Canadian authorities as a candidate for repatriation and spent two weeks in the French camps. Eventually, a Canadian or British government official arrived and quizzed Olynyk on his listed hometown of South Porcupine, Ontario. Satisfied that Olynyk knew enough details about this small northern mining town on the outskirts of Timmins to prove that he lived there, the official had him released.[24]

The final contingent of Canadian International Brigades volunteers to leave Spain were Franco's Canadian prisoners of war. Thirty-one were released on 5 April 1939.[25] With the war over and the Republic they had come to defend defeated, Jules Paivio, Percy Hilton, Nick Elendiuk, and the rest of the captured Canadians were no longer of any use to their captors. They were taken to the border with France and marched into freedom. A few others were released with volunteers from the United States, Britain, and the rest of Europe.

Several Canadians, however, were left behind. Charles Scarpello (known in Spain as Scanlan) was held until at least May 1939 but was released sometime later that year. James Cameron, who eluded capture by nationalists for ten weeks during the retreats of 1938, was finally freed in 1940. Mikalj Bukovi was held until 1941 or 1942, as was Paul Szucsko. Edvardas Zdanauskas was imprisoned long after hostilities ended in Spain. He had arrived safely in England by 1943, but his release date is unclear. According to Robert Dickie, a Canadian prisoner of war released in April 1939, Szucsko and Zdanauskas did not register with prison authorities as Canadians but as a Hungarian and a Lithuanian respectively. According to Dickie, this is why the two were not released with the rest of the Canadian prisoners in April. Bukovi was also born in Hungary and this might explain his prolonged detention. Cameron was reportedly held to be court-martialled for unspecified charges but was never tried.[26]

Part 3
Discipline in the International Brigades

Crimes

Singing was a popular pastime among volunteers in the International Brigades, as it has always been for soldiers in any army. At night Canadians could occasionally hear Moors or Spaniards singing in the trenches opposite them. A few of the internationals even had guitars and other musical instruments. Most of their songs were generic, if beautiful, odes to fighting fascism and working-class solidarity. Some were sung in Spanish; some were not. The American Finn Carl Syvanen recalls that in the predawn gloom before the internationals launched their attack on Brunete, a Canadian nicknamed K.O. because of his boxing talents broke the tension by shouting out the lyrics of Robert Service's classic poem "The Shooting of Dan McGrew." "A bunch of the boys were whooping it up in the Malamute saloon," he sang, reciting the story of a barroom shooting that happened one frozen night during the Yukon gold rush to several hundred men about to sweep across a scorching Spanish plain to attack a village bearing the familiar name of Cañada.[1]

None of this was particularly out of the ordinary in a war that had such an international character, and it certainly wasn't anything to worry the commanders and political commissars of the internationals in Spain. But some Canadians imported songs that soon caused consternation among their political bosses, such as this marching song:

Oh, I wanna go home
I don't wanna die
Machine guns they rattle
The cannons they roar
I don't wanna go to the front any more

Oh, take me over the sea
Where Franco can't get at me
Oh! My! I'm too young to die
I wanna go home![2]

Irving Weissman, a political commissar and leading American communist in Spain, decided, along with his fellow commissars, that it was unacceptable for anti-fascist volunteers to sing such lyrics and tried to stamp out the song.

"We commissars had a hell of a time because we had to fight that song," he said. "At least we thought – we were very solemn and strait-laced – we thought we had to fight it ... This song became the chant of the people who just felt, what the hell were they there for?"[3] Weissman did not say if the commissars' censorship campaign had any success, but it seems unlikely.

In truth, there was little seditious about the song. According to Weissman, it originated with Canadian soldiers in the First World War and was simply adapted to Spain. However, it is a good example of how the natural irreverence of the Canadian volunteers put them at odds with their commanders. This potential for conflict was made worse by the notable absence of Canadians in positions of command. "We didn't even have any goddamn Canadian officers. When I look back at it ... I think that we betrayed an enormous amount of chauvinism," said Weissman. "The leadership, both political and military, of the Mac-Paps was overwhelmingly American. We did not work in such a way to go and to recognize the leadership of Canadians, and they were just as good as we were."[4]

Some Canadians did rise to leadership positions in the International Brigades. Edward Cecil-Smith commanded the Mackenzie-Papineau Battalion for much of the unit's existence. Nevertheless, Canadians in Spain were frequently led by Americans, and the leadership of the 15th Brigade, both political and military, was predominantly British and American.

This situation was discussed in a report on the "political development of the International Brigades," written after demobilization by Abe Lewis, an American communist and political commissar in the 15th International Brigade. Lewis noted that tensions existed between national groups in the brigade. "This condition expressed itself chiefly among the Americans as it concerned their relationship and attitude towards the Latin Americans and Canadians," he wrote, adding that many Latin Americans chose to leave the 15th Brigade for other units:

> The Canadian comrades remained with the Brigade. They expressed their resentment in other ways. While this resentment was not shown during operations, in which they worked very well, it was sharply exhibited during discussions during periods of rest. In these discussions, the comrades raised the question of [the] lack of Canadian participation in the leadership of the Brigade.
>
> This complaint was never considered seriously ... They did not contend with it in a political manner. There was no distinction made between the developed and the backward Canadian comrades. However, the work of a number of our Canadian comrades decisively proved that they were sufficiently competent to assume leading positions although, in general, they were not given these positions.[5]

Lewis elaborated on the subservient position of Canadians in the 15th Brigade in another document, "Report on the Work of the North Americans in the XV Brigade." The Americans, he wrote, demonstrated "a feeling of superiority ... towards the Canadian, Latin American, Spanish, and Negro comrades." This attitude ultimately affected who led the Canadians in Spain. Wrote Lewis:

> The Canadian Battalion, Mackenzie-Papineau, throughout its entire history was led by Commissars who were from the United States. As far as officers were concerned, here too, we found a serious shortcoming in the development of Canadians. Was this due to the fact that we didn't have such leadership among the Canadians? It would be absolutely wrong to say [so]. Such leadership did exist but we did not discuss or collaborate in a policy of bringing them forward as leaders of the Mackenzie-Papineau Battalion. Yet despite its defects, it was one of the best fighting units in the Brigade.[6]

Many Canadians, both in leadership and among the regular soldiers, felt the same way. Speaking to party officials just before the repatriation of the surviving Canadian volunteers, Edward Cecil-Smith said,

> While it is undoubtedly true that the Party in Canada did not send out so many leading cadres as did the Party in Britain or the United States, nevertheless it does seem a little bit odd that after two years of fighting, in which the Canadians have not done so badly, we find 280 comrades waiting to go home with only three officers and four commissars among them. Of these, one officer and two commissars came from units other than the XV Brigade.

"To be perfectly frank there is an idea among the Canadian comrades that they have been overlooked and slighted on more counts than one," he continued, noting that the Canadian volunteers felt they were always the last to receive everything, from cigarettes and care packages from home to seats on a train. "There is also a long felt resentment over the matter of Canadian packages, a question which has not been sufficiently explained to anybody's satisfaction."[7]

The difference in leadership opportunities between the Canadian and American volunteers might also have been related to different attitudes toward authority among the two groups. "We Canadians had a rank and file consciousness ... It wasn't good, come to look back on it now," said John "Paddy" McElligott, an Irish-born Canadian volunteer. "The American boys, if they were put in charge of a detail ... well, next time you saw him he had stripes on." McElligott said part of the reason few Canadians were promoted was because the Canadians themselves had a desire to be "one of the boys." They were reluctant to either give or take orders. "I wouldn't call it disobedience," he said, "I would describe it as an independence. Just, 'We're Canadian; we're independent.'"[8]

According to Canadian volunteer Helge Meyer, the Canadians in Spain almost instinctively rebelled against authority because so many of them, especially from the West Coast, had spent time in relief or "Bennett" camps. "When they came over there, some of them, at least at the beginning, were still fighting the boss," he said. "Not the boss of the Bennett camps, but the boss of the company, the boss of the battalion ... They were more rebels. They took the boss complex with them, and they were still fighting the boss when they were over there."[9]

The Americans were also more dedicated communists, and party members held most leadership positions in the International Brigades. "I'm afraid they ruled the roost, pretty much," McElligott said. "That's what turned me against communism, against the Communist Party, they way it acted over there ... Any of the boys will tell you the same."[10]

McElligott recalled addressing a batch of new recruits and asking who among them had combat experience. Out stepped American Joe Brandt, a Communist Party secretary, wearing knee boots, jacket, a beret, and a Sam Browne belt. "He was more Spanish than the Spanish," McElligott thought, and he did not appear to know one end of a rifle from the other. Brandt told McElligott that he should be given a command position. McElligott asked why, and Brandt told him that he had been promised as much in New York. "This kind of annoyed me. I said, 'Comrade, this is Spain. This is not New York. There's a war on. If you have the ability to be an officer and you live long enough, you'll probably be one. In the meantime, the first thing you have to do is become a soldier.'" Brandt was put on brigade staff despite his lack of military experience. According to McElligott, he never became a good soldier.[11]

Most reports indicate that the rank-and-file Americans and Canadians got along well together – certainly more so than did the Irish and the British in the 15th Brigade, where relations once got so tense that a group of Irishmen demanded to be transferred to an American battalion. But animosity between the two groups did exist. The Americans tended to see the Canadians as a little rough around the edges. Some Canadians in turn derided the Americans for not being as tough as they were. In a 20 February 1938 letter to the Central Committee of the Communist Party of Spain, Jack Taylor, the Communist Party of Canada's representative in Spain, expressed dismay that while visiting the Mackenzie-Papineau Battalion he heard one of the Canadian soldiers refer to his American comrades as "New York ice cream boys."[12]

Some tension also appears to have existed between British commanders and Canadian soldiers in Spain. Bill Williamson, a Winnipeg man who fought with a Basque militia unit during the first months of the war, said that while he was a member of the International Brigades, he crossed paths with Jeff Mildwater, a British Communist Party functionary whom Williamson had met in London the previous summer. The two men liked each other, though Williamson found Mildwater to be a little dogmatic and self-important. In

Spain, Mildwater belonged to the British anti-tank battery. He told William-son that the group received special privileges and that he could arrange for Williamson to join the unit and receive the same.

Mildwater took Williamson to a stone barn where a company meeting was going on. At the centre of the barn stood the commander of the unit, whom Williamson described as "a little poppycock of a captain," and some kind of writer, probably the unit's commander Malcolm Dunbar or his second-in-command Hugh Slater. According to Williamson, the commander told his audience: "First of all, we've heard some very alarming reports, especially from the Americans, but even more so from the Canadians, about how ill-disciplined they are. Comrades, this is something that has got to be attended to."

Williamson said the captain continued his lecture for more than an hour before asking for comments and noting that a soldier has a duty to speak up if he disagrees. He noticed Williamson, a "visiting comrade from the Mac-Paps," in the audience and pressed him for his opinions. After initially declining to interfere because he was a guest, Williamson spoke up and cursed the British commander. Significantly, he was not rebuked or punished but applauded for his honesty. As they were leaving, however, Mildwater told Williamson he had blown his opportunity to join the British anti-tank battery.[13]

Canadian soldiers in Spain found themselves in a position where their irreverence and distaste for authority rubbed their usually non-Canadian commanders the wrong way. These attributes might have helped shape fine soldiers, capable of improvisation and bravery, but in Spain they also had negative political consequences. Canadians were often labelled by their commanders as politically undeveloped or as possessing anarchist tendencies. On occasion these kinds of judgments crossed the line from disapproval to condemnation. A sure sign that this had occurred was when reports no longer labelled the offending party as politically undeveloped but as a Trotskyist.

Just how serious political deviation when perceived to be Trotskyism was viewed by International Brigades leadership is made clear in the minutes of a 16 June 1937 meeting of political commissars in Madrid. At the meeting, Jean Barthol, then adjunct commissar of the inspector of the International Brigades, said that the notion of popular front unity must not stop the liquidation of Trotskyism. He especially praised the Soviet Union, then in the midst of a murderous purge that would kill hundreds of thousands, for its skill in disposing of these deviants. Barthol's comments are worth quoting at length because they help us understand how Canadians accused of Trotskyist tendencies were viewed by party leaders in Spain:

> It is certain that the Popular Front's unity, as well as international unity, depend on the liquidation of Trotskyism, a current of dividing elements that is responsible for bloody events such as those in Barcelona. Yes, for unity at the interior level and at the interna-

tional one, the elimination of Trotskyism is a conclusion that has to be deduced. These individuals must not be allowed to hide behind the Popular Front's wall with the most different currents of the people, communists, socialists, anarchists, anti-fascists, including our fellow comrades without party. All the differences in doctrine that may be seen within the Popular Front are not an obstacle to its unity because we are with the popular organizations; what we do not want is unity with the organizations of criminals, because it is not possible to admit within the Popular Front the accomplices of the fascists, those who have tried to sabotage the USSR and want to sabotage Spain. From this point of view, it cannot matter to us if we combat them, we must not allow them to hide behind our unity pacts. And I do not think I am moving away from the political framework of our army and the Popular Front if I state here that I wholeheartedly approve the energy of the USSR, which knows how to dispose of the elements that betray the cause of the people like the [Tukhachevskies] and other agents of Trotskyism and fascism. I am also persuaded that the Spanish government will be vigorous in order to maintain unity within our ranks, because unity is the condition for a quick victory over fascism.[14]

The concept of Trotskyism meant little to the average Canadian volunteer. Henry Scott Beattie was wounded in Spain and sent home by the party on a propaganda tour, but he renounced his party membership shortly after arriving back in Canada. "I was further coached to make certain statements about Trotskyists, for example: 'Trotskyists who stab wounded soldiers on crutches in the back,'" he said in his statement explaining his decision to leave the party. "And this despite the fact that while I was in Spain I had never seen or spoken to a Trotskyist."[15] In response, the party published an article in its *Daily Clarion* newspaper suggesting that Beattie was mentally unwell. "Poor boy. He sounds shell-shocked," Ted Allan is quoted as saying. "The boy is obviously in a bad nervous state and has been coached by Trotskyites who utilized his mental frame by getting him to make a complete ass of himself."[16]

Even if the average Canadian volunteer wasn't sure what constituted Trotskyism, International Brigades leadership thought it was a serious, even dangerous, crime. Yet it was a crime that they were remarkably quick to accuse many Canadians in Spain of committing. In an 8 September 1939 letter to André Marty, the pompous French communist leader of the International Brigades, in which he summarized the qualities of the Canadian volunteers, leading Canadian communist Tom Ewen said that 55 out of 354 returning veterans were rated "bad," which he classified as men who were drunks, Trotskyists, spies, or generally unreliable. Ewen also cited a report by Robert Dickie on the behaviour of thirty-two Canadians who were captured by the nationalists and became prisoners of war. Only six of the thirty-two were "reliable and steadfast to the Party and the struggle of Loyalist Spain under all conditions in prison." Nine were fair, while the remaining seventeen constituted "Trotskyist elements; drunks and immoral characters; tools of the prison fascist regime, who ingratiated themselves with the fascists etc, some of them aided the fascists by petty espionage against their fellow International Volunteers."[17]

The contents of these two reports cannot be taken seriously. Most of the Canadian volunteers would have had a hard time describing what a Trotskyist might be, and there is no evidence that any of the Canadian volunteers were spies against the Republic. Former prisoners also reported high levels of solidarity within the camps. But the reports show how quickly and how freely political authorities in the International Brigades threw around accusations of Trotskyism to describe almost anyone with whom they found fault. "One day you are working with a comrade, the next day he is a Trotskyite," wrote Canadian Robert Hamilton in an unpublished account of his time in Spain. "That one word covers everything."[18]

Volunteers could be suspected of Trotskyism simply because of the friends they kept. Pat Stephens, a Canadian in the Lincoln Battalion, recalled that in the spring of 1938 an American Jew named Morris Mickenberg was assigned to his unit. Stephens described Mickenberg as the "political philosopher" of the group and said that Mickenberg liked to mock "Uncle Joe" Stalin and the Communist Party hierarchy in Spain. Knowing that Mickenberg would be reported to the "appropriate people," Stephens advised him, without success, to be more careful about his jokes. When the company commissar took Stephens aside to question him about Mickenberg, Stephens told the commissar that Mickenberg's jokes were harmless and were not hurting the morale of the men.

Stephens was later approached by Doug Roach, a black comrade who was on his way home to the United States for propaganda purposes. Roach asked Stephens to take a walk with him outside their dugout, where he confided to Stephens that he was a member of military intelligence sent to spy on Mickenberg and Stephens. "He asked me to be very careful of what I said and if possible to get Micky out of my unit," Stephens said. "[Micky] was suspected of being a Trotskyite, and my friendship with him was suspect. He advised me to warn Micky and not to associate with him too closely. I thanked Doug for his warnings, but told him I had no fears; I had come to Spain to fight the Fascists, not the Communist Party." Stephens nevertheless took Roach's warnings to heart and became less friendly with Mickenberg.[19]

The military intelligence unit to which Roach belonged was the Servicio de Investigación Militar (SIM), the Republic's feared, communist-infiltrated secret police. The SIM's official role was to guard against spying and enemy sabotage, but much of its efforts were directed against supposed political deviants – primarily those who criticized the Communist Party or the Soviets. The Soviet NKVD exercised substantial control over the SIM, which employed thousands of agents, some of whom were not communists themselves.[20] Within the International Brigades, the SIM was led by an émigré Serb named Fein.[21] Fein reported directly to André Marty.

Stephens was recruited into the SIM in the spring or early summer of 1938. Summoned to brigade headquarters, he was told that because of the large number of new recruits, mostly Spanish and Catalan conscripts, a danger existed that fascist spies and agitators might infiltrate the Lincoln Battalion. Stephens' job was to establish a network of informers to ensure that this didn't happen:

> I was to set up agents in every company and they in turn would appoint someone in each platoon to act as informants. I would be assigned officially to Battalion Headquarters but would not be subject to Battalion command. My assignment was for SIM and under their direction. I was to submit a daily report on routine matters: the morale of the troops; the troops' confidence in their officers and any complaints about them; complaints about the food; rumors and who started them; the conditions and maintenance of arms; suspicious characters to be scrutinized and watched, and any information about their connections and their backgrounds; military effectiveness of the battalion; and the efficiency, conduct, and competence of the officers. These points would be transmitted to me by company agents, and I would prepare a daily report based on their information, and add my own summary and commentary. These would be taken personally to Brigade.[22]

Stephens said he did catch a spy – a conscript from Barcelona who had allegedly tried to smuggle out classified information by writing it in tiny script beneath a stamp on a letter he was mailing.[23] But despite what was clearly intensive surveillance, there is no evidence that these SIM agents and informers uncovered any genuine cases of treason or sabotage by internationals in the 15th Brigade.

Among Canadians in Spain, besides Pat Stephens, there is evidence that Ellis Fromberg also served with the SIM. A file on Fromberg in the Moscow archives notes that he was "discreet" and praises his skill at "conspiratorial work" during the party's period of illegality in Canada. His file says his name was put forward as a potential SIM recruit, but as Fromberg deserted in the spring of 1938, it is unclear whether he carried out this assignment.[24]

Peter Carroll estimates that about half a dozen men in the Lincolns served with the SIM at various times throughout the war.[25] According to Stephens' description of an agent in every company and an informant in every platoon, however, the total number was probably higher. Indeed, it appears that official SIM agents and trusted party members played similar roles in spying and reporting on their fellow soldiers. A February 1938 report on Canadian Harry Rayfield, who never deserted and who was later described as a comrade "with no apparent faults," is revealing:

> This comrade raised the problem within the cell of organizing a committee to go wherever it is necessary to seek to improve soldiers' conditions and even extend this action to

workers in the district ... He presents his items in an intelligent and concealed manner and bases his arguments on things that really exist. For example, some of the soldiers have to receive delayed payments. In the "complaint" he made at the second meeting, another comrade, whose name I don't remember, joined him. Despite having attended the [Party]'s meetings, he didn't pay the fee nor contribute. He didn't fill out his application either.

We believe this comrade is a Trotskyist or has Trotskyist tendencies and we ask that he be watched closely. About a week ago he was transferred from here to the division with twelve others whose names are stated in a separate list.[26]

The report is signed by members of the "5th Comp. cell committee." Such communist cells existed as part of a parallel party organization with the brigade.[27]

Of several other Canadians who were labelled Trotskyists in their individual evaluations, the case of John Grainger is instructive. Grainger arrived in Spain in July 1937. He worked in the auto park and the transport regiment, and for a while he drove an ambulance. By all accounts he did his job well. An evaluation in his file, dated 21 October 1938 and signed by Jim Bourne, John Gates, and A. Donaldson, rates his conduct as "satisfactory." He "worked well in auto park ... studied political questions and also learnt to speak Spanish." The reports says he is "slightly confused but willing to learn" and is "well liked by his friends." In summary, his political evaluators judged Grainger to be a "good anti-fascist" and "an element to be helped and advised from a political standpoint."[28] On 19 November 1938, in an evaluation of the non-communist Canadian volunteers awaiting repatriation, Grainger was listed as one of the "good" comrades, meaning "good anti-fascists in the military and political sphere, without serious weakness."[29]

At this time, as Canadians were awaiting repatriation at Ripoll, widespread discontent that had been simmering for weeks began to boil over. They had been withdrawn from the lines two months earlier but appeared to be no closer to getting back to Canada. Volunteer Fred Greysdale reportedly said their condition was approaching that of the Canadian soldiers who rioted in 1919 at Kinmel Camp in Rhyl, Wales, to protest the slow pace of demobilization.[30] In the midst of this unrest, Helge Meyer described Grainger as a Trotskyist, a label synonymous with traitor to the anti-fascist cause. Grainger had been on the verge of joining the Communist Party, Meyer said, but he had ripped up his application at the last moment and now "flourishes" a pin from the Federación Anarquista Ibérica – the largest anarchist organization in Spain. Grainger allegedly told Meyer he would even like to join the group.[31]

A few days later, on 15 December, Edward Cecil-Smith detailed Grainger's offences in a report titled "Activities of Group of Disrupters among Canadian Volunteers in Ripoll":

This clique of disrupters who have taken advantage of the recent situation among the

Canadian volunteers and of certain weaknesses in the leadership of the Canadians, have sought to create a grievance out of every little inconvenience, finally culminating in attempting to call two meetings on December 13 with the object of organizing some sort of demonstration against the command of this base and also against the leadership of the International Brigades.

Grainger, Cecil-Smith said, might not have been a member of this group, but he was at least guilty of "supplying them with arguments at meetings if not in the actual organization work."[32]

Despite more than a year of active service in the war without any blemishes on his record, in his final weeks in Spain John Grainger was labelled a Trotskyist and therefore an enemy of the Spanish people, for the crime of rejecting the Communist Party and complaining publicly about his military and political leaders. Grainger, however, was lucky. Although communist-affiliated unions in Canada no doubt received word of his anti-party attitudes, which might have hampered his search for work when he got home, there is no evidence that Grainger was punished in Spain.[33]

James McDowell was not so fortunate. A Scottish-born hotel and restaurant worker from Toronto, McDowell came to Spain in January 1938 and enlisted in the special machine-gun battalion of the 15th Army Corps. Sometime in May he got into a heated dispute with a political commissar. In his own words, written in a questionnaire after the Canadians had been withdrawn from the lines, he said he was punished for "telling company political delegate off."[34] A. Donaldson, who wrote an evaluation of McDowell, was a little more specific, noting that McDowell "practically called the commissar a fascist and refused to retract the statement."[35] In yet another report, R. Turner, who appears to have been with McDowell in the special machine-gun battalion, said McDowell "continually slurred and sneered at the leadership of both the International Brigades and the Party. Was a disruptive and demoralizing influence, finally sent back to 15th Brigade as undesirable."[36]

McDowell's punishment was two months in a labour battalion, a sentence he later called unjust. Perhaps understandably, by the time McDowell got to Ripoll to wait with the other Canadians for transportation back to Canada, he wanted little to do with the communists who controlled the brigade. A. Donaldson explained in the report on McDowell:

Since in Ripoll, Comrade has shown Complete Indifference to the Party. Informed by Responsible Comrade to discuss his Anti-Party position, Comrade McDowell failed to attend. Approached the 2nd occasion and advised of the importance of the meeting, McDowell stated he was not interested in what took place as far as he is concerned: Continues to Beef. Chronic Impossible ... Have concluded McDowell should be expelled.[37]

McDowell was expelled from the Communist Party at Ripoll, an outcome that probably did not bother him by that time.

What is most noteworthy, however, is that McDowell's commitment to Spain's fight against fascism, and his support for the Spanish government, did not waver. In the same questionnaire in which he complained that his sentence to the labour battalion was unjust, McDowell wrote that the "People's Front" policy was "very good ... the only way to defeat fascism in Spain and throughout the world." Spanish prime minister Juan Negrín's thirteen points outlining the goals of the Spanish Republic were similarly described as very good. Aside from McDowell's growing contempt for the party and its political commissars, it appears that his battlefield conduct was satisfactory. He did not drink or desert, and he fought in all the major engagements, from the initial offensive across the Ebro River to the battle in the Sierra de Cavalls. Even the Communist Party of Spain's representatives in the 15th Brigade, Jim Bourne, A. Donaldson, and John Gates, described his conduct as steady and said that he was liked.[38]

James McDowell's alleged crimes, which were serious enough to earn him the two-month sentence in a labour battalion, were political and personal offences rather than military shortcomings. In this respect he was not alone. The evaluations of returning Canadians are filled with phrases such as "anti-party element," "politically confused," "politically weak," "disruptive," "shows Trotskyist tendencies," "treacherous," and "potential fascist."[39] A few of these men might have been truly disastrous soldiers. Most were guilty of nothing more than a visceral dislike of authority and diminished faith in the Communist Party and its leaders. Arthur Ashplant, for example, said he was jailed for the crime of insubordination to the Communist Party.[40] Ashplant was not even a member of the Communist Party; his incarceration for disrespecting communism says much about the control wielded by the party within the International Brigades.

Even party members and long-time leaders in the Canadian labour movement were not immune from baseless accusations of disloyalty and Trotskyism. John "Paddy" McElligott, for example, was the epitome of an anti-fascist activist. His rebellion against authority began before he came to Canada, when he joined the IRA as a young teenager in Ireland. He emigrated in the 1920s and in 1934 joined the Communist Party of Canada. He spent the Great Depression drifting from place to place in search of work. He was also active in the labour and unemployed movements. He was variously a member of the Mine, Mill and Smelter Workers' Union, the Lumber and Sawmill Workers' Union, and the League against War and Fascism. He agitated regularly in relief camps and took part in numerous strikes and demonstrations, which led to his being jailed four times for offences such as obstructing police and inciting riots. His decision to fight in Spain required little contemplation. "Having become a member of the Communist Party, my interest in world affairs developed," he said. "I became aware we were gong to have to fight fascism on an international basis, and I figured Spain was a good place to start."[41]

McElligott's party membership and radical past, combined with a short stint in the Canadian militia, made him a natural candidate for military leadership in Spain. Upon arrival, he was immediately assigned the job of an infantry instructor. But McElligott did not enjoy shouting at the men he knew from Canadian relief camps as they marched around the parade square, and he soon arranged for a transfer to a fighting unit. There McElligott displayed both heroism under fire and the insubordination that would eventually get him sent to a disciplinary battalion.

None of McElligott's evaluations denies his courage and ability as a fighting man. He was cited for bravery in leading his section on a successful assault against an enemy position at Caspe. His evaluation sent to party district committees in Canada says he was "courageous at the front" but undisciplined.[42] An earlier evaluation on his skills as an infantry instructor says he is "very efficient but lacks a little politically in his approach to his men."[43] At the front, McElligott was initially assigned to the 15th Army Corps' special machine-gun battalion as a sergeant. For reasons that are not clear, he was demoted. From this point on, it appears that he was in open conflict with his commanders. A report by A. Donaldson says that he was twice guilty of "open indiscipline" in front of the men:

> In doing so he became popular because the men thought he was fighting for better conditions for them and taking a stand for them. On the first occasion when being tried he told the Commandante that his action of protest was in order to bring notice [to] the lack of proper military training in the unit – an obvious lie as a "get out." He was admonished on the first occasion but when he broke out on a later occasion he was sent to a disciplinary squad. A special meeting of the company was called to deal with his "martyrdom" and his support broken among the men.[44]

McElligott was also jailed and expelled from the party in Spain.[45] When released from the disciplinary squad, he had no intention of staying with the special machine-gun battalion and staged a "sit-down strike" to get transferred to the Mac-Paps, which was apparently successful.[46]

One of McElligott's final evaluations – completed on 20 October 1938 by representatives of the Communist Party of Spain, Gates, Donaldson, and Bourne – says that McElligott may still be of use to the movement at home, if he can overcome his "individualism." Nevertheless, Abe Lewis felt compelled to add his own judgment in a handwritten note scrawled on the top of McElligott's evaluation: "Trotskyist tendencies."[47]

A common and much more serious offence than insubordination and so-called political weakness among the Canadians in Spain was desertion. John Gates, commissar of the 15th International Brigade, addressed the problem on 6 September 1938 at a meeting with battalion and unit commissars in the brigade. "Regarding the issue of desertions, we have to explain that these deserters are not true representatives of the International Brigades," the commissars were told, according to minutes of the meeting signed by Gates. "They are adventurers, criminals, and cowards. We have to move away from these elements. We have to vote resolutions requesting the maximum punishment for these deserters and develop hatred towards them."[48]

If we are to take the commissars at their word, an extraordinarily high percentage of Canadians who volunteered to risk their lives fighting fascism in Spain were adventurers, cowards, and criminals. Based on records from the archives of the Communist International, at least 117 Canadians deserted or were accused of desertion.[49] In some cases, the allegation must be considered suspect. A soldier who tarried on an assignment to Barcelona, for example, might have earned himself the deserter label. At least one Canadian, seventeen-year-old Jean Paul Homer Matta, before deserting to Paris, attempted to desert to the front, so anxious was he to join the action.[50] It is nevertheless a substantial number of people when one considers that fewer than 1,700 Canadians served in Spain, and detailed records for hundreds of them – which would surely list more deserters – do not exist.[51]

Many who did not desert also wanted to leave. Scores wrote letters to Jack Taylor and others, asking to be sent home. "While I know that at about this time you will be receiving quite a number of applications, I would like you to consider my case," wrote Arthur Moffat, a lumberjack, miner, and construction worker, in the spring of 1938. "One year in Spain, eight months front line service, one serious wound and heartily fed up with war for a few years to come. I have had enough of it."[52]

James MacLean, a young man from Sioux Lookout, first wrote in January 1938 to Bob Kerr, a Canadian representative at the Albacete base, asking to be sent home. He said he had been kicked in the head by a runaway horse back in Canada, and now the old wound was starting to bother him again. He said he was promised when he volunteered that he could stay in Spain as long as he wanted and return to Canada when it suited him. "Of course, I kept my injuries quiet, not letting anyone know," he said of being kicked by a horse. He added that he was not a member of the Communist Party but intended to join when he got back to Canada; perhaps he could help out with the recruiting effort.[53]

Five months later, MacLean was still in Spain. He wrote another letter, this time to Jack Taylor, sounding more desperate. He noted that the comrades back in Toronto had assured him that Taylor was a "square" and upfront man. "I have not been treated humanely by the German doctors here. Probably it is because I do not speak their language or it is because they do not know their practice properly," he said. The doctors insisted he was fit for the front, but MacLean said that he was already half-blind and his vision was getting worse: "I mean business, I need an operation and I mean to have it done with, this damn thing has been bothering me too much ... The comrades back in Canada will see that I meant it when they find me immediately in a hospital undergoing another operation. These people here at Brigade, Comrade J. Gates, Com. Roger and Major Cecil Smith do not understand my condition."[54] Once again, MacLean argued that he would continue the fight against fascism in Canada. He could help with propaganda, he said, noting that he was now writing poetry. But MacLean was not sent home. He took part in the final campaign on the Ebro, was wounded, and was never seen alive again.

The reasons for desertion were legion and varied, and there does not seem to have been any pattern among the men who deserted. Young and old, party members and the apolitical, fled the front. All these men fought in horrendous conditions. Few who had seen action had not been wounded. Dysentery was rife. Many had running sores and loose teeth. There is little evidence that even deserters rejected or recanted their earlier commitment to fighting fascism. But under the conditions in which they fought it in Spain, many simply and understandably broke down and desperately searched for a way out.

Few volunteers have written candidly about desertion or their reasons for it. Hugh Garner did just this in a letter he wrote in the summer or early fall of 1937, asking for repatriation. Garner said that he arrived in Albacete on 17 February 1937 and was assigned the job of a telephone operator on the base. Most of his friends were with the Lincoln Battalion at the Jarama front, and he immediately applied for a transfer to join them. He got his wish in mid-February:

> I was a member of the machine gun company of the Lincoln Battalion until the end of May. (May 26 or 27th). Comrade [Oliver] Law who was acting commandant transferred five of us to the genie [engineer or labour] battalion. We were incensed when we found that the genie battalion was formed mostly of ex-prisoners. Our job was digging trenches in no-man's land. The work was torture to me. My nerves broke down completely. I suffered badly from abject terror of bullets and also the injustice of our transfer. I ran away to Madrid on June 6th. I joined the 39th mixed brigade [an anarchist unit]. They were out on rest. I hated being in it after three days. I went to Madrid on leave and saw Comrade [Ralph] Bates [assistant commissar of the 15th International Brigade] in the political bureau. I told him my whole story and he threatened to have me arrested and thrown from his office as a deserter. I told him I was not a deserter. I was still in a fighting unit and had come to him for the help that I thought he would afford me. He acted in a very boorish manner to me. I was now completely disgusted. I had no idea where to go.[55]

Garner went to the Central Committee of the Communist Party in Madrid, where someone arranged his transfer back to the 15th Brigade. At brigade headquarters, Steve Nelson, a popular political commissar, told Garner that if he did not want to go into the lines, perhaps he could get a medical examination that would excuse him. Garner, however, said that he wanted to go to the front. He returned to the lines and joined a Canadian section of the Lincoln Battalion:

> I felt fine. I was eager to go to the front. About a week there I began to drink heavily. My nerves went all to hell. I began to fear the front again. I told comrade Nelson. He said to stop drinking. I went to the doctor. He examined me and said my heart and lungs were fine but my nerves were very bad. He gave me some pills. I stopped drinking then.

Garner spoke to Bob Kerr, who also offered to try to get Garner a job behind the lines. Again, Garner refused and even followed his battalion into action at Brunete when he had been ordered to stay back to guard supplies:

> We went into action and I still felt good. In the afternoon of the first day I began to feel weak. My mouth was clogged with mucus. I could hardly talk. I suffered from shivering spells. My nerves broke down completely. Lieut. Hall[i]well ordered me to lie down in the shade near the first aid station. I did but I felt ashamed of myself. I wanted to help but I was terrified. I crawled along a trench to the machine gunners. We were firing at a sniper. Comrade Nelson told me to go out and ask either Comrade Law or the adjutant for instructions. I went out to where the adjutant was lying behind a slight rise in the ground. He gave me the information which I carried back to Comrade Nelson. I went back to the first aid post and lay down. The wounded were coming in. I wanted to help. I started helping the first aid men (getting stretchers, etc). I walked down toward the ambulances with a wounded Canadian named Moffat. He collapsed and I got three men to help me carry him. I borrowed a stretcher from a Spanish battalion. We carried him down to the stretcher-bearers post. There were many wounded there and no one to carry them so we decided to carry our man all the way. I think the distance was about seven or eight kilometers to the ambulances. It took us about four or five hours to carry him in. We were completely exhausted. My nerves were shot. I sobbed with vexation when no one else would help us. I knew he would die if we did not get him in soon. I fell asleep several times even when walking with the stretcher. We finally got him to an ambulance. We fell down exhausted on the ground and slept. In the morning I woke up with my limbs shivering violently. I was half-crazy. I felt a horror (probably caused by my exhaustion and nervous condition). I hated our own wounded men. I hated to look at guns or ambulances or anything else connected with war. I wanted to scream with disgust. I wanted to run, anywhere, to get away from the picture in my mind. I saw Toab coming up a road. He said he couldn't stand the noise of the guns. I said I couldn't go back. He said where will we go? I said I don't know but I'm going somewhere. We started to walk toward the highway. I intended to go to Brigade Headquarters, but I thought that they would send us back, and I wanted to get away from war altogether. I said we will go to Albacete and tell everything to our political commissars. We received a lift in a truck and came to Albacete.

I have thought everything over very carefully during the past week. I want to be repatriated. If my desertion merits punishment I do not wish to avoid it. It was caused by purely nervous and mental repugnance that is very difficult to understand or describe. I loathed myself for my action but I was powerless to prevent it.

My record in Spain is a bad one. I have given it all here very faithfully. Perhaps my whole record was a result of my nervous condition, or perhaps my condition was a result of some of these events. I don't know.

I am still of the same opinions politically and militarily as I was when I came to Spain. I have no axe to grind with anyone. I feel that I am not suited for the job here. I know also that a back-of-the-line job would bore me, and I could not keep it. I think that I could do more for the movement at home. I am liked and respected by the young socialists in my city. My actions were not caused by a desire to go home. I am too honest to try and fool others, and I have never fooled myself.

Hoping this rather lengthy case history meets with your approval and consideration.

I remain, Hugh Garner.[56]

Garner was discharged and sent home in October 1937. He was one of a few deserters who were repatriated. Indeed, how International Brigade leadership reacted to desertions and other offences varied greatly. Some commanders tried to keep their men unaware of desertions. If someone was absent, his comrades were encouraged to think he was wounded.[57] Many deserters were quietly reintegrated into their battalions, and some redeemed themselves in battle. Clifford Garrow, for example, reportedly deserted during the retreats of March and April 1938, but he was later praised for his bravery as a first-aid man on the last day of battle.[58] International Brigade command likely feared that publicizing the extent of desertion in the ranks might spread fear among those who remained. But fear was widespread. Even Edward Cecil-Smith, who led the Mackenzie-Papineau Battalion for more than a year, took desperate measures to avoid the front.

Cecil-Smith became the highest-ranking Canadian in Spain after he was given command of the Mackenzie-Papineau Battalion before the battle of Teruel. There he showed tremendous courage by rallying members of his headquarters staff to turn back a nationalist cavalry charge that threatened the entire battalion. One report praised his "serenity" during the chaos of the attack, which earned him a battlefield promotion.[59] Communist Party officials in Spain felt that Cecil-Smith was a good soldier but a half-hearted communist. Jim Bourne's evaluation of Cecil-Smith as having a "certain military capacity" but being "politically weak" is typical. Irving Weissman said Cecil-Smith resented Communist Party "help" in running the battalion, seeing it instead as interference and meddling – an assessment that was probably accurate.[60] The Mac-Pap commander, however, was accused of much more serious offences than rejecting party interference in military affairs. According to several reports, Cecil-Smith attempted to desert during the battle of Caspe, in March 1938.[61] He was also accused of shooting himself in the leg to avoid returning to the front. "There is no proof, but it follows all the indications," Jim Bourne wrote.[62]

Cecil-Smith's case presented a dilemma for the political leadership of the International Brigades. Officially, he had committed a crime for which the required punishment was clear. On 15 March 1937, Copic and Klaus issued an order explicitly dealing with the subject:

> Lately a number of self-mutilations has taken place in our Brigades. They can easily be recognized as such. From today all soldiers with self-inflicted wounds will be considered as traitors to the people and will be punished according to the military laws of Spain: Death by shooting.
>
> The commanders of the units must report to us before 19hrs tomorrow that this order has been brought to the notice of all officers and volunteers.[63]

But Cecil-Smith was already a protagonist in much of the party's propaganda; he could not be shot, or even publicly shamed. Instead, he led the battalion through its demobilization. On the back of Cecil-Smith's evaluation for the Communist Party of Spain, Frank Rogers, the political commissar of the Mackenzie-Papineau Battalion, wrote: "My opinion is that he should be used as a 'Front' by the Party – especially in connection with Spain campaigns. He should also be given some tasks strictly under Party control, to write his experiences in Spain, perhaps for the Party press."[64]

10

Punishments

Edward Cecil-Smith was luckier than many of his fellow international volunteers who were judged deserving of discipline or punishment in Spain. On 5 April 1937 an unnamed member of the International Brigades Judicial Commission wrote to Vladimir Copic to complain about the treatment of prisoners at a new "prevention house" that was home to an increasing number of international volunteers who had been sent there for punishment and re-education:

> The Judicial Commission calls the attention of Commander Copic in the most formal way regarding the fact that the Prevention House is not a bourgeois prison and that, in consequence, he should treat the prisoners, as well as his personnel, with moderation and fairness. Upon the first case of brutality through gestures or words, sanctions will be immediately proposed to the Chief of Staff.[1]

The official expanded on the nature of his complaints in the same letter. The prisoners must be sorted according to their crime and sentence, he wrote. Therefore, there must be separate cells for prisoners condemned or likely to be condemned to a simple prison sentence; those who have been designated to a "Labour Company" or are likely to be; those destined to an "Isolation Camp" or who have been sent back from the labour company; those "whom the Judicial Commission had requested ... be held in secret"; and, finally, prisoners in a "Control Cell," the nature of which is not explained.[2]

The prisoners' food, the official continued, is not good enough. As well, the prisoners, "except those who must be held in secret," should be allowed to go out at least half an hour a day in the fresh air. They should have free access to stamps, writing material, newspapers, and brochures – with the exception again of those prisoners "who must be held in secret."[3]

Numerous prisons and so-called prevention houses were established throughout republican Spain. Most Canadians ended up at Castillo de Fels, in an old castle overlooking the resort town of Castelldefels, south of Barcelona.

It had been converted into a prison for members of the International Brigades in April 1938, when Gallo decreed that a camp should exist for "undesirables."[4] Five months later, International Brigade command launched an investigation into abuses at the prison, where one official named Pedro Moreno said that the commander Marcel Lantez and the commissar Paul Dupont, both French, had "imposed a dictatorial, despotic regime ... always manipulating with threats, to the extent that the prisoners, soldiers of the guard, and others who visited the castle refused to make statements and declarations out of fear of possible retaliation by the indicated chiefs, who had subjugated them to constant coercion and terror."[5]

Guards and staff at the camps corroborated Moreno's testimony. They described a prison commander who savagely beat prisoners, stole from them, and also robbed both the family that lived in the castle and the civilian population from the nearby town. Civilian authorities who investigated were threatened with machine guns. Salvador Toscano, who worked in the prison storeroom, said,

> The commander abused [the prisoners] many times because the comrades could not say a word, and he always told me: "If you do not want to do as I order, I will put you in the dungeons like the rest." He also got drunk many times. His life consisted in going to the beach in the morning and returning at twelve [noon]. He ate and left again at two, remaining away until seven. When he interrogated the comrades, he beat them with a stick and a sandal.

Toscano said that volunteers who were released from the prison consoled themselves with thoughts of revenge and made a point of telling commander Lantez, "We'll see each other at some point in France."[6]

Lucien Courson, a guard at the prison, admitted to beating several prisoners but said they were all "concrete cases of Fascist spies, provokers and tenacious enemies of the Republic." If these bad elements were treated poorly, he said, it was because he knew what do "with the worst enemies of our cause to induce them to say all the ominous work they did against the Republic and because they were agents of Hitler and Mussolini."[7] Marcel Lantez similarly said that some prisoners had been beaten and imprisoned in the "dungeon," but they were all guilty of being defeatists, deserters, demoralizers, or Fascist agents. Everyone else, he said, he treated humanely.[8]

The investigators, however, concluded that Marcel Lantez was lying and that those who described a reign of terror at the prison were telling the truth. Investigator Alfredo Vinet wrote that the prison commissar Paul Dupont had already returned to France by the time the investigation concluded, taking with him property he had stolen from the prisoners. Lantez had not left Spain, though Vinet found that his suitcase contained a false bottom in which he carried official documents, maps, photos, two watches, and "gold objects of unknown origin."[9]

Vinet wrote in his report that Lantez's behaviour consisted of "a constant abuse of authority, employing violent and inhumane methods in all his actions; because he had no argument but to brandish his machine gun when someone dared not to immediately follow his orders." He thought that the witnesses who described Lantez's behaviour were credible. Ultimately, however, Vinet was required to trust only his own eyes:

> On one occasion on which we visited the dungeons, he showed us one of them, which could be compared to those of the Middle Ages, but it was empty, and the commander said no one was there; but a few days later and to my amazement, on occasion of another visit when I ordered that the aforementioned dungeon be opened, I saw that some ten men were coming out of it, one of whom had spent seventy-five days inside. The physical situation of this detainee was pitiful. When I asked the rest how many days they had spent inside that dungeon and the reason they were locked up, they all gave different dates and said they didn't know the reasons.[10]

By the time of Vinet's report, at least twenty-two Canadians had been jailed at Castillo de Fels. Others had been detained at the Carlos Marx prison, Camp Lukacs, or in one of the other prisons and labour camps throughout Spain.[11] That International Brigade authorities saw fit to investigate the mistreatment of prisoners demonstrates that the practice was not universally condoned, but this could not have been much comfort to those interned. At least one prisoner, the American Albert Wallach, was jailed at Castillo de Fels and never left.[12]

These camps and prisons were a dark secret among international volunteers in Spain. Few talked about them, but few doubted their existence. The camps operated outside the auspices of the Spanish government, and details about some of them were shrouded even during the war. In March 1937, an official at the Albacete base Judicial Commission wrote to Irving Weissman, who was responsible to the commission for the 15th Brigade. "I see that a certain number of comrades have been destined to the 'Labour Colony,' *arbeitskolonne*," the official wrote. "Could you tell me what it is about exactly, and what this new organization consists of, which must be interesting."[13]

A hint as to the nature of internment facilities for members of the International Brigades is revealed in an undated letter from "M" at the Judicial Commission to André Marty and Albacete base commander Augusto Vidal. The letter's author says that there were now more than twenty men, dangerous elements, who overburdened the "prevention house" and contaminated the good elements.

Two solutions were possible:

> a Send them back to the Spanish authorities, a solution that we do not recommend, because certain political influences could bring about the return of certain elements into circulation who should be kept as interns.

b Create an internment camp for the brigades, where, except for a stricter surveillance, the regime would be the same as in a labour camp.[14]

This network of prisons and camps for the international volunteers in Spain had more in common with Soviet prisons than with the "bourgeois" jails that the above-mentioned official invoked in an effort to improve conditions at Castillo de Fels. Prisoners were often held in barbarous conditions, frequently without charge or proper trial. The Canadian Robert Hamilton worked as a medic in Albacete. One of his duties was to treat prisoners held at the jail. They were kept in a filthy state, with excrement and maggots everywhere: "One man had been in four months because a party comrade thought he was a fascist, four months without even a hearing. Another got thirty days for entering a house to buy food where his superiors were eating. When I would ask most of the men how long they got, they would say they did not know. They had not been tried yet, men one to six months in jail, and never even seen a trial."[15]

For international volunteers who had come to Spain as idealists believing they would be building a new and better world, finding themselves locked up without trial by their supposed comrades was a bewildering experience. It offended their sense of justice and working-class solidarity, even if it did not diminish their enthusiasm for fighting fascism. On 3 July 1937, an imprisoned international volunteer wrote to the inspector of the War Commissariat of the International Brigades: "I am interested in knowing the charges ... against me, whether I'll be given a trial. Let's not forget, apart from the fact that we are at war, that we are still a part of the proletariat and that all individuals [must be treated] accordingly and not as they would under the Capitalist regime, locking a person in jail and throwing away the key." The imprisoned volunteer said he wanted to get back to the front to fight there, but if this was no longer possible, he said, then "I demand a release so I can get back to the States and do my share there."[16] Another imprisoned volunteer, a Frenchman who had been in jail for ten months without charge or trial, wrote to military authorities and said he would be going on hunger strike as of 17 February 1938 – the anniversary of his being wounded at Jarama. His goal, he said, was to force authorities to actually charge him with something so that he could hasten his return to the struggle.[17]

Fortunately for the scores of Canadians who fell afoul of authorities in Spain, the International Brigades had forms of punishment other than imprisonment. Many minor offences, such as drunkenness or petty insubordination, might earn a demotion or a brief stay in the guardhouse to sober up. Some deserters were treated with compassion rather than malice. On 18 April 1937, for example, Dr. William Pike, a physician with the American Medical Bureau, issued this evaluation of Francis North, a volunteer who had recently fled the front: "I am convinced that this Comrade was suffering from a severe, periodically recurring psycho-neurosis brought on by the intense nervous strain of artillery bombardment." The doctor added that North was not consciously responsible for attempting to "escape from the intolerable environment of war" and recommended that he not be punished but be removed from the front lines if possible.[18] It is unclear if Dr. Pike's advice was accepted. Of course, not all deserters were treated this well. Several of the Canadians languishing at Castillo de Fels were sent there because they had deserted.

Another common punishment was assignment to a disciplinary unit, also referred to as unit of engineers, a fortifications company, or a labour battalion. The Spanish Civil War was still fought to a large extent in trenches, often opposing each other across a no man's land of a few hundred metres or less. In such conditions, forward lines were in constant need of repairs – dangerous work best carried out in the middle of the night.

In March 1937, Copic and Barthol sent a directive to other commanders and commissars of units in the 15th International Brigade announcing the institution of "a disciplinary section for re-education" in the brigade:

> The guilty soldiers will be sent there on recommendation by the Judicial Commission and by order of the commander, for a period of ten days to three months or for an indefinite period.
>
> The soldiers sent to this section will be disarmed and immediately downgraded.
>
> This disciplinary section, well designed, will be used according to need during the day or at night, for work on terraces or other work at the Front, in the first lines or elsewhere and under very rigorous discipline.
>
> The soldiers sent to this section will remain in isolated places disposed to this effect at all times between work hours and under good guard.
>
> The detainees will be deprived of wages, wine and cigarettes.

Copic and Barthol concluded their directive with instructions that if the guilty soldier shows that he has, "with our help," corrected the defect that landed him in the disciplinary unit, his sentence might be reduced, or he might eventually be allowed to return to his unit. Soldiers who continued to misbehave, on the other hand, "will be subjected to very highly serious sanctions."[19]

The disciplinary units served another, unofficial, purpose beyond the fortification work and the "re-education" described by Copic and Barthol. It was risky digging trenches between the lines. The clanking of picks and the scraping of shovels attracted enemy fire, and those sentenced to these units could not be expected to last long. They therefore served as a convenient means to get rid of problem volunteers, though International Brigade commissars tended to describe the labour battalions' goal as isolating such men rather killing them:

> Labour Company: In order to clean units of any undesirable elements, a special company

of the Genie had been started. In it all undesirables from each battalion would be transferred and they would work there under the direction of the Chief of the Genie. There would not be sentences to this company, and the work would not be regarded as a sentence to punishments, but would be transference for undesirable elements.

Commissar Kobal further explained the necessity of a labour corps at the same meeting of political commissars:

Owing to the fact that the Labour colony in Albacete was closed, it would be necessary for us to solve our own problem of these undesirables, and therefore this formation of a special section was decided. The men will not be prisoners ... They will not serve any recognized time but will be transferred to other companies after they have proved themselves good anti-fascist soldiers.[20]

Hugh Garner's time in a labour company convinced him it was in reality a death sentence. The American Oliver Law assigned him to the unit. Garner suspected that Law disliked him because he had taken an extra-large portion of stew one night. He soon found himself in no man's land with other discipline cases and many French drunks:

It was a labour battalion, actually. And all of the non-conformists and drunks and so forth in the brigade were shoved into this outfit. And you used to go up at night with shovels and picks. And you'd go out into no man's land and dig trenches from the top down with the enemy less than fifty yards away. And so they'd just wipe us off. It was awful ...

[The French soldiers] didn't care. They'd be out there whistling and singing and picking and shovelling. And we were out there with them. And I remember Cox and I, we were digging fast enough to get down to China just to get down ...

It was certain death. You may last a week or you may last a month. But just by the law of averages, you're bound to be knocked off.[21]

At least fourteen Canadians spent time in a disciplinary unit. It is likely that more than this number did as well, but complete and detailed records do not exist.

While Garner toiled in no man's land, International Brigades officials tried to formally define the appropriate punishments for specific crimes. On 23 March 1937, the International Brigades base Judicial Commission sent this directive to Irving Weissman outlining appropriate sanctions:

1st Five days in prison with or without suspension of wages for light infractions. Sanctions decided by the head of the unit.

2nd Being sent to the Labour Company – from fifteen days to three months for more serious crimes, e.g., disorder without conscious will to sabotage, violations of ordinary law, desertion, repeat drunkenness.

3rd Being sent to an ISOLATION CAMP – (this is a concentration camp that is being created and whose name is not definite). Remaining there for the duration of hostilities.
For cases of 1st, conscious disorder.
  2nd individuals *suspected* of espionage (without formal evidence).
  3rd serious violations of ordinary law.

4th Appearance before the Military Tribunal, which could eventually lead to the death penalty.
Cases of 1st, pillage
  2nd, espionage
  3rd, treason
  4th, incitement to mutiny
  5th, and any other cases of a characteristic gravity.

The directive concluded with instructions that sentences carried out in cases involving an appearance before the Military Tribunal must have the agreement of the base Judicial Commission.[22]

As this directive makes clear, death was the ultimate penalty a volunteer in the International Brigades might face. Executions did take place throughout the war. On 20 April 1938, the Yugoslav-American Mirko Marcovicz, a former commander of the Washington Battalion, wrote to International Brigade command to complain about the execution of two men from the Djakovic Battalion, whom he said were shot on flimsy evidence of a rape. "Aside from these soldiers, in a lapse of a few days, some internationals have been executed in the same place under the command of Captain Dias and, according to my information, without having been examined and judged," he wrote. Marcovicz described the execution of the first convicted man: "[Oscar] Staer was executed in front of the whole battalion. Captain Dias commanded the execution. Before being executed, Staer shouted: 'Long live the Spanish Republic!'" After the first volley of rifle shots, which killed Staer, Marcovicz said Dias turned to the battalion with his fist held high and shouted, "Long live the Spanish people and the Spanish Republic!" "But the battalion did not reply," Marcovicz wrote. "This was the battalion's de facto expression of their disapproval of the execution."[23]

Executions were rare within the 15th International Brigade. They occurred most often in the spring of 1938, when Franco's forces broke through republican lines. Hundreds deserted in the ensuing chaos. In a report to the commissariat of the 35th Division, John Gates, commissar of the 15th Brigade, explained the measures he had taken:

One of the most important issues is that of the officer and commissar leading cadres. The action showed that these cadres left much to be desired. Most of them acted heroically but in almost all occasions control was lost. Some officers and commissars even ran alongside their men. Immediate measures have been taken to punish those who were weak. Two lieutenants and one sergeant were executed; three company commissars were downgraded; nine lieutenants and two sergeants were downgraded and two of these lieutenants are under investigation for a harsher punishment.[24]

There is clear documentary evidence that four men from the 15th Brigade were shot in the aftermath of the retreats. On 26 April, John Gates and 15th Brigade chief of staff Malcolm Dunbar announced their execution:

For treason to the Republic and the Spanish People in the fight against fascism, for defeatism and cowardice, insubordination, drunkenness and acts against the Republic, proven in the last operations and in the rearguard, the High Court formed by soldiers and officers from the brigade judged and after serious considerations sentenced the following soldiers to the death penalty.[25]

The condemned soldiers were Spaniard Manuel Pérez Montagud, allegedly an anarchist; a republican Moor named Sid Ben Amar Aboslam; American Paul White; and J.M. Smith.[26] The leaflet reports that the four were executed at six o'clock that morning, shot by a squad from each of the 15th Brigade's battalions: "Cowardice, desertion, provocation, and defeatism are allies of fascism, and for this reason it is a sacred duty of every anti-fascist to expel them from our lines."[27]

Of the four, only Smith served in the nominally Canadian Mackenzie-Papineau Battalion, but it is unclear if he was Canadian or American, as there were volunteers with the same first initial and family name from both countries. Most accounts of Paul White's execution do not mention a fourth victim. Smith was the only one not accused of desertion on the leaflet, but of "insubordination, provocation, disorder, defeatism and acts against the Spanish Republic." The American Joe Bianca reportedly expressed the sentiments of most members of the brigade when, upon receiving the leaflet with news of the executions, he wandered about shouting as loud as he could: "Those sons of bitches!"[28] Gerald Cook said that White was executed in part because he was a prominent communist and union organizer back home, of whom much was expected. "The purpose of shooting him was to set an example." According to Cook, the men in the brigade reacted to the news of White's execution with dislike – "but it wasn't strong enough to provoke a great outcry."[29]

Other men were shot during the retreats in an effort to stem the flow of deserters, sometimes without a court martial. Canadian Bill Matthews recalled, "Volunteers were asked for a firing squad to execute a deserter ...

I did not agree but they did get a firing squad from the Mac-Paps, and the person was executed. I do not know why he was executed – there were others that should have been as well."[30] Regular order and discipline broke down at this time. British volunteer Jim Fuhr recalled that a tall Canadian, dubbed "Rubio" because of his shock of blond hair, was shot on the spot by a British captain because the Canadian had mistakenly fired on his own men in the confusion of the retreats.[31] The Canadian Len Norris said a German, or a German-born Canadian, was shot following a hasty court martial after he had been caught with a thousand American dollars. He also recalled a Finn being shot, but this may have been Antti Nieminen or Paavo Oskari, discussed below.[32] Details about such matters are rare and written evidence almost never exists.

Much earlier in the war, a Canadian named Henry Shapiro was sentenced to die. Shapiro was condemned because of his role, in the late summer or early fall of 1937, in the theft of an ambulance, done with the intention of deserting. Shapiro and one of his American accomplices named Eisenberg were sentenced at a trial conducted on 4 and 5 October. According to a note-book kept by Sandor Voros, the Hungarian-born American who had worked in Canada as a Communist Party organizer, resolutions from all units in the brigade recommended death, as did Dave Doran, who presided over their trial: "We owe it to the Spanish people to be severe … death [by] shooting. This committee recommends death," Doran said.[33]

A separate document, a 9 October 1937 report from the War Commissariat of the 15th Brigade addressed to the political commissars, confirms that Shapiro was condemned to death. The report also claims that the trial was "utilized educationally to raise the struggle against desertions on to a higher level and to draw from this lessons on greater discipline and conduct from the soldiers."[34] However, the death sentence against Shapiro was not carried out, at least not immediately. He was still apparently alive, listed as missing, in January 1938. His fate is unknown.[35]

Finnish-born Canadians Antti Nieminen and Paavo Oskari definitely did not escape their death sentences. The two, and a Finnish American, were court-martialled and shot by an International Brigade firing squad on a beach outside Tarragona. Enough witnesses have testified to this shooting that there should be no doubt it occurred. Most accounts of the incident agree that the three had gone on a drinking binge in Tarragona. However, there might have been more to it than that. Several Canadian veterans allege that one, two, or all of the three had sexually assaulted a Spanish woman or child in the course of their drunken rampage.[36]

According to an American veteran, a Canadian medic was executed because he had stolen valuables from the bodies of dead volunteers at Jarama. The medic in question was always eager to creep into no man's land at night to bring back the dead. It was a grim and dangerous task, and fellow soldiers were suspicious as to why the Canadian wanted to do it. They searched his belongings and found several watches and a large amount of American money. They reported him to the authorities and he was removed from the lines. "Many years later I learned that he had been executed," one of the men later said. "In retrospect, I think that if I and the others who reported the medic to the authorities had any idea what they would do, we certainly wouldn't have taken such extreme measures."[37]

Other Canadians might have been executed, or murdered, by their commanders in Spain, leaving no records and with no witnesses left alive seventy years later to talk about it. It is a fact that "problem volunteers" were occasionally taken on a midnight walk and shot in the back of the head. The American Bernard Abramofsky was murdered this way.[38] Reports from returning Canadians who spoke to the RCMP suggest that the American Vincent Usera was also executed.[39] And Pat Stephens, in his memoirs, said that he warned two of his comrades not to file charges against their commander Oliver Law, after Law's incompetence had resulted in the death of one of their fellow soldiers. Law was a strong communist with powerful friends. Stephens knew nothing would happen to Law but feared his friends would be regarded as troublemakers and agitators. "This could be very dangerous," Stephens wrote, "as some agitators suspected of being Trotskyites were quietly executed at the back of the lines and no one ever knew what happened to them."[40]

There is a story about one such midnight walk that deserves further investigation. Historian Robert Rosenstone, who interviewed Lincoln veterans in the 1960s, said that a political commissar received instructions to "wipe out" an alleged Trotskyist during the battle of Teruel. The commissar accompanied the dissident on a night patrol, intending to kill him. But, the commissar said, the two became separated by a blizzard. He hoped the elements would take care of the problem but, in the morning, the soldier returned with a bad case of frostbite. He was immediately sent home, never knowing how close he came to dying.[41]

The story has a neat and tidy ending: the political deviant disappears, and no one has to murder anyone. It may well be true. However, the story also bears striking similarities to the case of Albert Ernest Burton, known in Spain by the nickname Yorkie. According to reports received by the Friends of the Mackenzie-Papineau Battalion in Canada, Burton went missing at Teruel.[42] The American writer Arthur Landis, a veteran of the Spanish Civil War, gave more details and said Burton was lost on a patrol in no man's land. A captured nationalist prisoner hinted that Burton had been caught and executed.[43] There is no evidence in the files of the Friends of the Mackenzie-Papineau Battalion that Burton returned safely home with a case of frostbite.

Finally, there is the intriguing case of a French Canadian named Lamont or Lamotte. Robert Hamilton, the Canadian medic who worked at the Albacete base, said that Lamont was a violent man who would often beat drunks he encountered in Albacete. He was eventually arrested for stealing money and deserting. "This time, he went to the wall," Hamilton wrote.[44] Hamilton's story about Lamont is corroborated elsewhere. In 1970, a researcher who was investigating international medical units in Spain wrote to Hamilton after reading his account. She said a Spanish Medical Bureau physician named Dr. Byrne told her that he had seen wanted posters for "Lamotte" and had later met him in a Valencia jail. The doctor, however, had thought Lamotte was French and had returned to France.[45] This still does not confirm Hamilton's assertion that he was executed. However, Ron Liversedge also recalled a French Canadian with some sort of medical authority in Albacete who was shot. "He was a fascist," Liversedge said.[46] There is no file on Lamont among records of Canadians in Spain in the Communist International archives. However, given that supporting evidence comes from three independent sources, it is probable that he was in Spain and was executed there.

Of the Canadians in Spain, therefore, it seems certain that several were executed or unofficially murdered by their commanders. Executing soldiers for the crime of raping or molesting a woman or child, should these allegations be proven, has long been standard practice in armies with a semblance of discipline and organized command; it certainly would have been the norm during the 1930s. Deserters from Canadian, British, and American armies have also faced the death penalty, though not with the frequency of volunteers in the International Brigades. Twenty-three Canadians were shot for desertion or cowardice during the First World War, out of over 600,000 who served. None was executed for desertion in the Second World War; one American was – out of more than 16 million who fought in the conflict. The problem with this comparison is that the International Brigades were not a Canadian or American army. The brigades were run in large part by Soviet-trained Europeans who came from a military tradition that looked on deserters with little pity. Deserters from most European or Soviet armies at the time could expect to be shot. Problem soldiers in a "bourgeois" Canadian or American army might have lived longer.

Deserters and shirkers must have enraged some volunteers in the International Brigades, who felt that those who fled endangered those who stayed in the lines. But the shooting of deserters appears to have deeply disturbed the majority of internationals. The American Harry Fisher said that he was tormented for decades after he was asked, and refused, to shoot his fellow American Bernard Abramofsky because Abramofsky had deserted. He did not think Abramofsky was a coward or a traitor, but someone who suffered fear so intense it was akin to sickness.[47] Volunteers in the International Brigades had come to Spain willing to both kill and die. Few expected, or would have accepted, that they might be asked to shoot their fellow volunteers or die at the hands of their comrades in a firing squad.

In the early 1980s, some of the surviving Canadian veterans decided to collect their stories in a book that veteran William Beeching was assigned to write. The process took several years, and Beeching and a few of the other veterans underwent a great deal of soul-searching and occasional conflict over what to include. In a 1984 letter to a fellow veteran, Beeching said it would be best not to discuss some of the dissident volunteers, whom he accused of espionage, because doing so would be "opening a Pandora's box."[48] For far too long, too much of the story of Canadians in Spain has remained locked in a similar Pandora's box. Issues such as desertion, prison camps, labour battalions, and executions do not feature in most accounts of Canadians in the International Brigades. This is unfortunate because it encourages a one-dimensional and rather unrealistic image of volunteers in the International Brigades as brave and selfless anti-fascists fighting in a utopian army untarnished by cruelty and fear.

The reality is much more complex. Most volunteers who went to Spain were brave and were committed to fighting fascism. They were also human. Some were simply unsuited to fighting a war, or at least to taking orders. Some drank. Poorly trained, poorly armed, and all too often sent on suicidal attacks by military incompetents, many deserted or asked to go home. Given the circumstances in which they fought and lived, it is perhaps surprising that more did not do the same. These deserters were not the adventurers, criminals, and cowards described by the brigade's commissars.

The righteous aura of the anti-fascist cause in Spain has similarly obscured uncomfortable truths about the way this cause was advanced among the International Brigades. The manner in which discipline was enforced and loyalty judged in the brigades too often had little to do with freedom or democracy. Canadians in Spain were maligned as Trotskyists for the crime of disparaging leading communists, and their loyalty could be questioned because of the friends they kept. Pat Stephens said that when he was a member of the SIM, the Republic's secret police, he was told to include in his daily briefings reports indicating who had complained about the food. Most Canadians reacted with characteristic irreverence. Asked by a political commissar if he liked his morning coffee, one Canadian responded, "It depends ... If I'm politically developed, comrade *commandante*, the coffee is very good. But if I am not politically developed, it tastes like horse piss."[49]

Often, however, the discipline imposed by brigade leadership could not be laughed off. Numerous Canadians ended up in labour battalions or prison camps, usually without any sort of trial and often in brutal conditions. In the most extreme cases, volunteers faced the possibility of death.

The issue of crimes and punishments in the International Brigades affected a minority of Canadians in Spain. Records from the Moscow archives suggest that about 150 Canadians were punished for one alleged offence or another

– usually desertion. The majority of Canadians in Spain suffered at the hands of their enemies only. Nevertheless, scores of Canadian volunteers wished to flee Spain, and many tried. These men and others guilty of nothing other than maligning communism or perhaps complaining about poor commanders and missing care packages risked the wrath of their superiors and were punished for offences ranging from insubordination to trumped-up charges of political weakness and Trotskyism. Most suffered nothing worse than a few days in a guardhouse. Some languished for weeks and months in filthy jails, or punishing work and re-education camps, without trial or even an explanation. Others were assigned potentially fatal jobs in labour battalions. An unfortunate few were executed.

27 Crowds in Montreal greet returning Canadian veterans.

28 Returning veterans disembark in Canada. "We kept a sharp watch for members of this unit who might have been injured in such a way as to become public charges," the RCMP reported.

29 Dolores and Carmen, two militia women with whom Canadian Bill Williamson fought during the early days of the war. Dolores, left, was killed in action.

30 Edward Cecil-Smith led the Mackenzie-Papineau Battalion and was the highest-ranking Canadian in Spain. He was a competent military commander, but was also strict and aloof with his men.

31 Jules Paivio, top right, arrived in Spain at the age of nineteen and fought for more than a year. He was then captured and spent another year as a POW in a nationalist prison camp.

32 New International Brigades recruits drilling before they had been given even rudimentary uniforms, c. December 1936-January 1937.

33 Spanish republican refugees in Le Perthus, France, are guarded by French regulars and North African cavalry, c. February 1939.

34 Members of the Mackenzie-Papineau Battalion cross the Ebro on 25 July 1938, the first day of the Ebro offensive. Bill Matthews is facing the camera.

35 When international volunteers could obtain footwear, it often consisted of rope-soled sandals known as *alpargatas*, shown here.

36 Bill Williamson, right, was the first Canadian to join the war. Here he poses with a Czech comrade, one of the few other foreigners to take part in fighting in the Basque and Asturian regions of Spain during the summer and fall of 1936.

37 Thomas Beckett was the first Canadian to die in Spain. He perished when a truck carrying volunteers to the front accidentally drove through enemy lines in February 1937.

38 Arriving in the Basque region of Spain one day after the war started, Bill Williamson encountered newly formed citizens' militias that included women and old men who took up arms to oppose the military uprising.

39 A Spanish youth group visits the Mackenzie-Papineau Battalion at Marçà in June 1938.

40 Mortimer Kosowatski, also known as Jack Steele, was sent home to Canada in October 1937 but was killed in action after returning to Spain the following spring.

41 "All the girls were dancing in their summer dresses, and many of them with their summer dresses on had a rifle on their shoulders and a red band around their arm," Bill Williamson recalled of his arrival in Portugalete on 19 July 1936. Within days, he joined the Ochandiano Column, shown here.

42 A memorial erected near the Jarama River. At least 18 Canadians were killed in fighting here between February and June 1937.

43 International volunteers rest in a dry riverbed beneath the nationalist stronghold of Mosquito Ridge during the battle of Brunete in July 1937. Their advance was stopped here.

Mackenzie-Papineau Battalion / LAC PA-194922

44 Members of the International Brigades salute at a British cookhouse in Albacete.

Courtesy of the Imperial War Museum, HU 71509

45 Paddy O'Daire, in peaked cap, introduced Canadians to his repertoire of Irish rebel songs during labour disputes in the 1930s. He was jailed and then deported from Canada in 1934 and came to Spain from England.

46 Norman Bethune visits republican troops near Madrid. The woman on his left is Kajsa Rothman, his lover, whom the Spanish secret police incorrectly suspected of consorting with fascists.

47 A wounded republican soldier is rushed to safety during the nationalist assault on Madrid, c. December 1936-January 1937.

Courtesy of the Imperial War Museum, HU 71665

48 An ambulance named after Tom Ewen, a leading Canadian communist, struggles through heavy snow near Teruel.

Courtesy of the Imperial War Museum, HU 34624

49 Vladimir Copic, the Yugoslav commander of the 15th International Brigade, was disliked by many volunteers because he insisted on sending them on doomed attacks but kept himself safely out of danger.

50 William Krehm at his home in Toronto in November 2004. Krehm spent three months imprisoned in Barcelona but never regretted going to Spain. "How can one regret one's life?" he asked.

51 Jules Paivio at a 2004 ceremony in Ottawa commemorating Canadian volunteers in the Spanish Civil War. "The thing is this, you look back through life – and I think you'll find this, too – it is the comrades and the people who you are impressed by. You almost fall in love with them."

Part 4
Renegades

The Photographer: Bill Williamson

Bill Williamson was rebellious as a child. He was intelligent, big for his age, and even as a boy possessed a questioning, anti-authoritarian streak. His mother died when he was a child, and so he was raised by an aunt in Winnipeg, surrounded by prairie and farms. Williamson skipped school regularly, spending much of the warmer months swimming in the nearby Assiniboine and Red rivers. When he attended classes he tormented his teachers with questions, especially if religion was on the curriculum. If the Earth is round, he asked, how did Jesus ascend to heaven? How could angels fly with such tiny wings? And, when history was taught, he would reflexively take the side of the underdog: the serfs against their king; the Americans against the British; Montcalm against Wolfe.

"I got on with the teachers all right," he said years later. "But I must have driven them up the wall."[1]

Williamson said that much of his early thinking was profoundly influenced by a man named Paddy, who was a friend of his aunt and a strong Irish republican. Williamson never knew if Paddy had been personally involved in political violence in Ireland, but he vigorously promoted the republican cause and found a receptive audience in young Williamson. "He had a sort of a hatred, or a dislike, of imperialism in general and in particular that of the British Empire, which he thought was enslaving the world," Williamson said. "I remember when I was a very young boy him pointing to the Union Jack flying over some building or the other, and he says, 'Look at that flag, boy. Wherever that flag flies there's misery and oppression.' And that had a great effect on me."[2]

Paddy plied the precocious Williamson with books. His favourites were novels by Jack London – *White Fang* and *The Call of the Wild* – but also books that tackled more profound topics, such as *The People of the Abyss*. By the time he was twelve, Williamson's aunt had married and Williamson was not getting along with her new husband. Inspired by Jack London's stories of hoboeing across the United States and a boy's fascination with trains, one morning before dawn he filled a small knapsack with food, water, and extra clothes and slipped out of the house. He walked to the freight yards and scrambled into the boxcar of a lumbering westbound train. It was late in the spring of 1921. Williamson was not yet thirteen years old and would not come home for many years.

Williamson almost immediately fell in with the Industrial Workers of the World, or the Wobblies, a union of a slight anarchist bent, consisting mostly of hoboes, ex-servicemen from the First World War, and transient workers. By the mid-1920s, the Wobblies were in decline and unable to compete with the energetic organization of the nascent Communist Party. But the Wobblies were still immensely popular in the hobo camps and among drifters riding the freight trains of western Canada. Williamson had heard about the Wobblies from his aunt's friend Paddy. He took to their camaraderie, and he loved the revolution-ary singalongs that took place nightly in the hobo jungles outside the rail yards, or while travelling in cold and windy boxcars. Williamson told everyone he was sixteen, but he was still a boy, and it felt good to belong to something.

Williamson spent the next several years travelling and working across North America. He began working on farms and ranches on the Canadian Prairies, often agitating with other Wobblies to obtain better pay and treatment for the mostly transient workers who planted and harvested on farms they did not own. He eventually made it as far west as the coast, where he got jobs in British Columbia lumber camps.

Despite the tough working conditions and often poor pay, he found the freedom of working and living in the bush satisfying. He was an agile and strong lumberjack, and he excelled at the most lucrative job, which required a man to climb to the top of the tree and saw off the uppermost tip to prevent the trunk from splitting when the tree is felled. "You could be two hundred feet up from the ground," he later recalled. "Once you've cut this top part of the tree off, it springs, just like the string of a bow. It swings in a terrific arch, at least thirty feet each way, the tree swings. And you've got to hang on like grim death until it stops swinging. Just like a pendulum, like an upside-down pendulum." It was dangerous work, and the other lumberjacks admired Williamson because he did it well. "You felt like a real kingpin," he said, "especially if you were really young."[3]

The Wobblies were falling apart by this time, and the most active unions in the lumber camps were affiliated with the Communist Party of Canada. Williamson tried to help organize his fellow workers, but he was mostly concerned with travelling and finding work himself. He crossed the border illegally and worked on ranches in the United States, from Washington to Texas. Then he slipped into Mexico and worked on ranches there, too:

I more or less hoboed my way, just getting jobs from time to time and sometimes not getting a job at all, often going hungry. But in spite of it, I enjoyed the thing, seeing all these sights. I went to all the great places, Yosemite and the Grand Canyon. Anywhere the railway went, I went. You'd get a job there. And when you got off the train, you'd go to the folks in the town. You'd knock on a door and say, "Lady, I'm really hungry. Can I do some jobs around the place for a meal?" ... I never at any time actually panhandled. I considered that degrading. That's begging. But I didn't see anything wrong with begging for food.[4]

Williamson was no less inquisitive as a young man than he was as a boy. He still read constantly, taking books from one library and returning them to another in whichever city he next found himself. Paddy had given him several books by Karl Marx, which Williamson had had difficultly understanding. But now he got a copy of the *Communist Manifesto* and carried it with him everywhere. In San Francisco, he joined the Communist Party but was still far too footloose to involve himself actively in the organization.

Whenever Williamson was in a port city, he hung around with the Greek and Portuguese sailors on the docks. He was fascinated with sailing ships – schooners and windjammers – and one day convinced the captain of a boat bound for Australia to hire him on. His experience as a lumberjack with no fear of heights paid off onboard: he was a natural working on the ship's riggings high above the rolling deck. It also no doubt helped him land a job in Sydney as a riveter, helping to build the city's sprouting skyscrapers.

In Sydney, Williamson socialized mostly with German communists. One Sunday morning, Williamson's friend Eric took him to a deserted warehouse to watch a secret screening of the Soviet propaganda film *The Battleship Potemkin*. The movie would change Williamson's life and eventually take him to Spain. While Williamson was impressed by the film's revolutionary message, what moved him most was its cinematography. Williamson decided he wanted to become a photographer. With the same headstrong obsessiveness that pushed him to ride freight trains and find a way to sail, he set about planning to get to the Soviet Union so that he could get a job with Eduard Tisse, the chief cinematographer for Sergei M. Eisenstein, director of *The Battleship Potemkin*.

In the meantime, Williamson continued to work and sail around the world. By now he had obtained a camera and was teaching himself photography. He even stowed away on a ship bound for Shanghai in a futile attempt to join the Chinese Red Army. After three weeks in Shanghai, during which time he was unable to communicate with any locals, Williamson returned to Australia, and from there sailed, by windjammer, to London and eventually back to Canada.

Williamson arrived in Halifax and joined the burgeoning unemployed movement. He worked in and organized relief camps before crossing the country to join the relief-camp workers' strike in British Columbia in 1935, eventually taking part in the On to Ottawa Trek. But Russia was always in the back of his mind: he still wanted to find the men responsible for producing the Soviet propaganda film he had seen in Australia. So he travelled back to Halifax and enlisted on a Norwegian ship bound for London.

Williamson had no luck in London finding a boat to take him to the Soviet Union, but fate intervened. It was the summer of 1936, and the newspapers in Britain were full of stories about the escalating political turmoil in Spain. Williamson decided to put his plans for Russia on hold and go to Spain instead. He did not foresee a war. He imagined street protests, surging crowds, and perhaps the odd street fight. He thought he might be able to take some good photographs.

Knowing that a few Basque ships were on strike in the Cardiff harbour, Williamson headed to Wales. He approached one of the strike leaders and, using the smattering of Spanish he had picked up in Mexico, asked if he could stowaway on his ship, which was sailing for Spain the next day. The strike leader agreed and said he would tell his men to turn a blind eye. Williamson climbed aboard and crept down ladders and staircases into the ship's hold. On the way, he stumbled upon four men playing cards at a small table in a dimly lit corner. "They sort of looked up in surprise when I came down and I gave a clenched fist salute," Williamson said. "They grinned, and I said the word in Spanish for coalbunker, and they just pointed the way. I went in amongst the coal and buried myself in it, and pulled my mackinaw coat over my head."[5]

The next morning, Williamson felt the boat lurch away from the dock. He waited until he guessed it was clear of the English Channel, then he climbed out of the bunker and turned himself in to the ship's captain. To Williamson's surprise, the captain seemed pleased to welcome him on board after he explained that he was going to Spain to help the struggling Spanish Republic. It was the morning of 18 July 1936.

At some point during the next twenty-four hours, the captain and crew got word that much of the Spanish military had rebelled against the government and war was threatening to engulf all of Spain. Details were sparse. When the ship arrived the following afternoon at the port town of Portugalete, about fifteen kilometres from Bilbao, a standoff ensued between the crew, now standing on the ship's deck, and the townspeople watching them from shore. Neither group knew which side those opposite them were on. Finally the ship edged into the harbour.

"It was an evening that will be forever etched in my mind," Williamson wrote to friends decades later. "Even now after more than 44 years the events of that evening are as clear as though it were yesterday ... As soon as we were abreast of the breakwater, the captain ordered a huge republican flag to be broken out on the main mast, amid the cheers and shouts that came to us from across the calm waters of the harbour."[6]

Williamson stepped into a town in the midst of a celebration. The war and the revolution were mere hours old, and the people of Portugalete had not yet suffered any of the horror and depredation that come with both. The city hall was festooned with republican flags, Basque flags, anarchist flags, and communist flags, and the streets were filled with people:

> I looked down into the square at this time. It must have been about three o'clock in the afternoon; and all the girls were dancing in their summer dresses; and many of them with their summer dresses on had a rifle on their shoulder and a red band around their arm; and I thought it was almost sacrilege in a way, because they were dancing to the strains of "The Internationale" ...
>
> And above everything else, I remember cars and trucks racing through the streets with their headlights on in bright daylight, and their sirens going and the claxons sounding, and all the time there was this terrific hullabaloo. It was almost as if it was the Russian Revolution happening all over again.[7]

The women in dresses and heels were gathering and distributing rifles, but when Williamson said that he wanted to enlist in a militia, he was directed to Bilbao. There he was taken to a government office and asked if he knew how to shoot a gun. Unlike most of the locals in Bilbao, but like thousands of other Canadians who grew up on the Prairies shooting groundhogs and small game, Williamson knew how to handle a rifle and was an excellent marksman. He proved this at a makeshift firing range someone had set up in the basement and, consequently, was given a prized Mauser rifle while others had to make do with shotguns and antiques.

Williamson joined a militia that dubbed itself the "Ochandiano Column," though its name would change at least twice. At the time, the political affiliation of his comrades seemed inconsequential. There was no real central command, and Williamson marched beside columns of men from anarchist, socialist, and Basque nationalist militias. They marched on San Sebastián, where the rebels still held a few strong points, mostly hotels. They cleared these out in several days of disorganized street battles, using homemade bombs, which often exploded before they could be thrown, and wagons full of burning hay, which they rolled into nationalist-held buildings.

Williamson spent the next nine months fighting on the Basque and Asturian fronts. Almost immediately he met a young Basque woman named Dolores, who fought in Williamson's column. They might have fallen in love, though Williamson described their relationship only as a close "association." Dolores was the last woman to remain in Williamson's column, as most of the others who had taken part in the fighting of July and August were transferred behind the lines. Late that fall, Dolores was sent on a mission away from the main column. She was wounded and died shortly afterward. In interviews more than fifty years later, Williamson said he was still sad and bitter that he was unable to attend her funeral. He also forged close friendships with two Basque men, Paco and Pepé. They gave Williamson the nickname Pancho Villa, and the three became known as the "three Ps."[8]

Their column took part in vicious fighting while retreating through the hills above Irun. They later attacked Oviedo in the Asturias and Vitoria, where Williamson was badly concussed in a bombing attack. Christmas 1936 was a brief, peaceful respite, though bitterly cold. Williamson's column found itself camped on a hillside opposite nationalist troops. Both armies risked hundreds of campfires, which illuminated the valley. It reminded Williamson of scenes described in Christmas carols. But the beauty was illusionary. There was no truce, and the fighting soon resumed. Williamson's column again assaulted Oviedo in February and March.

During the battle, Moors and troops from Spain's foreign legion stormed republican trenches in the middle of the night. Williamson took two bullets, which shattered his arm. In the smoke and darkness he could discern little more than masses of men streaming through their narrow trenches. With the pistol he had taken from a dead Frenchman who had been fighting with the nationalists, Williamson was able to shoot his way out of his trench and scramble, even with a numb and broken arm, to a safer position in second-line trenches.

Williamson was sent to a hospital in Durango, where, on 31 March 1937, he lived through air raids by the German Condor Legion. The attacks on the town followed the nationalist general Emilio Mola's threat to the Basque people: "I have decided to terminate rapidly the war in the north. Those not guilty of assassinations and who surrender their arms will have their lives and properties spared. But, if submission is not immediate, I will raze all Vizcaya to the ground, beginning with the industries of war."[9] German and Italian planes bombed the town's churches and chapels and strafed the streets with machine-gun fire. More than two hundred civilians were killed, including at least fifteen priests and nuns.[10]

The citizens of Durango were among the first inhabitants of Europe to suffer the terror bombing of a defenceless town. But this attack did not generate nearly as much outrage as did the German bombing of the Basques' holy town of Guernica, which was bombed, burned, and strafed a month later, on 26 April. By a twist of fate, Williamson was moved to a village only a few kilometres from Guernica and witnessed the raid on that town as well. "You could see the bombs glinting in the sunlight as they fell, but you couldn't actually see where they fell because that was down in a little valley," he said. "But you could hear the explosions. And afterwards a whole bunch of Messerschmitts would come over and scream down. It sort of terrified you, dive-bombing the town. And then they'd go away and then another wave." With his arm still in plaster, Williamson went into Guernica that night to help the wounded. Bodies lay on the street, and the town "was just a mass of flames and smoke."[11]

By this time, Williamson had heard rumours that other internationals were fighting elsewhere in Spain on the side of the government. These foreigners were, of course, the International Brigades, formed the previous autumn. But cut off from the rest of the country, Williamson knew little about them. Most of Williamson's friends from the summer of 1936 were no longer with him. Dolores was dead; Pepé and Paco had also been killed. Williamson decided to apply for a transfer. He was smuggled in a fast patrol boat into Saint-Jean-de-Luz, in France. From there he made his way to Paris, where he eventually found the headquarters of the International Brigades.

Williamson did not immediately enlist with the brigades. In the summer of 1936, before leaving for Spain the first time, he had visited the Communist Party of Great Britain's offices on King Street in London to ask for a letter of introduction to the Communist Party of Spain. The party secretary was "contemptuous" and refused to help, which left Williamson "fed up" with the whole organization.[12] Williamson also found many of the new recruits to be naive, and their party minders patronizing and bossy:

> I rather felt that many of the comrades that were coming at this time, they were people who hadn't beat their way all over the world ... They might have been college students, especially the Americans. A big percentage of them came from City College in New York, a lot of them Jewish. They didn't know anything about Europe or anything outside of their particular niche in the country. So most of them allowed themselves to be shepherded around by keepers, [who said] "Oh, well, you can do this, and you can have so much money. But you mustn't get drunk, and you mustn't do that."

Williamson still nursed a fierce independent streak, and he now decided to travel to southern France on his own. Ironically, he ended up in a train full of volunteers for the International Brigades – although, as he put it, "I didn't have to take orders from anyone."[13]

In southern France, Williamson took up with a French girl and decided to put off returning to war for a week or two so he could make the most of their liaison. But he did not waver in his conviction to get back into Spain. He must have eventually made his peace with the party, because he climbed the Pyrenees with other volunteers and formally enlisted in the International Brigades on the other side of the border in May.

Williamson fought with the 15th International Brigade for the duration of its existence, first with the Washington Battalion, then with the Abraham Lincoln Battalion, and finally with the Mackenzie-Papineau Battalion. He continued to have run-ins with authority figures. But by all accounts he was a good if unremarkable soldier, singled out by his commanders in Spain neither for praise nor for criticism.[14]

He returned to Britain when the International Brigades were withdrawn from Spain. Still a strong communist despite his earlier problems with the party, Williamson wanted nothing to do with the Second World War, until the Soviet Union was invaded. He then offered his services as a soldier at the

Soviet embassy in London, but was politely rejected. He next tried Canada House but was refused there as well, on account of wounds he had received in Spain. Finally, he tried the Free French, which did not bother giving Williamson a physical. He enlisted in a parachute battalion and trained with a Canada flash beneath the standard French insignia on his shoulder. But in 1944, before D-Day, he badly injured his back on a practice parachute jump and was discharged.

Williamson did not return to Canada but instead settled in London. He never forgot his original reason for going to Spain: photography. Williamson kept a camera with him throughout the war, and photos from his early days in Spain, including snapshots of Dolores and many more of his friends from the first militia column he joined, survive and are housed at Library and Archives Canada in Ottawa and at the Imperial War Museum in London. He also opened a small photography studio in London, where he worked almost until the day he died.

12

The Idealist: William Krehm

William Krehm was a bookish young man with literary tastes that ran toward political philosophy. He had read most of the writings of Karl Marx by the time he was sixteen, and he followed this up by reading Lenin and Leon Trotsky.[1] Like many young Canadians during the 1930s, Krehm's passions were inflamed by the political divisions and changes then engulfing Europe and the rest of the world. He became a committed leftist, intent on the ideal of socialist revolution. But the more Krehm read, the more he rejected the version of communism sanctioned and propagated by the Soviet Union. He found himself agreeing most with the anti-Stalinist revolutionary Trotsky and his supporters, but even Trotsky could not fully encapsulate Krehm's political convictions. In 1932, he enrolled in the University of Toronto. Four years later he had joined a small radical Marxist group called the League for a Revolutionary Workers' Party. The LRWP adhered to many, but not all, of Trotsky's principles and considered itself independent of his international network of supporters. "We were an extremely holy offshoot of an equally pious organization," Krehm said. "We of the dissident leftist socialist movement were starry-eyed about many things, but we had the correct line on communism."[2]

The LRWP had a brother party in the United States and occasionally cooperated with some of the other anti-Stalinist groups that were emerging in Toronto at the time. But unity among radical leftists was elusive and attempts at cooperation often broke down because of relatively minor political differences. Unlike the Communist Party of Canada and its affiliated organizations, the LRWP lacked the support of Moscow and the Communist Party's talent for mass organization. The LRWP itself remained tiny, and the radical anti-Stalinist left in Canada was only a marginal political force.

When the Spanish Civil War broke out in the summer of 1936, it briefly seemed that all this could change. In Barcelona and Madrid, the workers really had taken control of the streets. To Krehm it was as if the masses had liberated themselves and real social revolution was erupting – without Stalin, without the Soviet Union, and without Soviet communism: "It had that spirit because it was a phenomenon of the dawn. The world was not as old ... Part of the world had grown to fear certain aspects of Russian communism, and here there seemed to be a wonderful alternative. All the lines of all the labour songs that had been written seemed to have taken on flesh and spirit and to be marching in Spain. It was too good to be true."[3]

Krehm soon learned that the dawn of a new non-communist social revolution would not come easily and that the war in Spain presented as many obstacles as opportunities. Much of Canada was divided between supporters and opponents of the Spanish Republic, and the former did not have much patience for divisions among those fighting Franco. Krehm railed against the threat he believed communism posed in Spain, and every time the response was the same: Are you for the defeat of Franco, or are you not for the defeat of Franco? "Of course, one is for the defeat of Franco," Krehm said in 1965. "But one is also against having the worse aspects of the Franco regime painted red and established in Spain."[4]

An international conference of leftist groups opposed to Soviet communism was planned to take place in Brussels in October 1936, only a few months after the outbreak of war. The LRWP wanted to send a delegate, and Krehm was a natural choice:

I was twenty-two. I was a young socialist of a drastic sort, with my head on fire. I was looking forward to the millennium that would replace the rather depressing reality of capitalism as it existed. I was quite informed about the seamy sides of communism and even the dangers of power. And here Spain offered a solution to both of these things. It was not only that it was anti-fascist ... it was the beginnings of the socialist revolution, but also the social revolution that promised an alternative to Russia – that did not have heavy-handed tyranny connected with it.[5]

With so much happening in Spain, Krehm could not bear to stay in Brussels, waiting for the conference to begin. In September he crossed the anarchist-controlled Spanish frontier and spent five days in Barcelona. The city was everything he had imagined. "It was the sort of lyric, spring-like affair, where everything that a youthful, and hence naive radical might have dreamed of came to pass," he said. "These were the workers themselves who controlled things."[6] Krehm vowed to return to Spain and did so immediately after the Brussels conference. Rough plans had been made to hold another gathering a few months later, and Krehm decided it was not worth it to make the long trip back to Canada. Besides, he thought, the real action was in Spain.

Krehm spent most of the next eight months living in Barcelona and working informally for the Partido Obrero de Unificación Marxista, or POUM, the left-wing anti-Stalinist political party, usually labelled Trotskyist by members of the Communist Party, though Leon Trotsky had officially disavowed the group. Krehm lived in a large house formerly inhabited by a wealthy German with a group of other anti-Stalinist internationals, including a Greek, an Albanian, and an American. He spent long hours in Barcelona cafés, where he sometimes chatted with George Orwell. He visited the nearby Aragón front once or twice, but it was quiet at the time.

Krehm's working life consisted of translation work for the POUM and writing the occasional article for LRWP pamphlets back home. He also made a few radio broadcasts on behalf of the POUM, but most of the time he spent observing and, in his own words, trying to "show them the proper line." At the time, Krehm believed achieving socialist revolution was a simple matter of political philosophy. You just had to get on these rails, he said sixty-five years later, laughing at his younger self, and the train would take you the rest of the way.[7]

Krehm was an idealist who believed he could help change the world. But he was also earnestly serious and resented the fuss his Canadian comrades in the LRWP were making over him in their publications. "Stop plastering every page of the paper with announcements of my peregrinations and supposed return," he wrote to a friend at the *Workers' Voice,* an LRWP newspaper, in the autumn of 1936. "It is not only embarrassing to me here, but makes us as an excited bunch of kids endlessly thrilled that one of them has gotten to Europe."[8]

Krehm left Spain briefly to attend a small gathering of leftists in Paris (which he described as a failure), and then to visit London. There he met Charles Donnelly, an Irishman with whom he spent Christmas. Donnelly almost persuaded Krehm to join the International Brigades. Krehm was getting frustrated waiting for the planned anti-Stalinist conference, which never seemed to get any closer to fruition. And he was desperate to engage the fascists in Spain, even though he had an idea that communists organized the International Brigades. So Krehm made a decision that would prove monumental. He decided to return on his own.[9] Charles Donnelly joined the International Brigades and was killed. Krehm was luckier, but only barely.

Although there is no way he could have foreseen the outcome at the time, Krehm's problems began in May 1937, when mounting tensions between the various anti-fascist militias and political parties opposed to Franco erupted into a miniature civil war. On one side were far-left revolutionary and anarchist groups; on the other were communists, socialists, and Catalan nationalists, who were backed by the Catalan and republican governments. At root were conflicting visions of Spain's future and how the Republic might triumph in its immediate struggle against fascism. The majority of political groups in the republican zone favoured a conventional war fought by a centrally organized army. Anarchists and POUMists in Catalonia, however, wanted to protect and extend the revolution that had exploded in much of Catalonia during the war's early days, when farms and factories were collectivized and the authority of the central government was largely rejected.

The battle began on 3 May 1937. Truckloads of armed police attempted to take over the central telephone office in Barcelona, which was in the hands of an anarchist committee. Rodríguez Salas, the commissioner for public order, ordered the police on this mission and accompanied them himself.[10] The militiamen holding the telephone office resisted attempts to dislodge them, and fighting quickly spread across Barcelona. Anarchists and POUMists fought against communists and their allies, though tense standoffs between bewildered and jumpy groups of armed men were more common than were prolonged firefights.[11] Krehm, in Barcelona during the fighting, recalled huddling in doorways and only reluctantly venturing onto the streets, because it was impossible to know from which direction a shot might come.[12] A ceasefire was negotiated after three days; soon after, republican government troops took over the city.

Neither the Communist International nor the Communist Party of Spain had ordered the assault on the telephone office, but both had already decided to eliminate the POUM. In February 1937, the Executive Committee of the Communist International issued a directive to the Spanish party calling for the "complete and final crushing of Trotskyism." A month later, José Díaz, general secretary of the Communist Party of Spain, said that "the POUM must be removed from the political life of Spain."[13] Nothing happened at the time. But once the shooting began in Barcelona, there was no doubt which side the Spanish party would support and whom it would condemn.

Immediately, the communist press in Catalonia and in the rest of Spain launched a campaign depicting the street fighting as a revolt by Trotskyists whom it now claimed were allied with the fascists themselves. (An internal July 1937 report by the Servicio de Investigación Militar [SIM], written in German, claims to show links between the POUM, the German Gestapo, and Fascist Italy. Beside the statement was scrawled in German, "No evidence." It appears that even members of the Republic's secret police could not accept their own propaganda.)[14]

For the next five weeks, however, there was no assault against the POUM, and William Krehm could be excused for thinking that perhaps nothing more would happen. True, Juan Negrín became prime minister on 17 May, backed by socialists and communists, and the communists were tightening their control over the country's security and police forces. Party member Lieutenant-Colonel Antonio Ortega became director general of security, entwining the Republic's security forces with agents of Alexander Orlov, Stalin's NKVD representative in Spain.[15] The propaganda campaign against the POUM and other far left or anti-Stalinist parties also continued unabated. But the streets were calm. Krehm continued with his work. He visited his favourite cafés and felt safe.

Meanwhile, plotting the elimination of the POUM continued. A SIM report, again written in German, outlined these plans: "Work in relation to the POUM and the anarchists must be strengthened. This is particularly so for the foreign groups in the organization. One of the most important tasks for the section is to carry out the preparations for the POUM's illegality. We propose that a comrade be made responsible for this task."[16] William Krehm felt the full brunt of SIM's work early on the morning of 17 June 1937.[17]

Given the web of overlapping security services operating in Barcelona at the time, it is difficult to know exactly which organization arrested Krehm that morning at his house as part of a large sweep against the POUM and foreigners associated with it. Soviet personnel were involved, though there were not enough Comintern functionaries in Spain to have carried out, or even supervised, the POUM's repression without the support of the republican government.[18] However, the Soviets did concentrate their aggression on foreign dissidents, so it is possible that they targeted Krehm.[19] A SIM document written in German on 26 July 1937 refers to a "Special Brigade from Valencia" that carried out the arrests in mid-June.[20] Charles A. Orr, an American working with the POUM who was arrested in the same sweep as Krehm, possibly at the same house, said he was taken away by four police detectives. He claimed Russian experts directed the arrests and that he and other prisoners spoke to these Russians later, in prison.[21]

Krehm said the men who arrested him that morning were Spanish or Catalan but that he and his comrades were not taken to a government prison:

> There came a knock. Not at midnight when such knocks usually come. It was about seven o'clock in the morning. And they had lists of all people occupying that house. It had come from obviously communist spies who came from nowhere and disappeared into nowhere. Then there was a roundup, and we were taken – we were not allowed to take our belongings, and we were transferred to these newly carpentered cells in a basement … This was not a government prison. When we were finally extracted from there and put in a government prison, we were safe.[22]

Krehm's claim to have been initially held in some sort of private prison beyond the control of the government is plausible. The Communist Party of Spain ran its own jails. And the NKVD under Alexander Orlov developed an extensive prison network, using Spanish personnel, where dissident Spaniards and foreigners were interrogated, abused, and sometimes murdered.[23]

Documents from the Comintern archives describe a state of confusion about the foreign POUMists. Another SIM report, dated 26 July 1937, discusses the arrest of thirty-four foreigners. Of these, fourteen were set free after being interrogated; five were provisionally freed with the aim of later transferring them to a work camp; one was arrested and taken to hospital; seven were sent to Barcelona's Modelo Prison; and the remaining seven, "who are seriously suspected of espionage," were sent to Valencia. "Up to now, we have been unable to get hold of a list of all prisoners who were arrested in the course of the actions that were carried out against the POUM," the report continues. "We have only a list of those prisoners who were passed on by the Grupo de Información, but in this list, most of the names are incorrectly spelled."[24]

The report refers specifically to those arrested by "other services," noting that these prisoners were now missing. The overall result of all this was a certain amount of chaos. At least eleven men for whom the report writers had detailed information were imprisoned, but they did not know where. They knew the names and locations of another fifteen men who were in jail, but they did not know why they had been arrested.[25]

To make matters worse, from the perspective of the secret police, the prisons were too crowded to allow the prisoners to be sorted and isolated as they wished:

> The prison relations are such in the building of the Grupo de Información that the isolation of the prisoners is made impossible. In the building there are so many prisoners that there are up to sixteen people in each room and some are lodged in a garage. The hygienic conditions are under these circumstances insufficient ... In the interrogations, the newly found spies cannot be isolated because of lack of space.[26]

Krehm said that he and about eighty others, foreigners as well as Spanish POUMists and anarchists, were held in crowded cells, with plywood walls and no ventilation. He located this prison on the south side of the Plaza Catalunya. Conditions were unsanitary. The health of an elderly and tubercular Greek who was imprisoned with them deteriorated quickly, and he was soon coughing up blood and spittle.[27]

After approximately two weeks, Krehm and most of his fellow foreign prisoners were transferred to a government prison, where he said conditions were incomparably better, but still bad. At one point fifteen French and Flemish members of the International Brigades were jailed with them. They had oozing, infected sores from lice and were so starved that they sometimes fought over food.[28] A few of Krehm's fellow foreign POUMists, including Charles Orr, were released within a week.[29] Krehm and several other prisoners began a hunger strike to protest their imprisonment and the lack of judicial process. He was hospitalized as a result.

Krehm said he was never seriously interrogated during his incarceration. Once he lost his temper and was taken away and slapped. (He later recalled with bemused shame that his instinctive reaction was to shout: "You can't do that. I'm a British subject!")[30] But he said he was never beaten or forced to confess to any alleged crimes.

This lack of interrogation is puzzling, because some communist-affiliated security officials believed Krehm was a spy. Krehm's name appears several times in the SIM files, with notes about his hometown (Toronto) and his connections in Spain to the POUM and the Federación Anarquista Ibérica, an anarchist group that was particularly popular in Catalonia. His secret police file also notes that he was in Barcelona during the "May days."[31]

Another report on Krehm exists in a larger series of files on Canadians in Spain, also taken from the archives of the Communist International. Written in Spanish, it reveals details about Krehm's personal life, including the identity of his sister, and lists the people with whom Krehm had corresponded, noting, "It would be interesting to have news on these people's political activity."[32]

Krehm's file also notes the absence of an entrance stamp on his passport, which would have demonstrated that he had government authorization to enter Spain. The first time Krehm had come to Spain, in September 1936, he had used a proper visa. When he returned in January 1937, he crossed with the help of the POUM, which, along with anarchist militias, controlled many of the border posts.[33] According to the officials who wrote the report, however, Krehm's lack of entrance stamp proved one of two things: "Privileges granted by certain organizations to cross the border," or "Activity for a foreign group or spy ring." Neither option would excuse Krehm in the eyes of the secret police and of pro-communist security organizations. "Certain organizations" can be understood to mean the POUM or an affiliated group, and according to much of the communist propaganda circulating Barcelona at the time, membership in the POUM was virtually synonymous with being a fascist. The report's summary was explicit: "WK's case has symptoms of spying, so it would be advantageous to go through his residence ... to have complete information."[34]

William Krehm, who had come to Spain full of hope for its future, therefore found himself imprisoned, believed to be at the very least a political subversive, and perhaps even an enemy agent. His prospects did not look good.

Back in Canada, Krehm's comrades were frantic for his safety and were increasingly frustrated by the almost complete absence of reliable information about his fate. They corresponded frequently with Fenner Brockway, a British politician and secretary of the Independent Labour Party, which tended to side with the POUM and other non-communist leftists groups in the Spanish Civil War. Brockway arrived in Spain on a fact-finding mission shortly after Krehm's arrest and wrote a detailed day-by-day report:

> July 6th: I had information about only two British subjects under arrest for political offences – William Krehm, a Toronto neo-Trotskyist, and of Ethel MacDonald of Glasgow, an anarchist. I got the British Chargé d'Affaires to give me an introduction to the Minister of Interior and in his absence in Madrid obtained from his first secretary a letter on the matter to the Valencia Delegate of Public Order at Barcelona. Both the British prisoners are in Barcelona gaols ...

July 7th: Went to the Valencia Delegate and presented my letter from the Minister of the Interior. He promised to let me know by 8 p.m. whether Krehm and Ethel MacDonald would be released. If not, I could visit them. Returned at 8 p.m., waited to 9:30 p.m. Told they would probably be released tomorrow ...

July 9th: Heard that Krehm is free. Good. That's both the British prisoners for whom I've acted released.[35]

Krehm, however, had not been released, and would not be for another two months. The apparent confusion, even within the government, over Krehm's fate suggests that the crackdown on the POUM and other anti-Stalinist groups and individuals was not controlled by the republican government in its entirety. Brockway summarized his report by noting that the suppression of the POUM was directed and carried out by communist-controlled police and that non-party members of both the Catalan and central governments were disturbed by the communist takeover of security operations.[36]

When it became clear that Brockway was mistaken and Krehm was not free, Krehm's friends and co-workers in the LRWP and affiliated organizations scrambled to discover his fate and to obtain his release. They repeatedly pressed Brockway for information that might provide a clue to Krehm's whereabouts. Ultimately, however, Brockway could report back only on why he mistakenly believed Krehm had been freed, based on the assurances the Valencia delegate of public order had given him. Brockway explained his reasoning in more detail in a 30 July letter to B.J. Field (a former economist whose real name was Max Gould) at the American branch of the LRWP. He said that the day after he had been told by the delegate of public order that Krehm and Ethel MacDonald would likely be released, he saw MacDonald, free and out of prison, in Barcelona. "The next morning, I went to the British Consulate and while I was there a member of the staff telephoned the Hospital Clinico [where Krehm had been taken because of his hunger strike] and was informed that Krehm had been released," Brockway wrote. "Naturally after having seen Ethel MacDonald out of prison I was relieved to hear this and accepted it."[37]

Krehm's friends and co-workers were also in touch with the British consulate in Barcelona, which made inquiries on their behalf. They agonized over placing the expensive transatlantic telephone calls, as the calls produced little new information. But at least they confirmed that Krehm was alive. On 13 August, the British consul or a member of his staff informed Krehm's co-worker Ed Davis that a British member of the consulate had visited Krehm in prison. He said Krehm was being held without charges at Calle Corcega, 299, Barcelona, and appeared quite well. "We are in constant touch with the authorities, and he will be released as soon as possible," the diplomat said. Asked what "as soon as possible" meant, he replied, "presumably in a few days," a prediction that turned out to be too optimistic. Davis noted in his written report on the telephone conversation that it lasted five minutes and cost \$42.25, a small fortune.[38]

As the weeks passed with Krehm still in jail, his friends considered sending one of their own to Spain to look for him. But they had insufficient resources for this most ambitious plan and so were forced to appeal to Krehm's brother-in-law, Joseph Pick, a wealthy American living in Chicago with Krehm's sister, Ida. Pick did not sympathize with Krehm's politics. When Jim Martin, one of Krehm's fellow would-be revolutionaries, travelled to Chicago to appeal to Pick in person, the latter reluctantly agreed to part with a small sum of money, but insisted on dealing directly with Krehm's family members in Toronto. He also informed Martin that Krehm was only getting what was coming to him. "You will take it as definite that money will not be forthcoming here even if Krehm is to be shot the next day," Martin wrote of his meeting with Pick. "The strain of being polite to this bastard is getting me down."[39]

Krehm received help from the Canadian government, which worked through the British Foreign Office and the British consulate in Barcelona. On 14 August, after several letters and telegrams between British and Canadian officials in Spain, the United Kingdom, and Canada, Oscar Douglas Skelton, Canada's undersecretary of state for external affairs, informed Krehm's father, Hyman, that the British Foreign Office had "arranged for [Krehm's] comfort" and believed that Krehm would shortly be expelled from Spain.[40]

This prediction proved to be slightly premature. Krehm was released, but it was at least two more weeks before he was taken to the border and unceremoniously dumped in France, a free man.[41] What finally prompted Krehm's expulsion is unclear, although with the Spanish Republic eager not to antagonize Britain, the Foreign Office's intervention was presumably crucial. In another letter to Krehm's father, Skelton said that Spain's minister of the interior at Barcelona had personally demanded Krehm's release, but it is far from certain what effect this might have had in a country with often overlapping and conflicting security structures.[42] It is possible that Krehm, along with the other imprisoned foreigners, had simply become too much of an embarrassment to the Spanish government. This does not explain why Krehm was kept for nearly two months after Charles Orr and Ethel MacDonald, two foreigners caught up in the same sweep, were released. Perhaps, transferred to a hospital because of his hunger strike, he simply became lost among hundreds of other political prisoners in Barcelona at the time. It is unlikely we will ever know the whole story.

What is certain, however, is that despite a miserable incarceration, Krehm was lucky. We know from SIM documents that some foreign POUMists were sent to work camps. Bob Smillie, a military volunteer with the Independent Labour Party who was arrested before Krehm, was allowed to die in detention.[43]

Other politically suspect foreigners were imprisoned for much longer periods. George Kopp, Orwell's POUM militia commander in Spain, wasted away to little more than skin and bones during eighteen months in jail.

Krehm avoided all these fates. As soon as he made it safely to France, he began writing again for LRWP pamphlets and for the *Workers' Voice*. He crossed the Atlantic again and toured Canada and the United States, talking about his time in Spain. But by now, Krehm was fighting a losing battle. Public meetings and demonstrations about Spain held by anti-communist groups in Canada were broken up by party members, and the largest and most successful lobby and fundraising groups in Canada were fronts for or affiliated with the Communist Party. Krehm also got into a dispute with the Canadian government after refusing to repay expenses the British Foreign Office had expended to secure his release. Skelton wanted legal charges brought against Krehm but was persuaded to drop the matter. Krehm paid the debt a few years later.[44]

Emotionally exhausted and with $270 in his pocket, Krehm drifted south into Mexico, to rest and to "think things over." He was there when the Second World War broke out. Krehm says that he saw this new war as a natural extension of his own battle against fascism and wanted to join the fight. But, unable to get a visa to enter the United States, he was trapped in Mexico. He found work as a writer for *Time* magazine, filing reports on social upheavals and revolutions from across Latin America. Canadian government censors intercepted his letters home.[45] In 1947, as the Cold War heated up, *Time* fired Krehm. With a wife and young child in tow, he returned to Canada, "to lick my wounds and try to learn to play the violin again."[46]

The Doctor: Norman Bethune

All through the long, hot summer of 1936, Montreal doctor Norman Bethune followed the nationalist assault on republican Spain with restless dismay. Bethune was already a veteran of the First World War. He had been wounded, sent home, and enlisted again. In the years after the conflict, he pushed himself to become a renowned thoracic surgeon – until the Great Depression convinced him that improving the lives of the poor could save more lives than surgery. He established a free clinic for the unemployed; he joined the Communist Party; he visited the Soviet Union. Back in Canada, Bethune was something of an eccentric dandy. He painted, wore jaunty clothes, and moved in the same social circles as artists and activists who sometimes congregated at parties he hosted. Bethune was captivated by the war in Spain. He wanted to be there but could find no way to finance the trip. Bethune asked a friend for $200 but was refused. He then approached the Red Cross but was told it was not sending doctors.[1]

Meanwhile, Graham Spry, a leading member in the socialist Co-operative Commonwealth Federation (CCF), was watching the popularity of the Communist Party of Canada rise because of its vocal support for the Spanish Republic. Spry hoped to mimic the communists' success, and so he proposed that the CCF raise money to send medical staff and equipment to Spain.[2] He placed a notice in the CCF newspaper *New Commonwealth* on 26 September, announcing the creation of the "Spanish Hospital and Medical Aid Committee." Norman Bethune contacted Spry almost immediately. He was informed that the committee existed only in Spry's imagination, and Spry had no money to speak of.[3] Bethune was not deterred. He and Spry set about forming the Committee to Aid Spanish Democracy, which included both socialists and communists. Working so closely with his communist rivals surely irritated Spry, but he must have realized that he had little choice if he wanted his committee to reach a broad audience. Two Protestant ministers, Rev. Salem Bland and Rev. Benjamin Spence, chaired the committee and were its public face. Communists Tim Buck and Albert A. MacLeod were vice-chairmen and tended to stay in the background, though the Communist Party exercised a great deal of influence on the committee. Bethune was ready to leave for Spain within a month.

Shortly before sailing from Quebec on 24 October 1936, using the return portion of a steamship ticket given to Spry by a student, Bethune penned a short poem titled "Red Moon over Spain":

> And this same pallid moon tonight,
> Which rides so quiet – clear and high –
> The mirror of our pale and troubled gaze,
> Raised to a cool, Canadian sky,
> Above the shattered Spanish mountain tops
> Last night rose low and wild and red,
> Reflecting back from her illumined shield,
> The blood-bespattered faces of the dead.
> To that pale moon I raise my angry fist,
> And to those nameless dead my vows renew:
> Comrades who fall in angry loneliness,
> Who die for us – I will remember you.[4]

Bethune arrived in Madrid on 3 November 1936, the eve of the nationalist offensive against the Spanish capital.[5] Waiting for the doctor was Henning Sorensen, a Danish-born Canadian who had gone to Spain as a correspondent for the *New Commonwealth* and a Danish socialist paper. He had promised Spry that he would research the Republic's medical needs while in Madrid. Sorensen supported Spain's fight against fascism, but he was also a perpetually restless type, always seeking out new things to learn and experience. "Maybe I was an adventurer," he said many years later. "Maybe I was bored, needed some excitement. I was not Jesus Christ."[6] Sorensen got a cable from Spry asking if he would show Bethune around Madrid. He agreed.

Bethune and Sorensen spent the next few days visiting hospitals in Madrid to try to place Bethune on staff. None of the doctors they spoke to could offer Bethune more than vague commitments, and most told him to come back later. Bethune himself had no firm plans; it seems that he and Sorensen spent another week trying to find somewhere that wanted Bethune, and where Bethune wanted to work. According to Sorensen, in the midst of a nationalist assault on Madrid's University City, General Emilio Kléber (a foreign communist whose real name was Lazar Stern) promised Bethune a job as chief surgeon at the front, but then recanted a day or two later.[7] Bethune was also offered a job as a doctor with the International Brigades at the Albacete base, but he did not like the man in charge, a European, and thought he was incompetent. "I couldn't work with that bastard," he told Sorensen. "Let's get out of here."[8]

It is possible that in the chaos of a city under attack, Bethune was simply unable to find a hospital or medical service that could make use of his skills. But it is more likely that he wanted an assignment with a higher profile and more potential for fame. All those who knew Bethune in Spain described him as passionate and vain, with tremendous energy and little patience. Sorensen recalled Bethune complaining, "You don't give me enough importance when you introduce me."[9] Bethune eventually found his purpose on 14 November while sitting across a small table from Sorensen as the pair travelled by rail to Valencia. The two watched the landscape slip by their window, and then Bethune broke the silence: "Henning, I've got it!" He proceeded to describe his vision for a mobile blood transfusion service.[10] Sorensen decided to join him.

Within days, the pair had received approval from Spanish officials and from the Committee to Aid Spanish Democracy, which was funding their mission. They went to Paris to buy equipment, but Bethune soon lost patience with French bureaucracy and they proceeded to London. Here he bought the necessary supplies, read late into the night about the science of blood transfusion, and through the sheer force of his personality persuaded Hazen Sise, a young Canadian architect living in Britain, to accompany him to Spain. The three overloaded a Ford station wagon with medical equipment and baggage and drove it all the way back to Madrid. They set up their blood transfusion unit in a fifteen-room apartment that was located in a wealthy neighbourhood and had been given to them by the Socorro Rojo Internacional, a Spanish communist branch of a Comintern medical and relief agency.[11]

The trio immediately began gathering and supplying desperately needed blood to wounded soldiers and civilians, gradually expanding their operations to surrounding fronts. Since the outbreak of the conflict, republican doctors had made remarkable advances in blood transfusion work, especially under a Barcelona doctor named Frederick Duran Jorda. But Barcelona was far from the front lines.[12] Bethune crucially perceived the value of bringing blood to where it was needed most. Previously, wounded soldiers often bled to death before they could reach a hospital where a transfusion might be possible. Bethune's transfusion unit took blood to patients, which made all the difference in saving lives. Moreover, in a besieged city such as Madrid, the very act of donating blood gave Spanish citizens an opportunity to tangibly show their solidarity with the soldiers protecting them. Bethune's transfusion unit became a symbol of Madrid's defiance.

The transfusion unit was a medical success. But it was not without problems – many of which can be traced to Bethune's passionate and mercurial personality. The doctor seemed incapable of standing still, even to work steadily in the war-torn city. Shortly after Bethune had established the transfusion unit in Madrid, he and Sise spent three days working around the clock to transport desperate refugees who were fleeing from Malaga to Almeria. It was a brave, even heroic, action, but it also demonstrated Bethune's desire to be always where the action was hottest and the need most intense. When he was back in Madrid, Bethune frequently ran into conflicts with his staff, now mostly Spaniards.

"Norman Bethune was a magnetically attractive yet complex personality – gay and vivid at one moment and the next grim and stone-faced," Hazen Sise remembered in 1963. Before going to Spain, Bethune was "a man with a load of impatience, an angry man contemptuous of a society that seemed indifferent to suffering that he believed could be eradicated by political and economic means."[13] Bethune was consumed by Spain. He seemed to have little tolerance for those who did not possess the same zeal.

Ted Allan said that when he arrived at the blood transfusion unit early in 1937, he had already heard rumours of clashes between Bethune and the Spanish doctors working with him. Bethune told his old friend from Montreal that the Spaniards in his unit were lazy opportunists or even secret Franco sympathizers and that he was drinking Scotch whiskey so that he could tolerate working with them. Allan found Bethune courageous and as committed to his work as he always had been, but he remained an extremely difficult man to live with. "There were times I had loved him because he had been truly magnificent. There were times I hated him because he hadn't measured up to my ideal hero," Allan wrote. "I also remembered the night when Bethune, infuriated by the doctor with whom he'd had all the problems, gulped four straight whiskies, got drunk, and smashed his fist through the front-door window."[14]

Problems intensified in March 1937 as the Spanish republican government reorganized and took control of the many ad hoc groups that had flourished in the tumult of the war's early months. Bethune's transfusion unit was incorporated into the Spanish military on 2 March 1937 and placed under the control of two Spanish doctors and Bethune.[15] Tensions flared between Bethune, his Spanish staff, and his fellow Canadians. Raw nerves were often soothed by Henning Sorensen. Sise later recalled Sorensen fondly as "the hyphen" and "the peacemaker," calming everyone down in a soft Danish accent and keeping the unit focused on getting blood to the front.[16] Bethune, on the other hand, recoiled from the government-imposed control and bureaucracy, which cramped his style and autonomy. He was frequently absent from the transfusion unit and argued with staff when he was present.

Sise said Bethune had "contempt for little minds and for conventional hesitancies ... He would often go charging ahead to get something done, but in doing so would affront a great many bureaucrats and the bureaucratic type of mind." His conflicts with some of his Spanish colleagues became more intense, especially after he discovered that one of the doctors was collecting pay both from Bethune's unit and from another government organization. He drank. He fought with top military leaders, and he sneered at authority.[17] It is noteworthy that despite all this, Spanish doctors who worked with him described Bethune as a gentleman with enormous presence.[18] It seems his devotion to the anti-fascist cause was beyond reproach, and he was brave to the point of reckless-ness. But the pace took its toll; he was irritable and rundown.[19]

Eventually, perhaps inevitably, Bethune had to leave Spain. But the exact circumstances of his departure have always been shrouded in controversy. Officially, Bethune simply felt that the unit was now functioning well under Spanish control and he was no longer needed. In his letter of resignation to the chief of military health dated 9 April 1937, Bethune wrote,

> In view of the fact that the Instituto Hispano-Canadiense de Transfusión de Sangre as conceived by me in January is now operating as an efficient, well-organized institute, and as part of the Sanidad Militar [department of military health], it is clear to me that my function as chief of the organization here in Spain has come to a natural end. Since I am firmly of the opinion that all services of the Republican Army should be controlled by the Spanish people, I hereby offer my resignation as chief of the organization.

Bethune concluded his letter by noting the continued need for financial support from Canada, and therefore delegating his authority, as representative of the Canadian Committee to Aid Spanish Democracy, to Ted Allan, Hazen Sise, Henning Sorensen, and Allen May. May, another Canadian volunteer, had arrived at the unit in late February or early March.[20]

There may be some truth to this version of events. In a telegram to the Rev. Ben Spence at the Committee to Aid Spanish Democracy that Bethune wrote a week before resigning, he said that Sanidad Militar had taken over the Canadian unit and "our positions [are] now nominal ... Fortunately transfusion service is well established and can carry on without us." Beneath the surface, however, it is clear that not all was well at the institute. Indeed, in the same telegram, Bethune asked Spence to cable his authorization that Bethune be allowed to withdraw all Canadian medical personnel from Spain. He added that Spence should consider as legitimate only future telegrams from Bethune signed "Beth Bethune," clearly indicating his growing mistrust with the Spanish government.[21]

Over the years, other signs have emerged that Bethune was wearing out his welcome in Spain. The Canadian communist William Kashtan claimed that the party sent him and Albert A. MacLeod to Spain in 1937 with the assigned task of bringing Bethune back to Canada.[22] Bethune's personnel file in the Comintern archives confirms that Henning Sorensen and Ted Allan had writ-ten to the Communist Party of Canada to complain about Bethune and ask that he be replaced as director of the blood transfusion unit.[23] Hazen Sise said the Committee to Aid Spanish Democracy decided to bring Bethune home for a publicity tour.[24] However, Bethune had already resigned before Kashtan and MacLeod arrived in Spain. Whatever precipitated Bethune's resignation and eventual departure from Spain involved more than the orders of either the Communist Party of Canada or the Committee to Aid Spanish Democracy.

The diaries of Hazen Sise and the personal papers of Henning Sorensen reveal additional hints as to what took place. A diary Hazen Sise kept during his time in Spain contains this entry for 6 April 1937: "Got Beth to agree to get out."[25] Unfortunately, there is no further explanation. A similar day-by-day recollection by Henning Sorensen addressed, it seems, to Hazen Sise, confirms that on 6 April 1937, "we persuaded Beth to leave. He wrote letters of resignation to party." Little more can be pieced together by surrounding entries. Two days earlier, Sorensen wrote, "I arrived Madrid – things had happened."[26] Reading too much into this is speculative, but later entries in Hazen Sise's diary suggest Bethune had seriously crossed Spanish authorities.

Bethune left Spain for Paris around 16 May, after filming *Heart of Spain*, a propaganda film based on the blood clinic. But the doctor wanted to return to work on a project supporting Spanish war orphans in Bilbao. The Committee to Aid Spansih Democracy was unwilling to fund the mission.[27] Even without funding or support from Canada, Bethune felt compelled to return to Spain. On 29 May, he cabled his former colleagues and announced his intention to travel to Bilbao.[28] His former co-workers immediately tried to derail this plan. The remaining Canadians in the blood transfusion unit telegrammed Ben Spence and the Committee to Aid Spanish Democracy to advise that Bethune not be allowed to conduct further operations in Spain, noting though that he remained a valuable asset for propaganda in Canada.[29] Hazen Sise's diary entry for 30 May reads, "Finally got agreement on 2 telegrams indicating but not specifying serious trouble with Beth." The entry continues: "Had police (military) telegraph Paris to stop Bilbao trip. Had long chat with them. Saw and corrected Beth's dossier and discovered they would have put out order for his expulsion if he hadn't have left."[30]

From Sise's diary we can deduce that Bethune's conflicts with Spanish authorities had escalated to a point that he faced imminent deportation. But it was not until the Soviet Union opened the archives of the Communist International in the 1990s that the extent of the problem was made clear.

Bethune's Comintern file indicates that by July 1937 he was so determined and desperate to return to Spain that he planned to join the International Brigades, a fighting unit, at the age of forty-seven. His imminent arrival was greeted with some alarm by Hazen Sise, still at the blood transfusion unit, who wrote to a "Comrade Felipe," at the Communist Party of Spain's Madrid Provincial Committee, to inform him that Bethune was planning on returning to the country.

Spanish communist authorities were not pleased with the prospect of Bethune's arrival. On 17 August 1937, Juan Alcántara at the Madrid Provincial Committee sent Sise's letter to the Central Committee of the Communist Party. Alcántara attached a note in which he outlined reasons why Bethune should not be permitted back into Spain, and why he had left that spring:

This comrade was expelled by the [Committee] for Blood Transfusion and sent to Canada in a clever way because he was the person responsible for the Canadian Committee for assistance to Spain in Madrid.

1 For being immoral, among other things, he frequently got drunk and was never in a condition to lead a mission as delicate as blood transfusion.
2 He took jewellery under the pretext that he was going to hand them over to the SRI [Socorro Rojo Internacional] and then said he would sell it in Paris to raise funds for the institute, without nobody [sic] knowing to date what he did with those objects.
3 He happily squandered money without thinking that it came from the solidarity that the Canadian proletariat was showing to Spain and that in many cases this involved collecting cent by cent.
4 We always observed his great interest for going to the front whenever there were operations, but never with the good purpose of making transfusions.
5 He left Spain taking a film he had made on the different fronts without it passing through the censors.
6 There is much suspicion that BETHUNE may be a spy, according to a report that is already in the Central Committee of our party and in the Headquarters of Military Health.
7 He had frequent visits and interviews with a woman who was somewhat suspicious called "TAJSA," who we believe is at present in Valencia. This concrete report includes the most salient reasons why we believe that "NOREN" BUTHUNE should not come to Spain, and on this criteria there is agreement with the Canadian comrades and the Communist Cell from the Institute of Blood Transfusion in Madrid (located at Príncipe de Vergara No. 36, Telephone 59881).[31]

Another document on Bethune survives in the Comintern archives that provides some needed context for the accusations levelled against Bethune. It may in fact be the report referred to in the letter quoted above, which would suggest it originated at the Central Committee of the Communist Party of Spain or the Headquarters of the Sanidad Militar. Written by an anonymous Spanish official on 3 April 1937, it notes the growing conflicts between Bethune and Spanish military health authorities. It also refers to the suspicious activities of a woman named Kajsa, a Swede who was by then a fixture at the blood transfusion unit. According to the report, Kajsa made "frequent trips to the front, morning and afternoon and sometimes even at night." She did not live at the team's residence and where she went was unknown. The medical staff ignored her actions and she was accountable to no one, claiming only that she needed to inform herself about the medical needs on the front lines. "At present and by initiative of Kajsa, it is said that there are a series of very detailed maps in the team, similar to military maps," the report notes.[32]

Kajsa's full name was Kajsa Rothman, and what we know about her suggests she was a striking woman. A dancer and entertainer, she had toured Europe before her manager ran off and left her penniless. She then moved to Romania, where she worked for a while as a children's nurse. Apparently unable to stay put, Rothman travelled to Barcelona and established a travel agency; she was there when the war broke out.[33] She then worked for the Red Cross and a Swedish charity, and she also took up journalism, broadcasting in Swedish from Madrid and writing for a Swedish newspaper.[34] The Spanish official writes that, earlier in the war, Kajsa had worked as a nurse and with a Scottish ambulance unit. She was fired from her job at the ambulance unit, the official alleged, for immoral behaviour.[35] Other reports recall her penchant for riding motorbikes.[36] Most people described her as a redhead, and surviving photographs depict a woman with dark hair. Ted Allan, however, remembered her as a beautiful blond, who showed up at the blood transfusion unit wanting to write a book about Norman Bethune. Bethune and the Swede "exchanged long looks" and disappeared into the doctor's bedroom for two days, Allan said. He later stumbled upon them naked in bed. Occasionally, Bethune emerged to make his rounds. He said the journalist was conducting an in-depth interview, smirked, and then added, "or vice versa."[37]

A woman like Kajsa Rothman would have made quite an impression on Spanish society. It is tempting to think that the Spanish official who wrote the report might have been simply taken aback by the Swedish woman's brazen confidence and overt sexuality and consequently felt justified in implying she was a spy. But her name more ominously appears in a file kept by the Servicio de Investigación Militar, the Republic's secret police. She is identified as Kajsa Helin Rothmann and described as tall and thin, with a small face and blond hair. Her file says she was a former opera diva, a former governess in Sweden, and a Trotskyist "who had relations with fascist circles in Valencia and Barcelona."[38]

The report on Bethune contains additional dark warnings about the Canadian doctor. It refers to "a serious event of very special nature that speaks of the morality of these elements." The writer cautions that the details are alleged, not proven, but relates them anyway:

> A room in the apartment occupied by the team in Príncipe de Vergara 36 was sealed by the Chilean embassy. When he occupied the apartment, Bethune and another or others opened it by force. We know that two coffers that were there were also opened in one case and forced open in the other by these individuals, and it appears that there were jewels and documents in them whose present whereabouts are unknown.

The report then makes its most serious accusation against Bethune: "A suspicious piece of information that should also be taken into account is that Mr. Bethune, without concealing it, took detailed note of the state of bridges, road crossings, distances between certain points, the time it takes to travel them, etc., writing it all down carefully."[39] The implication here is that Bethune is a suspected spy – as indeed the later report, written in response to his desire to return to Spain, makes clear.

A closer look at these allegations, however, reveals them to be implausible nonsense. Bethune is damned for actions that were clearly part of his work delivering blood to various points on and behind the front lines. It should come as no surprise that he took careful note of distance and travel times: lives depended on it. At the time this report was written, in the spring of 1937, republican Spain was in the grips of anti-spy paranoia and many, especially foreigners, found their loyalty suspect. But even in this context, the evidence used to condemn Bethune is thin. It is remarkable that the accusations were evidently still taken seriously four months later, though it must be considered that some Spanish authorities were willing to accept whatever explanations might have helped ensure that Bethune stayed out of the country.

The documents from the Comintern archives allow us to answer – to the extent it will probably ever be possible – the question of how and why Norman Bethune left Spain. By April 1937, Bethune was no longer welcome in Spain by either his Canadian co-workers or the Spanish military health authorities. Even the police were ready to deport him. The details of this discord are unknown, but Bethune's headstrong independence, arrogance, contempt for authority, and drinking were crucial factors. The very personality traits that propelled him to Spain and that allowed him to flourish in the early days of the siege of Madrid caused him to flounder when he became a cog in a much larger bureaucracy.

Bethune's Canadian colleagues and Spanish hosts shrewdly realized they could not outright expel him without jeopardizing funding from Canada. It seems that the Sanidad Militar, along with Sise, Sorensen, May, and perhaps representatives from the Communist Party of Canada, conspired to remove Bethune from Spain "in a clever way," with a minimal amount of negative publicity, and without revealing the real reasons he had to go. That the circumstances of his departure remained hidden, and that Bethune himself seems to have been ignorant of the machinations against him, indicates how successful they were.

Norman Bethune was in Spain for less than six months, but he made a tremendous impact on the country and all those he encountered during his short time there. He saved lives, and he helped the Spanish government. He also inspired thousands of Canadians, including other doctors and medical workers, to help Spain – either directly and in person or through financial contributions. As a dedicated anti-fascist, he would have been pleased with this result.

Unlike Bethune, however, not all Canadian doctors had respectable careers in Spain. Eugene Fogarty worked as a medical officer in the 17th Battalion at a hospital in Villanueva de la Jara. His personnel file lists his citizenship as Canadian and indicates that he claimed to have a degree, presumably in medicine, from McGill University in Montreal. But reports on Fogarty conclude that he "is not a physician and did more harm than good." His file records numerous complaints aside from the most serious one of impersonating a doctor. He reportedly worked privately but drew pay from the International Brigades, he married a local girl and charged his wedding expenses to the International Brigades, he made enough money from his fraud to live in comfort, and he was a drug addict and trafficked in narcotics. Fogarty was dismissed from the International Brigades but stayed on in Villanueva de la Jara before disappearing sometime in the summer of 1937.[40] A search of records at McGill University revealed no trace of Fogarty ever having attended medical school there.[41]

It must also be said that problems at the blood transfusion unit were not solely of Bethune's making. On 21 July 1937, Sise, Sorensen, and May drafted a letter to Sr. Estrelles, director of Sanidad Militar in Madrid, and to the director of Sanidad Militar in Valencia to complain about many of the same problems that had so enraged Bethune. They were fighting with Spanish staff members, who did not want the trio of Canadians to be involved in running the unit, and the unit lacked any organizational support from military health authorities. "Though we agree that Dr. Bethune made many mistakes and might be said to have left the Institute in an unhealthy condition, yet he never tolerated slackness and always insisted that it was our duty to keep the hospitals well supplied with blood at whatever sacrifice of our own time and trouble," they wrote. The Canadians added that they did not think it was right that they should keep asking donors in Canada to send money to such a wasteful and disorganized unit.[42] The trio left Spain by the end of the summer.

As for Kajsa Rothman, she was no secret fascist. When Franco's forces won the war, she did not welcome them but fled the country with hundreds of thousands of Spaniards who feared Franco's reprisals. She found refuge in Mexico and died there thirty years later.[43] In the many letters Bethune wrote from Spain and China, he never mentioned her.

Spain left Bethune emotionally drained and detached, but also rededicated to continuing his vendetta against fascism. Two letters are revealing. On 5 May 1937, shortly before leaving the country, he wrote his friends in Canada an "Apology for Not Writing Letters." In it he attempts a philosophical discussion of the role of an artist in times of political turmoil but ends his letter abruptly: "But enough. Perhaps the true reason I cannot write is that I'm too tired ... Our first job is to defeat fascism – the enemy of the creative artist. After that we can write about it."[44] We know that Bethune tried twice after writing that letter to return to Spain – first to help orphaned children in Bilbao, then to serve as a soldier or doctor in the International Brigades. Both attempts were unsuccessful.

Six months later, as he prepared to leave for a new mission in China, Bethune wrote a farewell letter to an Elizabeth, a woman who must have been a former lover. He apologizes for not contacting her in person but says that he cannot risk emotional attachment. He sounds driven but no longer enthused. And it seems he is mentally preparing himself for a final and probably fatal mission. "My road ahead is a strange and dangerous one. You cannot come with me," he writes. "I don't want to attempt in my time – and in my time left – any serious emotional engagement. I am through with such things ... Now you can think about me kindly and sweetly. Do so. I loved you once. I have great affection for you now. Remember me as I will you – with quietness and respect. Beth."[45]

Norman Bethune successfully reached China and served in Mao Zedong's communist Eighth Route Army. He cut himself while operating on a wounded soldier in China's remote northwest. The wound became infected and blood poisoning set in. He died on 12 November 1939.

Part 5
Aftermath

14

Undesirables

We are getting rid of a lot of undesirables who may never return, but laws
should be enforced if possible.

RCMP commissioner James Howden MacBrien, 28 August 1937

Officially, Canadian survivors of the Spanish Civil War were criminals in
the eyes of the Canadian government. Legislation passed in 1937 outlawed
participation in the conflict, and the RCMP had spent large amounts of
time and resources compiling a case against the volunteers and those who
recruited them. Moreover, senior officials in the RCMP routinely pressured
the government to prosecute the volunteers. An 8 July 1937 letter from
RCMP commissioner James Howden MacBrien to Oscar Douglas Skelton,
undersecretary of state for external affairs, is typical of many:

> As you will agree, the presence in Spain of the individuals mentioned as having left
> Canada for that country would appear to be a breach of the spirit of the Non-Intervention
> Treaty and it would also seem that in making application for passport they must have
> given a false reason for leaving Canada and also a false destination ... In this connection
> our Officer Commanding at Regina, Sask., reports that a feeling prevails among the loyal
> spirited foreigners at that point that recruiting for the Spanish Government should be
> prohibited as it is felt that these youths are being sent to Spain largely for the sake of
> gaining experience in practical revolutionary work and will return to this country to form
> the nucleus of a training corps.[1]

The RCMP also reasoned that it might be able to prevent volunteers
who had already left for Spain from returning to Canada, especially if
the men in question were of the "foreign element." On 27 August 1937,
Inspector Charles Rivett-Carnac in the RCMP's Liaison and Intelligence
Section urged continued investigation of Communist Party recruitment
efforts because "the proof might be most useful from the point of view of

preventing the return of individuals who are not Canadian citizens to Canada from Spain."[2]

The RCMP commissioner himself made his feelings explicit in a 25 August 1937 letter to Ernest Lapointe, minister of justice. He conceded that a recent order-in-council banning Canadians from taking part in the Spanish war acted as a deterrent but noted that recruits were still leaving the country: "Any action, therefore, that the Immigration authorities could take in the manner described in our letter to the Under-Secretary of State would undoubtedly result in the exclusion of a certain number of individuals who had learned the essentials of revolutionary warfare in Spain and who might, at a future date, apply this education to local circumstances in this country." MacBrien told Lapointe that the RCMP did not concern itself with questions of foreign policy, "our interest in the matter being solely connected with the matter of legislation as laid down by the Immigration Act in this respect."[3]

Senior RCMP officials clearly wanted to build a criminal case against those responsible for sending Canadians to fight in Spain, but even the commissioner admitted that the departure of radical Canadians to fight in a dangerous foreign war had potential benefits. Attached to a note from the RCMP's Liaison and Intelligence Section suggesting the use of undercover agents is Commissioner James Howden MacBrien's response: "We are getting rid of a lot of undesirables who may never return, but laws should be enforced if possible."[4]

The government did finally decide to prosecute the recruiters in December 1937. On 16 December, Frederick J. Mead wrote to Assistant Commissioner Stuart Taylor Wood and urged him to be extremely selective about whom he hired as a counsel for the Crown. "We cannot go to Court with a case such as this with second-raters," said Mead, who also held the rank of assistant commissioner. "The question of who is appointed may be the making or breaking of our case and we cannot afford to fail." The barrister selected was François-Philippe Brais of Montreal.[5]

In February 1938, the Ministry of Justice informed Brais that his suggestion to charge the recruiters with conspiracy under article 573 of the Criminal Code had been approved. Brais immediately set about gathering as much information as possible about the Communist Party of Canada's country-wide recruitment network. He recommended that Detective Inspector Frank W. Zaneth at the RCMP's divisional headquarters in Montreal be dispatched to Toronto, Hamilton, Winnipeg, and Vancouver to liaise with officers in these cities, to gather information, and ensure that all future raids were conducted simultaneously.

"Before doing this, however, Inspector Zaneth will have to contact the various informers in order to properly develop the available information," Brais wrote in a 28 February 1938 letter to Mead in Montreal. He continued, "But what is more important is that he should make contact, if possible, with certain men who have now returned from Spain ... Needless to say, the chances of success of this prosecution will be further enhanced by evidence tending to show the ramifications of this conspiracy and to what extent it has involved from Canada young men who, under false pretences, are brought to Spain to fight in the cause of Communism."[6]

Inspector Zaneth did cross the country, gathering evidence and preparing for what he believed would be the RCMP's decisive confrontation with the Communist Party of Canada. "There is no doubt that we will be able to establish beyond a shadow of a doubt that the Communist Party is solely responsible for the breach of the act in question," he wrote to Rivett-Carnac from Regina in March 1938. "Once the system has been shown in court, all the leading lights of the Communist Party are equally and criminally responsible ... In other words, this crime was not committed by a group of individuals but by the Communist Party. We can, if we wish, charge as many and as few as we like."[7] Zaneth was no less confident in his letter to Wood, who took over as commissioner on 6 March after the death of James Howden MacBrien. Party members believed they had erected a wall of security around themselves, Zaneth wrote on 11 March. "In reality, they have left in their wake sufficient evidence to hang them."[8]

Zaneth was in for a disappointment. Regional RCMP branches across the country reacted with extreme disapproval when made aware of plans to raid Communist Party and affiliated offices in their areas. "The raids would be the means of arousing a moribund force into activity," wrote Raymond Cadiz, officer commanding at the RCMP's Vancouver branch, in a 25 March letter to the commissioner. Cadiz went on to claim, "It is erroneous to state that the Communist Party, at least as far as B.C. is concerned, has been recruiting volunteers for Spain."[9] This remark is baffling, as Vancouver was a major recruitment centre, and the RCMP must have been aware of this. Nevertheless, Cadiz's sentiments, protesting raids and prosecution of party members as counterproductive and a potential public relations disaster, were echoed in RCMP branches across western Canada. From Edmonton, William Hancock warned of repercussions in a province where the provincial government was sympathetic to the Communist Party: "The Social Credit and Communist Parties are so closely interwoven that any definite action such as is proposed will have an adverse effect on the good feelings which we have been able to create between the Provincial Government and this Force."[10]

Wood was ultimately swayed by these arguments. On 29 March, he wrote to Ernest Lapointe, minister of justice, recommending that all actions geared toward prosecuting volunteers and their recruiters "be left in abeyance for the present time." Wood argued that when plans to prosecute the recruiters began, large drafts of volunteers were being sent to Spain at regular intervals. "This situation has now changed completely as recruiting by Communist

Party functionaries has ceased and no volunteers are being sent." If recruiting were to resume, Wood said, they could reconsider. Now prosecutions would be too late to stop Canadian volunteers leaving for Spain. More important, Wood said, with the tide of war now turned in favour of the insurgents, "if the charges are proceeded with[,] ... public sympathy will be almost entirely on the side of the defending element and the prosecutions will merely have the effect of arousing antipathy in the public mind." Proceeding with the prosecutions might, Wood feared, push more moderate Canadians into the arms of the communists:

> In other words, it would appear that in proceeding with these prosecutions at the present juncture we would merely afford the Communist Party an instrument which that organization would put to useful purpose in attacking the government. Without doubt a very large number of persons hitherto unsympathetic towards Communism would defend the Communist stand on this point, and would thus be made the tools of the revolutionary element to the detriment of the eventual public welfare. Under the circumstances, no good would result and a great deal of harm might follow.

Finally, Wood said, searches and prosecutions carried out in the western provinces, with the consent of the attorney general, would cause friction between the provincial and federal governments. Even in eastern Canada, with the possible exception of Quebec, "the prosecutions would not be regarded as opportune in any matter or form."[11]

Days later, Ernest Lapointe instructed that no further actions be taken to prosecute those responsible for sending Canadians to Spain.[12] Prime Minister William Lyon Mackenzie King was a political survivor who owed his long success, in part, to his refusal to take a stand and by avoiding conflict. King correctly judged that the Spanish Civil War was a contentious issue in Canada, and he sidestepped it.

The RCMP did not entirely give up, however. If it was not possible to prosecute the recruiters, Wood reasoned, at least the force could discredit them. On 1 June, he sent a letter to Assistant Commissioner Mead in Montreal, suggesting that he take a statement from Lucien Latulippe, a former Canadian volunteer who had recently returned to Montreal after having a nervous breakdown on the front lines in Spain. The International Brigades proposed Latulippe's repatriation, though some notes in his personnel file say he left Spain on his own accord, which suggests he might have deserted. Wood told Mead that because Latulippe was a deserter, he "may have distinctly hostile feelings" toward those who sent him to Spain:

> When a statement has been obtained it will be possible to ascertain the state of mind of Latulippe, and if his information shows promise of disclosing the true state of affairs it might be well to discreetly place some reliable newspaper in possession of his address

so that his experiences, etc., may reach the public eye. You would undoubtedly be in a good position in Montreal to determine which newspaper could take best advantage of the information.[13]

The returning Canadian volunteers therefore faced no immediate legal ramifications on account of their fighting in Spain. The government even decided not to prevent the return of foreign-born volunteers – though most, depending on how long they had been away from Canada and their exact legal status, could have been kept out of the country. With the war in Spain all but over, the Canadian government wished to put the uncomfortable matter of Canadians fighting there behind it. A much larger European war was already brewing, and this was a war that Canada would not be able to avoid.

The Second World War broke out within months of the Canadians' return from Spain. Several veterans volunteered immediately. Edward Cecil-Smith pledged to lead the Canadian veterans back into battle against Hitler. But he spoke too soon for the Communist Party of Canada. Following instructions from the Communist International, the Canadian party declared that the new war was an imperialist conflict and urged Canadians to stay out of it. The Nazis, whom the Canadians had faced in Spain only a year before, were no longer the enemy, according to the Communist Party of Canada, such was its subservience to Moscow. Two years later, when Germany invaded the Soviet Union, the Canadian party reversed itself again and declared that the conflict was in fact a people's war, which Canadians should join in strength. Some stalwart party members followed the party line through all its twists and turns. Others were not so easily swayed.

Edward Cecil-Smith, although chastised by the party, did not publicly recant his support for the war. In a 26 December 1939 *Toronto Daily Star* article, carefully clipped and kept by the RCMP, the former Canadian commander is quoted as saying that many Canadian veterans of the Spanish Civil War were enlisting and cautioned that American Spanish Civil War veterans, who very publicly opposed the war, did not speak for the Canadian veterans. "Whether people of the United States want that country drawn into the war is up to them," he said. "But the opinions of the United States veterans are not necessarily the opinions of Canadians. We feel very differently about many things."[14]

Harvey Hall joined the Canadian army shortly after Germany invaded Poland. He felt that the Second World War was simply another round in the war against fascism he had begun fighting in Spain. "Many of us were not at that time, let us say late 1939 when we joined the Canadian army, we were not particularly pro-communist," he said.[15] Another veteran, a German emigrant who for years had watched the rise of Nazism in his homeland with fear, fell out with the party over its stand on the outbreak of a wider war in Europe. "I was an anti-fascist. Hitler was the enemy. And I got tired of all their political somersaults," he said.[16] Arne Knudsen felt the same way about Stalin's August 1939 pact with Hitler: "Well, Christ almighty, we had just fought the son of a bitch and now he was trying to make friends with him."[17]

That so many Canadian veterans of Spain enlisted when Canada declared war, regardless of the line dictated by the Comintern in Moscow, suggests that the Communist Party of Canada had a weaker hold on its Canadian members who fought in Spain, and especially on non-communist veterans, than did the Communist Party of the United States on the American veterans. This is consistent with evidence that emerged during the Spanish Civil War – particularly evaluations of Canadian volunteers by party officials, who singled them out as lacking "political education."

A desire to fight fascism a second time did not guarantee that a Canadian veteran of Spain would get a second opportunity, however. Arne Knudsen tried to enlist immediately after Canada declared war. The first unit he approached rejected him because he was not a Canadian citizen; the second turned him down because he had fought in Spain. "I thought that would have helped. But [the recruiting officer] stood up and said, 'Out! Out! Out! You're a Communist!'" Knudsen recalled. When he approached the recruiting officer for the Royal Canadian Artillery, Knudsen kept his mouth shut about Spain and claimed he had been born in an isolated Danish community in New Brunswick, which he said explained his accent. But his obvious combat skills gave Knudsen away once he got to Europe. His commanding officer, a man named Harrison, suspected Knudsen had previous military experience. When confronted, Knudsen admitted he had been in the Spanish war. "That's between you and me," Harrison said. "I was just wondering how come you're so good at it."[18]

Terrence Cunningham said that he too was turned away at a recruiting office after admitting he had fought in Spain.[19] Jules Paivio joined the forces and taught map reading to Canadian soldiers in Canada. He noticed that a man who was not one of the soldiers was often at the back of his classroom. Paivio assumed he was a friend of his commanding officer. After the war, the man told Paivio that he had been assigned to watch Paivio because of his Spanish connection.[20] On the other hand, civil war veterans William Krysa and Mike Storgoff said they did not hide the fact that they had fought in Spain and it never adversely affected them in the Canadian army. Milt Cohen was likewise upfront about his time in Spain and was still made an officer.[21]

Canadian government policy toward Spanish Civil War veterans serving with the Canadian armed forces was inconsistent to begin with and changed over the course of the war. Some Canadians, such as Knudsen and Cunningham, were rejected at recruiting offices when it became known they had fought in Spain. Other Spanish war veterans had no trouble. Scores served, fought well, and in many cases were honoured for their actions.

Canada's military high command clearly consulted the RCMP about admitting Canadian veterans of Spain. In December 1939, a high-ranking RCMP officer wrote to the Department of National Defence about Spanish Civil War veterans in the Canadian army. His reference to a recent visit to his office by a Major G.M. Morrison suggests that the Department of National Defence requested the help of the RCMP: "Out of the list provided, the following are on our records as having been members of the Mackenzie-Papineau Battalion, or having been connected with subversive movements ... They are men who, it is considered, with proper handling, would make good soldiers, and we see no reason why they should not be allowed to proceed with the Battalion to which they have now been attested." The list in question is about ten lines long but has been blacked out by Canadian government censors. The letter continues: "The following are reported as members of the Communist Party. They are known radicals and agitators. We would, therefore, recommend that they be struck off strength [removed from their units] and not permitted to proceed Overseas or receive any further training." This second list is shorter. All the names listed have similarly been censored, except one: Edward Cecil-Smith.[22]

A little over a year later, on 27 February 1941, Inspector Charles Batch, an RCMP intelligence officer, received a letter from a lieutenant-colonel in army intelligence, whose signature is undecipherable. It reads:

Dear Inspector,

This will acknowledge receipt of a list of Spanish War Veterans which we expressed a desire to secure on February 14th. The list forwarded by you may be of considerable value in detecting undesirables at present in the Forces or attempting to enlist, and I would like to thank you for your very kind co-operation in this matter.[23]

It is impossible to know the precise ramifications of this letter. Canadian veterans of the Spanish Civil War enlisted successfully before and after February 1941. There appears to have been no rigid policy. Some RCMP reports recommended that known communists not be discharged lest they enlist under different names. Better to keep these men under close surveillance, the reasoning went. "As soon as they undertake anything in the nature of subversive activities, they can be Court-martialed and dealt with," one report suggested.[24]

This confusion probably extended to individual recruitment centres. The recruiting officer who rejected Arne Knudsen as a communist might have been acting on his own initiative. Ironically, Knudsen had never been a member of the Communist Party. Edward Cecil-Smith, on the other hand, was discharged from the Royal Canadian Engineers in the first months of the war for "subversive activities," and it is now clear this happened because he was on a government and RCMP blacklist.

In the case of Cecil-Smith, and we can assume other barred veterans, the government and armed forces acted more on the basis of political prejudice than good intelligence. A document in Cecil-Smith's RCMP file contains a report on his activities in the Royal Canadian Engineers before his discharge:

> The Commanding Officer of the 2nd Field Company, R.C.E. [Royal Canadian Engineers] and C.A.S.F. [Canadian Active Service Force] is aware that Smith is a Communist, was surprised that he has been such a model outstanding Soldier. Between parades, and in the evening, Smith will have a group of green men around him, teaching them his knowledge on the different lines of Army life and work, of which he has a wonderful knowledge. He has been such a good Soldier that his [commanding officer] had to make him L/Cpl [Lance Corporal]. Since being in the Army, he has cultivated a large group of good friends and supporters. Any trouble which has arisen amongst the men, he has taken no part in it.[25]

Cecil-Smith was discharged anyway, and the Canadian army lost a good soldier.

A few Canadian communist leaders were jailed for a time early in the war, but Canadian and British authorities soon learned that they had a use for both the party and for veterans of the Spanish war. With most of mainland Europe occupied by Germany, Italy, and their puppet regimes, and with few immediate options available for a direct assault, the Allies sought to support and encourage partisan warfare behind enemy lines. In the Balkans and central Europe, powerful partisan militias, often communist, were forming to oppose the Nazis.

Among the surviving Canadian veterans of the Spanish Civil War were scores of emigrants from the Balkans and central Europe. They had combat experience and, more important, would be trusted by partisans in the mountains and forests of occupied Europe because of their family and party ties. At least six of these men were recruited by the British and Canadian governments to parachute behind enemy lines in the Balkans as part of the elusive Special Operations Executive, created by Winston Churchill to "set Europe ablaze."

The RCMP did not stop spying on Canadian veterans of Spain, or interfering in their lives, just because the government had elected not to prosecute them. Thick files, now declassified, albeit with large segments still censored, are full of RCMP surveillance reports and dark warning about what the veterans and their supporters might be up to – usually without any serious evidence to support the dire predictions. The reports begin in the 1930s and span at least six decades.

On 23 January 1939, RCMP commissioner Stuart Taylor Wood wrote to the Canadian Legion of British Empire Service League to warn that Spanish war veterans might try to infiltrate the organization.[26] Four days later, J.R. Bowler, general secretary of the Canadian Legion, wrote Wood to say that he had received Wood's "secret letter ... on the subject of combatants who have returned to Canada from the Spanish Civil War." Bowler assured Wood that service in Spain did not constitute a reason for membership in the legion and added: "We shall certainly be on the watch for any effort to penetrate the Canadian Legion, under any guise whatsoever, and should anything of interest come to our notice, will at once advise."[27]

In 1946, a special section of the RCMP's Toronto branch filed a report on a gathering of civil war veterans, conceding a couple of lines later, "this gathering could be called more of a social with much liquor, etc., in evidence." In case the report's recipient doubted that a handful of veterans getting drunk constituted a national security threat, the report cited an unnamed informer who said that meetings such as these constituted the nucleus of an underground movement should there be war with Russia.[28]

Several reports from 1947 claimed that the Mackenzie-Papineau Battalion was forming again as an armed force to fight in Spain and that the Communist Party of Canada had asked for money and soldiers. "It is reported that the aims of the new Battalion will be to organize and send recruits to fight in Spain and to collect money for medical supplies for Spain," reads an RCMP memorandum dated 19 December 1947.[29] It appears that the only evidence for this claim consisted of a few lines written by Walter Dent in the Canadian edition of *Volunteer for Liberty*, a newsletter for veterans of the Spanish Civil War. "Remember Comrade," Dent wrote, "we solemnly pledged to continue the struggle by whatever means within our power until Fascism is destroyed throughout the world and Spain regains her freedom." The RCMP also noted that the party organ *Canadian Tribune* had announced that Mackenzie-Papineau veterans were forming "a new national organization to continue their pledge to carry on the fight against Franco."[30]

The "new national organization" that the Canadian veterans were forming was the "Veterans of the Mackenzie-Papineau Battalion," essentially a social club that also lobbied against the Franco regime in Spain. It is difficult to believe that the RCMP could not tell the difference between a couple of lines of propaganda in a widely circulated veterans' newsletter and plans to raise an illegal militia.

Veterans were also pressured to become police informers, apparently with the cooperation of the Canadian government. "Members of the Mac-Paps who are in the Party have been approached by our contacts without result," reads a 4 January 1949 dispatch from the RCMP's special branch in Vancouver. "Similarly, a former Mac-Pap named [name has been censored] who had applied some time ago for a post in the Civil Service, was approached through [name has been censored] and while willing to discuss the matter, could supply no information of value."[31]

In 1970, Canadian veterans of the Spanish Civil War applied for formal incorporation as a non-profit organization called Mackenzie-Papineau Battalion – Veterans of the International Brigades. The stated aims of the organization, outlined in the application, included to "aid in the restoration of democracy to the Spanish Republic" and to "extend solidarity and aid to any national state or people whose independence and/or integrity is threatened by external aggression." The proposed organization also pledged to help fellow veterans who had fallen on hard times and to seek official government recognition as veterans.[32]

This application caused some alarm in Prime Minister Pierre Elliott Trudeau's Liberal federal government. The Department of Consumer and Corporate Affairs was consulted and concluded: "We are unaware of any international legal obligations owed by Canada to Spain or any other country which would have relevance to the above application." The report continues:

> However we are somewhat concerned about the possible external political implications arising from the incorporation of such an association whose objectives are antagonistic to the existing regime in Spain ... The incorporation of such an association seems to us inopportune at a time when our relations with Spain may be entering a new phase with that country's adoption of a more outward-looking policy. However it is for you to determine whether these external political implications should have a bearing on the application before you.

The report also notes that the RCMP has extensive files on the former volunteers and suggests they be consulted.[33]

The government had already contacted the RCMP. The police force was also opposed to the veterans' application. Assistant Commissioner Louis Raymond Parent, director of security and intelligence, wrote E.R. Rettie, the undersecretary of state for external affairs, outlining the history of the Mackenzie-Papineau Battalion, as understood by the RCMP. Parent noted that an organization calling itself the Veterans of the Mackenzie-Papineau Battalion became defunct in 1948 and then emerged again in 1967 with a total of twenty-six members. "Since the history of this organization has been greatly influenced by the Communist Party, it is suggested that the letters patent be discouraged," Parent wrote. "This organization would undoubtedly be utilized by the Communist Party of Canada as a front organization to further their cause."[34]

Yet the influence of the party among the Spanish war veterans had weakened dramatically from its already shaky foundations during the civil war, and there is little compelling evidence to suggest that an association of Canadian veterans would function as a communist front.

Nevertheless, on 15 December 1970, the Department of External Affairs concluded that the association, if formed, could hurt Canada's relations with Spain and therefore the application should not be accepted.[35] Evidently, the Canadian government so valued its relations with a squalid and fading dictator that it put Franco's concerns above those of its own citizens. It strains credulity to think that Francisco Franco would find out or even care about an application for non-profit status made by a group of one or two dozen senior citizens in Canada. But the very possibility was too much for Ottawa to countenance. The archives do not contain a copy of the Canadian government's formal response to the veterans' application. However, given the blanket opposition to their proposal in government circles, it is almost certain that it was turned down.

The RCMP kept files on the aging Canadian veterans until at least 1984, when most of those still living were in their seventies and eighties.[36] By the time they reached retirement age, Mac-Pap veterans who were still politically active were most interested in appealing for the end of Franco's now decrepit dictatorship, gathering material for a book, and planning reunions with their former comrades. What the RCMP discovered can hardly be classified as a national threat: "Of 1,200 Canadians spending time in Spain from 1936 on with the Mac-Pap Battalion, only 150 are presently alive and they are scattered around Canada," reads a 1980 memorandum. "The majority of these men do not belong to the party, however their political motivations are more in keeping with the NDP philosophies."[37]

This report was written more than forty years after the Spanish Civil War ended. There may well be more recent files that have not yet been declassified. For all their human faults, and for all the ugly complexities in the war they chose to fight, the Canadians who fought in Spain had the moral clarity to face the rising menace of fascism when most of their countrymen chose to look away. They joined a war of which their government and the RCMP did not approve. It seems they were never quite forgiven.

Conclusion

Sometimes lost causes are worthwhile.

George Watt, CBC interview with Mac Reynolds, c. 1965

The ultimate fate of all of the almost 1,700 Canadians who fought in Spain will never be known with certainty. More than 400 were killed or went missing and can be presumed to have perished. But scores of bodies were never recovered, and none has a marked grave. Most survivors did not escape unharmed by either wounds or sickness. The war carved mental scars as well. At least four volunteers later committed suicide. Art Siven, who left his home in Port Arthur expecting not to live, survived unscathed, as did his friend who reassured him that there has never been a war in which everyone dies. But many of their fellow miners and lumberjacks from northern Ontario did not come home. It was a tremendous collective sacrifice, for both the dead and the living.

Few who took part, however, expressed regret. "It's probably one of the only decent things I've ever done as an adult," said Victor Himmelfarb, who worked with a medical unit in Spain.[1] "I don't regret anything I did," echoed Fred Kostyk. "I tried to do something for humanity, for the Spanish people."[2]

This does not mean that veterans were immune to doubts about how the war was fought. In 1977, one veteran said that what he learned about the Soviet Union in the years after the Spanish Civil War caused him to re-evaluate his decision to fight in a largely communist army:

> In retrospect I do wonder, if the Spanish Republic would have been victorious over Franco, whether the civil war would have ended there, or whether the Communist Party would have fought on to its political victory over all the other elements in the Spanish spectrum. That feeling first occurred to me when we went to Barcelona in the spring of 1937, and I suppose at that time I would have gone along with that, blindly perhaps, because in those days Stalin was still a Saint ... However, I believe that at the time in 1937 I did the right thing.[3]

For many Canadian survivors of the war, including those who did not join veterans' groups or attend commemorations, Spain remained the central experience of their lives, a time when youth, idealism, and the intensifying experience of war coalesced. Like soldiers everywhere, some found returning to peace difficult. One Canadian, Mortimer Kosowatski (Jack Steele), could not handle living in Canada as a civilian after his return in October 1937. He sailed again for Spain in spring of 1938. "I know what the problem was," Walter Dent told an interviewer in 1980,

> I know exactly what it was. If I tried to explain to you what we were going through … what do you see? You've got an idealistic picture of a bunch of men out there fighting for liberty and fighting for freedom and all these things. You don't know about the dirt and the mud and the flies on the mess tent, and the latrines when we couldn't get lime to cover them properly … How do you explain this to people? How do you tell them, people who never had to go through anything of this type? How do you explain it to them? And you know that you can't. And this bothered Jack Steele so much that he just could not adapt to normal life again here in Canada. He requested to be returned to Spain and he was killed the first month after he got back.[4]

For others, even as the years passed, memories of the war periodically forced themselves back into the veterans' day-to-day lives. John "Paddy" McElligott returned to his life as a sailor after the Second World War. In 1947, his ship stopped at Barcelona. Walking through the city, he saw one of his former civil war commanders now working as a street-side shoe shiner. McElligott sat at his commander's stool and, although the two men recognized each other, they said nothing. The Spaniard, however, scrawled an address on a scrap of paper and tucked it inside McElligott's pant leg. When McElligott arrived at the address, in Barcelona's red light district, ten former members of the International Brigades, all Spaniards, were there to meet him. They hugged and kissed him and, as McElligott recalled years later, "tears just rolled down my goddamned cheeks."[5]

Thirty years later, the Canadian veteran Jim Higgins was unexpectedly contacted by a Spaniard who had moved to Canada. It was Manuel Alvarez, the young boy whom Higgins had saved from a flash flood after the nationalist bombing of a water reservoir in Corbera during the Ebro offensive of 1938. Alvarez had spent forty years trying to find Higgins and was finally successful. The two spent a weekend together at Higgins' home in Peterborough, Ontario. Higgins said their reunion made him believe in miracles.[6]

After Francisco Franco's death in 1975, which ended a dictatorship that had persisted for almost forty years, Canadian veterans began returning to Spain in greater numbers. During one visit to Teruel in 1979, Fred Mattersdorfer met a former nationalist officer who had also come to Teruel to confront and relive wartime memories. The Spaniard showed Mattersdorfer still-visible bullet holes in Teruel's walls, and the two veterans reminisced about the battle. The officer eventually invited Mattersdorfer to come back to his house, but Mattersdorfer could not bring himself to accept the hospitality of his former enemy.[7] On the same visit was George Fiwchuk, who had fought in Teruel with the Mackenzie-Papineau Battalion. He toured the battlefield with the aid of a cane, his face showing great strain as he laboured over the steep and rocky terrain. He frequently stopped to swallow pills for his weak heart. Fiwchuk suffered an attack and died that night. His comrades buried him in Spain.[8]

Few Spaniards wanted to confront the legacy of their civil war in the years immediately after Franco's death. For Spaniards, unlike the internationals who came to Spain, the civil war pitted families and neighbours against each other. And Franco's war against his political opponents did not end with the nationalist victory in 1939. Tens of thousands of republicans were executed after hostilities ceased; many others were imprisoned and used as slave labour. Deep fissures still ran through Spanish society when Franco died, and some feared that probing them too deeply might rupture the country. An unspoken *pacto del olvido,* an agreement to forget, governed Spain's relationship with its past. In recent years, however, this has changed. In Marçà and Falset, the Catalan villages where Canadians were stationed before and after the Ebro offensive of 1938, small commemorative events have been held. The grave of John Cookson, an American veteran of the International Brigades, has been cleared of the undergrowth that hid it for decades, and fresh flowers are periodically placed on his tombstone. The ashes of an Argentine veteran were scattered there in 2005. Many foreigners attend these events, but local residents are beginning to come as well. It has been seventy years, and for much of that time they said little about it, but Spaniards cannot forget their civil war or those who fought it. "Sí, hombre," an elderly man told a visiting researcher in a village near Marçà in 2003. "I remember the Canadians. I remember everyone who came here."

But what did the International Brigades and the Canadians who fought in its ranks actually accomplish? It is a difficult question – and a painful one for many veterans. "We didn't accomplish what we started out to do," Ron Liversedge said thirty years after the war, when asked if he had any regrets. His voice, recorded on an old reel-to-reel audiotape, sounds on the verge of breaking. "We didn't achieve what we set out to achieve ... I don't know how to express it. All that we have left is that we failed."[9] On one level, Liversedge is unavoidably correct. Despite the sacrifices of thousands of internationals and tens of thousands of Spaniards, the Spanish Republic lost the war.

Some veterans of the International Brigades have said that the Spanish Civil War was the first battle of the Second World War. In this interpretation of history, the International Brigades played the same role as the legendary King Leonidas and his three hundred Spartans who faced a Persian invasion of

Greece and fought to the death at Thermopylae while the rest of the country rallied behind them. "We lost," Fred Kostyk said, and then added, "I made up for it in the Second World War."[10]

The democratic world, however, failed to rally behind the Spanish Republic. Britain, France, Canada, and the United States did not rouse themselves to confront fascism's growth despite the stand that thousands of their countrymen made in Spain. The democracies avoided war until it was forced on them. The Canadians who recognized the danger of fascism and volunteered to fight it were abandoned and ultimately defeated. Those who did so can claim only a moral victory – the belief, as George Watt put it, in the epigraph that opens this chapter, that even lost causes can be worthwhile.

Postscript

When I began researching this book in 2002, fewer than ten Canadian veterans of the Spanish Civil War were known to be living. In the twilight of lives that are already far longer than the time allotted to most men, the survivors now dwell not so much on the politics of the war as on the memories of lost friends. "There are people right through life who you feel close to and you want to know better, but perhaps you hadn't the opportunity," Jules Paivio said recently in an interview at his Sudbury home that stretched long into the evening. "The thing is this. You look back through life – and I think you'll find this, too – it is the comrades and the people who you are impressed by. You almost fall in love with them."[1] Other veterans return Paivio's affection. The American Mac-Pap veteran Carl Geiser asked after him when I spoke with Geiser over the phone in 2002. They stood beside each other and faced a firing squad; it is a difficult thing to forget.[2]

Paivio, slim and wiry with a soft voice and bright blue eyes, is still actively involved in commemorative activities and recently saw through to completion the erection in Ottawa of a statue dedicated to Canadian veterans of the Spanish Civil War. It is unlikely that building such a monument in the Canadian capital would have been possible at any point in the last sixty years.

I visited Fred Kostyk twice in Montreal, where he lived with his daughter and son-in-law before passing away in October 2005. "I'm doing as good as I can in this goddamned son-of-a-bitchin' capitalist system," he said, and he laughed to show he was not completely serious. He also joked about a comrade in Spain who demanded to be buried face down so the world could kiss his arse. "He was hit. And we did bury him like that," Kostyk said.[3] He later served in the Canadian army and fought with such bravery across Normandy and northwest Europe that a lake in the Prairies was named after Kostyk and his brothers. He had few mementos from his time in Spain and offered to give them away. He named his pet budgie Pablo.

William Krehm, the young man who travelled alone to Spain hoping to witness the dawn of a social revolution and instead spent three months in a

Barcelona jail, today lives in a handsome house in the east end of Toronto. His home is filled with natural light, colourful carpets and tapestries, and large antique-looking religious artifacts – Byzantine-style paintings and Jewish menorahs. Krehm achieved a degree of financial independence through a construction business that he started upon his return to Canada and has been able to spend much of the last twenty or thirty years indulging his passion for studying and writing about economic history and reform. He publishes a regular journal on the topic.

Spain and the Spanish Civil War are no longer focal points of Krehm's life and have not been for many decades. He's had a full life since and is now as committed to the study of economics as he once was to combating fascism. Krehm has also had success relearning how to play the violin, as he wanted to do some sixty years ago. The last time I saw him, in November 2004, he was hosting the four other members of a string quintet, who were meeting at his home that evening to practise. Krehm has no regrets about taking part in the Spanish Civil War. He believed in the anti-fascist cause. Going to Spain gave him a window on history as it unfolded. And besides, he asked, "How can one regret one's life?"[4]

In the summer of 2002, I telephoned David Constant, the son of Maurice Constant – a former student at the University of Toronto who became a scout in the International Brigades and remained in Barcelona until moments before Franco's troops marched through the city. I explained to David that I was beginning a doctorate at the University of Oxford in the fall and that I was hoping to speak with his father about his experiences in Spain.

"Well, there's a problem," David said. "My father's dying."

I apologized and was about to hang up the phone when David interrupted. "You don't understand. I think he'd like to speak with you."

Maurice Constant did want to speak with me. The next day I reached him by phone at the palliative care wing of Grand River Hospital in Kitchener-Waterloo. His voice was weak and airy. He needed to stop for breath every few words. He told me to come see him in the afternoon: earlier in the day the pain was too severe for him to talk much; later the morphine made him groggy.

I visited Constant a few days later, on a hot and breezeless August day with no hint of the approaching fall. I had seen in archived personnel files a grainy black-and-white photograph of Constant as he looked during the war – a young man with thick, swept-back hair, large thoughtful eyes, and a mouth set in what is either a grimace or a barely suppressed smile. Sixty-five years later, lying in his hospital bed, Constant appeared tiny and frail. His hand when I shook it felt weightless. On the walls surrounding him were photographs and memorabilia from the Spanish Civil War – the things he wanted to keep with him at the end of his life. His wife, almost blind, watched over him.

We both knew he was dying, but Constant wanted to impart as much infor-mation as possible. He coolly tried to work out how long he had left – weeks only – and how many more times I could visit before he would be unable to help more. We spoke for about an hour, stopping frequently so Constant could rest. He would drop his head onto the pillow, close his eyes, and breathe audibly for several seconds before waving his fingers and whispering, "Okay. Let's continue …"

Toward the end of the interview, I had been pressing him to tell me more about the role of the Communist Party in the International Brigades and his relationship with the party. It is an important issue, but for decades Franco apologists dismissed foreign volunteers in Spain as Stalin's dupes, and Constant was clearly getting sick of discussing the topic. He looked even more exhausted than he had when I arrived. I changed the subject and we concluded the interview.

But leaving the palliative care wing, I realized I had forgotten a notebook in Constant's room and retraced my steps to get it. He looked only moderately surprised to see me when I re-emerged beside his bed.

"You know, there's one more thing," he said, his voice hoarse and a little louder now. "They said we were legends. They called us the legends of the International Brigades."

Maurice Constant was not a vain man, and I do not think he ever considered himself a legend. I think his point was simply that there was a time and a place when people thought he was a legend and that all the men who came to Spain to fight fascism deserved the term. Such a time and place must have felt a long way away from the palliative care wing of a suburban Ontario hospital.

Standing there at the foot of his bed, I wanted to say something that sounded reassuring instead of accusatory, to tell him I thought that what he did was brave and good. But I did neither of these things. I simply thanked him again and walked out of his room. And, of course, Constant had seen and done far too much to really care what I thought of him. But thinking back now, five years later, I wish I had told him just the same.

Appendix
Canadian Volunteers

NAME	HOME	ETHNICITY	DATE OF BIRTH	OCCUPATION	FINAL STATUS
Abocheski, George	–	Ukrainian	–	miner	MIA, Gandesa, Apr. 1938
Abramovic, Jural	Cooksville, ON	Croatian	2 Feb. 1901	–	survived
Abramson, Samuel	Montreal	Canadian, Jewish	16 Jan. 1909	driver, writer	WIA, survived
Adamic, Joseph	Edmonton; Vancouver	–	10 Oct.1915	bookkeeper	KIA, Sept. 1938
Adamic, Michael	–	–	–	–	MIA, Retreats
Aleksic, Petar	–	Serbian	–	–	survived
Alexiuk, Dimitro	Vita, MB	Canadian	11 Feb. 1916	–	MIA, Gandesa, Apr. 1938, fate unknown
Aiksnys, Boleslavas	Calgary; Lethbridge	Lithuanian	20 Aug.1906	–	KIA, Brunete, 6 July 1937
Allan, Ted	Montreal	Canadian, Jewish	25 Jan. 1916	journalist	survived
Allen, James	Winnipeg	–	c.1897	–	fate unknown
Allstop, Geoffrey	Stoney Mountain, MB	English	26 Feb. 1904	–	KIA, Caspe, Mar. 1938
Ambroziak, Petar	Montreal	Canadian	21 Oct. 1917	worker	survived
Ames, Bruce	Vancouver; Kenora, ON	–	c. 1913	miner	survived
Anderson, Harry	Capelton, QC; Winnipeg	Canadian	8 July 1902	lumberjack, steelworker	WIA, survived
Anderson, Hugh	Timmins, ON; Regina	–	–	–	survived
Anderson, Ivor "Tiny"	Vancouver	Danish	11 Jan. 1909	miner	KIA, Sierra de Pàndols, Aug. 1938
Anderson, Samuel	Vancouver	Irish	3 June 1904	painter	survived
Anderson, V.B.	Winnipeg	–	–	–	survived
Andreeff, Ivan	Toronto	Macedonian	12 June 1910	cook	survived
Angell, William	Winnipeg; Brandon, MB	–	c. 1917	truck driver	survived
Anst, Wilfred	Ottawa; Edmonton	–	c. 1909	–	WIA, survived
Antoniuk, Pavlo	Toronto; Kapuskasing, ON	Ukrainian	11 Apr. 1911	lumberjack	survived
Anttila, Erland	Port Arthur, ON	Finnish	c. 1893	–	WIA, survived
Ardelsh, P.	Schumacher, ON	Ukrainian	–	–	fate unknown
Aristov, Grigor	–	Slavic	–	–	fate unknown
Armit, Andrew	Hamilton	Scottish	6 Jan. 1907	miner	KIA, Brunete, 6 July 1937
Armitage, Joseph	Vancouver	English	c. 1902	coal miner	fate unknown
Armitage, Lucien	–	–	–	–	survived
Asalt, Arthur	–	–	–	–	survived
Ashplant, Arthur	Calgary	English	6 Nov. 1897	worker	survived
Aspey, William	Toronto	English	c. 1904	auto mechanic, sailor	survived
Atanasoff, Naiden	Toronto	Bulgarian	c. 1904	–	survived
Atanasoff, Nikola	Toronto	Macedonian	24 May 1906	–	survived
Aucoin, Thomas	b. Joliette, QC; Vancouver	French Canadian	20 Apr. 1915	worker	survived
Auerbach, Louis	Toronto; New York	Canadian	1 Jan. 1910	–	WIA, survived

Name	Location	Nationality	Date	Occupation	Fate
Augusta, Tony	Vancouver	—	—	—	WIA, fate unknown
Ausborn, Paul	Winnipeg	German	c. 1888	—	survived
Aviezora/Avinger, Elias	Montreal	Belarusian, Jewish	c. 1899	driver	KIA, Jarama, 22 Feb. 1937
Aylward, Lee (woman)	—	—	—	—	fate unknown
Babic, Anto/Tony	Vancouver	Croatian	c. 1900	—	KIA, Retreats, Apr. 1938
Babij/Costello, Frank/Bobby	Montreal; Vancouver	Canadian	24 Oct. 1914	road worker	survived
Bacic, Karlo	Noranda, QC; Montreal	Croatian	c. 1905	—	KIA, Fuentes de Ebro, Oct. 1937
Backler, Lionel Charles	Vancouver; Victoria	English	28 July 1913	journalist	KIA, died in Murcia hospital, Aug. 1937
Backman, Edvin	Vancouver	Finnish	9 Sept. 1901	miner	WIA, survived
Bagics, Jozsef	—	Hungarian	—	—	fate unknown
Bailey, Frank Thomas/Tom	Regina; Moose Jaw	English	1 Aug. 1901	salesman	WIA, survived
Bajuk, Martin	Timmins, ON	Slovenian	c. 1899	—	survived
Balciar, Pavel	—	Slovak	29 July 1898	—	survived
Balderson, James	Britannia Beach, BC; Vancouver	—	8 Nov. 1911	—	KIA, Teruel, Jan. 1938
Bally, Thomas	Toronto	Macedonian	c. 1892	—	KIA, died of wounds in Canada
Balogh, Ferenc	—	Hungarian	—	—	fate unknown
Balogh, Janos	Toronto	Hungarian	—	—	fate unknown
Balogh, Mihaly	Windsor; Toronto	Hungarian	9 Oct. 1901	worker	survived
Balos, Miha	Port Arthur, ON	Czechoslovakian	1 Sept. 1895	—	survived
Baltic, Luka	Port Arthur, ON; Toronto	Serbian	30 May 1900	shoemaker	survived
Balwar, Volodymar	Sudbury; Toronto	Ukrainian	17 June 1909	cook	survived
Bambrick/O'Hara, Arthur J.	Vancouver; Kirkland Lake, ON	Irish	14 Oct. 1915	miner, machinist	survived
Banic, Karlo	Toronto	Yugoslav	—	—	survived
Banner, Charles	New York	Canadian	—	—	MIA, Gandesa, Apr.1938, fate unknown
Barak, George	Toronto; Calgary	Czech	c. 1904	—	fate unknown
Baranowski, Joseph	several small towns in SK; Toronto	Canadian	26 Feb. 1909	—	survived
Barcena, Isidore/Frank	Toronto; New York	American	11 Aug. 1895	cigar maker	WIA, survived
Barilot	Toronto	—	—	—	KIA
Barna	—	Hungarian	—	—	fate unknown
Barski, Ben	—	—	—	—	MIA
Bartolotta, Charles	Hamilton	Canadian	28 Oct. 1917	student	KIA, Sierra Cavalls, Sept. 1938
Barton, Albert	Vancouver	—	—	—	MIA, Feb. 1938
Bartski, Joseph	Winnipeg	—	—	—	survived
Bartus, Ignac	Toronto	Hungarian	19 Oct. 1901	cook	WIA, survived
Baryla, Franciszek	Toronto; Kenora, ON; Winnipeg	Ukrainian	c. 1908	—	survived
Baryluk, Michael/Theodore	Fort William, ON; Winnipeg	Ukrainian	c. 1904 or 1907	—	KIA

NAME	HOME	ETHNICITY	DATE OF BIRTH	OCCUPATION	FINAL STATUS
Basic, Anton	Noranda, QC	Croatian	c. 1910		KIA
Batson, Percy	Hamilton	English	c. 1915	truck driver	KIA, Teruel, died of wounds, Feb. 1938
Batymer, Fred					MIA, Retreats
Baudy, Jack	Toronto				fate unknown
Baurman, E.	Vancouver				fate unknown
Baxter, Frank	b. NB; Crows Nest Pass, BC	Canadian	9 May 1898		WIA, survived
Bayden, James	Winnipeg	English	5 Aug. 1895	farmer	WIA, survived
Baynham, Ralph		Australian			KIA
Bazin, Jozsef		Hungarian	c. 1902		survived
Beamish					fate unknown
Beasor, Charles	Nanaimo, BC	English	c. 1913	painter	WIA, survived
Beattie, Henry Scott	Nanaimo, BC	Canadian	21 Mar. 1913	baker, printer	WIA, survived
Beaulieu, Albert/Bob/Bert	Vancouver; Montreal; Trois Pistoles, QC	French Canadian	19 Aug. 1906	lumberjack	POW, survived
Beaumont, John					fate unknown
Beckett, Thomas	Moose Jaw	Canadian	c. 1915	construction worker	KIA, Jarama, Feb. 1937
Bedard, Joseph	Hawkesbury, ON; Montreal	French Canadian	c. 1895	accountant	survived
Beeching, William	Regina	Canadian	22 June 1913		survived
Beegachewski, Taras	Toronto	Ukrainian			fate unknown
Begelia, Vladimir	Port Arthur, ON; White River, ON	Russian	15 June 1911	lumberjack, worker	KIA
Beke, Daniel	Lethbridge	Hungarian	17 Mar. 1913 farmer	coal miner, driver,	survived
Bélanger, Joseph	Montreal; Winnipeg	French Canadian	13 Aug. 1915	auto mechanic worker	survived
Bell, Alfred	Toronto	English	19 Mar. 1896		survived
Bell, John/James	Salmon Arm, BC; Vancouver	Scottish	c. 1905	mechanic, steelworker	WIA, survived
Bellie, J.					MIA
Benham, Lionel	b. Glace Bay, NS; Vancouver				fate unknown
Benko, Petru	Edmonton	Ukrainian	16 July 1900		survived
Benter, Michael	Winnipeg	Austrian	4 Sept. 1899	factory worker, railway worker	KIA, Gandesa, 1938
Bepirstis, Petras	Toronto; Cochrane, ON	Lithuanian	16 Sept. 1891	carpenter, farmer	survived
Berenic, Ivan	Vancouver	Croatian	c. 1908		KIA, July 1937
Berezca, Michael	Toronto	Ukrainian	11 Aug. 1903		WIA, survived
Berg, Nels	Bloomfield, NS	Swedish			fate unknown

Name	Location	Ethnicity	Birth date	Occupation	Fate
Bergeron, Edmond	Quebec; Montreal; Winnipeg	French Canadian	18 May 1909	lumberjack, steel rigger	survived
Bernstock, George	–	German	–	–	fate unknown
Berthusz, Paul	Hamilton	Hungarian	6 Oct. 1900	worker	survived
Bethune, Norman	Gravenhurst, ON; Montreal	Canadian	3 Mar. 1890	doctor	survived
Bibrechan, F.	–	Ukrainian	–	–	fate unknown
Bidiuk, Ivan	Toronto	Ukrainian	18 May 1904	–	survived
Biglow, Peter	b. Nairn Centre, ON; Vancouver	Canadian	25 Apr. 1904	electrician	WIA, survived
Bigras, Alcide	Timmins, ON; Winnipeg	French Canadian	c. 1914	worker	KIA, Quinto, 24 Aug. 1937
Bigwood, Ernest	b. Montreal; Vancouver	Canadian	26 June 1901	electrician	survived
Biles, Norman	–	–	–	–	fate unknown
Bileski, William	Port Arthur, ON	Ukrainian	–	–	fate unknown
Bilka, Pavel	Hamilton; Chatham, ON	Slovak	c. 1899	–	hospitalized, survived
Billigan, Bert	–	–	–	–	fate unknown
Bilodeau, Roger	Quebec; Montreal	French Canadian	26 Mar. 1905	office worker, pilot	hospitalized, survived
Bilous, Nicholas	Kirkland Lake ON	Ukrainian	c. 1905	miner	KIA, Quinto, Aug. 1937
Bishop, Michael	Montreal	–	c. 1914	lumberjack	survived
Black, James	Kingston; Toronto	–	16 Jan. 1911	masseur	KIA, Retreats, Mar. 1938
Blackburn, Tommy	Vancouver	–	–	–	KIA, Retreats, Apr. 1938
Blackley, Harry	Renfrew, ON	Scottish	1 Aug. 1906	–	survived
Blackman, Frank "Trapper"	Edmonton; Valemount, BC	–	5 Mar. 1913	trapper	POW, survived
Blaho, Imrich	Montreal	Czech	15 Feb. 1899	–	survived
Blaskiewicz/Blake, Stanley	b. Rossburn, MB; moved to US	Canadian	28 Sept. 1914	construction worker	fate unknown
Blazevich, Marko	Cadomin, AB	Croatian	c. 1902	miner	WIA, survived
Bier, Jack	Edmonton	–	–	–	KIA, Brunete, July 1937
Bichfeldt, Hendrick	–	Danish	–	machinist	fate unknown
Block, Joseph	Winnipeg; Toronto	Canadian	3 Nov. 1908	driver, linotype operator	survived
Bloom, John Oscar	Edmonton	–	c. 1913	–	KIA, Brunete, 6 July 1937
Bodnar, Walter	Toronto	Hungarian	–	–	fate uknown
Bodnarczuk, Mykhailo	Edmonton	Ukrainian	c. 1901	railway worker	WIA, survived
Bogner, Julius	Toronto	Hungarian	30 Mar. 1898	farmer, worker	survived
Bohmer, Walter	Toronto	German	c. 1905	–	KIA, Brunete, July 1937
Boivin, Edward	Winnipeg; Vancouver	French Canadian	25 Mar. 1906	baker	WIA, survived
Bojinoff, James	–	Bulgarian	–	–	KIA, Battle of the Ebro, 1938
Bolamchuk, John	–	–	–	–	fate unknown

NAME	HOME	ETHNICITY	DATE OF BIRTH	OCCUPATION	FINAL STATUS
Boland, Duncan	Vancouver; Montreal	Scottish	8 May 1902	printer	KIA, Teruel, 20 Jan. 1938
Bolf, Matija	Toronto	Croatian	13 Apr. 1900	miner	survived
Bollo, Jozsef	Toronto; Kapuskasing; Coldwater, ON	Hungarian	16 June 1905	driver, factory worker	survived
Borics, Jozsef	Montreal, Chatham, ON	Hungarian	c. 1902	–	KIA
Boss, Ray	Regina	–	c. 1899	–	WIA, fate unknown
Bothwell, Joe	Midland, ON	–	–	–	survived
Boulting	–	–	–	–	fate unknown
Bowman, Volodymyr	–	Ukrainian	–	–	fate unknown
Bowen, Cromwell	Toronto; Kirkland Lake, ON	Canadian	15 Mar. 1895	mechanic	POW, survived
Bowzailo, Harry	Athabasca, AB	Ukrainian	9 Dec. 1901	–	POW, survived
Boxer, Harry	Smith Falls, ON	Canadian, Jewish	7 Oct. 1909	salesman	fate unknown
Boyko, S.	Toronto	Ukrainian	–	–	survived
Boyuk, William	Copper Cliff, ON; Sudbury	Canadian	27 Sept. 1918	driver	survived
Bozinovic, N./Pande	Toronto	Macedonian	24 Feb. 1906	tailor	fate unknown
Brackenbury, Edward	Vancouver	English	c. 1899	driver	WIA, survived
Bradley, William	Montreal	Scottish	c. 1900	miner	survived
Brais, Napoleon	Toronto	French Canadian	5 Nov. 1905	–	survived
Bramberg, Ephraim	Toronto; Sudbury	Polish, Jewish	–	–	hospitalized, fate unknown
Brennan, William	b. Cobourg, ON;	Canadian	6 Mar. 1917	construction worker	WIA, survived
Brent, John/Jack	moved to Scotland as a child	Canadian	c. 1912	–	WIA, survived
Brezovik/Brusovitch, Albert	Pittsburgh, PA; Toronto	American	c. 1905	–	KIA, Battle of the Ebro, July 1938
Brisevac, Vaso	Port Arthur, ON	Serbian	15 Aug. 1895	lumberjack, mechanic	survived
Briski, Anton	Chicago	Yugoslav	–	–	KIA, Jarama, Mar. 1937
Bromberg, E.	Toronto	–	–	–	fate unknown
Brotman/Brown, Elie/Kenneth	St. Paul, MN	Canadian, Jewish	12 July 1911	barber	KIA, Fuentes de Ebro, Oct. 1937
Brown, Allan Clive	Calgary	Canadian	27 June 1913	–	KIA, died of wounds, June 1938
Brown, James Basil	b. NB; Vancouver; Winnipeg; Toronto	Canadian	18 Apr. 1899	farmer, worker	survived
Brown, Joseph	Vancouver; Toronto	Scottish	c. 1909	–	KIA
Brown, Len	Rockglen, SK	–	–	–	KIA, 1938
Brown, Richard de Witt	Hamilton; Vancouver	Scottish	c. 1915	miner	survived
Brown, Robert	–	–	–	–	MIA, Retreats, Mar. 1938
Brown, Samuel	Winnipeg; Vancouver	Irish	5 Mar. 1912	machinist	WIA, survived
Brown, William	Windsor	Canadian	–	–	fate unknown
Brown, William/John "Pop"	Windsor	–	c. 1893	–	survived

Name	Residence	Nationality	Birth date	Occupation	Fate
Brownlee, Robert	Vancouver; Smiths Falls, ON	Canadian	c. 1888	surveyor	hospitalized, survived
Brozovic, Sresko Filip	Toronto	Croatian	20 May 1905	shoemaker	KIA, Gandesa, Apr. 1938
Brudzhinsky, Felix	–	–	–	–	fate unknown
Brugere, Alfred	–	French Canadian	–	construction worker	KIA, Jarama, Feb. 1937
Brunet, Paul-Henri	Montreal	French Canadian	5 June 1904	–	MIA, Caspe, Mar. 1938
Brunner, Emeric Jack	Winnipeg	Hungarian	c. 1909	–	survived
Brusic, Anton T., aka Oscar Brikich	Kirkland Lake, ON	Croatian	6 Nov. 1905	miner	survived
Bubanecz, Janos	Lethbridge	Hungarian	c. 1900	–	survived
Buchanan, Stanley	Paris, ON; Winnipeg	–	c. 1909 or 1913	–	KIA
Bucior, Stanislaw	Port Arthur, ON	Polish	c. 1902	–	MIA, Caspe, Mar. 1938
Buckwell, Clifford	Vancouver	Canadian	24 Oct. 1909	teacher	survived
Buczkowski, Wazsyl	South Porcupine, ON	Ukrainian	15 Jan. 1912	worker	survived
Budgen, Clifford	Toronto	Canadian	c. 1913	truck driver	fate unknown
Budsinovitch, Jim	Toronto	Macedonian	–	–	hospitalized, survived
Budynkiewicz, Stefan	Toronto	Ukrainian	21 Feb. 1907	construction worker	survived
Budzinsky, Joseph	Toronto	–	c. 1901	chemist	fate unknown
Buhovics, Matyas	–	Hungarian	c. 1894	–	POW, survived
Bukovi, Mikalj	Montreal	Hungarian	c. 1904	worker	survived
Bullock, J.H.M.	–	–	–	–	WIA, survived
Buric, Ivan	Kirkland Lake, ON	Croatian	10 Nov. 1898	–	WIA, survived
Burke, Lee	b. Sydney, NS; Winnipeg; Toronto	Canadian	c. 1910	clerk, dockworker	POW, survived
Burns, Paul	Montreal	–	–	–	fate unknown
Burns, Samuel	–	English	21 Sept. 1904	–	KIA, Teruel, Jan. 1938
Burton, Albert Ernest "Yorkie"	Vancouver	English	11 Aug. 1908	miner	WIA, survived
Buss, Roy	Regina	German	c. 1906	carpenter	MIA, Retreats, Apr. 1938
Butler, Benjamin	Vancouver	Canadian	19 Aug. 1913	mechanic	survived
Butrey, Ivan	Toronto	Ukrainian	15 Aug. 1893	–	KIA, Gandesa, Apr. 1938
Butrimas/Butrim, Bolis/William	Winnipeg	Canadian	1 May 1912	–	MIA, Retreats, Mar. 1938
Butymer, Frederic	Timmins, ON	–	–	–	WIA, survived
Butyniec, Teodor, Fred	Fort William, ON	Ukrainian	c. 1898	–	fate unknown
Bzumik, Michael	–	–	–	–	survived
Cacic, Tomo	Toronto	Croatian	25 Sept. 1896	–	POW, survived
Cameron, James	Vancouver	Scottish	7 May 1910	fisherman	WIA, survived
Campbell, Charles	Hamilton	Scottish	19 June 1903	worker	survived
Campbell, George	Vancouver	English	5 Feb. 1900	–	KIA, Gandesa, 27 July 1938
Campbell, Joseph	Montreal	French Canadian	6 Jan. 1893	leather cutter	KIA, Jarama, 27 Feb. 1937

NAME	HOME	ETHNICITY	DATE OF BIRTH	OCCUPATION	FINAL STATUS
Campbell, Morrison	Kincardine, ON; Windsor	Canadian	11 Aug. 1914	–	survived
Carberry, Dominic	Calgary	Irish	c. 1907	–	survived
Carlson, Arvid	Port Arthur, ON	American	c. 1909	–	KIA, died of wounds sustained at Teruel
Carlson, Joseph	Delhi, ON	Swedish	c. 1885	–	KIA, Teruel, Jan. 1938
Carlstad, Earl	Calgary	Norwegian	–	–	WIA, survived
Carreteri, Tony Martin, aka José Fuentes	Montreal; Vancouver	Spanish	28 Mar. 1904	–	survived
Carter, James	Vancouver	Canadian	–	–	POW, survived
Cawston, John/Jack	Vancouver; Oregon	Canadian	1 Feb. 1899	mechanic	KIA, Retreats, Mar. 1938
Cecheff, Nicola	–	Bulgarian	–	–	fate unknown
Cecil-Smith, Edward	Toronto	English	3 Oct. 1903	journalist, machinist	WIA, survived
Chadanysiak, John	Windsor	–	–	–	fate unknown
Chalimoniuk, Stefan	Toronto	Polish	c. 1899	–	KIA, Battle of the Ebro, Aug. 1938
Chambers, Alex	Winnipeg	Scottish	2 Mar. 1898	grocer	WIA, survived
Chapin, M.	–	–	–	–	fate unknown
Charczuk, Feofan	Vancouver	Ukrainian	c. 1907	lumberjack	KIA, Feb. 1938
Chaudoin/Chardon, Norman	Vancouver; Prince George, BC	American	30 May 1916	mill worker	KIA, Retreats, Mar. 1938
Chega, William	Brockville, ON	Canadian	3 Aug. 1916	truck driver	WIA, survived
Cherep, Petro	–	Ukrainian	–	–	fate unknown
Cherrie, Charles	Regina; Toronto	–	c. 1903	machinist	hospitalized, survived
Chevalier, Alexander	Montreal; Yukon	Canadian	31 Dec. 1906	lumberjack	WIA, survived
Chiesz, G.	–	Ukrainian	–	–	fate unknown
Chizyk/Cizek, Mykola/Nicholas	Winnipeg; Toronto	Ukrainian	19 May 1909	butcher	survived
Chodur, Michael	Port Colborne, ON	Hungarian	c. 1886	–	KIA when *Ciudad de Barcelona* was torpedoed, 30 May 1937
Chollaux, Armand	–	French Canadian	–	–	survived
Christie, H.	b. Glace Bay, NS; Vancouver	–	–	–	survived
Christie, Timothy	Vancouver	Scottish	5 Jan. 1899	electrician	survived
Christoff, Gregory	Toronto	Macedonian	15 Aug. 1903	hotel worker	MIA, Retreats, Mar. 1938
Christy, Richard	Vancouver	Canadian	6 Mar. 1900	lumberjack	fate unknown
Cisko, Andy	Lethbridge	Hungarian	c. 1903	–	hospitalized, survived
Clarke, James William	Port Credit, ON; Toronto	Irish	c. 1900	printer	fate unknown
Clarkson, Red	–	–	–	–	MIA, Mar. 1938
Clement, T.	–	–	–	–	fate unknown
Cleveland, Ralph	Toronto	–	c. 1891	–	fate unknown

Name	Places	Nationality	Date	Occupation	Fate
Cleven, Randolph	Veteran, AB; Edmonton	Canadian	17 Apr. 1914	worker	WIA, survived
Cluny, Joshua Ward	b. Hillsboro, NB; Hamilton	Canadian	5 Feb. 1905	gardener	survived
Cochrane, James	Brussels, ON; Windsor	Canadian	4 July 1904	—	KIA, Segura de los Baños, Feb. 1938
Cochrane, Thomas "Pop"	Windsor	Irish	10 Dec. 1885	auto mechanic	WIA, survived
Cohen, Joseph	—	Jewish	—	—	survived
Cohen, Milton	Winnipeg; Montreal	American, Jewish	17 Feb. 1915	pharmacist	survived
Cohen, Saul Bernard	b. St. John, NB; Montreal; Chicago	Canadian, Jewish	22 June 1906	social worker	WIA, survived
Cohen, Sidney	Edmonton; Vancouver; Winnipeg	Canadian, Jewish	22 Dec. 1912	pharmacist	MIA, Apr. 1938
Coleman, Bryce Lloyd	Vanguard, SK; Regina	Canadian	5 May 1908	farm and ranch worker	KIA, Brunete, 6 July 1937
Collens/Cullen, Michael	Calgary	Ukrainian	28 Nov. 1897	farm worker, railway worker	WIA, survived
Conroy, Roy Edward	Vancouver	English	19 Dec. 1912	miner	survived
Constant, Maurice	Toronto	Canadian, Jewish	7 Jan. 1914	student, writer	WIA, survived
Cook	—	—	—	—	KIA
Cook, George	Toronto	Canadian	c. 1916	—	survived
Cookings, William Spencer	Toronto; Victoria	English	c. 1909	—	KIA, Feb. 1938
Coops, Jan William	Vancouver; Lynn Valley, BC; Saskatoon	Canadian	15 Dec. 1913	auto mechanic, driver	WIA, survived
Cop, Alojz	Toronto; Montreal	Croatian	c. 1902	miner	survived
Corak/Chorok, Ivan	Fort William, ON; Winnipeg	Croatian	c. 1904	restaurant worker	survived
Costone, Frank	—	—	—	—	fate unknown
Cote, Gilles	—	English	27 Apr. 17	—	fate unknown
Cowan, Tim	Toronto	English	c. 1917	—	survived
Cowan, Wilfred	Toronto; Winnipeg	Scottish	4 Oct. 1911	dockworker, painter	WIA, survived
Cowie, Charles	Douglas, Alaska	Aboriginal (American)	c. 1890	painter	hospitalized, survived
Cox, Thomas	—	—	—	—	MIA
Cressman, Elmer Allen	b. Regina; Nanaimo; Vancouver	Canadian	24 Feb. 1904	cowboy, farm worker, lumberjack	WIA, survived
Croll, John Watson	Regina	Scottish	7 Mar. 1907	carpenter	POW, survived
Crossley, Clyde Raymond	Nanaimo	American	24 Mar. 1916	worker	WIA, survived
Crozier, Eugene	Vancouver	—	—	lumberjack	hospitalized, survived
Csaszar, Jozsef	—	Hungarian	—	—	fate unknown
Cseriszuyes/Csizmar, Sandor	East Coulee AB	Hungarian	c. 1909	mechanic, miner	KIA, Sept. 1938

NAME	HOME	ETHNICITY	DATE OF BIRTH	OCCUPATION	FINAL STATUS
Cserny, Joseph	Lethbridge; Winnipeg; Regina	Hungarian	c. 1903	–	KIA, Sept. 1938
Csirmaz, Mihaly	Montreal	Hungarian	c. 1902	farm worker	survived
Csoke, Andras	Welland, ON	Hungarian	30 Nov. 1898	farmer	MIA, Retreats, Apr. 1938
Csulak, Andras	–	Hungarian	–	–	fate unknown
Csurgala, Jozsef	–	Hungarian	–	–	fate unknown
Csusko, Pal	–	Hungarian	–	–	fate unknown
Cullen, Eugene	b. Montreal; moved to US	Canadian, Jewish	12 Feb. 1913	engineer, union organizer	fate unknown
Cunningham, Andrew	Toronto	Scottish	c. 1906	–	KIA, Gandesa, 1938
Cunningham, George	Toronto; Milton, ON	Scottish	30 Dec. 1912	–	POW, survived
Cunningham, Terrence	Vancouver	English	c. 1913	lumberjack, miner	WIA, survived
Czyzewski, Jan	Mundare, AB; Toronto	Polish	c. 1903	–	WIA, survived
Dack, Steve	–	Polish	–	–	fate unknown
Dagesse, Percival	St. Catharines, ON	English	18 July 1914	–	POW, survived
Dahl, Eskil	Vancouver	Finnish	19 Jan. 1907	–	KIA, Retreats
Dale, Joseph	–	–	–	–	survived
Dalog, Fedor	Toronto; Sudbury	Ukrainian	16 Jan. 1893	–	survived
Dames, James	Montreal	Greek	12 Dec. 1896	salesman	WIA, fate unknown
Danek, Tom	Winnipeg; Windsor	Canadian	12 Nov. 1917	electrician	survived
Daneliuk, Michael	Hamilton	Ukrainian	–	–	fate unknown
D'Arcy, Owen	–	Scottish	c. 1907	–	WIA, survived
Da Silva, Joaquin	Vancouver	Canadian	24 Dec. 1906	worker	fate unknown
Dasit, R.C.	–	–	–	–	fate unknown
Dasovic, Steve	South Porcupine, ON; Vancouver	Croatian	c. 1901	–	KIA, Jarama
David, Reginald Charles	Vancouver	Welsh	30 Oct. 1909	medic	survived
Deck, John	New Westminster, BC	German	c. 1904	engineer	KIA, Brunete, 9 July 1937
Delaney, Gerald	b. Halifax; Montreal; Vancouver	French Canadian	04 Feb. 1909	–	POW, survived
Delaney, William	Sudbury	French Canadian	c. 1901	driver, factory worker, lumberjack	MIA, Retreats, Apr. 1938
Demers, Charles	–	English	10 May 1908	–	fate unknown
Demetrou, Demetres	–	Greek	–	–	KIA, Gandesa
Demianchuck, Nazar/Nikolai	Winnipeg	Ukrainian	2 Mar. 1906	lumberjack	KIA, 1937
Demianchuk, Peter	Toronto; Fernie, BC	Ukrainian	13 July 1907	driver, miner	survived
Demidiuk, Ivan	Sudbury	Belarusian	c. 1903	–	KIA
Denby, John	Toronto	–	c. 1902	clerk	survived

Name	Location	Ethnicity	Birth date	Occupation	Fate
Dent, Walter Everett	Parry Sound, ON; Toronto	Canadian	c. 1917	carpenter	WIA, survived
Dentry, Ernest William	Winnipeg	English	c. 1907	–	KIA, Retreats, Apr. 1938
Depope, Mate	Connaught, ON	Croatian	5 July 1906	miner	WIA, survived
Derawchuk, Peter	–	Ukrainian	–	–	hospitalized, fate unknown
Derencinovic, Johan	Vancouver	Croatian	18 Aug. 1905	miner	survived
Derkach, Ignatii	Val d'Or, QC; Timmins, ON	Ukrainian	c. 1899	miner	MIA
Derkacz, Nestor	–	Ukrainian	–	–	fate unknown
Derry, Joe	Toronto	–	–	–	fate unknown
Dettrich, Joseph	Vancouver	German	c. 1898	carpenter	MIA
Dewitt, Thomas	Windsor	Irish	17 Nov. 1903	clerk	survived
Diamond, James	Victoria	Scottish	11 May 1905	miner	survived
Dickie, Robert	Kirkland Lake, ON; Montreal	Scottish	12 Feb. 1898	–	POW, survived
Dietrich/Zacharik, Jacob/Joseph/Jack	Kamloops	Canadian	3 Oct. 1903	carpenter	WIA, survived
Djajic, Jovan	Timmins, ON	Croatian	14 Sept. 1903	–	survived
Dmitruk, Bartflom	The Pas, MB; Fort William, ON	Ukrainian	6 Nov. 1906	worker	survived
Dobrovolsky, Samuel	Val d'Or, QC; Toronto	Ukrainian	30 Jan. 1904	–	survived
Dobson, James Harry	Calgary; Vancouver	Canadian	19 Aug. 1913	construction worker	WIA, survived
Doherty, Bill	–	–	–	–	survived
Dolanchuk, John	Sudbury; Toronto	Ukrainian	c. 1895	worker	survived
Dolyniuk, Petro	Edmonton	Ukrainian	16 June 1904	truck driver	survived
Dometro, Steven	Toronto	–	c. 1898	electrician	fate unknown
Domjnovic, Mile	Delhi, ON	–	c. 1896	–	survived
Doroszuk, Stefan	Port Arthur, ON	Ukrainian	c. 1894	carpenter	KIA, Teruel, Jan. 1938
Douloff, John	Toronto	Macedonian	c. 1907	–	survived
Drasner, Anton/Tony	Toronto; Kirkland Lake, ON	Croatian	c. 1903	–	KIA
Dratva, Jan	Chatham, ON	Slovak	25 Dec. 1900	–	survived
Dregiel, Jewticki	Geraldton, CN; Sudbury; Kirkland Lake, ON	Ukrainian	c. 1886	miner	survived
Droch, Matao	Fort William, ON	Polish	8 Nov. 1901	blacksmith, lumberjack, mechanic	survived
Drolet, Maurice	Quebec	French Canadian	23 Apr. 1915	–	survived
Duan, Kelvin	BC; US	Canadian	–	sailor	KIA
Dubel/Duviel, Vincent	Toronto; Windsor	Polish	c. 1901	–	fate unknown
Dubic, Franjo	Schumacher, ON	Croatian	–	–	survived
Dubois	–	French Canadian	–	–	KIA

NAME	HOME	ETHNICITY	DATE OF BIRTH	OCCUPATION	FINAL STATUS
Dudka, Ivan	The Pas, MB	Ukrainian	6 July 1907	lumberjack	WIA, survived
Dufour, Paul	Montreal	French Canadian	9 Apr. 1918	steelworker	POW, survived
Dumas, Laurent	Quebec City; Montreal	French Canadian	8 July 1887	carpenter	hospitalized, survived
Dunlop, John	Winnipeg	Canadian	–	accountant	survived
Dunne, James	–	–	–	–	WIA, fate unknown
Dupak/Dupiak, Petro	Sudbury	Ukrainian	4 Dec. 1906	miner	survived
Duranchuk, Joe	–	Ukrainian	–	–	fate unknown
Dyer, Robert	Winnipeg	English	28 July 1908	worker	MIA, Retreats, Mar. 1938
Dyrovy, Mykhailo	Toronto	Ukrainian	c. 1901	shoemaker	fate unknown
Dziki, Michal	Fort William, ON	Ukrainian	2 Dec. 1900	farm worker	survived
Dzumaga, Michael	Winnipeg	Ukrainian	c. 1912		survived
Eacott, Charles	Coleman, AB	Canadian	23 Jan. 1910	miner	survived
Edwards, Lionel	b. Pine Lake, AB; Vancouver; Edmonton	Canadian	23 Oct. 1910	accountant	WIA, survived
Edwards, Thomas	Montreal; US	Canadian	12 June 1902	barber	survived
Edwardsen, Sverge/Eddie	Winnipeg	Norwegian	7 Oct. 1906	cook, CPC official, jeweller	WIA, survived
Efremov, Joseph	Toronto	Bulgarian	c. 1913	hotel worker	survived
Elams, Tauno	–	Finnish	–	–	KIA
Eldon, John	BC	–	–	–	fate unknown
Elendiuk, Nick/Mykola	Winnipeg	Canadian	2 Apr. 1911	cowboy	POW, survived
Elomaki, Matti	Copper Cliff, ON; Port Arthur, ON	Finnish	24 June 1902	lumberjack, miner	KIA, Fuentes de Ebro, Oct. 1937
Emery, Alf	–	–	–	–	MIA
Engstrom, Edwin	Lappe, ON	Finnish	3 Sept. 1907	–	survived
Epstein, Edward	–	Jewish	–	–	KIA, Retreats, 1938
Epstein, Hyman	b. Montreal; Ottawa; Vancouver; US	Canadian, Jewish	17 Jan. 1900	sailor	KIA, Retreats, 1938
Epstein, Milton	–	American, Jewish	8 May 1912	–	KIA, Brunete, July 1937
Epstein, Ruth (woman)	Toronto	Canadian	20 Mar. 1905	nurse	survived
Erdei, Gabor/Gabriel	Montreal	Hungarian	c. 1890	cook	survived
Erdeljack, Petar	Timmins, ON; Schumacher, ON; Kirkland Lake, ON	Croatian	13 July 1903	–	WIA, survived
Erenoff, A.	Toronto	Bulgarian	c. 1906	CPC official, journalist	fate unknown
Erick, Muni, aka Jack Taylor	Montreal	Ukrainian, Jewish	21 Mar. 1906		survived
Evans, Lloyd	b. Hamilton, PE; Regina; Winnipeg	Canadian	16 Apr. 1913		hospitalized, survived

Name	Location	Ethnicity	Birth date	Occupation	Fate
Evashuk, Max	Clair, SK	Ukrainian	7 July 1909	farm worker	WIA, survived
Ewen, James/Jim	Vancouver	Scottish	24 Dec. 1915	sailor	survived
Ewen/McEwen, William Alexander/Bruce	b. Waldeck, SK; Toronto	Canadian	31 July 1917	machinist	survived
Fabrituius, Tauno Leo	Toronto	Finnish	8 Nov. 1912		survived
Fairbanks, Wilfred	Winnipeg	English	c. 1912	miner	fate unknown
Falkowski, Nikodem	Toronto	Polish	18 Aug. 1909	miner	survived
Farkas, Alex/Sandor/Pal/Paul	Toronto	Hungarian	–		survived
Farkas, Ferenc	–	Hungarian	–		fate unknown
Farkas, Laszlo	–	Hungarian	c. 1914		fate unknown
Faulkner, Percy Howard	Vancouver	Canadian	31 Aug. 1908	lumberjack	WIA, survived
Feasy, Robert	–	–	–		hospitalized, fate unknown
Fedorchak, Michal	Hamilton	Slovak	10 Oct. 1888	mill worker	survived
Feher, Jozsek	–	Hungarian	c. 1907		fate unknown
Felton, Allan Field	b. Sooke, BC; Victoria	Canadian	12 Nov. 1914	pilot	hospitalized, survived
Fenton, Harry "Scotty"	Courtenay, BC; Edmonton	Scottish	8 Oct. 1904	lumberjack, union organizer	WIA, survived
Ferencz, Janos/Istevan	Taber, AB	Hungarian	c. 1905	miner	KIA, Sierra de Cavalls, Sept. 1938
Ferguson, John	Edmonton	Scottish	c. 1893	student, worker	KIA
Ferrier, William/Marcelin	b. Montreal Toronto; Regina	French Canadian	23 Mar. 1918	coal miner	survived
Filkohazi, Emerich	Drumheller, AB	Hungarian	8 Apr. 1903	blacksmith	KIA, Retreats, Apr. 1938
Finnigan, John	Winnipeg	Irish	28 Mar. 1909	truck driver	MIA, Retreats, Apr. 1938
Firmin, John Charles	Calgary; Travers, AB; Lethbridge	English	c. 1914	truck driver	POW, survived
Fiwchuk, George	Timmins, ON	Ukrainian	10 Jan. 1914	lumberjack	WIA, survived
Fleming, Sheridan	Cochrane, ON	Canadian	15 Sept. 1915		KIA, died in hospital of wounds sustained at Gandesa, Aug. 1938
Flovecheff, Gregor	Vancouver; Toronto	–	–		survived
Flynn, Richard	Halifax; Vancouver	Canadian	c. 1912	worker	KIA, Retreats
Fobert, Cecil Laurence	Saskatoon; Vancouver	Canadian	1 May 1914		WIA, survived
Fodey, William	b. Lansdowne, ON; Toronto	Canadian	20 Oct. 1900		WIA, survived
Fogarty, Eugene	Vancouver; Montreal	Canadian	c. 1897	doctor, possibly fraudulent	fate unknown
Foley, Harry	b. Collingwood, ON; Calgary; Windsor	Canadian	15 Mar. 1909	sailor, tanner	survived
Foma, Alex	–	Ukrainian	–		fate unknown
Forrest, William	–	–	–		survived

NAME	HOME	ETHNICITY	DATE OF BIRTH	OCCUPATION	FINAL STATUS
Forsman, Walter	–	Finnish	c. 1912	–	KIA, possibly of sickness, July 1938
Fournier, Ed	Montreal	French Canadian	–	–	fate unknown
Fowle, John	Toronto	English	c. 1902	journalist, salesman	MIA, Retreats, Mar. 1938
Foy, Laurence	Montreal	French Canadian	3 May 1909	lumberjack, painter, teacher	hospitalized, survived
Franchuk, Jozef	Winnipeg	Polish	c. 1910	barber, lumberjack	survived
Francis/Fronczysty, Karl/Karol	Winnipeg	Polish	c. 1903	farm worker	KIA when Ciudad de Barcelona was torpedoed, 30 May 1937
Frantisek, Maxim	Chatham, ON; Delhi, ON	Slovak	15 Nov. 1901	–	fate unknown
Fraser, Don	Calgary	–	–	–	fate unknown
Frederick, William	b. Ottawa; Vancouver; Toronto	Canadian	15 Jan. 1914	worker	WIA, survived
Friend/Frund, Charles	Hamilton	–	c. 1910	journalist, textile worker	KIA
Fromberg, Ellis	Vancouver	Swedish	8 May 1904	lumberjack, telegrapher	survived
Gabor, Erdar	–	–	c. 1892	–	fate unknown
Gabryluk/Gabriel, Stepan/Steve	Port Arthur, ON	Ukrainian	20 Oct. 1895	–	survived
Gabrylyk/Gabriel, Danilo	Kenora, ON; Port Arthur, ON	Ukrainian	27 Dec. 1903	blacksmith, lumberjack, railway worker	WIA, survived
Gahm, Sven	Halifax	–	–	–	fate unknown
Gainhorst, T.	Timmins, ON	–	–	–	fate unknown
Gal, Janos	Lethbridge	Hungarian	–	–	survived
Galka	Fort William, ON	Polish	–	–	fate unknown
Gallagher, Leo	Toronto	–	–	–	fate unknown
Gallow, John Alexander	Vancouver	Scottish	19 June 1910	–	WIA, survived
Gangarossa, Giuseppe	Montreal	Canadian	22 May 1911	–	survived
Garcia, Andres Menandes	Montreal; US	Spanish	c. 1900	–	KIA, Jarama, 27 Feb. 1937
Gardiuk, John	Winnipeg	–	–	–	WIA, survived
Garner, Hugh	Toronto	Scottish	22 Feb. 1913	salesman	hospitalized, survived
Garrow, Clifford	b. Lac du Bonnet, MB; Vancouver	Canadian	28 June 1911	–	survived
Garrow, George	b. Winnipeg; Vancouver	Canadian	16 Aug. 1913	–	survived
Garzyz, Fedor	Toronto	Ukrainian	–	–	fate unknown
Gasgrovaz, John	–	–	–	–	fate unknown
Gaspar, Ladislav	Hamilton	Czechoslovakian	c. 1905	–	survived

Name	Place	Ethnicity	Birth date	Occupation	Fate
Gasparac, Ivan	Sudbury	Croatian	12 Dec. 1904	miner	survived
Gawda, Wladyslaw	Port Arthur, ON	Polish	c. 1909	–	KIA, Mar. 1938
Gawliuk, Thomas	Guelph, ON	Canadian	19 Apr. 1910	–	MIA
Gawrycki, Walter	Vancouver	Belarusian	7 Mar. 1907	lumberjack	WIA, survived
Gendy	–	Polish	–	–	fate unknown
Genge, Josep	Montreal	Romanian	1 May 1906	–	MIA, Mar. 1938
Gergonne, Carl	Toronto	Finnish	–	–	survived
Germain, Jerry	Montreal; Toronto	French Canadian	–	–	survived
Gesjetgm, G.	Vancouver	–	–	–	survived
Getchoff, Nikola	Timmins, ON; South Porcupine, ON	Bulgarian	30 Apr. 1903	–	survived
Gibbons, Joseph	–	English	–	–	fate unknown
Gibson, Patrick	–	Irish	–	–	survived
Gideon, Maynard	Montreal	–	–	–	survived
Gieblich, George	–	–	–	–	ill, fate unknown
Gilbank, Jack	Duncan, BC	–	–	–	fate unknown
Gillian, Andras	Timmins, ON; Driftwood, ON	Hungarian	c. 1904	blacksmith	KIA, Retreats, Mar. 1938
Gilligan, Bert	Vancouver	English	18 Nov. 1904	–	hospitalized, survived
Gillis, Roderick	Winnipeg; Glace Bay, NS; Thorold, ON	Scottish	11 Dec. 1900	miner	KIA, Fuentes de Ebro, 13 Oct. 1937
Gillstrap, John	Vancouver; Winnipeg; Saskatoon	–	c. 1910	medical student	WIA, survived
Girard, Joseph-Lucien	–	–	c. 1915	driver	fate unknown
Gislason, Harold	Vancouver	–	c. 1912	–	fate unknown
Gleadhill, Thomas	Vancouver	English	c. 1915	–	WIA, survived
Glenn, Joseph	Toronto	Canadian	17 Mar. 1915	machinist	survived
Glow, Gerald	Winnipeg	Canadian, Jewish	7 June 1913	musician, upholsterer	WIA, survived
Glowacki/Glogowski, Bazyli/Wasil	–	–	–	–	KIA
Godin, Emery	b. St. Léolin, NB; Timmins, ON	Polish	2 June 1900	worker	survived
Goguen, Emil	b. NB; Vancouver	French Canadian	1 July 1900	construction worker, lumberjack	WIA, survived
Gold, Irving	–	–	–	–	MIA
Goldenberg, Israel/José	Winnipeg; Toronto	Ukrainian, Jewish	13 Oct. 1909	furrier	WIA, survived
Goldiawecz, William	Winnipeg	–	–	–	fate unknown
Goldman, Emma (woman)	Canada; US	Lithuanian, Jewish	–	–	survived
Gombas, Antal	Windsor	Hungarian	c. 1905	–	fate unknown
Gongora, Emilio	–	Spanish	c. 1903	–	survived

NAME	HOME	ETHNICITY	DATE OF BIRTH	OCCUPATION	FINAL STATUS
Goodison, Michael	–	–	–	–	MIA
Gordon, Joe	–	–	c. 1914	–	WIA, survived
Gordon, Robert James	Douglastown, SK; Timmins, ON	Canadian	14 June 1914	driver	KIA, Gandesa, July 1938
Gordon, William	Montreal	Canadian, Jewish	c. 1915	mechanic	survived
Gordziejuk, Ignacy	Winnipeg	Polish	15 July 1900	–	WIA, survived
Gosselin, Ernest	Montreal	French Canadian	c. 1910	–	KIA when *Ciudad de Barcelona* was torpedoed, 30 May 1937
Goszbonyi, Ferenc	Winnipeg	Hungarian	c. 1891	–	survived
Gouette, Ernest	Victoria Harbour, ON; Timmins, ON; Toronto	French Canadian	19 May 1903	–	survived
Gough, Joe	Montreal	–	–	–	fate unknown
Grabchuk, Hendrick	–	Ukrainian	–	–	survived
Graham, Walter James	Vancouver	English	25 June 1912	–	WIA, survived
Grainger, John Douglas	b. Fort William, ON; Winnipeg	Canadian	21 Feb. 1906	car salesman, clerk, driver, journalist	survived
Grainger, Percy	Toronto; Hamilton	Scottish	c. 1889	–	survived
Grant, Lewis Charles	Calgary; Vancouver	German	16 May 1905	–	POW, survived
Grassl, Adolf	Montreal	Canadian	3 Oct. 1898	–	hospitalized, survived
Gray, Arthur	Toronto	Canadian, Jewish	31 Jan. 1911	clerk	POW, survived
Greenberg, Russel, aka Ross Russell	b. Toronto; Montreal	Lithuanian	c. 1903	miner	WIA, survived
Gregore/Gregorvich, Frank	Winnipeg; Vancouver; Bienfait, SK	French Canadian	18 Jan. 1913	worker	KIA, died of wounds in hospital, Mar. 1938
Grenier, Amedee/Joseph	Sault Ste. Marie	English	12 Aug. 1894	–	WIA, survived
Greysdale, Frederick	Vancouver	–	c. 1917	–	WIA, survived
Griffin, Winston	Toronto	Canadian	6 Apr. 1914	businessman	survived
Griffiths, John N.	b. Montreal; Vancouver	Scottish	8 June 1912	–	WIA, survived
Grondels, Ross George	Toronto; Windsor	Serbian	15 Sept. 1904	–	hospitalized, fate unknown
Gruic, Branco/Bronte/Stanko	Montreal	Czech	–	–	survived
Gulley, George John	Victoria; Vancouver	Swedish	c. 1905	carpenter, driver	survived
Gunerod/Gunervo, Trygve/Ted/Ed	Vancouver	Swedish	24 Dec. 1902	–	survived
Gustafsson, Axel	Milk River, SK	Hungarian	25 Feb. 1906	worker	survived
Gyuricza, Matyas	–	Hungarian	c. 1901	mechanic	survived
Gyurkovics, Istvan	b. Toronto; Winnipeg	Canadian	7 Feb. 1907	–	WIA, survived
Haas, Andrew	–	–	–	–	MIA
Haber, Rudy	Toronto	–	28 Sept. 1894	engineer, sailor	survived
Hackett, Frederick					

Name	Place(s)	Nationality	Date of birth	Occupation	Fate
Hadaszi, Karoly	Lethbridge	Hungarian	9 July 1904	–	KIA, Sierra de Cavalls, Sept. 1938
Hadesbeck, Frank	Regina; Lethbridge; Taber, AB	German	15 July 1906	farm worker	hospitalized, survived
Haferbier, Jens	Vancouver	Danish	c. 1903	–	WIA, fate unknown
Hagerty, B.	Vancouver	–	–	–	survived, detained in France and did not reach Spain
Haldane, Marcus	Vancouver; Kamloops, BC	Aboriginal (Canadian)	c. 1910	diamond driller, lumberjack	WIA, survived
Hale, Robert	Vancouver; Liverpool, UK	Canadian	c. 1912	student	survived
Haleta, Mykola/Nick	Val d'Or, QC; Kirkland Lake, ON	Ukrainian	12 May 1905	miner	survived
Halimoniuk	–	Polish	–	–	fate unknown
Hall, George Francis	Toronto	English	10 Apr. 1910	–	MIA, Retreats, Mar. 1938
Hall, Harvey/William/Harry	Ottawa; Kingston; Belleville, ON	Canadian	1 Jan. 1911	railway worker	WIA, survived
Hallikanen, Einno	–	Finnish	–	–	WIA, fate unknown
Halliwell, William	Edmonton; Vancouver	English	c. 1894	–	WIA, survived
Halmberg, Karl	Vancouver	Swedish	c. 1905	–	fate unknown
Halyniuk, Stepan	–	Ukrainian	–	–	fate unknown
Hamilton, Edward	Salmon Arm BC; Vancouver	Scottish	c. 1905	–	WIA, survived
Hamilton, Steve	Montreal	–	–	–	survived
Hamilton, William	Moose Jaw	–	c. 1919	student	survived
Hamilton/Bell, Robert, aka Tommy Burns	Winnipeg; Vancouver	Scottish	18 Oct. 1910	tailor	survived
Handziuk, Nick	Toronto	Ukrainian	c. 1899	miner	survived
Haney, George	Vancouver; Timmins, ON	–	c. 1900	–	survived
Hanni, Matti	Port Arthur, ON	Finnish	29 Feb. 1908	lumberjack, miner	fate unknown
Hannon, Thomas	Vancouver; Sudbury	English	20 Sept. 1914	lumberjack	survived
Hansbout, Urbain	Winnipeg; Swift Current, SK	Belgian	25 Jan. 1902	–	POW, survived
Hansen, Henrich/Hans	Winnipeg	Danish	12 Dec. 1908	machinist	survived, returned June 1938, died Apr. 1939
Harasimchuk, Pawel	Val d'Or, QC	Ukrainian	c. 1899	–	survived
Harbocian, Nicholas	Windsor	Romanian	–	–	KIA, Brunete, July 1937
Hardy, George	Victoria	Canadian	2 Oct. 1910	printer, shop steward	MIA
Harper	Kingston	English	c. 1901	–	fate unknown
Harris, Abraham	Winnipeg	English	–	–	survived
Harris, Ilija Gromovnik	–	Croatian	–	–	fate unknown
Harris, Ray	Winnipeg; New York	Canadian, Jewish	10 Jan. 1910	nurse	survived
Harris, Sydney	Toronto; Chicago	English	–	–	POW, survived

NAME	HOME	ETHNICITY	DATE OF BIRTH	OCCUPATION	FINAL STATUS
Harrison, William	Vancouver	Scottish	c. 1911	–	WIA, survived
Harrost, Steve	Toronto; Val d'Or, QC	Ukrainian	26 Nov. 1903	worker	POW, survived
Harvey, David	Vancouver	Scottish	c. 1898	carpenter	WIA, survived
Hasiuk, Stefan/John	Montreal	Ukrainian	11 Feb. 1905	–	survived
Haslett, Howard	Toronto	–	c. 1913	–	survived
Hatala, Imre	–	Hungarian	–	–	survived
Hautaharju/Hemminki, Lee/Leo	Port Arthur, ON	Finnish	5 Jan. 1902	–	WIA, fate unknown
Havryliuk, Stepan	–	Ukrainian	–	–	fate unknown
Havrylyk, Danylo	–	–	–	–	survived
Hayes, George	Winnipeg	–	c. 1896	miner	survived
Heaney, John Hugh	Edmonton	Irish	4 Mar. 1913	cook	fate unknown
Hébert	Montreal	–	–	–	KIA, Retreats, Mar. 1938
Heikka/Heikki, Eino/Tuovinen	Port Arthur, ON	Finnish	c. 1896	–	MIA
Heinche, Lawrence	b. Winnipeg; Windsor	Canadian	16 Dec. 1916	mechanic	WIA, survived
Hellund, Walter	Vancouver	Finnish	c. 1903	–	WIA, survived
Henderson, Raymond/Roy/James	b. Huntingdon, QC; Brantford, ON; Saskatoon; Calgary	Canadian	17 Dec. 1902	cook, farm worker, lumberjack, salesman	KIA, Retreats, Apr. 1938
Henderson, William Stanley	St. Catharines, ON; Calgary	Canadian	17 Feb. 1905	truck driver	KIA, Retreats, Apr. 1938
Henrickson, Sulo	Winnipeg	Finnish	c. 1912	–	fate unknown
Herczog/Hristov, Gyorgy	–	Hungarian	–	–	fate unknown
Herton/Herter, Adam	Windsor	Hungarian	8 June 1900	waiter	survived
Hesketh, Henry	Vancouver	English	2 Jan. 1906	steelworker	POW, survived
Higgins, James	Peterborough, ON; Saskatoon	English	26 July 1907	carpenter, painter	WIA, survived
Hihn, Michael	Winnipeg	Romanian	c. 1899	construction worker	survived
Hill, George	Saskatoon; Vancouver; Toronto	Canadian	24 Nov. 1908	shoemaker	POW, survived
Hill, Herbert	Saskatoon	English	4 Oct. 1907	mechanic	KIA, Gandesa, 30 July 1938
Hilton, Percy	Vancouver	English	2 Sept. 1903	baker	POW, survived
Himmelfarb, Victor	Toronto; US	Canadian, Jewish	11 July 1909	pharmacist	survived
Hinta, Leo	Toronto	–	–	–	fate unknown
Hitchcock, D.	–	–	–	–	MIA
Hlady/Hladki, Mykhailo/Michael	Winnipeg; Toronto	Ukrainian	2 Jan. 1902	worker	WIA, survived
Hlohovsky, Vasyl	Winnipeg; Kenora, ON	Ukrainian	–	–	KIA
Hushak	Toronto	Ukrainian	–	–	fate unknown
Hlywa, Wasyl	Montreal	Belarusian	4 Dec. 1902	–	survived
Hnatkiw, Ivan	Montreal	Ukrainian	1 Apr. 1911	worker	KIA, Gandesa, 26 July 1938

Name	Location	Ethnicity	Birth date	Occupation	Fate
Hodge, Robert	Vancouver	English	15 Sept. 1907	construction worker	survived
Hodgson, Edward	Vancouver; Dunster, BC	Canadian	26 Feb. 1901	–	survived
Hoffheinz, Arthur	b. Cumberland, BC; Vancouver	Canadian	4 Aug. 1907	–	POW, survived
Hogarth, Arthur Paul	Vancouver; England	Canadian	c. 1917	–	survived
Hohm, Mihaly	–	Hungarian	–	–	fate unknown
Hoinov, S.	Timmins, ON	Ukrainian	–	–	fate unknown
Holaek, Josif	–	Yugoslav	–	–	fate unknown
Holdyshchuk, Ivan	–	Ukrainian	–	–	fate unknown
Holmstead, Selwin	–		–	–	fate unknown
Holowaczak, Mykieta	Red Lake, ON	Ukrainain	21 Mar. 1904	miner	WIA, survived
Homer, Stewart, aka Paddy O'Neil	Vancouver; Toronto	Irish	18 Dec. 1900	lumberjack	KIA, Brunete, 6 July 1937
Hondorf, Mykhailo	Montreal	Canadian	c. 1915	–	KIA when *Ciudad de Barcelona* was torpedoed, 30 May 1937
Horanic, Pavel/Michal	Toronto	Slovak	22 Jan. 1905	carpenter	survived
Hordy, Alexander	Lethbridge	Slovak	30 Apr. 1913	–	survived
Horrell, Robert	Vancouver	English	23 June 1905	cook	MIA, Retreats, Apr. 1938
Horvath, Ylko	Toronto	–	10 Oct. 1895	–	survived
Horwath, Vendal	Winnipeg	Hungarian	–	–	survived
Hoshooley, John/Jack	b. Montreal; Toronto; Guelph, ON	Canadian	c. 1912	textile worker	WIA, survived
Howard, Allan Robert	Toronto; Montreal	Canadian	18 Aug. 1917	driver	MIA, Retreats, Apr. 1938
Hrab, M.	Toronto	Ukrainian	25 Dec. 1898	–	fate unknown
Hrodetskyi, Danylo	Sudbury; Kirkland Lake, ON	Ukrainian	–	–	WIA, survived
Hrstic/Hurstick, Petar	Toronto; Por. Arthur, ON	Croatian	c. 1896	worker	KIA, Segura de los Baños, Feb. 1938
Hryszczyshin, Stefan	–	Ukrainian	–	–	fate unknown
Hrytsiuk, Ivan	–	Ukrainian	c. 1910	–	fate unknown
Hubb, Jack	–	–	–	–	MIA
Huhtala, Sulo/Kalle/Sam	Montreal; Kirkland Lake, ON; Sudbury	Finnish	15 Jan. 1911	journalist	WIA, survived
Hula/Goola, Oleksa/Alex	Toronto	Ukrainian	c. 1890	–	survived
Huosianmaa, Oskaria/Oskar	Port Arthur, ON	Finnish	1 July 1895	lumberjack	survived
Hurrell, R.	–	–	–	–	MIA
Hyduk, Mike/Mykhailo/Emil	b. Innisfree, AB; Edmonton	Canadian	12 Oct. 1910	restaurant worker, worker	WIA, survived
Hylkinen, Vaino J.	Port Arthur, ON	Finnish	8 Mar. 1907	–	survived
Hyrniak, Michael	Toronto	Ukrainian	c. 1905	–	KIA, Feb. 1938
Hyyppa, Sauli	Vancouver	Finnish	23 Mar. 1905	–	KIA, Retreats, Mar. 1938

NAME	HOME	ETHNICITY	DATE OF BIRTH	OCCUPATION	FINAL STATUS
Ibing, Hans	Toronto; Winnipeg	German	c. 1911	truck driver	WIA, survived
Ichelson, Isaak	Montreal	Russian, Jewish	10 Mar. 1901	worker	survived
Ilchyshyn, Stefan	Toronto	Ukrainian	c. 1901	–	WIA, survived
Illes, Paul	Raymond, AB	Hungarian	c. 1908	–	fate unknown
Illmori, Arne	Port Arthur, ON	Finnish	30 July 1902	lumberjack	fate unknown
Inge, William	Winnipeg	English	6 Jan. 1900	–	survived
Ioannu, Toula (woman)		Greek Cypriot	–	nurse	fate unknown
Irving/Gilroy, Edward "Shorty"	Regina	English	c. 1903	machinist	KIA, Retreats, Apr. 1938
Isohanni, Matti	Cochrane, ON; Port Arthur, ON	Finnish	29 Feb. 1908	lumberjack	survived
Iszcuk, Stefan/Steve	Hamilton; St. Catharines, ON	Ukrainian	6 Jan. 1912	teacher	MIA, Gandesa, Apr. 1938
Iuuiichuk, Vasyl	Toronto	Ukrainian	–	–	KIA, Sept. 1938
Ivanisevik/Evanishvech, Nikola	Toronto; Sudbury	Croatian	c. 1902	worker	survived
Ivankik, John	Toronto; Montreal	Czech	–	–	fate unknown
Ivanoff, Ante/Anto	Tillsonburg, ON	Macedonian	15 Mar. 1905	worker	survived
Ivanov, Georgi	–	Macedonian	–	–	KIA
Ivanov, Kuntcho	–	Macedonian	–	–	KIA
Ivanychuk, Stepan	–	Ukrainian	–	–	fate unknown
Ivashchuk, Maksym	Winnipeg	Ukrainian	8 Sept. 1909	–	survived
Iven, James	–	–	c. 1913	–	fate unknown
Jablonski, Volodymyr	Port Arthur, ON	Ukrainian	c. 1901	–	KIA, 1938
Jablowski, Hendryk	–	Polish	–	–	fate unknown
Jacko, H.	–	Czech	–	–	fate unknown
Jacobs, John E.	Calgary	–	c. 1895	–	MIA
Jacquat, Pierre	Edmonton	Swiss	c. 1913	–	WIA, survived
Jaczku/Yakzku, Istvan	Taber, AB	Hungarian	c. 1904	–	fate unknown
Jakab, Laszlo	–	Hungarian	–	–	fate unknown
Jakovcic, Matto/Mike	Coxville, ON	Croatian	c. 1902	worker	KIA
Jakovievic, Sretan	Vancouver	Serbian	c. 1890	worker	survived
Jakub, Michal	Montreal	Slovak	16 July 1904	–	survived
Jakubec, Jan	Chatham, ON	Czechoslovakian	30 Dec. 1907	–	survived
James, Percy Martill	Vancouver	Welsh	c. 1905	–	POW, survived
Jameson, Clarence W.			5 Oct. 1896	–	survived
Janas, Jan	Chatham, ON; Toronto	Czech	24 Oct. 1900	–	survived
Janei, Gabor	Timmins, ON; Hamilton	Hungarian	c. 1901	blacksmith	KIA, July 1937

Name	Location(s)	Nationality	Date	Occupation	Fate
Janicki, Eurgeniusz	Welland, ON; North Battleford, SK; Toronto	Ukrainian	12 May 1907	–	survived
Janicki, Sewerin	–	Polish	4 May 1903	–	MIA
Janik, Stanislaw	Winnipeg	Ukrainian	c. 1899	–	fate unknown
Janiszewski, Frantiszek	St. Catharines, ON; Port Arthur, ON	Polish	c. 1905	–	WIA, survived
Janneson, Osborn	Port Arthur, ON	Swedish	c. 1907	–	survived
Jardas/Yardas, Eduard	Toronto	Croatian	30 Jan. 1901	journalist	WIA, survived
Jarrow, George	Winnipeg; Vancouver; US	Canadian	16 Sept. 1914	fish packer, miner, relief camp cook	fate unknown
Jaskari, Arvo	Vancouver; Ladysmith, BC	Finnish	30 Aug. 1904	lumberjack, miner	survived
Jelic, Lazar/Louis	Winnipeg; Port Arthur, ON	Croatian	2 Mar. 1901	miner	survived
Jergovic, Mate	Port Arthur, ON; Rouyn, QC	Croatian	25 Aug. 1906	miner	WIA, survived
Jeruche, Eugene	Toronto	–	–	–	survived
Johanson, Hannes	Toronto	Finnish	–	–	fate unknown
Johanson, Veikko	Toronto	Finnish	–	–	KIA
John, Leonard		Canadian	17 Jan. 1917	clerk	POW, survived
Johnson, Arthur Selim	Toronto	Canadian	30 Nov. 1915	–	KIA, Gandesa, 30 July 1938
Johnson, John George	Montreal; Vancouver	Canadian	29 July 1911	lumberjack	survived
Johnston, Peter	Vancouver	–	–	sailor	KIA, Jarama, May 1937
Jokela/Jokinen, Hekki/Henry	Vancouver; Fort Arthur, ON	Finnish	20 Jan. 1908	–	KIA, Retreats, 11 Mar. 1938
Jokvach, Joseph	Toronto	Hungarian	–	–	fate unknown
Jones, Clare	Edmonton		–	–	fate unknown
Jones, Richard/John Edward	Montreal; Winnipeg; Calgary	Canadian	22 May 1896	telephone operator	POW, survived
Jordan, Bill	Winnipeg; Toronto	–	–	–	survived
Jordan, Frank Benjamin	Calgary	American	9 Apr. 1895	–	survived
Jorgensen, Hans Peter	Port Arthur, ON	Danish	13 June 1899	lumberjack	WIA, survived
Joutsen, Matti	Port Arthur, ON	Finnish	29 Dec. 1905	carpenter	KIA, Gandesa, Apr. 1938
Juk, Jozsef	Winnipeg	Hungarian	c. 1921	shoemaker	survived
Jukasz/Juhas, Sandor/Alex	Montreal; Toronto	Hungarian	14 Sept. 1898	–	survived
Junkala, Eino	Sudbury	Finnish	18 June 1910	lumberjack, trapper	hospitalized, survived
Jurisic, Miho	–	Yugoslav	c. 1896	–	fate unknown
Jyunkovics, Istvan	Edmonton	Hungarian	c. 1902	–	survived
Kabatoff, Alexander Ronald, aka Alex Forbes	b. Kamsack, SK; Toronto; Regina; Vancouver	Canadian	15 Nov. 1915	worker	WIA, survived
Kache, Ivan	–	Slavic	–	–	fate unknown
Kack, Axel	Vancouver	Swedish	14 Apr. 1895	–	fate unknown

NAME	HOME	ETHNICITY	DATE OF BIRTH	OCCUPATION	FINAL STATUS
Kaipainen, Onni Emil	Port Arthur, ON	Finnish	c. 1898	–	fate unknown
Kakos, Mihaly	Edmonton; Drumheller, AB	Hungarian	c. 1901	–	survived
Kalanj, Ivan	Vancouver	Croatian	10 Oct. 1902	–	survived
Kalapatsa/Kalapud, Volodymyr	Rainy River, ON	Ukrainian	7 Mar. 1909	miner	survived
Kalisnikoff, William	Vancouver	–	c. 1914	–	fate unknown
Kalke, Karl	Toronto; Buffalo, NY	Canadian	4 Jan. 1910	mechanic, truck driver	survived
Kaltschmidt, Hans		Canadian	4 May 1914	–	WIA, fate unknown
Kambides, John	Montreal	Polish	c. 1906	–	POW, survived
Kandia, Anthony	Winnipeg		c. 1902	–	survived
Kane, James "Scotty"	Toronto		c. 1915	–	KIA, Brunete, 6 July 1937
Kantola, Emil	Sudbury	Finnish	c. 1908	–	fate unknown
Kaplan, Joe			11 Dec. 1897	farmer	KIA, Retreats, Mar. 1938
Kardash, Theodore	Winnipeg	Ukrainian	6 Oct. 1912	farm worker, mechanic	KIA, Retreats, Apr. 1938
Kardash, William/Vasyl, aka Arturo Edwards	Winnipeg	Canadian			WIA, survived
Karikka, Taimi/Evert/Ernest	Port Arthur, ON; Toronto	Finnish	28 Aug. 1909	lumberjack	WIA, survived
Karpuk, Peter	Fort William, ON	Ukrainian	14 Oct. 1902	lumberjack	survived
Kaska, Tom	Drumheller, AB	Ukrainian			KIA
Kasza, Janos	Creston, BC; Drumheller, AB	Hungarian	26 May 1900		survived
Kaufman, L.		–			MIA
Keenan, Archibald Patterson	Cumberland, BC	Scottish	19 Jan. 1898	miner	survived
Keenan, William	Toronto	Irish	c. 1901		KIA, July 1938
Keenan/Keeguan, Gordon	Cumberland, BC; Vancouver	Scottish	14 Feb. 1908		KIA, Gandesa, July or Aug. 1938
Kelly, Aubrey Kirby	Vancouver	American			fate unknown
Kelly, Joseph	Vancouver	Irish	4 Feb. 1900	lumberjack, miner	WIA, survived
Kelly, Michael	Edmonton				KIA
Kelly, Thomas Anthony	Vancouver	English	20 Sept. 1914		WIA, survived
Kempa, Walerian	Montreal; Windsor	Polish	27 Sept. 1905		survived
Kennedy, Frank	St. Vital, MB	Canadian	19 Nov. 1898		MIA, Retreats, Mar. 1938
Kenyon, Robert Jackson	Kitchener; Vancouver	English	c. 1897		fate unknown
Kerdiak, Ivan	South Porcupine, ON	Ukrainian	14 Jan. 1905	miner	survived
Kerkkonen, Kalle/Karl	Toronto	Finnish	18 June 1911	auto mechanic, farm worker, lumberjack	hospitalized, survived
Kerr, Bob Joseph/Robert	Vancouver	Scottish	c. 1897	lumberjack	survived
Kessner, Aaron/Archie	Toronto; US	Canadian, Jewish	11 Aug. 1915	aviation mechanic	KIA, Sept. 1938

Name	Residence	Nationality	Birth date	Occupation	Fate
Kestick, Franck	Toronto	Hungarian	c. 1902	–	survived
Keto, Antti Wiljo	Port Arthur, ON	Finnish	c. 1901	–	fate unknown (conflicting information)
Keto, Reino Waldemar	Worthington, ON	Finnish	c. 1909	construction worker, farm worker, gymnastics instructor	survived
Kezele, Alexandar	–	Croatian	–	–	fate unknown
Kezele, George	–	Croatian	–	–	fate unknown
Kiegway, Gordon	Cumberland, BC	Canadian	14 Feb. 1908	–	KIA
Kierpaul, Casimir K.	Toronto	Polish	c. 1906	–	survived
Kietaranta, Johannes	Port Arthur, ON; Toronto	Finnish	26 Apr. 1894	worker	survived
Kiiskinen, Antti	Sudbury	Finnish	29 Mar. 1910	lumberjack	survived
Kipen, Stephen/John	Kirkland Lake, ON	Ukrainian	24 July 1913	auto mechanic	survived
Kiraly, Istavan/Estevan/Steve	Windsor	Hungarian	12 July 1905	carpenter	survived
Kirkich, Ignatz	Val d'Or, QC	–	–	–	fate unknown
Kiroff, Istevan	Toronto	Bulgarian	22 Mar. 1907	worker	survived
Kisielis, Liudes/Louis	Port Arthur, CN; Bienfait, MB	Lithuanian	29 July 1902	farm worker, miner	WIA, survived
Kiss, Andrew	Lethbridge	Hungarian	c. 1900	–	MIA
Kit, Nick/Mykola	Toronto; Sudbury	Ukrainian	10 Nov. 1905	cook	survived
Kivi, Matti	Drumheller, AB; Toronto	–	–	–	fate unknown
Kivimaki, Eemeli	Port Arthur, CN	Finnish	c. 1904	worker	fate unknown (conflicting information)
Klago, Ludevit	Winnipeg	Slovak	9 Oct. 1903	–	survived
Kluchewski, George	Kamloops, B.C.; Val d'Or, QC	Ukrainian	5 Mar. 1909	miner	WIA, fate unknown
Knack, A.G.	Crowsnest Pass, AB	–	–	–	WIA, survived
Knaut, Helmut	Calgary	German	c. 1898	–	survived
Knight, Allan	–	–	c. 1916	–	survived
Knudsen, Arne/Augustinius	Vancouver	Danish	c. 1910	–	survived
Kobaly, Andrew	Toronto	Ruthenian	7 Jan. 1899	carpenter	KIA
Kobe, Michael	Toronto; South Porcupine, ON	Slovenian	c. 1911	–	KIA
Kochma, Joseph/Joe	Port Arthur, ON	Czech	c. 1898	–	fate unknown
Kojshak, M.	Port Arthur, ON; Winnipeg	Slovak	–	–	fate unknown
Kokko, Vilho Armas	Toronto	Finnish	17 Dec. 1905	–	fate unknown
Kokovskyi, Stephan	–	Ukrainian	–	–	WIA, survived
Kokura, Ivan/John	Edmonton; Sudbury; Coleman, AB	Ukrainian	1 Dec. 1905	farmer, painter	survived
Kolbasko, Maksym	Regina; Val d'Or, QC	Ukrainian	c. 1901	miner	survived
Koleszar/Kolgar, Geza	Lethbridge; Drumheller, AB	Hungarian	3 Jan. 1915	–	survived
Kollensky/Kolens, Michael	Winnipeg	–	–	–	fate unknown

NAME	HOME	ETHNICITY	DATE OF BIRTH	OCCUPATION	FINAL STATUS
Kolody, Alex	Windsor; Toronto; Detroit	Russian	7 June 1894	–	survived
Komodowski, Edward/John	Winnipeg; The Pas, MB	Canadian	20 May 1912	teacher	survived
Koncz, Janos	–	Hungarian	c. 1899	–	fate unknown
Kondas, George	Toronto	Hungarian	23 June 1899	farmer	survived
Koni, J.	Toronto	Czech	c. 1902	–	fate unknown
Kopp, Ferdinand	South Porcupine, ON; Schumacher, ON	Croatian	c. 1900	miner	WIA, survived
Koradi/Koryto, Alex	–	Hungarian	–	–	fate unknown
Korascil/Johnson, Andrew	Vancouver	Canadian	15 Jan. 1915	worker	KIA, Sept. 1938
Kordan, A.	Winnipeg	–	–	–	fate unknown
Kore, Janos/Jozef	Toronto	Hungarian	c. 1902	–	KIA, Battle of the Ebro, 1938
Koricki, Nikita	Winnipeg	Ukrainian	c. 1904	–	survived
Korinsky, Joseph/Osyp	b. Ottawa; Kirkland Lake, ON	Canadian	18 Feb. 1912	miner	POW, survived
Kormos, Nandor	–	Hungarian	–	–	fate unknown
Korneichuck, Stepan	Montreal	Ukrainian	c. 1903	–	KIA
Kos, Mykhailo	Weekes, SK	Ukrainian	11 Nov. 1904	–	KIA, Teruel, Jan. 1938
Koscic, Franjo	Timmins, ON; Schumacher, ON	Croatian	22 July 1902	miner	WIA, survived
Koskela, Emil	Toronto; Port Arthur, ON	Finnish	c. 1907	–	KIA, Sept. 1938
Koski, Hugo	–	Finnish	c. 1907	–	survived
Koskinen, Paavo, aka Gunnar Ebb	–	Finnish	–	construction worker	survived
Koslowsky, Stefan	Toronto; Kitchener, ON	Polish	c. 1907	teacher	KIA, Sept. 1937
Kosmik, Peter	–	Ukrainian	–	–	fate unknown
Kosowatski, Mortimer/Thomas, aka Jack Steele	Montreal; Toronto	Jewish	c. 1906	farm worker, steelworker	KIA, Battle of the Ebro, July 1938
Koss, G.C.	Vancouver	–	–	–	fate unknown
Kostaniuk, Petro	Winnipeg	Canadian	12 Apr. 1917	mechanic	WIA, survived
Koster, William	Sunderland, ON; Port Arthur, ON	Ukrainian	c. 1906	baker	MIA
Kostoff, George	Toronto	Macedonian	c. 1909	cook	survived
Kostyk, Fred	b. East Selkirk, MB; Winnipeg	Canadian	17 Mar. 1916	auto mechanic, factory worker, welder	WIA, survived
Kotniuk/Kostiuk, Vasyl	Winnipeg	Ukrainian	1 Feb. 1901	worker	hospitalized, survived
Kotyk, Jan	Port Hammond, BC	Ukrainian	25 July 1908	railway worker	survived
Kovacic, Josip/Joseph	Hamilton	Croatian	c. 1909	worker	survived
Kovacs, Istvan	Toronto; Lethbridge	Hungarian	23 Sept. 1903	mechanic	survived, Canadian Army WWII
Kovacz, Yurko	Winnipeg	Slovak	23 Sept. 1903	worker	survived

Name	Location	Ethnicity	Date	Occupation	Fate
Kovelas, George	Montreal	–	–	–	fate unknown
Kowalchuk/Nesteruk, Mikhail	Timmins, ON; Edmonton	Ukrainian	c. 1901	worker	KIA
Kozak, Martin	Port Arthur, ON	Czech	c. 1890	–	fate unknown
Kozel, Victor	Valley Centre, SK; Toronto	Slovak	23 Aug. 1901	worker	survived
Koziel, Alexander	Toronto; Windsor; Kapuskasing, ON	Croatian	c. 1911	–	WIA, survived
Koziol/Kozlov, Nick/Mikolas	Fort William, ON	Belarusian	c. 1902	–	survived
Kozlov, Alexander	New Westminster, BC	Macedonian	c. 1911	–	survived
Kozma, Denes	Porcupine Plain, SK	Hungarian	11 Jan. 1896	farmer	hospitalized, survived
Kral, Otto	Montreal	Slovak	19 Oct. 1898	railway worker	survived
Krehm, William	Toronto	Canadian, Jewish	23 Nov. 1913	journalist	survived
Krein, Jozef	Windsor	Hungarian	–	–	fate unknown
Krepsz, Jozef	Ottawa	Hungarian	–	–	fate unknown
Kristiansen/Kristian, Emanual	Vancouver	Norweigan	c. 1894	carpenter	hospitalized, survived
Krizan, Jozef	Fort William, ON	Hungarian	16 Nov. 1902	farmer	survived
Krizsan, Antal	Welland, ON; Toronto	Hungarian	c. 1897	–	KIA, Brunete, July 1937
Kromholc, J.	Port Arthur, ON; Vancouver	Slovak	–	–	fate unknown
Kronchak, Joseph	Winnipeg	–	–	–	fate unknown
Krousement, Edward	–	Estonian	25 Dec. 1905	–	POW, survived
Kruth, Niilo	–	Finnish	–	–	survived
Krysa, William	Winnipeg; Estevan, SK	Ukrainian	17 July 1904	coal miner	WIA, survived
Kryshany, Anthony	–	–	c. 1899	–	fate unknown
Kszysztowczak, Piotr	Hamilton	Belarusian	c. 1901	worker	survived
Kubinec, Michael	Vancouver; Fernie, BC	Canadian	18 Aug. 1912	worker	MIA, Retreats, Mar. 1938
Kucherepa, Volodymyr	Toronto	Ukrainian	c. 1913	–	survived
Kuchmy, Mykailo	Montreal	Ukrainian	9 Dec. 1902	mechanic	survived
Kucz/Kurc, Mikhail	Montreal	Polish	c. 1903	painter	WIA, survived
Kudebski, Michal	Montreal	Polish	c. 1902	–	survived
Kuebler, Harold	Vancouver	American	9 Nov. 1908	farmer	survived
Kulikowsky	Montreal	–	–	farmer	fate unknown
Kulmala, Feliks	South Porcupine, ON	Finnish	13 Mar. 1902	miner	WIA, survived
Kumpulainen, Esko/Emil	Vancouver	Finnish	7 Mar. 1906	lumberjack	WIA, survived
Kuncho, John	–	Bulgarian	–	–	survived
Kuokka, Uuno	Port Arthur, CN; Toronto	Finnish	c. 1904	worker	survived
Kupchik, Isidore	Montreal; Toronto	Canadian, Jewish	c. 1912	salesman, truck driver	KIA
Kupusinac, Alex	Toronto	Serbian	c. 1899	–	KIA, Dec. 1937

NAME	HOME	ETHNICITY	DATE OF BIRTH	OCCUPATION	FINAL STATUS
Kuryk, Harry John	Edmonton	Ukrainian	5 Apr. 1895	carpenter, miner, railway worker	KIA, Retreats, Mar. 1938
Kwiatek, Antoni	–	Polish	c. 1890	–	fate unknown
Kydnia, T.	Winnipeg	Ukrainian	–	–	fate unknown
Kyyny, Yrjo/George	Port Arthur, ON	Finnish	23 Feb. 1907	lumberjack	KIA
Kyzniak, John	Saskatoon	–	–	–	fate unknown
Laakso, Uno/Johan/Erick	–	–	–	–	KIA, Retreats, Mar. 1938
Laakso/Jaakonsaari, Valdo	Port Arthur, ON	Finnish	c. 1908	firefighter	KIA, Retreats, Mar. 1938
Lacelle, Lionel J.	b. Ottawa; Toronto	French Canadian	14 Mar. 1909	–	survived
LaChapelle, William	Vancouver; Sudbury	French Canadian	c. 1910	lumberjack	survived
Lackey, Frederick	b. Manitou, MB; Toronto	Canadian	23 Dec. 1904	auto mechanic	KIA, Jarama, 27 Feb. 1937
Lacko, Jan	Sault Ste. Marie; Hearst, ON	Slovak	c. 1900	–	survived
Lafazanov, Krusto	–	Macedonian	–	–	KIA
Lagstrom, Edwin	Port Arthur, ON	Finnish	c. 1909	lumberjack	fate unknown
Lahdekorpi, Yrjo/Korpi/George	Port Arthur, ON	Finnish	10 Nov. 1911	lumberjack, miner	survived
Lahti/Lakti, Vilpas	Port Arthur, ON	Finnish	–	–	survived
Lahue, Albert	–	–	–	–	survived
Lajure/Lazure, Omer/Omar	Howick, QC; Glenn Falls, NY	French Canadian	20 Apr. 1905	steel and cement worker	KIA, Gandesa, 30 July 1938
Lamont	Montreal	French Canadian	–	–	KIA, executed
Lamper, Josef	Windsor	Czech	c. 1897	–	fate unknown
Langley, Samuel	Toronto; deported to England 1931	English	10 Mar. 1895	sailor	WIA, survived
Lapinskas, Ernestas	Montreal	Lithuanian	–	–	survived
Lapscuk, Myroslaw	–	Canadian	13 Jan. 1912	–	survived
Laszab, Ferenc	–	Hungarian	–	–	fate unknown
Latulippe, Lucien	Montfort, QC	French Canadian	28 June 1908	cook	survived
Lauradin, Roy	Rimouski, QC; Rouyn, QC	French Canadian	c. 1911	–	KIA, Fuentes de Ebro, Oct. 1937
Laurin, Joseph	Toronto	French Canadian	c. 1912	painter	WIA, survived
Lawrence, Tom	Vancouver	–	–	sailor, salesman	fate unknown
Lawson, Jack/John	Vancouver; Victoria	Scottish	1900	sailor	survived
Laziwich, Marko	Vancouver	Croatian	–	–	survived
Lazzerman, Arthur	–	–	–	–	WIA, fate unknown
LeBlanc, Wilfrid	Windsor; Tecumseh, ON	French Canadian	c. 1916	–	MIA
LeClerc, Joseph	b. Frampton, QC; Montreal; Quebec City	French Canadian	c. 1908	–	detained in France, not clear if made it to Spain, fate unknown

Name	Location	Nationality	Birth date	Occupation	Fate
Lees, John	Hamilton	Scottish	–	lumberjack	survived
Legge, Walter "Scotty"	Vancouver	Finnish	c. 1916	farmer, miner	survived
Lehtovirta, Hugo	South Porcupine, ON; Timmins, ON		2 Feb. 1902		KIA, Retreats, 17 Mar. 1938
Leige, Clare	Toronto	–	c. 1912	sailor, truck driver	KIA, Jarama, 27 Feb. 1937
Lemal, Arthur	b. Inverness, NS; Drumheller, AB, Newcastle AE	Canadian	8 Aug. 1916	miner	KIA
Lemke, Edgar/George	Fort Fraser, BC; Vancouver	Russian	26 Nov. 1883	surveyor	survived
Lenek, Joseph	Montreal	Czech	2 Jan. 1899	mechanic	survived
Leppanen, Viljo Armas	Port Arthur, ON	Finnish	30 July 1900	lumberjack	survived
Lerner, Arthur	–	–	–	–	fate unknown
Leslie, Albert	Toronto	Irish	–	–	survived, arrested in France and did not reach Spain
Leslie, Robert Duncan	Toronto; Regina	Canadian	c. 1910	blacksmith	WIA, survived
Levens, Harold John "Dirty Duke"	Vancouver	Canadian	14 Feb. 1911	medic	KIA, Segura de los Baños, Feb. 1938
Levitt, Ralph	–	–	–	–	fate unknown
Levy, Bert "Yank"	Hamilton; Windsor	Canadian, Jewish	5 Oct. 1897	driver	POW, survived
Lewandowski, Tadeusz/Alex		Polish			fate unknown
Lewczuk, Maksym	Toronto	Ukrainian	24 Apr. 1902	painter, machinist	survived
Lewilsky/Levitzki, Joseph	Montreal	Ukrainian	c. 1900	railway worker	fate unknown
Lewis, Alexander	Toronto	English	15 Nov. 1905	mechanic	survived
Leye, W.					MIA
Liaskovsky, Yury/George/Bill	Toronto; Waterloo, ON	Ukrainian	6 July 1899	barber	KIA, Jarama, 27 Feb. 1937
Lieber, Wasyl/Michael	Toronto	Ukrainian	c. 1896	textile worker	KIA, 1938
Lightheart, William/George	b. Hamilton; Toronto	Canadian	28 Dec. 1901	machinist	hospitalized, survived
Linardic, Ivan	Toronto; Hamilton	Croatian	23 Aug. 1906	–	WIA, survived
Lind, Tauno	Toronto; Nak na, ON	Finnish	c. 1892	–	KIA, Brunete, 7 July 1937
Linton, Arthur	b. Montreal; Windsor; London	Canadian	2 Nov. 1916	sailor	WIA, survived
Lisk, Fred	Sudbury	Ukrainian	5 Feb. 1905	lumberjack, miner, worker	fate unknown
Lisko, Alexander	Drumheller, AB	Hungarian	17 Feb. 1906	coal miner	fate unknown
Lisowik/Oliswik, Joseph	b. Hamilton; Windsor	Canadian	15 Feb. 1917	auto mechanic	survived
Lisset, John	–	–	–	–	survived
Liversedge, Ronald/Rowland/Rodney	Vancouver	English	12 Apr. 1899	CPC organizer, miner	hospitalized, survived

NAME	HOME	ETHNICITY	DATE OF BIRTH	OCCUPATION	FINAL STATUS
Livingston, Donald/Ronald	Vancouver	–	c. 1904	lumberjack	KIA, died in hospital, Sept. 1938
Llewellyn, Eugene	Terrace, BC	American	c. 1918	lumberjack, sailor	survived
Loch, Jacob	Waterloo, ON; Guelph, ON; Kitchener, ON	German	c. 1903	carpenter	KIA, 2 Sept. 1937
Lockwood, David	–	–	–	–	fate unknown
Logovsky, Vasil	Kenora, ON	Ukrainian	c. 1901	–	KIA, Brunete, died in hospital, July 1937
Loiselle/Regan, John/Johnny	Vancouver	French Canadian	27 Dec. 1915	–	MIA, Retreats, Mar. 1938
Lombart, Herman	Edmonton	German	26 Nov. 1904	worker	survived
Lompik/Lompich, Jakob/James	–	Belarusian	–	–	WIA, survived
Lonho, T.	–	–	–	–	KIA
Looser, William	Chilliwack, BC	Swiss	4 Apr. 1909	–	survived
Loser, Creso	–	–	–	–	KIA, July 1938
Losodor, Steve	Windsor	Irish	–	–	fate unknown
Loughran, "Pop"	–	Bulgarian	–	–	fate unknown
Loviereff	Toronto	English	–	–	fate unknown
Lucas/Dutton, James	Vancouver; Surrey	English	c. 1911	lumberjack	survived
Lucasiewicz, John	Montreal; Rouyn, QC	Polish	c. 1909	miner	KIA, Battle of the Ebro, July 1938
Ludanic/Ludevit, Kolous/Kalert	Montreal	Slovak	c. 1910	–	fate unknown
Ludkin, Ernest	Hamilton	English	–	–	fate unknown
Luho, David	Port Arthur, ON	–	–	–	fate unknown
Lukac, Samuel/Simon	Windsor	Slovak	2 July 1901	–	KIA, Retreats, 11 Mar. 1938
Lukas, Franjo	–	Yugoslav	–	–	fate unknown
Lukas, Janos	–	Canadian	c. 1907	–	MIA, Sept. 1937
Lulic, Bozo	Vancouver	Croatian	25 Mar. 1901	miner	survived
Lungel/Lurgel, Michael	Toronto	Ukrainian	3 Oct. 1908	auto mechanic, driver, lumberjack	fate unknown
Luoma, Emil	Port Arthur, ON; Vancouver	Finnish	24 May 1895	lumberjack	WIA, survived
Luoto, Kalle/Frank	Montreal	Finnish	–	lumberjack	KIA, Retreats, Apr. 1938
Lutesan, Mike	Montreal	Czech	–	blacksmith, lumberjack	fate unknown
Lynch, Patrick	–	–	–	–	fate unknown
Lyons, Thomas/William	Edmonton	English	9 Nov. 1903	lumberjack	WIA, survived
Lypka/Lypky, Ivan/John	Montreal	Ukrainian	c. 1900	–	KIA
Lys, Jan	Toronto	Ukrainian	c. 1907	–	survived

Name	Place	Nationality	Date of birth	Occupation	Fate
Lysetz/Lyetski/Leguet, Hryhori/Gregory	Winnipeg; Toronto	Ukrainian	6 May 1915	pilot	WIA, survived
Lyska, Fedir	Estevan, SK	Ukrainian	5 Feb. 1905	miner	hospitalized, survived
MacDonald, A.	–	–	–	–	survived
MacEacron, Paul	–	–	–	–	fate unknown
MacGregor, James	Vancouver	Scottish	19 Apr. 1903	miner	WIA, fate unknown
Mack, Henry	–	Finnish	–	–	survived
Mackenzie, Jack	Gilbert Plains, MB	Scottish	26 Oct. 1919	–	KIA, Gandesa, 26 July 1938
Mackenzie, Roderick	Sudbury; Toronto	Scottish	–	mechanic	WIA, survived
Mackie, Alfred George	Deloraine, M3; Vancouver	–	26 Aug. 1910	miner	survived
MacLean, James	Hamilton; Sioux Lookout, ON	Scottish	5 Mar. 1907	lumberjack, miner, printer, road worker	WIA, fate unknown
MacLeod, Donald	Hamilton; Va·couver	–	c. 1913	auto mechanic	survived
Madaire, Charles	–	French Canadian	c. 1899	–	fate unknown
Madden, Harry	Glace Bay, NS	Canadian	c. 1894	–	WIA, survived
Madley, Russell/Ross	Toronto	Canadian	22 Jan. 1918	printer at *Daily Clarion*	WIA, survived
Madsen, Neils/Isaac Christian	Vancouver	Danish	11 Dec. 1899	lumberjack, miner	POW, survived
Maenpaa/Maki, Karlo/Kalle	Port Arthur, ON; Silver Mountain, ON	Finnish	25 Apr. 1900	worker	hospitalized, survived
Magid, Aaron	Toronto; Winnipeg	Canadian, Jewish	4 May 1905	doctor	survived
Magid, Ethel (woman)	b. Balcarres, SK; Winnipeg	Canadian	–	nurse	survived
Magill, Joseph	Toronto	Irish	6 July 1907	–	survived
Magyar, Jozsef	Julian, AB; Taber, AB	Hungarian	1 May 1907	–	WIA, fate unknown
Mahanchuk, John	Montreal	Ukrainian	–	–	fate unknown
Major, Vince	Timmins, ON	Finnish	c. 1917	journalist, lumberjack, miner	KIA, Caspe, died in hospital of wounds, March 1938
Makela, Niilo Johannes	Port Arthur, ON; Toronto; Sudbury	Finnish	23 Apr. 1899	journalist, miner	WIA, survived
Makela, Untamo	–	Finnish	c. 1885	–	KIA
Maki, Uuno	Toronto	Yugoslav	–	–	WIA, fate unknown
Makovic, Mato	–	–	–	–	fate unknown
Makura, John	Port Arthur, ON	Lithuanian	30 July 1905	worker	KIA, Caspe, Mar. 1938
Malickas, Juozas/James	Winnipeg; Tcronto	Ukrainian	4 Oct. 1902	road worker	POW, survived
Malicki/Malytski, Mykhailo/Michael	Toronto	Ukrainian	c. 1897	shoemaker	WIA, survived
Malko, Ivan/John	Winnipeg; Windsor	American	28 May 1912	–	KIA, Retreats, Apr. 1938
Mallon, Thomas	Vancouver	Hungarian	c. 1895	–	fate unknown
Malnar, Imre		Irish	17 Feb. 1912	driver	WIA, survived
Malone, John					

NAME	HOME	ETHNICITY	DATE OF BIRTH	OCCUPATION	FINAL STATUS
Malson, J.	Winnipeg	–	–	–	fate unknown
Mandel, Emanuel	–	Jewish	–	–	KIA, Feb. 1938
Mangel, David	Toronto; Montreal	Polish, Jewish	9 Oct. 1900	painter	WIA, survived
Mangotic, Anthony/Anto	Timmins, ON; Schumacher, ON	Croatian	19 June 1914	–	POW, survived
Manien/Maneer, J.J.	Toronto	Irish	–	–	survived
Manko, Ondrej	–	Ukrainian	c. 1892	–	fate unknown
Mantell, James Percy	Vancouver	Welsh	–	–	survived
Mantero, Asser	–	–	–	–	WIA, fate unknown
Maranda, Charles Edward	St. Sauveur, QC	Canadian	26 Feb. 1896	–	fate unknown
Marchuk, Walter	Regina	Canadian	10 Mar. 1914	painter	KIA, Gandesa, Apr. 1938
Marier	–	French Canadian	–	–	fate unknown
Mariniuk, Walter	Toronto	Ukrainian	c. 1896	–	fate unknown
Marinoff, Nicholas	Montreal	Bulgarian	c. 1897	tailor	KIA, Jarama, 27 Feb. 1937
Markoff, Joseph	Toronto	Bulgarian	25 Jan. 1907	–	survived
Markowski, Daniel	Val d'Or, QC; Montreal	Canadian	3 June 1916	truck driver	survived
Markowski, George/Jerzy	Toronto	Ukrainian	20 Nov. 1904	miner	POW, survived
Markowsky, Andrew	Toronto	Ukrainian	–	–	KIA, Sept. 1938
Marsh, Ted/Edouard	Winnipeg	Swiss	13 May 1899	blacksmith	WIA, survived
Marshall, Albert	Vancouver; Winnipeg	Finnish	c. 1906	driver	survived
Martilla, Helge	Vancouver	Finnish	1 Nov. 1899	–	POW, survived
Martin, Christopher	Toronto	Irish	25 Dec. 1907	–	survived
Martin, Robert	–	English	c. 1913	journalist	survived
Martin, Tony	Vancouver	English	–	–	survived
Martineau, Robert/Rosario	Montreal; Quebec; Valcartier, QC	French Canadian	7 Nov. 1900	boiler fireman	WIA, survived
Martinuk, Anton	Winnipeg; Toronto	Ukrainian	c. 1906	foundry worker, miner	KIA, Feb. 1938
Martlins, Bernard	–	–	–	–	fate unknown
Martinssen, Svene	–	–	27 Oct. 1911	–	MIA, Retreats, Apr. 1938
Martyniuk, Anton/Tony	Toronto	Ukrainian	c. 1908	miner	survived
Martyniuk, Wladyslaw/Walter	Montreal	Polish	10 Oct. 1901	plumber	survived
Matesic, George/Jurij	Timmins, ON	Slovenian	c. 1903	worker	WIA, survived
Mateychuk/Matyjozyk, Mykola	Sudbury	Belarusian	c. 1897	–	survived
Matich, Jovo	Vancouver	Yugoslav	c. 1885	–	fate unknown
Matiak, Jozef	Toronto	Polish, Jewish	c. 1901	–	KIA, Retreats, died in hospital, Mar. 1938
Matosic, Ivan	–	Croatian	–	–	survived
Matson, Isaac	Vancouver	Swedish	2 Feb. 1898	lumberjack, miner	POW, died in prison

Name	Residence	Nationality	Birth date	Occupation	Fate
Matson, Karl	Winnipeg	Finnish	c. 1897	student	hospitalized, fate unknown
Matta, Jean Paul Homer	Windsor	Canadian	14 Sept. 1920		hospitalized, survived
Mattersdorfer, Fred	b. Springhill, NS; Vancouver; Burnaby, BC; Fernie, BC	Canadian	28 Jan. 1915	mill worker, road worker	survived
Matuska, Jan	Montreal	Slovak	18 May 1894	blacksmith, steelworker	WIA, survived
Matvenko/Matthews, Vasyl/Bill	b. Kamsack, SK; Sudbury; Calgary; Blairmore, AE	Canadian	30 May 1913	amateur boxer, miner	WIA, survived
Maunumaki, Uuno/Walter	Port Arthur, ON	Finnish	c. 1907	miner	KIA, Battle of the Ebro, July 1938,
Max, J.T.	Chatham, ON	–		–	fate unknown
Maxiam, Frantisek	Elfros, SK; Toronto	Slovak	c. 1902		survived
May, Allen	Vancouver	–		journalist	survived
Maynard, Roger	Hamilton; Montreal	Canadian	24 Jan. 1902	carpenter	survived
Mazeppa, Peter	Edmonton	Ukrainian	c. 1902	–	MIA, Battle of the Ebro, July 1938
Mazurkiewicz, Volodymyr	Vancouver	Ukrainian	c. 1898		survived
McAlister, Patrick	Carlyle, SK	Irish	11 Aug. 1909	lumberjack, waiter	WIA, survived
McBride, John	Vancouver	Scottish	3 Oct. 1908	lumberjack, painter	survived
McCallum, James	Vancouver	Scottish	c. 1915	driver	KIA, Retreats, 1938
McCallum, Thomas	Vancouver	Scottish	8 Feb. 1906	lumberjack, painter	WIA, survived
McCarthy, Cormac	–	Australian	c. 1898		KIA, Retreats, Mar. 1938
McChesney, Isaiah	Vancouver; Margo, SK	Canadian	9 Jan. 1907	auto mechanic	survived
McClaren, Beverley F. Slats	Vancouver; Brantford, ON	Canadian	31 Oct. 1916	lumberjack, clerk	WIA, survived
McClure, Alexander Crocher	Montreal	New Zealander	c. 1909		KIA, Fuentes de Ebro, Oct. 1937
McCrystal, William	Vancouver	Irish	28 Dec. 1905	tailor	MIA, fate unknown (conflicting information)
McDonald, Charles Wellrose	Toronto	Canadian	18 July 1901	baker	KIA, Teruel, Feb. 1938
McDonald, Joseph	–	–		–	MIA, Gandesa, Apr. 1938
McDonald, Thomas	Toronto	Canadian	27 Feb. 1909	machinist, railway worker	WIA, survived
McDonald, William	b. New Brunswick; Vancouver; Calgary	Canadian	20 June 1912	driver	MIA, Retreats, Mar. 1938
McDowell, James Hamilton	Toronto	Scottish	14 Jan. 1911	hotel and restaurant worker	survived
McElligott, John Patrick "Paddy"	Vancouver; Nanaimo, BC; New Westminster, BC; YK	Irish	21 May 1905	farm worker, miner, sailor	hospitalized, survived
McGowan, William	Vancouver	–		painter	survived
McGrandle, John "Scotty"	Vancouver	Scottish	10 May 1912	driver, lumberjack	survived,

NAME	HOME	ETHNICITY	DATE OF BIRTH	OCCUPATION	FINAL STATUS
McGrath	Calgary	Scottish	c. 1911	–	fate unknown
McGrath, John Freeman	b. Chatham, NB; Edmonton	Canadian	28 Mar. 1905	lumberjack	survived
McGregor, Hugh	Vancouver; Victoria	Scottish	28 Apr. 1911	baker, farm worker	WIA, survived
McGuire, Patrick	Vancouver	Irish	28 Apr. 1907	auto mechanic	WIA, survived
McInnis, Neil/Henry	Vancouver	–	c. 1912	–	WIA, fate unknown
McIntyre, Thomas	Sudbury; Glace Bay, NS	Canadian	c. 1917	–	MIA, Retreats, Mar. 1938
McKay, John P.	Vancouver	Canadian	3 July 1908	construction foreman	MIA, Retreats, Mar. 1938
McKenzie, Jack	Vancouver	–	c. 1919	–	survived
McKenzie, Thomas	–	–	–	–	survived
McLaren, Alexander	–	–	–	–	detained in France, unclear if he made it to Spain, fate unknown
McLaughlin, Matthew	Hamilton	Scottish	25 Jan. 1901	–	KIA, Retreats, Mar. 1938
McLaughlin, Michael P.	Hamilton	–	–	–	WIA, survived
McLean, Donald/Slats	Regina; Vancouver	–	–	–	WIA, survived
McLeod, Daniel	Regina; Vancouver	Scottish	23 Aug. 1903	bartender, tanner	WIA, survived
McLeod, George	Regina; Vancouver	Scottish	14 Feb. 1903	carpenter	survived
McMann, Francis Henry	Vancouver	English	13 Oct. 1901	electrician	KIA, 26 July 1938
McNeil, Frederick James	b. Arcola, SK; Vancouver; Saskatoon	Canadian	c. 1899	teacher	survived
McNutty, John Brown	Vancouver; Calgary	Scottish	21 Sept. 1909	baker	WIA, survived
McRae, Donald	b. Westbourne, MB; Regina	Canadian	17 Jan. 1916	public servant	WIA, survived
McVicar, Reid, G.W.	b. Dauphin, MB; Winnipeg	Canadian	6 Aug. 1911	clerk, student	WIA, survived
Medgyse, Charles/Karoly	Windsor	Hungarian	19 Mar. 1896	mechanic	POW, survived
Melajeznik, Mike	–	–	–	–	fate unknown
Melanson, William/Wilfred	Yarmouth, NS	French Canadian	28 Nov. 1904	farm worker	MIA, Retreats, Apr. 1938
Meleschuk, Pavel	Toronto; Sudbury; Chicago	Russian	3 Mar. 1909	auto mechanic	survived
Melnick, Alex	Port Arthur, ON	Ukrainian	c. 1902	–	fate unknown
Melnychenko, Oleksander/Alexander	Toronto	Ukrainian	3 July 1904	dish washer, union organizer	WIA, survived
Melville, Patrick	b. Howe Island, ON; Vancouver; Melville, SK	Canadian	c. 1901	worker	WIA, survived
Menard, Gideon/Leo	Montreal	French Canadian	25 Nov. 1887	auto mechanic	survived
Mennel, Morris	Calgary; Vancouver	Canadian	7 May 1913	telegrapher	survived
Menzies, John	Vancouver	Scottish	23 Oct. 1909	lumberjack	survived
Mercelin, Ferrer	Regina; Montreal	French Canadian	23 Mar. 1918	worker	survived

Name	Location	Ethnicity	Birth date	Occupation	Fate
Merges, Elmer Stephen	Toronto	Hungarian	14 Aug. 1912	worker	WIA, survived
Merisalo, Einor	Port Arthur, ON	Finnish	c. 1905	–	survived
Meurs, Arnie	Lethbridge	Dutch	20 June 1901	miner	KIA, Gandesa, 27 July 1938
Meyer, Helge/Henry	Vancouver; Kirkland Lake, ON; Timmins, ON	Danish, Jewish	9 Feb. 1896	medic, painter	survived
Mezei, Benjamin	Coquitlam, BC; Lethbridge; Milk River, AB	Hungarian, Jewish	c. 1903	–	survived
Michna, Mihaly	Montreal	Hungarian	c. 1901	–	KIA, Brunete, July 1937
Mihaichuk, Mykhailo Ivanovich	Brantford, ON	Ukrainian	18 Jan. 1910	carpenter, steelworker	WIA, survived
Mikinnen, Vaino	–	Finnish	–	lumberjack, miner	fate unknown
Milas, Nikola	Winnipeg	German	14 Nov. 1897	carpenter	survived
Miljkovic, Joseph	Port Arthur, ON	Croatian	c. 1903	–	KIA, Brunete, July 1937
Miljkovic, Jure	–	Yugoslav	–	worker	KIA, Jarama, 27 Feb. 1937
Miller, Alexander	Edmonton	Canadian	c. 1896	baker, carpenter	WIA, survived
Miller, Allan	Toronto	Scottish	31 Mar. 1912	clerk, miner	WIA, survived
Miller, Ernest	Vancouver	–	–	–	POW, survived
Miller, John	Windsor	Scottish	20 June 1898	painter	WIA, survived
Mironchuk, Michael	Winnipeg; Fort Frances, ON; Kapuskasing ON	Ukrainian	17 Dec. 1904	lumberjack	survived
Mironiuk, Aleksy/Martin	Ottawa; Toronto; Kirkland Lake, ON	Ukrainian	21 Oct. 1907	–	survived
Mitchell, John Eric	Vancouver	Australian	30 Mar. 1894	dockworker	survived
Mitchie, Thomas	b. Sherbrooke, QC; Montreal; Toronto	Canadian	c. 1911	steelworker	MIA, Jarama, 27 Feb. 1937, fate unknown
Mitrenko, Bill	–	Ukrainian	–	–	fate unknown
Mizowets, Sam/Leon/Sebastian	Montreal	Ukrainian	18 Dec. 1901	painter	WIA, survived
Moczik, Istvan	Lethbridge	Hungarian	5 Dec. 1899	–	KIA, died in hospital of wounds, Aug. 1938
Modic, Matija	Timmins, ON	Slovenian	c. 1900	baker	KIA, Battle of the Ebro, July 1938
Moffat, Arthur	Edmonton; Vancouver	English	19 Sept. 1905	construction worker, lumberjack, miner	WIA, survived
Molineux, Andres/Pat	Vancouver	Irish	22 Oct. 1906	mill worker, worker	WIA, survived
Molnar, Imre/Jim	Windsor	Hungarian	–	–	KIA
Montgomery, Harry Robert	Vancouver; Toronto	Scottish	27 July 1906	driver, painter	hospitalized, survived
Moore, Charles, William	Vancouver	–	c. 1910	welder	MIA, Retreats
Moore, Howard George "Skinny"	Toronto	Canadian	5 Oct. 1916	machinist	KIA, died of wounds in hospital, Oct. 1938
More, Joseph	Montreal	–	–	–	survived
Morency, Jean B.R.	Montreal; US	French Canadian	c. 1903	engineer	fate unknown

NAME	HOME	ETHNICITY	DATE OF BIRTH	OCCUPATION	FINAL STATUS
Morin, François	Montreal; Saint-Hubert, QC	French Canadian	c. 1903	lumberjack	KIA when *Ciudad de Barcelona* was torpedoed, 30 May 1937
Moroz, Feodor	Calgary	Ukrainian	c. 1904	–	survived
Morris, Arthur	Blairmore, AB	Canadian	–	miner, union organizer	KIA, Jarama, 27 Feb. 1937
Morris, Harry	–	–	–	–	fate unknown
Morris, Leonard	Hamilton	English	c. 1904	lumberjack	survived
Morrow, William	–	Scottish	c. 1901	dockworker, miner	hospitalized, survived
Morton, Paul	NS	–	–	–	fate unknown
Moser, George	Vancouver	–	c. 1902	anesthesiologist	fate unknown
Moskaliuk, Petro	–	Ukrainian	11 Dec. 1907	clerk	POW, survived
Mowbray, Fred Clarence	b. Montreal; Winnipeg	Canadian	5 Nov. 1912	shoemaker	KIA, died in hospital of wounds, Mar. 1938
Mozer, Jozsef	Montreal	Hungarian	21 Oct. 1898	–	survived
Mudry, Hryhorii	Toronto; Winnipeg	Ukrainian	c. 1901	locksmith, machinist, railway worker	WIA, survived
Muellers, Ernest	Vancouver	Swiss	10 Jan. 1903	electrician	POW, survived
Mullen, Lawrence	Niagara Falls, ON	–	c. 1904	railway worker	survived
Munro, Alexander	Vancouver	Scottish	c. 1907	truck driver	KIA
Murawsky, Andrii	Winnipeg	Ukrainian	15 Mar. 1895	worker	KIA
Murray, Ben	Toronto	Irish	c. 1896	newspaper salesman	KIA, Retreats, Mar. 1938
Murray, Edward	Vancouver	English	22 Nov. 1898	mechanic	survived
Murtch, John	–	–	–	–	POW, survived
Myers, Roy St. Clair	b. Cobalt, ON; Kirkland Lake, ON	Canadian	19 June 1913	miner	WIA, survived
Myllykangas, Arvi/Arne	Toronto; Edmonton	Finnish	1 Mar. 1908	worker	KIA, Battle of the Ebro
Myllymaki, Arvi	Toronto	Finnish	31 Jan. 1908	farmer, lumberjack, railway worker	KIA, Battle of the Ebro
Mynttinen, Aarne	–	Finnish	c. 1896	carpenter	KIA, Retreats, Mar. 1938
Myroniuk, Martyn	Ottawa	Ukrainian	–	–	survived
Myroniuk, Nicholas	b. Andrew, AB; Vancouver; Edmonton	Canadian	19 May 1915	blacksmith, mechanic	WIA, survived
Nadanicsek, Janos	Notch Hill, BC	Hungarian	1 Sept. 1899	miner	survived
Nagorny, Sedor	Val d'Or, QC	Polish	16 Feb. 1904	miner	survived
Nash, Arden Claude	b. Camrose, AB; Notch Hill, BC	Canadian	7 Aug. 1918	farmer, lumberjack	WIA, survived
Naumov, Ilja	Toronto	Macedonian	c. 1897	worker	survived
Nawalowsky, Stefan	Leamington, ON	Ukrainian	25 Nov. 1901	worker	survived
Nedvar, Joseph	–	Lithuanian	–	–	fate unknown

Name	Residence	Nationality	Birth date	Occupation	Fate
Neilson, Peter Sorin	Vancouver	Danish	27 June 1897	lumberjack	survived
Nelson, Hyman, aka Kosmos Stavrous	Montreal	Jewish	c. 1903	glass worker	survived
Nelson, Thomas	Vancouver	Icelandic	c. 1901	–	fate unknown
Nelson, Thomas Howard	Montreal	–	13 Sept. 1914	laboratory assistant	survived
Neshev, Nikola	–	Bulgarian		–	survived
Neufeld, Abram	Delhi, ON	–	c. 1907	–	KIA, Brunete, 9 July 1937
Nicholson, Charles	Vancouver	Danish	c. 1903	–	survived
Nielsen, Kristian	Winnipeg	Finnish	c. 1900	blacksmith	fate unknown
Niemi, John	–	Finnish	c. 1903	–	survived
Niemi, Toivo	–	Finnish		–	fate unknown
Nieminen, Antti/Niemi	Toronto; Port Arthur, ON	Finnish	10 Aug. 1903	–	KIA, executed, Apr. 1938
Nieminen, Emil	Port Arthur, ON	Finnish		–	survived
Nihtila, Kauko	–			–	KIA, Retreats, Mar. 1938
Nikephorou, Elene (woman)	–	Greek		nurse	fate unknown
Nikita, Nick		Ukrainian		–	fate unknown
Nikolao, Maria/Marika (woman)		Greek		–	fate unknown
Nikolaychuk, Peter	Winnipeg	Ukrainian	c. 1903	–	fate unknown
Nikoloff, Bojan	Port Arthur, ON	Bulgarian	c. 1904	–	survived
Nikoltcheef, John/Anto	–	Bulgarian	c. 1906	–	survived
Nimmo, Jean	Hamilton	–		–	MIA, Retreats, Mar. 1938
Nivirisnsky, Nicholas	Edmonton	Ukrainian	9 Sept. 1915	diamond driller	KIA
Norman, Stanley Gilbert	Vancouver	English	c. 1899	cook, mechanic	WIA, survived
Norris, John Alexander	Winnipeg; New York	Canadian	14 Apr. 1909	salesman	fate unknown
Norris, Leonard/Lenan	Vancouver; Yorkton, SK; New Westminster, BC	English	6 Aug. 1894	sawmill worker	hospitalized, survived
Norum, John	Winnipeg	Norwegian	30 Aug. 1904	worker	KIA, Belchite, died in hospital, Sept. 1937
Novosel, Janko	Calgary	Croatian	c. 1902	–	survived
Numi, E.	Toronto	–	c. 1897	–	fate unknown
Nunemaker, Willis	b. Welland, ON; Toronto; Vancouver	Canadian		truck driver	POW, survived
Nurisalo, Matti Einao	Port Arthur, ON	Finnish	5 June 1914	carpenter, lumberjack	WIA, survived
Nus, Olik	–	Polish	19 May 1905	–	fate unknown
Nutt, Alexander	Hamilton	Scottish		farm worker, machinist	KIA, Teruel
Nuttal, B.	Regina	–	27 Mar. 1910	–	fate unknown
O'Boyle, Pat Stewart	–	Irish		–	WIA, survived
O'Brien, John Thomas	Montreal	Canadian	6 jan. 1914	printer	survived

NAME	HOME	ETHNICITY	DATE OF BIRTH	OCCUPATION	FINAL STATUS
O'Brien, Sanford Byron	Vancouver	Canadian	c. 1908	machinist, mechanic	MIA, Gandesa, Apr. 1938
O'Connor, James "Paddy"	Vancouver	Irish	c. 1906	worker	KIA, Retreats, 11 Mar. 1938
O'Daire, Patrick "Paddy"	Saskatoon; England	Irish	c. 1904	worker	WIA, survived
O'Dorne, Frank	Regina	–	–	–	survived
Offer, John Harry William	Vancouver	English	16 Feb. 1906	cannery worker	WIA, survived
Ojabru, Vaino	Port Arthur, ON	–	–	–	survived
Ojala, Steve	Sudbury	Finnish	c. 1892	–	survived
Ojanem, Armas Johan	–	Finnish	c. 1904	firefighter	WIA, survived
Okonski, Jakob	Winnipeg; Edmonton	Polish	4 June 1912	miner	WIA, survived
Olchyshyn, Steve	Toronto	–	–	–	fate unknown
O'Leary, Earl	Midland, ON	Irish	c. 1909	sailor	fate unknown
O'Leary, Frank Earl Roderick	Midland, ON; Toronto; Sprague, ON	Canadian	6 Sept. 1909	lumberjack, sailor	WIA, survived
Olsen, J.	–	–	–	–	fate unknown
Olynyk, Konstantin "Mike"	South Porcupine, ON	Ukrainian	4 July 1904	worker	survived
O'Mahony, Patrick	Calgary	Canadian	9 Oct. 1890	masseur, nurse	fate unknown
Opanowski, Kazimir/Kostur	Toronto	Polish	23 Dec. 1905	blacksmith, welder	hospitalized, survived
Oppenheim, Antal	Montreal	Hungarian	14 Nov. 1904	–	survived
Oppenheim, Cimer	–	Hungarian	–	–	fate unknown
Oraschuk, Hendrick/Henry	Edmonton; Entwhistle, AB	Ukrainian	–	musician	survived
Ordog, Ferencz	Mission, BC	Hungarian	18 Feb. 1894	farmer	survived
Orlovitch/Osemlak, Filip	Vancouver	Polish	29 Apr. 1901	–	survived
Oshchypko/Oszczypko, Fedir/Teodor	Sudbury; Toronto	Ukrainian	17 Nov. 1903	worker	survived
O'Shea, John "Paddy"	Toronto	Irish	6 Mar. 1904	shoemaker	KIA, Teruel
Osirmaz, Mihaly	Montreal	Hungarian	29 Jan. 1903	worker	survived
Oskari, Paavo	South Porcupine, ON; Schumacher, ON; Toronto	Finnish	c. 1915	–	KIA, executed, Apr. 1938
Ostovic, Nikola	–	Canadian	26 Oct. 1914	–	survived
Ostry, Harry	Winnipeg	Russian, Jewish	–	doctor	survived
Osuchowski/Ossowski, Joseph B.	Vancouver; Calgary	German	22 Feb. 1897	bookkeeper, lumberjack, prospector	survived
O'Sullivan, Paddy	–	–	c. 1911	–	KIA, Gandesa, 31 July 1938
Ouelette, Germain	Winnipeg; Toronto; Montreal	French Canadian	–	–	survived
Owen, Darcy	Vancouver	–	c. 1907	clerk	WIA, survived
Paakko, Vilhelm /Johan	–	Finnish	–	–	KIA, Azuara, Mar. 1938

Name	Location	Ethnicity	Date of birth	Occupation	Fate
Pacholczak, Stefan	Winnipeg; Ottawa	Ukrainian	c. 1898	carpenter	POW, survived
Pacsuta, Gyorgy	Toronto; Branford, ON; Proctor, BC	Hungarian	8 Sept. 1900	machinist	WIA, survived
Pacyna, Jozef	–	Polish	–	–	fate unknown
Padowsky, Nicholas	b. Blaine Lake, SK; Winnipeg	Canadian	24 Oct. 1899	mechanic	MIA
Page, George Henry	Vancouver; Hamilton	English	14 May 1899	steelworker	fate unknown (conflicting information)
Page, John	Edmonton; Wetaskiwin, AB; Vancouver	–	19 Jan. 1916	tailor's apprentice	survived
Painter	–	–	–	–	survived
Paivio, Jules Pekka	Sudbury; Matawa; ON	Canadian	30 Apr. 1917	clerk	POW, survived
Pajdak, Mladan	Toronto	Serbian	c. 1901	worker	WIA, survived
Pakkala, Frans	Port Arthur, ON	Finnish	c. 1897	–	WIA, survived
Palak, Stanislaw	Winnipeg	Polish	–	–	fate unknown
Palavter, Andre	–	Ukrainian	–	–	fate unknown
Pangracz, Martin	Vancouver	Slovak	c. 1899	worker	survived
Panosuik, S.	Fort William, ON	Ukrainian	–	–	fate unknown
Panteluk, Wasyl John	Bellevue, AB	Ukrainian	–	–	survived
Papiernik, Pavel	Montreal	Slovak	30 Oct. 1904	carpenter	survived
Papp, Ferenc/Frank	Windsor	Hungarian	c. 1900	–	POW, died of pneumonia, 27 June 1938
Papp, Gyula	–	Hungarian	c. 1912	–	fate unknown
Parker, Charles	Vancouver; Winnipeg	English	c. 1901	sports instructor	KIA, Quinto, 24 Aug. 1937
Parker, Douglas	Toronto	–	c. 1896	–	fate unknown
Parker, Frank Reilly	Vancouver	American	–	pilot	survived
Parlington, Frank	Hamilton	–	–	–	fate unknown
Paroczai, Sandor/Alexander	Windsor	Hungarian	c. 1901	–	KIA, Gandesa, 26 July 1938
Parsons, Francis Harold	Calgary	Canadian	11 Jan. 1914	radio technician	survived
Pascall, Jack Abie/Isaac	Montreal	Canadian, Jewish	6 July 1912	sailor, textile worker	survived
Paterson, Harry C.	Fenelon Falls. ON; Toronto	Canadian	9 July 1915	truck driver	survived
Paterson, Robert "Scotty"	Calgary	English	27 Jan. 1909	lumberjack	WIA, survived
Paterson, Thomas Edward	Vancouver	English	17 Jan. 1904	lumberjack, truck driver	WIA, survived
Paton, George	Fernie, BC; Coleman, AB	Scottish			KIA, Retreats, Apr. 1938
Patrick, Daniel	Vancouver	Canadian	18 Nov. 1914	–	KIA, Retreats, Mar. 1938.
Patryluk, Vasyl/Bill	Toronto; Winnipeg	Ukrainian	23 May 1908	miner	hospitalized, survived
Patterson, Edward/Theodore	Vancouver; Edmonton	Irish	28 Aug. 1904	harness maker	KIA, Gandesa, 28 July 1938
Patterson, Thomas	Vancouver	English	21 Dec. 1900	–	MIA

NAME	HOME	ETHNICITY	DATE OF BIRTH	OCCUPATION	FINAL STATUS
Pattison, Pat	–	–	–	–	fate unknown
Paulsen, Harry	Winnipeg	–	–	–	fate unknown
Pavelic, Paul	Port Arthur, ON	Croatian	c. 1901	–	WIA, survived
Pawliuk, Theodore	Toronto	Ukrainian	8 Mar. 1894	barber	hospitalized, survived
Pawliuk, Thomas/Timothy	Toronto; Guelph, ON	Ukrainian	9 July 1910	machinist	MIA, Retreats, Mar. 1938
Peacock, Jack	Churchill, MB	–	–	–	fate unknown
Pearce, Robert	Vancouver	–	–	–	fate unknown
Pearson, Alexander	Winnipeg	English	–	worker	fate unknown
Pearson, John	Vancouver	–	c. 1918	–	fate unknown
Pekkalin, Arvi	–	–	–	–	hospitalized, fate unknown
Penchaff/Pencho/Ponchoff	Toronto	Bulgarian	c. 1898	driver, worker	WIA, survived
Penn, Marvin	Winnipeg	Lithuanian, Jewish	9 Aug. 1913	furrier, miner	WIA, survived
Pennycade, Edward	Huntsville, ON; Toronto	English	c. 1912	machinist	WIA, survived
Penrod, J.	–	–	–	–	MIA, Retreats, Mar. 1938, fate unknown
Perala, Juho Ludvig	Port Arthur, ON	Finnish	c. 1906	farmer	survived
Perdue, Carl Raymond	b. Clinton, ON; Calgary; Lethbridge	Canadian	15 Sept. 1903	factory worker	survived
Peressini, Antonio	Blairmore, AB	Canadian	12 Apr. 1914	miner	KIA, Battle of the Ebro, Aug. 1938
Perles, Harry	Montreal	Ukrainian	–	–	fate unknown
Pesyshanski, S.	Winnipeg	Welsh	28 Mar. 1915	sailor	fate unknown
Peterson, Robert James "Bob"	Toronto	Danish	4 Oct. 1908	gardener	WIA, survived
Peterson, Anker Magnus	Vancouver; Port Arthur, ON	Bulgarian	c. 1905	steelworker	KIA, Teruel, 15 Jan. 1938
Petkoff, Ivan	Montreal	Czech	c. 1906	hospital orderly	fate unknown
Petric, Vilijam	–	Scottish	c. 1896	waiter	fate unknown
Petrie, William	Vancouver	Ukrainian	c. 1903	–	survived
Petruk, Onismim	Winnipeg	English	21 Dec. 1900	–	survived
Petterson, Thomas	Vancouver	–	–	–	MIA
Pettier, Louis	Vancouver	Irish	–	–	fate unknown
Pickards, J.	–	Canadian	9 Oct. 1904	nurse, social worker	fate unknown
Pike, Florence Mildred Stevenson (woman)	b. Paris, ON; Montreal				survived
Piliuk, Ivan	Winnipeg	Ukrainian	25 May 1899	carpenter, cook	survived
Pilo/Pulo, Martti/Matti/Mack	Port Arthur, ON; Silver Mountain, ON	Finnish	7 Dec. 1914	lumberjack	survived
Plafter/Plakht, Andrei	Beaupré, QC	Ukrainian	3 Nov. 1905	worker	survived
Plese, Juraj	Montreal	Croatian	25 Feb. 1898	worker	WIA, survived
Pocik, Steve	Lethbridge	Hungarian	c. 1896	–	WIA, fate unknown

Name	Location	Ethnicity	Birth date	Occupation	Fate
Poikulainen/Holopainen, Erik Armas/Jussi	Port Arthur, CN; Toronto	Finnish	c. 1910	sailor	survived
Poirier, François X.	Montreal; Labelle, QC	French Canadian	c. 1899	teacher	WIA, survived
Polic, Stjepan	–	Croatian	1 Mar. 1902	–	WIA, survived
Polichek, John	Vernon, BC; Vancouver	Canadian	20 Mar. 1907	miner	KIA, Gandesa, 30 July 1938
Pollington, Hiram/Frank	b. Fulton, ON; Hamilton	Canadian	2 Nov. 1909	printer	survived
Pollock, Herbert/Harry	Windsor	Irish	2 Mar. 1899	boilermaker	hospitalized, survived
Polozyk, Fred	Winnipeg	Ukrainian	–	–	fate unknown
Pomeroy, Joseph Wilson	b. Grand Falls, NF; Vancouver; Montreal	Newfoundlander	23 Jan. 1911	miner	WIA, survived
Pongalos	–	Russian	–	–	fate unknown
Poniedzilsky, Joseph	Montreal	Polish	3 Mar. 1907	artist	survived
Potvin, Edward	b. Wetaskiwin, AB; Edmonton	French Canadian	–	driver, mechanic	WIA, survived
Pozniak, Jan/John	Saskatoon	Ukrainian	23 Sept. 1893	worker	survived
Prange, Robert "Red"	Vancouver; Ottawa	Canadian	c. 1911	butcher	hospitalized, survived
Preer, Martin	Toronto	–	–	–	survived
Prentice, Roger	Vancouver	–	–	–	survived
Pretz, Adam	Toronto; Delhi, ON	Hungarian	c. 1901	–	KIA, Brunete, 17 July 1937
Princz, Joseph	Lethbridge	Hungarian	10 Nov. 1899	–	KIA, Retreats, Mar. 1938
Pritchard, David/Pat	Saskatoon	Irish	c. 1906	–	MIA, Retreats, Mar. 1938
Procyk, Michael	Calgary	Ukrainian	16 Aug. 1908	–	WIA, survived
Prokopets/Prokopiuk, Mike/Nick	Young, SK; Toronto	Ukrainian	15 Nov. 1897	–	POW, survived
Provlovich, Paul	–	–	–	–	WIA, fate unknown
Przedwojewski, Joseph	Winnipeg; Montreal	Canadian	8 Apr. 1916	aviation mechanic	POW, survived
Punko, Paul	Fernie, BC; Vancouver	Ukrainian	c. 1898	–	survived
Purdek, Peter	Fort William, ON	–	c. 1896	–	survived
Puska, Franja	–	Finnish	–	–	KIA, Azuara, 11 Mar. 1938
Puttonen, Alex	Port Arthur, ON	Finnish	2 Aug. 1897	worker	KIA, Retreats, Apr. 1938
Pyhaluoto, Franz Luoto	Port Arthur, ON	Finnish	16 Mar. 1905	lumberjack	KIA, Sierra de Cavalls, 23 Sept. 1938
Quarrie, Roy	Delhi, ON	–	–	–	KIA
Queen, James	Geraldton, CN	English	18 July 1912	–	survived
Raatikinainen, Eino	Port Arthur, ON	Finnish	c. 1903	lumberjack	WIA, survived
Racki, Ivan	Kirkland Lake, ON	Croatian	c. 1905	worker	KIA, Brunete, 6 July 1937
Racz, Imre/James	Delhi, ON	Hungarian	c. 1897	–	KIA when *Ciudad de Barcelona* was torpedoed, 30 May 1937
Ragvacs, Janos	Toronto	Hungarian	3 Oct. 1903	farmer	KIA, Retreats, Apr. 1938

NAME	HOME	ETHNICITY	DATE OF BIRTH	OCCUPATION	FINAL STATUS
Raisanen, Lauri August	Port Arthur, ON	Finnish	c. 1906	–	WIA, survived
Rajamaki, Bruno Albert	Toronto; Port Arthur, ON	Finnish	c. 1905	worker	survived
Rajki, Matyas	Toronto	Hungarian	19 Feb. 1900	worker	survived
Ramonovich, Stanley	Toronto	Polish	c. 1903	–	survived
Ramuelson, Baruch/Bert	Edmonton	Ukrainian, Jewish	22 Mar. 1910	lawyer	WIA, survived
Rank, Victor John	Toronto; Hamilton	Canadian	4 July 1915	worker	WIA, survived
Ranti, Yohan	Port Arthur, ON	–	–	–	survived
Rasmus, Mattias	Port Arthur, ON; Parry Sound, ON	Finnish	c. 1913	worker	survived
Ratkovic, Dragutin	Mountain Park, AB	Croatian	2 Sept. 1904	miner	survived
Raves, Otto	–	–	–	–	MIA
Rawicz, Michael	–	Polish	12 Jan. 1915	mechanic	KIA, Segura de los Baños, Feb. 1938
Rayfield, Hedron/Harry	Toronto	English	12 Dec. 1908	accountant, musician	WIA, survived
Rayner, Stanislas	Edmonton	–	c. 1910	truck driver	fate unknown
Reid, James	Vancouver; Saskatchewan	–	–	worker	fate unknown
Reilly, Frank Parker	Vancouver; Terrace Bay, BC	American	c. 1909	–	survived
Reinholm, Alex	–	–	–	–	hospitalized, fate unknown
Relev, Dimitar	–	Bulgarian	–	–	survived
Renner, Henry Arthur	Edmonton; Vancouver; US	Canadian	11 Apr. 1905	plumber, railway worker	hospitalized, survived
Reutta, Len	Toronto	–	c. 1913	–	fate unknown
Reznowski, Edward	b. Dauphin, MB; Toronto; Vancouver; Winnipeg; Chicago	Canadian	28 Dec. 1904	electrician	survived
Ribas	–	Hungarian	–	–	fate unknown
Rice, Benjamin	Toronto	Polish	c. 1907	–	survived
Ricetts, Lee	–	–	–	–	MIA
Richards, George E.	Alberta	English	5 Sept. 1914	–	survived
Richardson, T.	Verdun, QC	–	–	–	fate unknown
Rickards, Joseph	Winnipeg	French Canadian	5 Apr. 1917	worker	survived
Righton, Leonard	Toronto	–	c. 1908	auto mechanic, driver	survived
Riley, Joe	Vancouver	–	–	–	survived
Rivard, Lucien	–	French Canadian	–	–	fate unknown
Robbins, Carl William	Dresden, ON	Canadian	12 Feb. 1913	driver, sailor	survived
Robbins, Tom	Winnipeg	–	–	–	fate unknown
Roberts, Charles	Winnipeg	–	c. 1910	–	KIA, Fuentes de Ebro, Oct. 1937
Roberts, Thomas	Lethbridge; Calgary	Canadian	31 Mar. 1915	–	WIA, survived
Robertson, James Keith	Edmonton	Scottish	c. 1897	cook	MIA

Name	Location	Nationality	Birth date	Occupation	Fate
Robertson, Shand/Shane	Vancouver; Nanaimo, BC	Canadian	13 Nov. 1888	worker	survived
Robeson/Robertson, Wilfred Jackson	Vancouver; Montreal; Halifax	English	21 Dec. 1900	miner, sailor	survived
Robinson, Digley/Digby	–	–	–	–	KIA, Battle of the Ebro
Robson, Albert Edward	Vancouver	Australian	c. 1911	–	WIA, survived
Rockman, Harvey	Montreal	Canadian, Jewish	6 Jan. 1915	driver, salesman, student	WIA, survived
Rocziak, Stanislaw	Hazelridge, MB; Sioux Lookout, ON	Canadian	31 Dec. 1904	–	MIA, Retreats, Mar. 1938
Rodd, Wilfred G.	Winnipeg; Vancouver	–	c. 1913	–	WIA, fate unknown
Roden, Frank	Vancouver; Winnipeg	Scottish	13 Mar. 1899	dockworker	survived
Rogers/Henderson, Frank	Regina; Toronto	–	–	–	survived
Rogers, Jim	Guelph, ON	–	–	–	survived
Rolloff/Ralloff/Rally/Nicoloff, Ivan/Jim	Toronto	Macedonian	c. 1913	cook, waiter	survived
Roman, Danylo	Toronto	Ukrainian	c. 1903	blacksmith	WIA, survived
Romanishin, Dan	Toronto	Ukrainian	–	–	survived
Romaniuk, Alexander	Montreal	Ukrainian	29 June 1902	worker	survived
Romaniuk, Gabriel	Montreal	Ukrainian	–	–	KIA, Oct. 37
Romaniuk, Mikolaj/Nick/ Emanuel/Eugene	Val d'Or, QC; Port Arthur, ON	Ukrainian	5 Feb. 1902	lumberjack	WIA, survived
Romaniuk, Mykhailo/Michael	Val d'Or, QC	Ukrainian	14 Jan. 1908	miner	survived
Romanovich, Stanley	Toronto	–	–	–	hospitalized, survived
Romanuk, A.	Montreal	–	–	–	KIA
Romk	Vancouver	–	–	–	WIA, fate unknown
Ronczowsky, Harry/Gregor	Camrose, AB; Edmonton	Ukrainian	12 July 1913	worker	survived
Roschly, Charles W.	Vancouver	Swiss	c. 1903	–	MIA
Roschuk, Steve	Winnipeg	Ukrainian	c. 1898	–	survived
Rose, Arthur	Drumheller, AB; Blairmore, AB	–	–	miner	KIA
Rose, Earl	Vancouver; Cold Lake, AB	American	22 Nov. 1886	machinist, trapper	WIA, survived
Rose, Richard	Hamilton	English	19 Aug. 1900	painter	MIA, Retreats, Mar. 1938
Rose, Leo	–	–	–	–	KIA, Teruel, 20 Jan. 1938
Rosenberg, Louis Walsh	Toronto	Jewish	c. 1909	–	survived
Rosenthal, Leon	San Francisco	American, Jewish	c. 1919	warehouse worker	fate unknown
Ross, Allan	Winnipeg; Vancouver	Canadian, Jewish	22 Aug. 1917	mechanic	hospitalized, survived
Ross, George Crandles "Scotty"/ Charles	Vancouver	Scottish	6 Aug. 1912	lumberjack	survived

NAME	HOME	ETHNICITY	DATE OF BIRTH	OCCUPATION	FINAL STATUS
Ross, James	Vancouver; Winnipeg	English	c. 1905	miner	MIA, Retreats, Apr. 1938
Rucashevich, John	Montreal; Rouyn, QC	–	–	–	fate unknown
Rudnykiewicz, Stefan	–	Ukrainian	–	–	survived
Rudzinskis, Felixs	Windsor	Polish	c. 1899	–	WIA, survived
Ruggiero, Vincenso/Jimmy	Guelph	Canadian	24 June 1920	student	WIA, survived
Ruitta, Al	–	–	–	–	MIA
Ruohohen, Armas Henrik	Port Arthur, ON	Finnish	c. 1905	lumberjack	WIA, survived
Rupcic, Franjo/Frank	b. Schumacher, ON; Timmins, ON	Canadian	17 Feb. 1915	painter	survived
Rushchak, Mykola/Nick	Toronto	Ukrainian	5 Dec. 1902	worker	survived
Rushton, Harry/Albert	Toronto; Hamilton	English	26 Oct. 1892	salesman	WIA, survived
Russel, Tomasz/Thomas	Montreal; Toronto	Polish	c. 1899	carpenter	survived
Russell, Francis Michael	Toronto	Canadian	16 Mar. 1920	auto mechanic	survived
Russell, Michael	Montreal	Irish	c. 1910	cook	fate unknown (conflicting information)
Rutherford, Frank	Vancouver	–	c. 1913	–	survived
Rutkowski, Joszef	Edmonton	Polish	c. 1896	–	KIA
Ruuskka, Vaino	Port Arthur, ON	Finnish	24 Aug. 1893	lumberjack	KIA, Caspe, 14 Mar. 1938
Ruzic, Jerolim Franjo	–	Croatian	c. 1894	–	KIA
Ryan, Larry/Lawrence	Toronto; Burk's Falls, ON	–	c. 1903	typesetter	WIA, survived
Ryant/Rubin, Tommy	Edmonton; Montreal	–	c. 1913	–	KIA
Ryback, Steve	b. Elma, MB; Fort William, ON	Canadian	1 Feb. 1910	driver, lumberjack, mechanic	WIA, survived
Rychuk, Fedir	Red Lake, ON; Winnipeg	Belarusian	c. 1903	foundry worker, miner	WIA, survived
Rye, Malinowsky	Toronto	Ukrainian	–	–	survived
Ryynanen, Toivo	b. Sunshine, ON; Port Arthur, ON	Canadian	21 May 1917	driver, lumberjack, miner	KIA
Saari/Jaakonsaari, Toivo	Toronto	Finnish	c. 1898	electrician	survived
Sabo, Albert	Windsor	Hungarian	23 May 1902	–	WIA, survived
Sabo, Jan	Toronto	Slovak	13 Apr. 1912	–	survived
Sakland, Erich	–	Estonian	c. 1905	–	POW, fate unknown
Salemko, Oleksa	Brandon, MB	Ukrainian	c. 1905	worker	WIA, survived
Salminen, Vaino Johannes	Port Arthur, ON; Sudbury	Finnish	1907	–	survived
Salo, Alexsius	Port Arthur, ON	Finnish	11 Mar. 1905	–	fate unknown
Salvail, Arthur	b. St. Majorique, QC; Montreal	French Canadian	31 Dec. 1901	painter, printer	WIA, survived
Samuolis, Antana	Lethbridge; Sudbury; Edmonton	Lithuanian	c. 1903	–	survived
Sanchis, Vincent	–	–	–	–	WIA, fate unknown

Name	Location	Origin	Birth date	Occupation	Fate
Sarvas, Juraj/George	London, ON	Slovak	25 Apr. 1903	shoemaker	survived
Satiz, Joe	Drumheller, AB	Hungarian	–	–	survived
Saunders, Charles Adshead	Vancouver	English	24 Oct. 1906	farmer	WIA, survived
Saunders, Murray Charles	Hamilton; Kyle, SK; Edmonton; US	Canadian	11 Oct. 1906	driver, farm worker	survived
Sauriol, Jean Vianney	Winnipeg; Montreal	French Canadian	28 Nov. 1914	–	MIA, Gandesa, Apr. 1938
Savikko, Johan	Port Arthur, ON	Finnish	7 Dec. 1890	–	hospitalized, survived
Sawkiw, Stefan	Toronto	Ukrainian	c. 1916	driver	survived
Saxer, Charles Marin	Lethbridge	English	17 Jan. 1901	printer	survived
Scarpello/Scanlan, Charles Anthony	b. Kingston; Toronto	Canadian	23 Nov. 1910	worker	POW, survived
Schatz, Issac	Toronto	Ukrainian, Jewish	5 Apr. 1903	sailor	WIA, survived
Scheretrum, Walter	–	Hungarian	–	–	fate unknown
Schiffer, Ferenc–	–	Hungarian	–	–	fate unknown
Schmeltzer, George/Gyorgy	Toronto; Montreal	Hungarian	2 July 1902	–	survived
Schmidt, Joseph	Edmonton	Hungarian	17 Jan. 1904	mechanic	hospitalized, survived
Schneider, Janos	Lethbridge	Hungarian	1 Oct. 1912	driver, mechanic	WIA, survived
Schoen, Joseph	b. Steinbach, MB; Winnipeg	Canadian	27 Apr. 1911	factory worker, farm worker, lumberjack	WIA, survived
Schofield, Ronald	Toronto	English	26 Dec. 1912	baker	POW, survived
Schwartzmann, Janos	–	Hungarian	–	–	fate unknown
Scott, Stuart Maurice	b. Grandview, MB; Vancouver; Powell River, BC	Canadian	28 Mar. 1902	carpenter	WIA, survived
Sczczyk, Stepan	Winnipeg	Ukrainian	c. 1914	teacher	POW, survived
Sekerek, Elias	Winnipeg	Czech	c. 1901	–	MIA
Seminoff, Walter	Toronto; Schumacher, ON	Canadian	5 Sept. 1916	petroleum chemist	survived
Seppanen, Arvi	Port Arthur, ON; South Porcupine, ON	Finnish	5 May 1904	lumberjack, miner	survived
Serdar Stevan	Port Arthur, ON; Val d'Or, QC	Croatian	c. 1908	miner	WIA, survived
Serdar, Filip	Port Arthur, ON	Croatian	c. 1903	miner	WIA, survived
Serdar, Milan/Mike	Timmins, ON; Schumacher, ON	Croatian	c. 1905	miner, railway worker	KIA, Brunete, 10 July 1937
Serhiievych, Maksym	Winnipeg; Fed Lake, ON	Ukrainian	25 Oct. 1900	worker	survived
Seviceski, Harry	–	Ukrainian	–	–	fate unknown
Sezia, Charles	–	Ukrainian	–	–	fate unknown
Shapcott, James	Toronto	–	c. 1880	–	survived
Shapiro, Henry/Saul	Montreal	Jewish	–	–	MIA, Teruel, 21 Jan. 1938
Shapiro, Saul Meyer	Montreal; New York	American, Jewish	c. 1916	tailor	WIA, survived

NAME	HOME	ETHNICITY	DATE OF BIRTH	OCCUPATION	FINAL STATUS
Shea/Moore, Gerald Charles	Vancouver; Glace Bay, NS; Port Morien, NS	Canadian	3 May 1918	cannery worker, fisherman, lumberjack, miner	survived
Sheppherd, Fred	ON	Canadian			survived
Sheridon, Fleming	b. Haileybury, ON; Vancouver; Cochrane, ON	Canadian	15 Sept. 1915	lumberjack	KIA, Battle of the Ebro, died of wounds in hospital
Sherwood, William	SK; Wisconsin	Ukrainian	–	–	fate unknown
Shevchuk, Joseph	The Pas, MB; Fort Frances, ON	Ukrainian	–	–	survived
Shevchuk/Sheweluk/Sheveliuk, Oleksander/Alex	Toronto	Ukrainian	2 Aug. 1913	carpenter, printer	WIA, survived
Shevshky, John	–	Ukrainian	–	–	survived
Shields, Robert Frank	–		–	–	KIA
Shirley, Edward	Vancouver		–	–	WIA, survived
Shlemko, Ivan/John	Drumheller, AB	Ukrainian	28 Aug. 1909	miner	fate unknown (conflicting information)
Shpyrka, Pavlo	Ottawa	Ukrainian	3 Apr. 1903	–	survived
Shumeker, John	Winnipeg	Ukrainian	c. 1898	–	survived
Shumik, Samuil/Stefan	Winnipeg	Ukrainian	c. 1904	–	KIA, Caspe, Mar. 1938
Shush, Havrylo	Montreal	Ukrainian	c. 1900	–	KIA
Sidney, Walter	–		–	–	POW, survived
Sidor, Michael	b. Winnipegosis, MB; Saskatoon	Canadian	21 Mar. 1912	barber, fisherman	WIA, survived
Sidor, Victor	Toronto; Fort William, ON	Polish	11 Dec. 1903	–	survived
Sidun, Michael	Port Arthur, ON	Czech	c. 1903	–	KIA, Retreats, Apr. 1938
Sillanpaa, Franz Johan	Port Arthur, ON	Finnish	28 Dec. 1904	truck driver	KIA, Teruel
Siitala, Vilho Artturi	Vancouver	Finnish	30 July 1899	–	KIA, Sierra de Cavalls, 23 Sept. 1938
Silverman, Ivan/Max	–	Canadian	9 Mar. 1910	bookkeeper	MIA, Retreats, Apr. 1938
Sim, Charles	Vancouver	Canadian	c. 1886	–	survived
Simic, Anton.	Timmins, ON	Croatian	10 Feb. 1900	–	survived
Simionoff, Boris Theodoroff	South Porcupine, ON	Bulgarian	15 Jan. 1894	worker	WIA, survived
Simmonds, Percival	Regina	English	c. 1903	–	survived
Simms, Thomas Patrick	Vancouver; New Westminster, BC	Irish	c. 1903	miner	KIA, Retreats, Mar. 1938
Sipponen, Ilmari	Port Arthur, ON	Finnish	30 July 1902	lumberjack	survived
Sirdar, Tony	Port Arthur, ON	Finnish	–	–	fate unknown
Siren, Aarne	Montreal	Finnish	–	–	survived
Sirko, Louis Stephen	New Waterford, NS; Drumheller, AB	Hungarian	29 Dec. 1905	miner	survived
Sisco, Alexander/Sandor	Drumheller, AB; Bellevue, AB	Hungarian	17 Feb. 1906	coal miner	WIA, survived

Name	Place	Nationality	Birth date	Occupation	Fate
Sise, Hazen Edward	Montreal; England	Canadian	c. 1906	—	survived
Siskonen, Karl	—	Finnish	—	—	MIA, Retreats, Mar. 1938
Siveatre, M.	—	—	—	—	MIA
Siven, Arthur Johannes	Port Arthur, ON; Vancouver	Finnish, Jewish	26 June 1908	sailor, truck driver	survived
Skawulak, Dmytro	Toronto	Ukrainian	c. 1915	driver	survived
Skibinski, Stanislaw	Toronto	Polish	c. 1904	—	survived
Skinner, Baden	Vancouver	Welsh	20 May 1900	miner	KIA, Sierra de Cavalls, 23 Sept. 1938
Skinner, William C. George	b. Owen Sound; Winnipeg	Canadian	27 Apr. 1905	blacksmith, lather	survived
Skoloda, Joseph	Montreal	Slovak	15 Aug. 1894	worker	survived
Skopljec, Ivan	—	Croatian	c. 1888	—	KIA, June 1937
Skriniar, Yuray/Juraj	Montreal	Slovak	5 Oct. 1901	—	survived
Skup/Scott, Paul	Montreal	Canadian, Jewish	6 June 1916	student	POW, survived
Slamen, S.	—	Slovak	—	—	fate unknown
Slater, Frederick W.	Hamilton	English	9 Feb. 1908	—	survived
Slobodzian/Woodman, Walter	Port Arthur, ON	Polish	27 Mar. 1905	construction worker, steelworker	WIA, survived
Slotin, Louis	Winnipeg	Canadian, Jewish	c. 1910	—	survived
Smalec, Jozef	Fort William, ON	Polish	c. 1900	—	survived
Smi, Joseph	—	—	—	—	survived
Smibrer, Alex	Toronto	Ukrainian	25 Mar. 1903	—	MIA, Retreats, Mar. 1938, fate unknown
Smiechowicz, Dorofiej/Mick	Port Arthur, ON	Ukrainian	c. 1908	—	survived
Smith, Benjamin Carr	Toronto	English	6 Oct. 1914	—	KIA
Smith, Fred Ernest	Edmonton	—	—	—	MIA, Retreats, Mar. 1938, fate unknown
Smith, Joe	—	—	—	miner	fate unknown
Smith, Lloyd Stewart	Vancouver; Montreal	Canadian	24 Apr. 1913	lumberjack	WIA, survived
Smolko, Jan	Montreal	Slovak	8 Jan. 1902	worker	survived
Smutylo, Vasyl/William	Toronto	Ukrainian	24 Apr. 1893	worker	WIA, survived
Smythe, Daniel	Toronto	Scottish	5 Oct. 1911	—	KIA, Gandesa, 1 Apr. 1938
Sneer, Martin	Toronto	—	—	—	fate unknown
Snihur, Alex	—	—	c. 1903	—	fate unknown
Socha, Frank	Toronto	—	—	—	survived
Soltesz, Jozsef	Lethbridge	Hungarian	c. 1900	engineer	fate unknown
Somers, Lou	Vancouver	—	—	—	fate unknown
Sorensen, Henning	Vancouver	Danish	14 May 1901	journalist	survived
Southgate, James	Hamilton	English	c. 1906	crane operator	survived
Spamberger, Adam	Montreal	Yugoslav	15 May 1895	—	survived

NAME	HOME	ETHNICITY	DATE OF BIRTH	OCCUPATION	FINAL STATUS
Spark, Leonard	Vancouver	–	c. 1905	–	KIA
Sparks, Harold Christopher	Toronto	Canadian	c. 1908	electrician	survived
Spencer, Cyril C.	b. London, ON; Toronto	Canadian	3 Mar. 1910	upholsterer	survived
Spirovic, Djorije/George	–	Bulgarian	c. 1903	worker	KIA
Spiwak, Teodor/Fred	Toronto; Windsor	Ukrainian	14 Mar. 1899	mechanic	survived
Srein, Jozsef	Montreal	Hungarian	–	–	fate unknown
Stamm, Morris	Calgary	Ukrainian	c. 1904	–	survived
Stanton, Michael	Winnipeg	Canadian	8 Feb. 1914	–	MIA, Retreats, Mar. 1938
Staub, Arnold	Estevan, SK	Swiss	c. 1907	jockey	WIA, survived
Steer, George	Chatham, ON; Toronto	English	c. 1900	tailor	WIA, survived
Stefan, Florian	–	–	c. 1911	–	survived
Stefaniuk, Sam	Winnipeg; Toronto	Ukrainian	c. 1907	waiter	WIA, survived
Stefansky, John/Bill	Toronto; South Porcupine, ON	Canadian	9 Dec. 1912	clerk, driver, prospector	WIA, survived
Steiner, Janos	–	Hungarian	c. 1900	–	fate unknown
Steiner, Sandor/Alex	Montreal	Hungarian	27 May 1905	–	survived
Stenberg, Tauno H.J.	Montreal	Finnish	1 Sept. 1907	–	fate unknown
Stenko, Michael	Montreal	Czech	c. 1897	–	KIA, Retreats, Mar. 1938
Stepanian/Stephens, Douglas Badrig/Pat	Toronto; Detroit	Armenian	22 Nov. 1910	accountant	survived
Stepanyshyn, Mykhailo/Nick/Saul	Drumheller, AB	Ukrainian	1 Nov. 1897	lumberjack, miner	WIA, survived
Stern, Franz Einar Bertrand	Vancouver	Swedish	c. 1909	lumberjack	MIA, Retreats, Mar. 1938
Stern, Jervo/Jano	–	Hungarian	–	–	fate unknown
Sternichuk, Peter/Piotr	Val d'Or, QC	Ukrainian	c. 1903	–	survived
Stetina, Frantisek/Frank	Montreal	Slovak	1 Apr. 1905	–	survived
Stewart, Douglas	Toronto; Oakville, ON	–	–	–	survived
Stewart, William Gilmore	Wayne, AB; Saskatoon	–	c. 1906	miner	fate unknown
Stillman, John	The Pas, MB	Canadian	–	–	fate unknown
Stimac, Ivan/John	Beardmore, ON	Croatian	8 Aug. 1902	miner	WIA, survived
Stivic-Stuco, Franjo	Port Arthur, ON; Toronto	Croatian	c. 1906	–	WIA, survived
St. Louis, Narcisse/Narciso	b. Astorville, ON; Edmonton	French Canadian	15 Mar. 1902	barber	survived
Storgoff, Mikhail/Misha/Mike	Kamsack, SK; Geraldton, ON; Winnipeg; Sudbury; Calgary	Canadian	9 Aug. 1918	worker	survived
Storozhak, Ivan	–	Ukrainian	–	–	survived
Stoycheff, George	Toronto	Macedonian	c. 1913	cook	KIA, Caspe, Mar. 1938

Name	Location	Nationality	Birth date	Occupation	Fate
Straub, Gyorgy/George	Vancouver; Crowsnest Pass, AB	Hungarian	26 Feb. 1908	blacksmith	survived
Stromilo, Ivan/Hromila/John	Toronto	Ukrainian	15 July 1893	lumberjack	survived
Suchy, Andrej	Chatham, ON; Toronto	Slovak	c. 1905	—	survived
Suchy/Sych, Andrei	Toronto; Val d'Or, QC; Kirkland Lake, ON	Ukrainian	c. 1903	miner	survived
Sueby, Andre	Montreal	Slovak	27 May 1897	—	survived
Suhaida, Frank	Toronto	Finnish	c. 1914	—	KIA
Sundsten, Tono Arvid	Port Arthur, ON	Finnish	c. 1909	—	WIA, survived
Suni, Toivo	Vancouver	Finnish	11 Nov. 1902	lumberjack	survived
Suomela, Otto	Port Arthur, ON; Toronto	Finnish	c. 1908	—	KIA, Retreats, Mar. 1938
Suoniemi, Toivo Julis	Montreal		c. 1906	—	WIA, survived
Sus, Harry/Gregorii/Grzegorz		Ukrainian		—	KIA
Sustar, Vinko		Croatian		—	survived
Swain, Richard Joseph	Edmonton; Coal Creek, BC; Fernie, BC	Canadian	5 May 1902	construction worker, painter, sailor	WIA, survived
Swan, Art	Port Arthur, ON			miner	fate unknown
Swanson, Harry	Edmonton	Ukrainian		—	fate unknown
Swatak, Frank				—	fate unknown
Sweeney, Bernard/Pat	East Coulee, AB; Vancouver	Irish	12 June 1908	driver, farm worker, miner	KIA
Swiderski, Gregory/Harry/Walter	Sudbury	Ukrainian	c. 1914	miner	KIA, Teruel, Jan. 1938
Synyshyn, John	Edmonton			—	survived
Sypka, Jan				—	fate unknown
Syrjalainen, Veikko Kantola	Sudbury	Finnish	c. 1915	—	survived
Syurkovics, Istvan	Edmonton	Hungarian	26 Feb. 1902	—	survived
Szabari, Gabriel/Gabor/Michael	Lethbridge; Winnipeg	Hungarian	22 Nov. 1902	miner	survived
Szabo, Jan	Toronto	Ukrainian	10 Sept. 1899	—	survived
Szamylo, Aleksy		Ukrainian	c. 1904	—	fate unknown
Szepesi, Sandor		Hungarian	c. 1911	—	survived
Szewczyk, Jozef/Stepan	Winnipeg; Fort Frances, ON	Ukrainian	20 Dec. 1899	worker	fate unknown
Szewitch, John/Luke	Montreal	Ukrainian		—	survived
Szkara, Danil	Winnipeg	Ukrainian	10 Sept. 1906	worker	KIA, Segura de los Baños, Feb. 1938
Szlapek, Michael	Toronto	Ukrainian	15 Aug. 1902	miner	KIA, Retreats, Mar. 1938
Sztumic, Samuel/Stefan				—	
Szucsko, Paul	Delhi, ON; Hamilton; Toronto	Hungarian	8 July 1912	factory worker	POW, survived
Szysz, Gabriel	Montreal	Ukrainian	c. 1900	—	KIA

NAME	HOME	ETHNICITY	DATE OF BIRTH	OCCUPATION	FINAL STATUS
Tait, James Reid	Rouleau, SK	Scottish	c. 1915	student	WIA, survived
Takacs, Janos	–	Hungarian	c. 1913	–	KIA, 22 Apr. 1937
Takas, Gyorgy	–	Hungarian	11 Mar. 1902	–	survived
Tarasoff, William	Victoria	Russian	–	–	survived
Tarnawsky, Mykola/Nick	Winnipeg; Niagara Falls, ON	Ukrainian	8 Mar. 1910	mechanic	survived
Tassaman, Arthur/Ambrose	Vancouver	Canadian	22 Oct. 1882	electrician	WIA, survived
Taylor, George James	Saskatoon	English	13 June 1915	secretary	survived
Taylor, Lawrence Michael	b. Newcastle, NB; Vancouver	Canadian	5 Apr. 1917	worker	MIA, Retreats, Mar. 1938
Taylor, Norman	Regina	English	c. 1905	–	MIA, Retreats, 1938
Tellier, Louis	b. Montreal; Nanaimo, BC; Vancouver	French Canadian	27 Nov. 1915	construction worker, plumber	survived
Temelkoff, Simeon/Simon	Toronto	Macedonian	c. 1912	restaurant worker	survived
Terno, Vangel	–	Slavic	–	–	fate unknown
Teuhunen, David	–	Finnish	–	–	fate unknown
Thanner, George	–	–	–	–	MIA
Therien, Joseph	b. Emerson, MB	Canadian	c. 1897	–	survived
Thirkettle, Francis/Frank	Vancouver	English	c. 1909	clerk	WIA, survived
Thomas, George Albert	Drumheller, AB; Saskatoon; Regina	English	25 Feb. 1915	–	KIA, shot after capture
Thomas, Jack	–	Welsh	c. 1902	miner	KIA, shot after capture
Thompson, Frank Walter	Drumheller, AB	English	25 Sept. 1900	miner	WIA, survived
Thompson, Matthew Oswald	Vancouver	English	8 Sept. 1913	lumberjack, miner	survived
Thorinferany, M.	Vancouver	–	–	–	fate unknown
Thornton, David	Calgary	Irish	20 Nov. 1905	–	survived
Thorton, Frank	–	Irish	26 Oct. 1911	bookseller, shoemaker	WIA, fate unknown
Tierney, Francis Josep/Frank	Vancouver	Irish	–	–	WIA, survived
Tiger, Raymond	–	–	c. 1910	–	fate unknown
Tirpak, Joseph	Toronto	Hungarian	c. 1896	–	survived
Titleman, Nathan	b. Canada; Camden, NJ	Canadian, Jewish	15 Dec. 1910	–	KIA, Retreats, Apr. 1938
Titus, William	Grand Rapids, MI	–	–	–	KIA, Feb. 1938
Tlatloff, Nicholas	Vancouver	Canadian	25 Oct. 1915	restaurant worker	WIA, survived
Tlustiak, Michal	Toronto	Slovak	8 Aug. 1905	–	survived
Toikka, Taavetti	Port Arthur, ON	Finnish	–	–	fate unknown
Tolnai, Bela	–	Hungarian	–	–	fate unknown

Name	Place	Ethnicity	Birth date	Occupation	Fate
Tomas, Michal	Port Arthur, ON	Slovak	7 Sept. 1904	worker	survived
Tomas, Mihaly/Mike	Port Arthur, ON	Hungarian	—	worker	survived
Tornikoski, Eino	Toronto	Finnish	c. 1904	—	KIA Retreats, Mar. 1938
Torok, Jozsef	—	Hungarian	c. 1899	—	fate unknown
Toroshenko, Phillip	—	Ukrainian	—	—	KIA
Tosikosky, Frank	b. Cook's Creek, MB; Winnipeg	Canadian	20 Oct. 1907	—	survived
Toth, Dezso	Toronto	Hungarian	6 Jan. 1897	—	survived
Toth, Georges/Estevan/Steve	Minto, NB; Windsor	Hungarian	15 Jan. 1900	miner	WIA, survived
Toth, Gyorgy	Toronto	Hungarian	c. 1903	—	KIA
Tough, William/Andrew	Vancouver	Scottish	1 May 1898	miner	survived
Tourunen, Sulo/Heikki	Port Arthur, CN	Finnish	16 Feb. 1900	worker	KIA, Gandesa, 28 July 1938
Trakalo, Volodymyr	Kirkland Lake, ON	Ukrainian	5 July 1910	baker	WIA, survived
Traynor, Thomas	Toronto	Irish	5 June 1897	worker	WIA, survived
Treer, Martin	Toronto	Hungarian	c. 1905	worker	WIA, survived
Triteran, Mike	—	—	—	—	fate unknown
Trudeau, François/Hector	Vancouver; Montreal	French Canadian	c. 1901	—	fate unknown
Tuho, Tevi	—	Finnish	c. 1904	—	fate unknown
Tuovinen, Heikki	Port Arthur, CN	Finnish	27 Jan. 1901	—	WIA, survived
Tupper, Patrick	Sudbury	Canadian	24 Feb. 1911	waiter	KIA, Gandesa, 30 July 1938
Turkowsky, Vasyl/Bill	Toronto	Ukrainian	14 Jan. 1913	dockworker, waiter	WIA, survived
Turnbull, Joseph Aubrey	b. Grand Valley ON; Guelph, ON	Canadian	1 Sept. 1915	construction worker, sailor, letter carrier	hospitalized, survived
Turner, Robert	Vancouver; Extension, BC; California	English	25 Dec. 1900	lumberjack, mechanic, sailor	WIA, survived
Turner, William	Toronto	—	—	—	survived
Tuz, Imre/James	Windsor	Hungarian	—	worker	survived
Tymus, Stefan	Winnipeg	Ukrainian	c. 1900	—	survived
Udden, Sten Fabian/Svens	Vancouver; Port Arthur, ON	Swedish	2 Jan. 1909	—	WIA, survived
Ugren, Charles Karlo	—	Croatian	c. 1914	mechanic	KIA
Ugrow, Mike	—	—	—	—	fate unknown
Usher, John	Hamilton	English	c. 1906	—	KIA
Usher, Robert Edward S.	Vancouver	Canadian	c. 1912	mechanic	WIA, survived
Vack/Vacku, Istvan	—	Hungarian	—	—	fate unknown
Valent/Voljant, Ludvik/Ledevit/Louis	Montreal	Slovak	9 Nov. 1901	painter	survived
Valentincic, Ivo/John	—	Slovenian	—	—	KIA, Jarama, 1937
Van, Jack	Lac Megantic, QC	Canadian	—	—	survived

NAME	HOME	ETHNICITY	DATE OF BIRTH	OCCUPATION	FINAL STATUS
Van der Brugge, Adrian	St. Catharines, ON	Dutch	c. 1904	architect, engineer	KIA, Jarama 23 Feb. 1937
Van der Roest, William Allan	New York	–	–	worker	KIA, Brunete, July 1937
Vandzala, Andrej	Montreal	Czech	1 Jan. 1900	worker	survived
Van Orren, Jansen	England	Canadian	c. 1907	horse trainer	survived
Van Rensalaier, Chase	b. Calgary; US	Canadian	1 June 1914	–	POW, survived
Varchuk, P.	Winnipeg	Ukrainian	–	–	fate unknown
Varga, Andreas	Taber, AB; Fort William, ON	–	15 Mar. 1903	–	survived
Varga, Gyorg/Geza	New Aberdeen, NS	Hungarian	c. 1893	miner	survived
Varro, Ferencz/Frank	Regina	Hungarian	30 Aug. 1908	–	survived
Vasas, Zoltan	Calgary; Winnipeg	Hungarian	c. 1913	–	fate unknown (conflicting information)
Vaselev, Naum/Norman	–	Macedonian	–	–	KIA
Vaskiw, Jan	–	Ukrainian	c. 1906	–	survived
Vasovic, Vukasin	–	Croatian	–	worker	survived
Vassileff, Tonas/Tom	Toronto	–	–	–	survived
Vasylchyshyn, Hryhori	Edmonton; Timmins, ON	Ukrainian	c. 1902	worker	WIA, survived
Velichko, Mike	Winnipeg	–	c. 1902	miner	WIA, survived
Vernon, Stanley James	b. Kamloops, BC; Vancouver	Canadian	1 Apr. 1918	–	survived
Vitez, Jozsef, Joe	Windsor	Hungarian	c. 1902	–	survived
Vlasic, Nikola Ivan	Timmins, ON; Kirkland Lake, ON	Croatian	c. 1896	worker	KIA, Belchite, Sept. 1937
Volaric, Mate	Vancouver	Croatian	2 July 1900	worker	survived
Voros, Sandor	Hamilton; US	Hungarian, Jewish	7 Jan. 1900	journalist	WIA, fate unknown
Vosenchuk, Mykhailo	–	Ukrainian	–	–	fate unknown
Vrabec, Stefan	–	Czech	c. 1898	–	survived
Vukelic, Petar/Stepan/Paul	Port Arthur, ON	Croatian	16 Sept. 1902	miner	fate unknown
Waichuk, I.	Windsor	Ukrainian	–	–	survived
Walker, Frederick, aka Dan Wilson	Vancouver	–	c. 1902	steelworker	fate unknown
Walsh, Charles	–	–	–	–	fate unknown
Walsh, James "Red"	Vancouver; New York	American	c. 1904	steelworker	WIA, survived
Walsh, William Francis	Toronto	English	18 May 1911	pipefitter	WIA, survived
Walters, Phillip Joseph	Calgary	Canadian	c. 1897	worker	MIA
Walthers, Charles Henry Sands	Vancouver	German	2 Dec. 1902	gunsmith, miner	KIA, Belchite, 6 Sept. 1937
Wandzilak, John/Ivan	The Pas, MB	Ukrainian	–	lumberjack	KIA, Gandesa, 27 July 1938
Warner, Stanley	Calgary	Canadian	–	mechanic	survived
Waselenchuk, Manolii	Port Arthur, ON	Ukrainian	c. 1904	–	KIA, Jarama
Washington, George Alexander	Vancouver	–	25 Dec. 1907	worker	KIA, Retreats, Mar. 1938

Name	Origin/Residence	Nationality	Date of birth	Occupation	Fate
Watchman, David	b. Regina; Edmonton; Crane Valley, SK	Canadian	15 Oct. 1913	farm worker, lumberjack, truck driver	WIA, survived
Watson, Isaak	Vancouver	–	–	–	fate unknown
Watson, Stanley	Regina	–	–	–	fate unknown
Watt, Charles	Vancouver	Scottish	29 Aug. 1893	railway worker	WIA, survived
Watts, Jean Myrtle Eugenia, aka Jim Lawson (woman)	Toronto	Canadian	3 May 1909	journalist	survived
Watts, Jim "Taffy"	–	–	–	–	survived
Waxwood/Waywood, Walter	Winnipeg; Vancouver	Russian	22 July 1909	–	hospitalized, survived
Webster, Henry Thomas	Vancouver	English	19 June 1901	–	KIA, died in hospital
Weikkola, Vaino	Sudbury; Port Arthur, ON	Finnish	c. 1894	carpenter	survived
Weir/Patterson, Robert "Scotty"	Calgary	Scottish	14 Apr. 1908	mechanic	WIA, survived
Weldon, John Cecil	b. Thornhill, MB; Vancouver; Banff	Canadian	27 Oct. 1901	carpenter, lumberjack	survived
Wellesley, Arthur	Edmonton	English	27 June 1913	shoemaker	KIA, Battle of the Ebro, 1938
Welsby, Frank Maximilian	Winnipeg	English	16 Dec. 1913	worker	KIA, Gandesa, July 1938
Werner, Peter	Toronto	–	–	–	fate unknown
West, Wilfred	b. Ottawa; Edmonton	Canadian	4 July 1908	shoemaker, trapper	WIA, survived
Westlund, Gustav Adolf	–	Swedish	–	–	fate unknown
Wharmby, James	Vancouver	English	1 May 1902	hospital orderly	KIA, Battle of the Ebro, Sept. 1938
Wheatly	Crane Valley, BC	–	–	–	survived
Whiteside, Frederick	Toronto	Scottish	22 Jan. 1915	chemist	MIA, Retreats, Mar. 1938
Whitfield, Frank	Vancouver; L.S; Lake Louise, AB	English	28 Nov. 1896	–	KIA, Retreats, Mar. 1938
Wiebe, Bernard	b. Aberdeen, SK; Winnipeg; Vancouver	Canadian	14 Dec. 1904	miner	WIA, survived
Wiitaniemi/Vitaneimi/Niemi, Jukka/Jussi/Hugo	Toronto; Kirkland Lake, ON	Finnish	c. 1913	worker	survived
Wijatyk, Antoni Filip	Fort William, ON	Polish	c. 1898	–	KIA, Mar. 1938
Wilk, Frank	–	Polish	c. 1897	–	KIA
Williams, John D.	Winnipeg	English	c. 1909	–	fate unknown
Williamson, Edgar William "Bill"	Winnipeg	Canadian	17 Sept. 1908	lumberjack, photographer, sailor, construction worker	WIA, survived
Willoughby, William Everett	Vancouver	Canadian	1 Apr. 1908	steelworker	KIA, Retreats, Mar. 1938
Wilson, James	Edmonton	Irish	c. 1897	plumber	WIA, survived

NAME	HOME	ETHNICITY	DATE OF BIRTH	OCCUPATION	FINAL STATUS
Wilson, John Stillman	b. Kenora, ON; Vancouver; The Pas, MB	Canadian	4 Sept. 1914	-	KIA, Retreats, Mar. 1938
Wilson, Leslie Warren "Curly"	b. Kenora, ON; Vancouver; The Pas, MB	Canadian	20 Jan. 1912	-	POW, survived
Wilson, William	Calgary	Scottish	1 Sept. 1901	farm worker	MIA, Retreats, Mar. 1938
Winchewski, Stanley	Winnipeg; Regina; Toronto	Ukrainian	13 Nov. 1895	miner	WIA, survived
Winkelmans, Joseph Arnold	Vancouver	Belgian	21 July 1904	clerk	fate unknown
Winsky/Vinsky, Alfred/Albert	-	German	c. 1908	painter	survived
Witczak, Ignacy	Leamington, ON; Windsor	Polish	10 Apr. 1906	worker	survived
Wladek, M.	Edmonton	-	-	-	fate unknown
Wojnar, Piotr	Timmins, ON	Ukrainian	c. 1898	miner, tailor	WIA, survived
Wolek, John	Winnipeg	Polish	c. 1902	-	fate unknown
Wolf, Sam	Kingston; Winnipeg	-	c. 1912	-	survived
Wolfe, James	Vancouver	Irish	c. 1900	lumberjack	KIA, Belchite, Sept. 1937
Wollington, Frank	Hamilton	-	-	-	fate unknown
Woloncewicz, Vincent/Stefan/William	Toronto; Fort William, ON	Polish	12 Dec. 1898	worker	survived
Wood, Bill	-	-	-	-	survived
Wood, Frank C.	Vancouver	Canadian	9 May 1915	-	POW, survived
Wood, John Kenneth	Vancouver	English	8 June 1911	-	hospitalized, survived
Woolgar, Stanley	Crane Valley, SK	-	c. 1895	truck driver	survived
Wosniuk, Danilo	Montreal	Ukrainian	c. 1901	-	KIA, Quinto, 24 Aug. 1937
Yacemec, Ivan	Val d'Or, QC	Ukrainian	24 May 1907	driver	survived
Yakimchuk/Jakimczuk, Mikolaj	Port Arthur, ON	Ukrainian	c. 1902	-	KIA
Yalovcheff, Gligor/Greger	Toronto	Bulgarian	16 May 1905	cook	survived
Yarash, Ilych/William	Toronto	Ukrainian	c. 1900	-	survived
Yaroshuk, Joseph	St. Paul, AB; Toronto	Ukrainian	3 Oct. 1916	baker	WIA, survived
Yarrington, George	Hamilton	-	c. 1912	-	fate unknown
Yarysz, Theodore	Toronto	Ukrainian	11 Nov. 1900	hotel worker, restaurant worker	survived
Yaskiw, John	Winnipeg	Ukrainian	15 Sept. 1906	painter	survived
Yates, James Oscar	Halifax; US	Canadian	3 May 1904	sailor	hospitalized, survived
Yaworski/Jaworski, Stanley	Winnipeg; Toronto	Ukrainian	11 July 1916	worker	WIA, survived
Yilkyla, Axel-Nikolai	Toronto; Fort William, ON	Finnish.	20 Dec. 1906	truck driver	survived
Yohanchuk, John	-	Ukrainian	-	-	WIA, fate unknown

Name	Place	Ethnicity	Birth date	Occupation	Fate
Yulkoff/Wulkoff, Ivan	Toronto	Macedonian	10 Oct. 1903	cook	KIA, Retreats, Apr. 1938
Yurchyk/Jurczyk, Paul	Winnipeg; Red Lake, ON	–	c. 1900	miner	WIA, survived
Yurischuk, Prokop/Peter	Winnipeg; Edmonton	Ukrainian	7 July 1904	worker	survived
Zagar, Mijo	Montreal	Croatian	c. 1904	miner	WIA, survived
Zaharik, Dmytro	Regina	Canadian	9 Jan. 1914	construction worker	WIA, survived
Zahornasky/Zeronas, Andy	Port Arthur, ON	Czech	–	–	fate unknown
Zakharuk, Dmytro Illich	–	Ukrainian	2 Oct. 1894	farm worker, furrier	survived
Zaluski/Zalacki, Gerasim/Herasim	Montreal	Ukrainian	17 Oct. 1905	–	WIA, survived
Zapkar, Petar	Hamilton; Port Arthur, ON; Soviet Union (deported from Canada)	Croatian	c. 1897	miner	KIA
Zaremba, Jan	Hamilton	Polish	c. 1898	–	fate unknown
Zastawni, Theodore	Toronto	Ukrainian	c. 1899	carpenter	KIA
Zaversheniuk, John	Timmins, ON	Ukrainian	–	–	survived
Zdanauskas, Edvardas	Lethbridge; Edmonton; Hillcrest Mines, AB	Lithuanian	1 Feb. 1904	coal miner	POW, survived
Zdybel, Wojcicek	Sudbury	Polish	c. 1903	–	survived
Zemek, Jan	Winnipeg	Czech	9 June 1902	–	survived
Ziemski, Jan	Winnipeg	Polish	1 June 1914	–	MIA, Retreats, Apr. 1938
Zojda, Bogdan	–	Polish	–	–	fate unknown
Zubak, Juraj	Toronto	Slovak	27 Oct. 1910	–	survived
Zuberec, Frantisek	–	Slovak	–	–	fate unknown
Zygarowicz, Kornil	Toronto	Polish	c. 1899	roofer	KIA, Mar. 1938

Notes

Abbreviations

ALBA (Moscow)	Microfilm copies of material from the International Brigade Collection at the Russian State Archive of Social and Political History in Moscow, held at the Abraham Lincoln Brigade Archive, New York University's Tamiment Library, New York
CBC RA	Canadian Broadcasting Corporation Radio Archives, Toronto
IWM DD	Imperial War Museum Department of Documents, London
IWM SA	Imperial War Museum Sound Archive, London
LAC	Library and Archives Canada, Ottawa
LAC (Moscow)	Microfilm copies of material from the International Brigade Collection at the Russian State Archive of Social and Political History in Moscow, held at Library and Archives Canada, Ottawa
TFRBL	Thomas Fisher Rare Book Library, University of Toronto

Preface

1 Several days of street battles took place in Barcelona in May 1937 between factions within Spain's anti-fascist coalition. Canadian William Krehm, discussed in Chapter 12, was caught up in these events.
2 Hugh Thomas, *The Spanish Civil War* (London: Penguin Books, 1977), 977-78.
3 Quoted in Judith Keene, *Fighting for Franco: International Volunteers in Nationalist Spain during the Spanish Civil War, 1936-39* (London: Leicester University Press, 2001), 7.
4 Thomas, *The Spanish Civil War*, 978-79.
5 LAC, Record Group [RG] 146, vol. 4183, CSIS files 95-A-00088, Recruiting for Spanish Army Canada, part 7, box 58, newspaper clippings.
6 Wilson is mentioned several times in Frank Thomas, *Brother against Brother: Experiences of a British Volunteer in the Spanish Civil War,* ed. Robert Stradling (Thrupp: Alan Sutton Publishing, 1998). See also Keene, *Fighting for Franco,* 101. Thomas, in *The Spanish Civil War,* 980, says that Wilson emigrated to Canada; it is possible that he did so after the war, though Keene identifies the deserter from a British ship in Gibraltar as a Canadian. This book focuses exclusively on Canadians who served on the side of the Spanish Republic.
7 Thomas, *The Spanish Civil War,* 984.
8 Soviet military support was paid for with Spain's stockpile of gold, which was shipped to Russia in October 1936. According to some historians, notably Gerald Howson, the Soviet Union defrauded the Spanish Republic of millions of dollars by selling it weapons at falsely inflated prices. See Gerald Howson, *Arms for Spain: The Untold Story of the Spanish Civil War* (London: John Murray, 1998). This interpretation of events is supported by Stalin's agent Alexander Orlov, who coordinated the gold shipment. See Alexander Orlov, *The March of Time: Reminiscences* (London: St. Ermin's Press, 2004).
9 Throughout this book, the two opposing sides in the Spanish Civil War are referred to as "nationalists" and "republicans." This is by no means a perfect definition given the ideological

diversity arrayed on both sides of the conflict, but I believe it is the most accurate description available.

10 Denis Smyth, "Soviet Policy towards Republican Spain: 1936-1939," in *The Republic Besieged: Civil War in Spain, 1936-1939,* ed. Paul Preston and Ann L. Mackenzie (Edinburgh: Edinburgh University Press, 1996), 95.

11 Ibid., 95.

12 See Paul Preston, *A Concise History of the Spanish Civil War* (London: Fontana Press, 1996), 104-8; Thomas, *The Spanish Civil War,* 580, 686-87.

Introduction

1 For a more detailed discussion, see Paul Preston, "War of Words: The Spanish Civil War and the Historians," in *Revolution and War in Spain 1931-1939,* ed. Paul Preston (New York: Methuen, 1984).

2 Among the most important of these books are Gerald Brenan, *The Spanish Labyrinth: An Account of the Social and Political Background of the Spanish Civil War* (Cambridge: Cambridge University Press, 1943) and Hugh Thomas, *The Spanish Civil War* (London: Penguin Books, 1977). Both these books were smuggled into Spain during the Franco era.

3 This has changed in the last ten to fifteen years. A recent addition to the historiography on the International Brigades in Spanish is Santiago Alvarez, *Historia politica y militar de las Brigadas Internacionales* (Madrid: Compañía Literarira, 1996).

4 Victor Hoar with Mac Reynolds, *The Mackenzie-Papineau Battalion* (Toronto: Copp Clark, 1969).

5 William Beeching, *Canadian Volunteers: Spain 1936-1939* (Regina: Canadian Plains Research Center, 1989).

6 Mark Zuehlke, *The Gallant Cause: Canadians in the Spanish Civil War 1936-1939* (Vancouver: Whitecap Books, 1996).

7 D.P. (Pat) Stephens, *A Memoir of the Spanish Civil War: An Armenian-Canadian in the Lincoln Battalion,* ed. Rick Rennie (St. John's, NF: Canadian Committee on Labour History, 2000); Greg Lewis, *A Bullet Saved My Life: The Remarkable Adventures of Bob Peters, an Untold Story of the Spanish Civil War* (Torfaen: Warren and Pell Publishing, 2006); Stanley Harrison, *Good to Be Alive: The Story of Jack Brent* (London: Lawrence and Wishart, 1954)

8 Files pertaining to Canadian volunteers from the International Brigade Collection at the Russian State Archive of Social and Political History in Moscow are now on microfilm and housed at Library and Archives Canada in the Mackenzie-Papineau Battalion Fonds. Microfilm copies of some the Moscow documents are also housed at the Abraham Lincoln Brigade Archive at New York University's Tamiment Library. Although I consulted microfilm copies of the Moscow files at the London School of Economics, I have not cited these in the notes. The documents in the LAC personnel files, and in the Moscow files in general, range from reports written in several different languages, to semi-formal letters and notes scrawled on scraps of paper.

9 The Canadian Security Intelligence Service, formed in 1984, took over duties related to the surveillance of alleged subversives from the RCMP and inherited the relevant files. This is reflected in notes sourcing "CSIS files."

10 Most of these interviews were conducted by Mac Reynolds and used by Victor Hoar in his 1969 book *The Mackenzie-Papineau Battalion.* Unfortunately, some of the tapes are incorrectly labelled. Copies of many of the interviews are also housed at Library and Archives Canada.

Chapter 1: Who Were the Canadian Volunteers?

1 LAC, Mackenzie-Papineau Battalion collection, R2609-0-0-E, vol. 2, file 7, Walter E. Dent papers, letter from Beckett to "Audrey," 17 January 1937.

2 Victor Hoar with Mac Reynolds, *The Mackenzie-Papineau Battalion* (Toronto: Copp Clark, 1969), 71. Hoar estimates that there were forty Canadians in the Lincoln Battalion at the time. He bases this figure on several interviews. I can account for about half this many Canadians dying at Jarama, which makes forty a reasonable estimate for the number of Canadians there in February. Bob Kerr, however, in a 19 October 1937 document, "Discussions with Bob Kerr, Canadian Political Commissar," estimated that only nine Canadians were among the first group of Americans sent to Jarama. This figure is hard to square with their subsequent death toll, and Kerr himself noted that the first Canadian volunteers were so integrated with their American comrades that little was known about them. ALBA (Moscow), 545/3/469.

3 LAC, RG 25, External Affairs, vol. 1833, file 1937-291-B, "Protection in Spain of T. Beckett." I thank Stephen Burgess-Whiting for alerting me to this material.

4 LAC, Mackenzie-Papineau Battalion collection, R2609-0-0-E, vol. 2, file 7, Walter E. Dent papers, letter from Margaret Grant to R.E. Beckett, 22 February 1938.

5 LAC, Mackenzie-Papineau Battalion collection, R2609-0-0-E, vol. 1, file 16, Edward Cecil-Smith papers, letter from Ryan to Reid and Jessie Beckett, 21 October 1937.

6 Carl Geiser, *Prisoners of the Good Fight: The Spanish Civil War 1936-1939* (Westport, CT: Lawrence Hill and Company, 1986), 1.

7 LAC (Moscow), MG10-K2, 545/6/545, questionnaire completed by Cullen, in his personnel file.

8 LAC (Moscow), MG10-K2, 545/6/549, questionnaire completed by Goldenberg, in his personnel file.

9 ALBA (Moscow), 545/3/569, "Discussions with Bob Kerr, Canadian political Commissar," 19 October 1937. The document is signed with the initials P.W.

10 LAC (Moscow), MG10-K2, 545/3/509-12, "Detailed Questionnaires of the Historical Commission of the International Brigades," completed in August 1937.

11 The database lists the names of anyone who lived in Canada before joining the Spanish Civil War. This includes hundreds of men who arrived in Canada as immigrants in the 1920s, and several who spent only a few months or years in Canada before emigrating or being deported elsewhere. To count only those who had spent their entire lives in Canada would be to ignore the high number of volunteers who were immigrants and would misrepresent the population of Canada itself, of which more than 20 percent were immigrants at the time. Canadians who visited Spain as part of a delegation or propaganda tour are not listed, nor are journalists, though agents for the *Daily Clarion*, the Communist Party of Canada organ, are. Several Canadians who died before reaching Spain when their ship *Ciudad de Barcelona* was torpedoed are listed, as is a Canadian who volunteered to fight in Spain but was arrested in France and never made it across the border.

I would like to thank Myron Momryk, now retired from LAC, for his help as I compiled my database. He freely shared all the information he has discovered about the personal histories of Canadians in Spain, and my profile of the Canadian volunteers would be much less complete without his assistance. Additional notes citing my database will refer to "author's database."

12 I am happy to share biographical information on individual volunteers with readers of this book. The publisher, UBC Press, will have my up-to-date contact information on file.

13 Almost two-thirds of the American volunteers were thirty years of age or younger, and more than one-third were twenty-five or younger. See Peter N. Carroll, *The Odyssey of the Abraham Lincoln Brigade: Americans in the Spanish Civil War* (Stanford, CA: Stanford University Press, 1994), 15-16. The average age of the British volunteers was twenty-nine, and their most common age was twenty-three. See Richard Baxell, *British Volunteers in the Spanish Civil War: The British Battalion in the International Brigades, 1936-1939* (London: Routledge, 2004), 16. The average age of the French volunteers was just under thirty. See Rémi Skoutelsky, *L'espoir guidait leur pas: Les volontaires français dans les Brigades Internationales, 1936-1939* (Paris: B. Grasset, 1998), 141.

14 Information is available on the ages of 1,250 Canadians.

15 Eugene Fogarty, who fell under the suspicion of Spanish republican authorities, claimed to be a medical doctor in Canada and a graduate of McGill's medical school. A search of McGill's medical school's graduation records revealed no trace of Mr. Fogarty. See Chapter 13 for more details.

16 See James Hopkins, *Into the Heart of the Fire: The British in the Spanish Civil War* (Stanford, CA: Stanford University Press, 1998), 224-32. Despite tensions among the British volunteers, there was probably more successful class integration among the British in Spain than anywhere in Britain itself.

17 Robert Rosenstone, *Crusade of the Left: The Lincoln Battalion in the Spanish Civil War* (New York: Pegasus, 1969), 104.

18 LAC (Moscow), MG10-K2, 545/6/559, John McGrandle's personnel file. This quote is attributed to McGrandle in a report by Helge Meyer.

19 Quoted in *Los Canadienses*, directed by Albert Kish, 58 mins. (Ottawa: National Film Board of Canada, 1975).

20 LAC (Moscow), MG10-K2, 545/6/569, Edward Cecil-Smith, "Precis of Statement Made by Myself during a Meeting with Comrades Lewis and Elliott of the Central Committee." The report is not dated, but the letter from the Foreign Cadres Commission suggesting Cecil-Smith discuss the issue is dated 30 December 1938.

21 Data on the education obtained are available for only 208 volunteers, though those with education were more likely to have this noted than were those without.

22 This volunteer was Karlo Maenpaa.

23 *Canadian Jewish News*, 9 April 1981; *New York Times*, 5 September 1965.

24 A list of former inmates, from the Records of the Bureau of Prisons, is posted online by the American National Archives at http://www.archives.gov/pacific/san-francisco/finding-aids/alcatraz-alpha.html#u.

25 LAC (Moscow), MG10-K2, 545/3/511, "Detailed Questionnaires of the Historical Commission of the International Brigades," completed in August 1937.

26 LAC (Moscow), MG10-K2, 545/6/574, Walker's personnel file, translated from French.

27 LAC (Moscow), MG10-K2, 545/6/541, completed questionnaire, in Aucoin's personnel file.

28 Myron Momryk, "'For Your Freedom and for Ours': Konstantin (Mike) Olynyk, a Ukrainian Volunteer from Canada in the International Brigades," *Canadian Ethnic Studies/Études Ethniques au Canada* 10, 2 (1988): 125.

29 Myron Momryk, "Ukrainian Volunteers from Canada in the International Brigades, Spain, 1936-39: A Profile," *Journal of Ukrainian Studies* 16, 1-2 (Summer-Winter 1991): 189.

30 Ibid.

31 Unpublished memoirs in possession of the author.

32 CBC RA, Zack McEwen, interview with Mac Reynolds, c. 1965.

33 Information exists about the homes of approximately 1,400 Canadian volunteers.

34 It is likely that some volunteers without a permanent address listed Toronto as their home because the Central Committee of the Communist Party of Canada was in the city and mail could be held there until the volunteers returned.

35 *Canadian Jewish News*, 9 April 1981, and *New York Times*, 5 September 1965.

36 Richard Baxell, "The British Battalion of the International Brigades in the Spanish Civil War 1936-1939" (PhD diss., London School of Economics, 2002), 313-14; Skoutelsky, *L'espoir guidait leurs pas*, 148-53.

37 Carroll, *The Odyssey of the Abraham Lincoln Brigade*, 65, cites a July 1937 survey of 1,745 American volunteers, of whom a substantial 34 percent had formal military experience. Only 45, however, were war veterans.

38 Information is available on the birthplace or ethnicity of approximately 1,400 Canadian volunteers. The year of immigration is known for approximately 540 volunteers.

39 In the database, a volunteer is considered ethnically Canadian, or French Canadian, only if he or she was born in Canada. Some volunteers considered themselves part of an ethnic group that did not correspond to the formal borders of the countries in which they were born; they are listed in the database according to how they defined themselves.

40 Carroll, *The Odyssey of the Abraham Lincoln Brigade*, 18; Rosenstone, *Crusade of the Left*, 110. Rosenstone says that 30 percent of the American volunteers had been born into Jewish homes.

41 Carroll, *The Odyssey of the Abraham Lincoln Brigade*, 16.

42 Randy Gibbs Ervin, "The Men of the Mackenzie-Papineau Battalion: A Case Study of the Involvement of the International Communist Movement in the Spanish Civil War" (MA thesis, Carleton University, 1972), 16.

43 Information exists on the political parties to which 877 Canadian volunteers belonged. At least 613 were full Communist Party members before they arrived in Spain, and 56 belonged to the Young Communist League. Most joined the Communist Party in Canada, but ten did so in the United States, four in Britain, one in Ireland, and one in Yugoslavia. Seven had been party members but were expelled or left the party on their own accord before volunteering.

44 The dates volunteers joined the Communist Party are known in 467 cases.

45 LAC (Moscow), MG10-K2, 545/6/560, letter from Meyer to "Comrade Lewis," sent from Ripoll.

46 LAC (Moscow), MG10-K2, 545/2/199, Sandor Voros notebook entry, c. September 1937.

47 Carroll, *The Odyssey of the Abraham Lincoln Brigade*, 71.

48 Skoutelsky, *L'espoir guidait leurs pas*, 154.

49 Baxell, *British Volunteers*, 15.

50 Robert Stradling, *The Irish and the Spanish Civil War, 1936-1939: Crusades in Conflict* (Manchester: Manchester University Press, 1999), 129-30.

51 CBC RA, several American veterans, including Irving Weissman, interview with Victor Hoar, New York, c. 1965.

52 Carl Geiser, telephone interview with the author, 2 October 2002.

Chapter 2: Why Did They Fight?

1 LAC, Mackenzie-Papineau Battalion collection, MG30-E173, vol. 3, file 3, "To My Son in Spain," by Aku Paivio, 1938.

2 Maurice Constant, interview with the author, Kitchener-Waterloo, Ontario, August 2002.

3 LAC (Moscow), MG10-K2, 545/3/438, Parker to Jack Taylor (Muni Erlick), 18 June 1938. Canadian Bob Kerr and American William Lawrence were political commissars at the International Brigades base at Albacete.

4 Jules Paivio, interviews with the author, Sudbury, September 2002, and Toronto, October 2003. Paivio did not remember the volunteer's name but believes it was Roy as either a first or last name. Paivio did not think it was Canadian volunteer Roy Lauridin.

5 Arne Knudsen, telephone interview with the author, October 2002.

6 LAC (Moscow), MG10-K2, 545/6/540, "Report of Party Life of Canadians Taken Prisoner by Franco Forces and Individual Characteristics of Canadians Who Were War Prisoners and Have Now Returned," undated. It is unclear who wrote this report. Woods reportedly made the above comment to an officer in the British Battalion.

7 CBC RA and LAC, Ron Liversedge, interview with Mac Reynolds, c. 1965.

8 LAC (Moscow), MG10-K2, 545/3/437, letter from Nelson to Taylor, undated but seems to be from early 1937.

9 Bill Waiser, *All Hell Can't Stop Us: The On-to-Ottawa-Trek and Regina Riot* (Calgary: Fifth House, 2003), 12-13.

10 Ibid., 25, 26.

11 Ibid., 37.

12 CBC RA, Frank Roden, interview with Mac Reynolds, c. 1965.

13 Waiser, *All Hell Can't Stop Us*, 188-89, 246.

14 William Beeching, *Canadian Volunteers: Spain 1936-1939* (Regina: Canadian Plains Research Center, 1989), 7-8. My database contains the names of fifty-two Canadian participants of the On to Ottawa Trek who fought in Spain, though the true number is certainly higher.

15 LAC (Moscow), MG10-K2, 545/3/509-12, "Detailed Questionnaires of the Historical Commission of the International Brigades," completed in August 1937.

16 CBC RA, Harvey Hall, interview with Mac Reynolds, c. 1965.

17 CBC RA and LAC, Ron Liversedge, interview with Mac Reynolds, c. 1965.

18 CBC RA, Nick Elendiuk, interview with Mac Reynolds, c. 1965.

19 CBC RA, Frank Hadesbeck, interview with Mac Reynolds, c. 1965.

20 Gregory S. Kealey and Reg Whitaker, eds., *R.C.M.P. Security Bulletins: The Depression Years, Part IV, 1937* (St. John's, NF: Canadian Committee on Labour History, 1997), 20 January 1937 bulletin.

21 CBC RA, Ed Shirley and John "Paddy" McElligott, interview with Mac Reynolds, c. 1965.

22 Ibid.

23 Fred Kostyk, interview with the author, Montreal, September 2002.

24 CBC RA, Jules Paivio, interview with Mac Reynolds, c. 1965.

25 CBC RA, Walter Gawrycki, interview with Mac Reynolds, c. 1965.

26 Ibid.

27 Jules Paivio, interview with the author, Sudbury, September 2002.

28 John Peter Kraljic, "The Croatian Community in North America in the Spanish Civil War" (MA thesis, City University of New York, 2002), 41-42.

29 Ibid., 25-26.

30 Ibid., 22-30.

31 Quoted and translated from Croatian in ibid., 52.

32 Ibid., 52-53, 53.

33 Ibid., 54-57.

34 Robert Stradling, *The Irish and the Spanish Civil War, 1936-1939: Crusades in Conflict* (Manchester: Manchester University Press, 1999), 138.

35 Ibid., 139.

36 Ibid., 138.

37 Ibid., 209-10.

38 LAC (Moscow), MG10-K2, 545/3/511, "Detailed Questionnaires of the Historical Commission of the International Brigades," completed in August 1937.

39 Frank Ryan, ed., *The Book of the XV Brigade: Records of British, American, Canadian, and Irish Volunteers in the XVth International Brigade in Spain 1936-1938* (Madrid: Commissariat of War, XV Brigade, 1938), 194.

40 See, for example, Victor Hoar with Mac Reynolds, *The Mackenzie-Papineau Battalion* (Toronto: Copp Clark, 1969), 35.

41 Ryan, *The Book of the XV Brigade*, 36.

42 CBC RA, Art Siven, interview with Mac Reynolds, c. 1965.

43 CBC RA, Walter Gawrycki, interview with Mac Reynolds, c. 1965.

44 "With the Mackenzie-Papineau Battalion in Spain," a scrapbook of memoirs and photos, gathered by Canadian volunteer Edward Komodowski, apparently after a reunion of veterans in Winnipeg in 1980. It was in the possession of former volunteer Fred Kostyk, who made it available to me.

45 LAC (Moscow), MG10-K2, 545/3/510, "Detailed Questionnaires of the Historical Commission of the International Brigades," completed in August 1937.

46 Anonymous, interview with the author, 2002.

47 Randy Gibbs Ervin, "The Men of the Mackenzie-Papineau Battalion: A Case Study of the Involvement of the International Communist Movement in the Spanish Civil War" (MA thesis, Carleton University, 1972), 31.

48 LAC (Moscow), MG10-K2, 545/3/510, "Detailed Questionnaires of the Historical Commission of the International Brigades," completed in August 1937.

49 McMaster University, Hannah Chair for the History of Medicine, Oral History Archives, Ethel Sage Colter Duff [Magid], interview with Charles Gordon Roland, 4 December 1981, no. HCM 19-81.

50 Myron Momryk, "Ukrainian Volunteers from Canada in the International Brigades, Spain, 1936-39: A Profile," *Journal of Ukrainian Studies* 16, 1-2 (Summer-Winter 1991): 6.

51 Hywel Francis, *Miners against Fascism* (London: Lawrence and Wishart, 1984), 170.

52 LAC (Moscow), MG10-K2, 545/6/573, Jack Taylor's personnel file. Taylor notes that he was sent to Spain by the Central Committee of the Communist Party of Canada. He also notes in an 11 June 1938 report that Bob Kerr was "sent" to Spain by the party.

53 Quoted and translated from Croatian by Kraljic, "The Croatian Community in North America," 62.

54 William Beeching and Phyllis Clarke, eds., *Yours in the Struggle: Reminiscences of Tim Buck* (Toronto: NC Press, 1977), 266.

55 Gregory S. Kealey and Reg Whitaker, eds., *R.C.M.P. Security Bulletins: The Depression Years, Part III, 1936* (St. John's, NF: Canadian Committee on Labour History, 1996), 12 November 1936 bulletin.

56 LAC (Moscow), MG10-K2, 545/6/534, Edward Cecil-Smith, "Activities of Group of Disrupter among Canadian Volunteers in Ripoll," 15 December 1938.

57 LAC, Mackenzie-Papineau Battalion collection, R2609-0-0-E, vol. 1, file 16, Edward Cecil-Smith papers, letter from Martineau describing his time in Spain, written on 17 May 1939 after his return to Canada.

58 LAC (Moscow), MG10-K2, 545/6/536, list of volunteers with biographical information, undated.

59 LAC (Moscow), MG10-K2, 545/6/537, letter to party representatives in Alberta, signed "J.W.," undated.

60 LAC (Moscow), MG10-K2, 545/3/509-12, "Detailed Questionnaires of the Historical Commission of the International Brigades," completed in August 1937; see also questionnaires completed in the spring and autumn of 1938, in volunteers' personnel files.

61 LAC (Moscow), MG10-K2, 545/6/558, Makela's personnel file.

62 LAC (Moscow), MG10-K2, 545/6/575, Vasylchyshyn's and Watchman's personnel files.

63 Kealey and Whitaker, *R.C.M.P. Security Bulletins: Part IV*, 6 January 1938 bulletin.

64 Hoar, *The Mackenzie-Papineau Battalion*, 38-39. Hoar incorrectly identifies Trotsky's assassin.

65 John Earl Haynes and Harvey Klehr, *Venona: Decoding Soviet Espionage in America* (New Haven, CT: Yale University Press, 1999), 183-84.

66 Ibid., 333-34.

67 Jules Paivio, interview with the author, Sudbury, September 2002, and subsequent conversations in Toronto, October 2003, and by telephone, March 2004.

68 Marx Memorial Library, London, box A 15, file 10, Ron Liversedge's unpublished 1966 memoir.

69 FBI file 65-HQ-60356, "Subject: Lester B. Pearson," August 1951-February 1952.

70 Elizabeth Bentley's FBI deposition of 30 November 1945 in FBI file 65-14603. See also FBI file 65-HQ-60356, "Subject: Lester B. Pearson," August 1951-February 1952. I am grateful to John E. Haynes for sending me a copy of Bentley's file.

71 Historians differ over whether Sise was a knowing source. John E. Haynes, in an email to me, said he believes Sise knew the information he was telling Bentley would reach the Soviets, adding that it is difficult to imagine what other reason Sise would have for meeting with her. Amy Knight describes Bentley's allegations against Sise as "more fantasy than fact" and says that Sise would not have merited the attention of Soviet intelligence. See Amy Knight, *How the Cold War Began: The Gouzenko Affair and the Hunt for Soviet Spies* (Toronto: McClelland and Stewart, 2005), 217-21.

72 LAC (Moscow), MG10-K2, 545/6/548, Fenton's personnel file, evaluation, translated from French.

73 LAC (Moscow), MG10-K2, 545/6/537. Evaluations on McElligott and Tierney are included with those of volunteers from Vancouver; Hall is listed with the volunteers from southern Ontario.

74 LAC (Moscow), MG10-K2, 545/6/569, Edward Cecil-Smith, "Precis of Statement Made by Myself during a Meeting with Comrades Lewis and Elliott of the Central Committee." The report is not dated, but the letter from the Foreign Cadres Commission asking that he discuss the Canadian volunteers is dated 30 December 1938.

75 LAC (Moscow), MG10-K2, 545/6/537, report by Edward Cecil-Smith to the Vancouver Committee of the Communist Party of Canada, c. December 1938.

76 LAC (Moscow), MG10-K2, 545/6/537, report by Irving Weissman, undated.

77 LAC (Moscow), MG10-K2, 545/6/557, Lucas' personnel file, translated from Spanish.

78 Various documents from the International Brigade collection at the Russian State Archive of Social and Political History in Moscow, 545/6/165. I am grateful to historian James Hopkins for sending me notes on this file.

79 Maurice Constant, interview with the author, Kitchener-Waterloo, ON, August 2002.

80 LAC (Moscow), MG10-K2, 545/3/511, "Detailed Questionnaires of the Historical Commission of the International Brigades," completed in August 1937.

81 LAC (Moscow), MG10-K2, 545/3/509, "Detailed Questionnaires of the Historical Commission of the International Brigades," completed in August 1937.

82 LAC (Moscow), MG10-K2, 545/3/510, "Detailed Questionnaires of the Historical Commission of the International Brigades," completed in August 1937.

83 LAC (Moscow), MG10-K2, 545/6/540, "Report of Party Life of Canadians Taken Prisoner by Franco Forces and Individual Characteristics of Canadians Who Were War Prisoners and Have Now Returned," undated. It is unclear who wrote this report.

84 Fred Kostyk, interview with the author, Montreal, 10 September 2002.

85 LAC (Moscow), MG10-K2, 545/6/572, Tellier's personnel file.

86 LAC (Moscow), MG10-K2, 545/6/566, Rose's personnel file.

87 Maurice Constant, interview with the author, Kitchener-Waterloo, ON, August 2002.

88 Ibid.

89 All details about Malraux's visit to the university and of Constant's reaction come from an interview I conducted with him in Kitchener-Waterloo, ON, August 2002. The RCMP in its weekly security bulletins noted Malraux's speeches at Massey Hall and at the American Presbyterian Church in Montreal but not his speech at Hart House. It is possible Constant was referring to Malraux's speech at Massey Hall and has confused the locations, but given his excellent memory, this seems unlikely.

90 Maurice Constant, interview with the author, Kitchener-Waterloo, ON, August 2002.

91 LAC, Ron Liversedge, interview with Mac Reynolds, c. 1965.

92 Constant joined the Communist Party for the first time in Spain.

93 Kealey and Whitaker, *R.C.M.P. Security Bulletins: Part IV*, 24 February 1937 bulletin.

94 Ibid., 7 April 1937 and 14 April 1937 bulletins.

95 Ibid., 16 September 1937 bulletin.

96 Ibid., 17 August 1937 bulletin.

97 Ibid., 8 September 1937 bulletin.

98 CBC RA, Frank Hadesbeck, interview with Mac Reynolds, c. 1965.

99 CBC RA, Hugh Garner, interview with Mac Reynolds, c. 1965.

100 Anonymous, interview with the author, 2002.

101 Ibid.

Chapter 3: Going to War

1 CBC RA, Art Siven, interview with Mac Reynolds, c. 1965.

2 Ibid.

3 CBC RA, Peter Hunter, interview with Mac Reynolds, c. 1965.
4 CBC RA, Walter Gawrycki, interview with Mac Reynolds, c. 1965.
5 LAC, RG 146, vol. 4183, CSIS files 95-A-00088, Recruiting for Spanish Army Canada, part 2, box 58; *Moose Jaw Times*, 30 March 1937.
6 LAC (Moscow), MG10-K2, 545/6/551, Hamilton's personnel file, translated from French.
7 LAC, Hugh Garner, interview with Mac Reynolds, c. 1965.
8 Hugh Garner, *One Damn Thing After Another: The Life Story of a Canadian Writer: An Autobiography* (Toronto: McGraw-Hill Ryerson, 1973), 33-34.
9 CBC RA and LAC, Hugh Garner, interview with Mac Reynolds, c. 1965.
10 LAC, RG 146, vol. 4183, CSIS files 95-A-00088, Recruiting for Spanish Army, part 1, box 58.
11 LAC, RG 146, vol. 4183, CSIS files 95-A-00088, Recruiting for Spanish Army, part 1, box 58. The RCMP memorandum was attached to an 18 January report from RCMP Montreal branch's Corporal Alcide Lamothe. The memorandum appears to have been signed by the commissioner, but the signature is unclear. The memorandum writer says that upon receiving the report he proceeded to the office of Laurent Beaudry, acting undersecretary of state for external affairs. Beaudry said he would take the subject up with Oscar Douglas Skelton, undersecretary of state for external affairs. Beaudry reportedly said it was too late to stop the draft, which had been scheduled to leave the previous day, and furthermore, he said, the policy of the government regarding Spain was, as far as he was aware, "undecided."
12 LAC, RG 146, vol. 4183, CSIS files 95-A-00088, Recruiting for Spanish Army Canada, part 3, box 58, letter from MacBrien to Lapointe, 1 September 1937.
13 LAC, RG 146, vol. 4183, CSIS files 95-A-00088, Recruiting for Spanish Army Canada, part 2, box 58, letter from Lapointe to MacBrien, 15 September 1937.
14 LAC, RG 146, vol. 4183, CSIS files 95-A-00088, Recruiting for Spanish Army Canada, part 3, box 58, letter from Wood to officer commanding F division, 2 September 1937.
15 LAC, RG 146, vol. 4183, CSIS files 95-A-00088, Recruiting for Spanish Army Canada, part 3, box 58, memorandum from Rivett-Carnac to Wood, [attached forwarding note dated 28 August 1937].
16 LAC, RG 146, vol. 4183, CSIS files 95-A-00088, Recruiting for Spanish Army Canada, part 3, box 58, note from Wood to MacBrien, 28 August 1937.
17 LAC, RG 146, vol. 4183, CSIS files 95-A-00088, Recruiting for Spanish Army Canada, part 3, box 58, memorandum to RCMP Montreal branch, 22 October 1937. The identity of the sender is unclear.
18 Glenn Wright, in the RCMP's historical section, searched the RCMP's records for evidence of a member named Joseph Berubé who served in 1938 and could find none.
19 LAC, RG 146, vol. 4183, CSIS files 95-A-00088, Recruiting for Spanish Army Canada, part 5-A, box 58, Wood to RCMP Winnipeg branch, 16 February 1938.
20 CBC RA and LAC, Ron Liversedge, interview with Mac Reynolds, c. 1965.
21 LAC, Hugh Garner, interview with Mac Reynolds, c. 1965.
22 CBC RA, Nick Elendiuk, interview with Mac Reynolds, c. 1965.
23 CBC RA, William Beeching, interview with Mac Reynolds, c. 1965.
24 CBC RA, Percy Hilton, interview with Mac Reynolds, c. 1965.
25 CBC RA, Joe Schoen, interview with Mac Reynolds, c. 1965.
26 Ibid.
27 CBC RA and LAC, Ron Liversedge, interview with Mac Reynolds, c. 1965.
28 Peter N. Carroll, *The Odyssey of the Abraham Lincoln Brigade: Americans in the Spanish Civil War* (Stanford, CA: Stanford University Press, 1994), 125.
29 CBC RA, Lionel Edwards, interview with Mac Reynolds, c. 1965. The perception of Spain as a literal and metaphorical new dawn was not limited to the Canadians; see Josie McLellan, *Antifascism and Memory in East Germany: Remembering the International Brigades 1945-1989* (Oxford: Oxford University Press, 2004), 14-15.
30 CBC RA, Percy Hilton, interview with Mac Reynolds, c. 1965.
31 CBC RA, Frank Hadesbeck, interview with Mac Reynolds, c. 1965.
32 Sandor Voros, *American Commissar* (Philadelphia: Chilton, 1961), 310-15.
33 LAC, Konstantin Olynyk, interview with Mac Reynolds, c. 1965.
34 ALBA (Moscow), 545/3/469, "Conversation on the Brigade Participation in Combat Operations (with Commissars And Volunteers) in Albacete," under subheading "Discussion with Bob Kerr, Canadian Political Commissar, Oct 19, 1937." It is unclear who wrote the report.

35 LAC (Moscow), MG10-K2, 545/6/570, St. Louis' personnel file, questionnaire completed by St. Louis on 11 November 1938.

36 LAC (Moscow), MG10-K2, 545/1/3, memorandum from Regler in the 12th Brigade's commissariat, 24 April 1937.

Chapter 4: Protecting Madrid

1 This account of the Jarama battle draws heavily on Antony Beevor, *The Spanish Civil War* (London: Orbis Publishing, 1982), 220-27. Details on Levy come primarily from postwar newspaper profiles and obituaries, including those in *Canadian Jewish News*, 14 September 1981, and in *New York Times*, 5 September 1965.

2 Victor Hoar with Mac Reynolds, *The Mackenzie-Papineau Battalion* (Toronto: Copp Clark, 1969), 70.

3 LAC (Moscow), MG10-K2, 545/1/4. Luigi Gallo's complaints about equipment are contained in an 11 August 37 report.

4 CBC RA, Hugh Garner, interview with Mac Reynolds, c. 1965.

5 Peter N. Carroll, *The Odyssey of the Abraham Lincoln Brigade: Americans in the Spanish Civil War* (Stanford, CA: Stanford University Press, 1994), 98-99.

6 CBC RA, Walter Dent, interview with Mac Reynolds, c. 1965.

7 Hugh Thomas, *The Spanish Civil War* (London: Penguin Books, 1977), 591.

8 Carroll, *The Odyssey of the Abraham Lincoln Brigade*, 100.

9 Ibid., 101, 102. Carroll says that before the attack, the battalion totalled 263 men; it was then reduced to 150. Others report higher casualty rates. Cecil Eby, for example, cites American veteran Robert Gladnick, who estimated that the Lincoln Battalion totalled only 80 effectives the morning after the attack. See Cecil Eby, *Between the Bullet and the Lie: American Volunteers in the Spanish Civil War* (New York: Holt, Rinehart, and Winston, 1969), 64-65.

10 CBC RA, Hugh Garner, interview with Mac Reynolds, c. 1965.

11 LAC (Moscow), MG10-K2, 545/3/435, minutes of 15th Brigade commissars' meeting, 26 March 1937.

12 LAC, (Moscow), MG10-K2, 545/3/435, report on difficulties in the brigade's political work, signature obscured, c. June 1937, translated from French.

13 LAC (Moscow), MG10-K2, 545/6/565, Rayfield's personnel file, questionnaire, 30 October 1938.

14 LAC (Moscow), MG10-K2, 545/6/559, McGregor's personnel file.

15 LAC, Mackenzie-Papineau Battalion collection, R2609-0-0-E, vol. 1, file 9, Victor Howard (Hoar) papers, Jules Paivio's memoir, c. 1939.

16 CBC RA, Walter Dent, interview with Mac Reynolds, c. 1965.

17 LAC, Mackenzie-Papineau Battalion collection, R2609-0-0-E, vol. 1, file 9, Victor Howard (Hoar) papers, David Mangel's memoir, c. 1939; LAC (Moscow), MG10-K2, 545/6/534, draft history, "Canadians in Spain," produced during the war by Edward Cecil-Smith. ALBA (Moscow), 545/3/469, "Discussion with Bob Kerr, Canadian political Commissar," 19 October 1937, is the source of the assertion that one Lincoln company had a Canadian majority.

18 LAC (Moscow), MG10-K2, 545/6/534, Edward Cecil-Smith, draft history, "Canadians in Spain"; ALBA (Moscow), 545/3/469, "Discussion with Bob Kerr, Canadian political Commissar," 19 October 1937. Bob Kerr said thirty Canadians were in the Washington Battalion at Brunete and noted that the battalion's commander feared having too many Canadians in his unit, as he expected he would later lose them to the Mackenzie-Papineau Battalion.

19 LAC, Mackenzie-Papineau Battalion collection, R2609-0-0-E, vol. 2, file 9, Walter E. Dent papers, letter from Dent to Len Norris, c. 1982.

20 The final wartime edition of the *Volunteer for Liberty*, for example, refers to a Canadian company of the George Washington Battalion, under the command of Lieutenant "Vardos" [Jardas] from Toronto. Canadian Tom Bailey also said he trained with the Canadian company of the Lincoln Battalion, which he says was dubbed the "Mackenzie-Papineau Company." However, when Bailey arrived in Spain, the Lincolns were at Jarama, so if there was a Mackenzie-Papineau Company, it probably belonged to the Washington Battalion. On the other hand, Steve Nelson, a respected and highly placed American, in interviews with Mac Reynolds (CBC RA) recalled no designated Canadian sections in either battalion.

21 ALBA (Moscow), 545/3/426, orders of the day 25 June 1937.

22 Arthur Landis, *The Abraham Lincoln Brigade* (New York: The Citadel Press, 1967), 173; Edwin Rolfe, *The Lincoln Battalion: The Story of the Americans Who Fought in the International Brigades* (New York: Random House, 1939), 86.

23 Antony Beevor, *The Battle for Spain: The Spanish Civil War 1936-1939* (London: Penguin Books, 2006), 274.
24 Ibid., 275. Prieto's cooperation later waned.
25 Beevor, *The Spanish Civil War*, 286-90.
26 LAC, Steve Nelson, interview, probably with Mac Reynolds, though this is not certain, c. 1965; the interviewer might have been Victor Hoar.
27 ALBA (Moscow), 545/3/444, "TO ALL THE COMRADES OF THE XV BRIGADE," statement signed by Aitken and Copic, 5 July 1937.
28 Author's personal correspondence with veteran Bob Peters, 2004.
29 LAC, RG 146, vol. 1880, CSIS files 95-A-00088, Friends of the Mackenzie-Papineau Battalion of Canada, part 6, box 59, article clipping, *Canadian Forum* (October 1979).
30 Imperial War Museum Department of Documents (IWM DD), London, "A Salute to Unrecognized Comrades," J. Turnbull file, 95-39-1.
31 LAC, Mackenzie-Papineau Battalion collection, R2609-0-0-E, vol. 1, file 16, Edward Cecil-Smith papers, letter from Bailey to Maurice Constant, c. 1939. Hoar lists five Canadians who died in the assault; my research has revealed several more fatalities.
32 CBC RA and LAC, Hugh Garner, interview with Mac Reynolds, c. 1965.
33 CBC RA, Jack Lawson, interview with Mac Reynolds, c. 1965.
34 Carroll, *The Odyssey of the Abraham Lincoln Brigade*, 142.
35 Thomas, *The Spanish Civil War*, 716.
36 ALBA (Moscow), 545/3/426, memorandum from Klaus and Aitken to the battalion commanders and heads of units, 12 July 1937, translated from Spanish.
37 LAC (Moscow), MG10-K2, 545/1/4, report by Luigi Gallo, 11 August 1937.
38 Beevor, *The Battle for Spain*, 237-38.
39 CBC RA, Ron Liversedge and Abe Smorobin, interviews with Mac Reynolds, c. 1965.
40 ALBA (Moscow), 545/3/469, "Discussion with Bob Kerr, Canadian Political Commissar," 19 October 1937. Kerr estimated that the original Mackenzie-Papineau Battalion was 60 percent American and 40 percent Canadian.
41 Joe Dallet, *Letters from Spain: An American Volunteer to His Wife* (New York: Workers Library Publishers, 1938), 52-53.

Chapter 5: Aragón Battles

1 Antony Beevor, *The Spanish Civil War* (London: Orbis Publishing, 1982), 300-1; Hugh Thomas, *The Spanish Civil War* (London: Penguin Books, 1977), 725.
2 CBC RA, Marvin Penn, interview with Mac Reynolds, c. 1965.
3 CBC RA, Louis Tellier, interview with Mac Reynolds, c. 1965.
4 Carl Geiser, *Prisoners of the Good Fight: The Spanish Civil War 1936-1939* (Westport, CT: Lawrence Hill and Company. 1986), 30-32.
5 Peter N. Carroll, *The Odyssey of the Abraham Lincoln Brigade: Americans in the Spanish Civil War* (Stanford, CA: Stanford University Press, 1994), 156.
6 Ibid.; Victor Hoar with Mac Reynolds, *The Mackenzie-Papineau Battalion* (Toronto: Copp Clark, 1969), 136.
7 Carroll, *The Odyssey of the Abraham Lincoln Brigade*, 158.
8 CBC RA, Carl Geiser, interview with Mac Reynolds, c. 1965; Geiser, *Prisoners of the Good Fight*, 33. The Falange Española, or Spanish Phalanx, was a far right Spanish political party that shared many characteristics with Italian fascism. However, it was more conservative and traditional, and placed greater emphasis on the Catholic Church. See Antony Beevor, *The Battle for Spain: The Spanish Civil War 1936-1939* (London: Penguin Books, 2006), 40-41, for a detailed explanation. Franco took control of the Falange in April 1937 and merged it with the anti-modern Catholic Carlists, after which time it became the only permitted political party in nationalist Spain.
9 CBC RA, several American veterans, interview by Victor Hoar, New York, c. 1965. Hoar interviews a group of American veterans in one session in New York. Irving Weissman was one, and while I am reasonably certain of the identities of the others, the audiotape is not accurately labelled.
10 CBC RA, George Watt, interview with Mac Reynolds or with Victor Hoar, c. 1965.
11 CBC RA, John McGrandle, interview with Mac Reynolds, c. 1965; LAC, Mackenzie-Papineau Battalion collection, R2609-0-0-E, vol. 1, file 3, Victor Howard (Hoar) papers, letter from Cane to Victor Hoar, 19 April 1966.

12 Alvah Bessie, *Men in Battle* (New York: Veterans of the Abraham Lincoln Brigade, 1954), 60.
13 LAC, George Watt, interview with Mac Reynolds or Victor Hoar, c. 1965.
14 Carroll, *The Odyssey of the Abraham Lincoln Brigade*, 160-61. Carroll's description of Dallet is confirmed in several interviews with veterans conducted by Mac Reynolds and now housed at CBC RA and LAC.
15 CBC RA and LAC, Ron Liversedge, interview with Mac Reynolds, c. 1965.
16 CBC RA, Ron Liversedge, interview with Mac Reynolds, c. 1965.
17 LAC (Moscow), MG10-K2, 545/3/434, letter from Vladimir Copic to General Walter. Copic claimed the artillery barrage hit its own positions. This may be true, but veterans of the attack did not mention it in subsequent interviews.
18 CBC RA, several American veterans, interview by Victor Hoar, New York, c. 1965.
19 CBC RA, Lionel Edwards, interview with Mac Reynolds, c. 1965.
20 LAC (Moscow), MG10-K2, 545/3/434, report by Vladimir Copic to General Walter.
21 LAC (Moscow), MG10-K2, 545/2/120. This document lists thirty-one internationals who formed an international tank unit, though it states that their job was to be instructors. All the internationals – Czechs, Bulgarians, Austrians, Serbs, and one Canadian – are listed with a Spanish *nom de guerre* in brackets beside their real, or party, name. Kardash is listed by his party name Arturo Edwards, with the Spanish name José Revillo Blanco given as well.
22 My research suggests that at least five Canadians came to Spain from the Lenin School. Peter Hunter, in an interview with Mac Reynolds, an audiotape which now housed at CBC RA, estimated that six or seven Canadians left Moscow for Spain. Hunter too was at the Lenin School but did not fight in Spain.
23 LAC (Moscow), MG10-K2, 545/2/120, list of *tanquistas*; CBC RA, William Kardash, interview with Mac Reynolds, c. 1965. Kardash's interview is the source of his statement that he was trained by Soviet instructors.
24 CBC RA, William Kardash, interview with Mac Reynolds, c. 1965.
25 Ibid.
26 LAC (Moscow), MG10-K2, 545/3/434, report by Vladimir Copic for General Walter.
27 LAC (Moscow), MG10-K2, 545/3/508.
28 Cecil Eby, *Between the Bullet and the Lie: American Volunteers in the Spanish Civil War* (New York: Holt, Rinehart and Winston, 1969), 184. Eby says the Mac-Paps lost sixty dead and one hundred wounded, while American veterans interviewed by Victor Hoar (CBC RA) say sixty died and two hundred were wounded.
29 Author's database. The majority of this information is taken from files from Communist International archives, which often list the date and location of death for deceased volunteers.
30 LAC (Moscow), MG10-K2, 545/3/507, biographies on medical staff in the Mackenzie-Papineau Battalion.
31 LAC (Moscow), MG10-K2, 545/3/508, report by Thompson for Copic, providing list of comrades cited for bravery in last action.
32 CBC RA, Hugh Garner, interview with Mac Reynolds, c. 1965.
33 LAC (Moscow), MG10-K2, 545/3/508.
34 LAC (Moscow), MG10-K2, 545/3/434, report by Vladimir Copic for General Walter, translated from Spanish.
35 Ibid.
36 Ibid.
37 Arthur Landis, *The Abraham Lincoln Brigade* (New York: The Citadel Press, 1967), 321-22.
38 Edwin Rolfe, *The Lincoln Battalion: The Story of the Americans Who Fought in the International Brigades* (New York: Random House, 1939), 134.
39 LAC, Irving Weissman, interview with Mac Reynolds, c. 1965.
40 LAC, Mackenzie-Papineau Battalion collection, R2609-0-0-E, vol. 1, file 4, Victor Howard (Hoar) papers, letter from Cane to Hoar, 19 April 1966.
41 Eby, *Between the Bullet and the Lie*, 195; Hoar, *The Mackenzie-Papineau Battalion*, 165.
42 LAC (Moscow), MG10-K2, 545/1/3, letter from Gallo to War Commissariat, 10 January 1938, translated from Spanish.
43 CBC RA, William Beeching, interview with Mac Reynolds, c. 1965.
44 Hoar, *The Mackenzie-Papineau Battalion*, 166-67.

45 CBC RA, Lionel Edwards, interview with Mac Reynolds, c. 1965.

46 CBC RA, Percy Hilton, interview with Mac Reynolds, c. 1965.

47 This story is corroborated in several interviews conducted by Mac Reynolds and Victor Hoar and held at CBC RA, and also in a document at LAC, Mackenzie-Papineau Battalion collection, R2609-0-0-E, vol. 1, file 3, Victor Howard (Hoar) papers, letter from Lawrence Cane to Victor Hoar, 19 April 1966.

48 Matthew Halton, *Ten Years to Alamein* (Toronto: S.J. Reginald Saunders and Company, 1944), 56-59, quotation from 56.

49 CBC RA, Lionel Edwards, interview with Mac Reynolds, c. 1965; Halton, *Ten Years to Alamein*, 56-59.

50 ALBA (Moscow), 545/3/448, report by Maurice Constant to 35th Division, 19 January 1938, log from 12:00 to 16:00, translated from Spanish.

51 ALBA (Moscow), 545/6/11, letter from Jack Taylor to the "Commission of work among Internationals" at the Central Committee of the Communist Party of Spain, 20 February 1938.

Chapter 6: Retreats

1 Antony Beevor, *The Spanish Civil War* (London: Orbis Publishing, 1982), 325.

2 CBC RA, Bill Matthews, interview with Mac Reynolds, c. 1965.

3 Cecil Eby, *Between the Bullet and the Lie: American Volunteers in the Spanish Civil War* (New York: Holt, Rinehart and Winston, 1969), 208.

4 Victor Hoar with Mac Reynolds, *The Mackenzie-Papineau Battalion* (Toronto: Copp Clark, 1969), 179-80.

5 CBC RA, Percy Hilton, interview with Mac Reynolds, c. 1965.

6 CBC RA, John "Paddy" McElligott, interview with Mac Reynolds, c. 1965. Interviews with Bob Hamilton and Ed Shirley are on the same tape.

7 LAC, Mackenzie-Papineau Battalion collection, R2609-0-0-E, vol. 3, file 3, Walter E. Dent papers, Sulo Huhtala's recollections.

8 See Angela Jackson, *At the Margins of Mayhem: Prologue and Epilogue to the Last Great Battle of the Spanish Civil War* (Torfaen, UK: Warren and Pell Publishing, 2007); quotation from CBC RA, John McGrandle, interview with Mac Reynolds, c. 1965; LAC, Mackenzie-Papineau Battalion collection, R2609-0-0-E, vol. 1, file 3, Victor Howard (Hoar) papers, letter from Lawrence Cane to Victor Hoar, 19 April 1966.

9 CBC RA, Mike Storgoff, interview with Mac Reynolds, c. 1965. Interviews with Joe Schoen and William Krysa are on the same tape.

10 LAC, (Moscow), MG10-K2, 545/3/507, letter from Geiser to Doran, 30 March 1938.

11 Hoar, *The Mackenzie-Papineau Battalion*, 187.

12 Jules Paivio, interview with the author, Sudbury, September 2002.

13 This episode has been related by Geiser and Paivio, among others, in interviews, unpublished memoirs and, in Geiser's case, published works. Most of the details come from a September 2002 interview I conducted with Paivio in Sudbury.

14 CBC RA, Nick Elendiuk, interview with Mac Reynolds, c. 1965.

15 Carl Geiser, *Prisoners of the Good Fight: The Spanish Civil War 1936-1939* (Westport, CT: Lawrence Hill and Company, 1986), 259-67.

16 CBC RA, Jack Lawson, interview with Mac Reynolds, c. 1965.

17 Peter Kemp, *Mine Were of Trouble* (London: Cassell, 1957), 170.

18 CBC RA, Peter Kemp interview. It is unclear who the interviewer is, though she has a British accent; the approximate date it was recorded is also unclear.

19 LAC, RG 146, vol. 1880, CSIS files 95-A-00088, Friends of the Mackenzie-Papineau Battalion of Canada, part 3, box 59, report on 29 May 1939 speech Charles Bowen gave in Kirkland Lake, Ontario, about his time as a prisoner in Spain. According to Bowen, the camp commander ordered that the beatings of prisoners, which were particularly savage after an escape attempt, be stopped.

20 Jules Paivio, interview with the author, Sudbury, September 2002.

21 Geiser, *Prisoners of the Good Fight*, 144.

22 *The Guardian* (London), 1 November 2002.

23 Geiser, *Prisoners of the Good Fight*, 187-91.

24 Hoar, *The Mackenzie-Papineau Battalion*, 191.

25 CBC RA, Mike Hyduk, interview with Mac Reynolds, c. 1965.

26 CBC RA, William Beeching, interview with Mac Reynolds, c. 1965.

27 Hoar, *The Mackenzie-Papineau Battalion*, 191.

28 CBC RA, John "Paddy" McElligott, interview with Mac Reynolds, c. 1965; CBC RA, Bill Matthews, interview with Mac Reynolds, c. 1965.

29 CBC RA, George Watt, interview with Mac Reynolds, c. 1965.

30 Geiser, *Prisoners of the Good Fight*, 235-36.

31 LAC (Moscow), MG10-K2, 545/1/3, report by Gallo, 6 April 1938.

32 LAC, Mackenzie-Papineau Battalion collection, R2609-0-0-E, vol. 3, file 11, Walter E. Dent papers, Sulo Huhtala's recollections.

33 ALBA (Moscow), 545/3/429, memorandum from John Gates and Vladimir Copic to the commanders and commissars of the 15th Brigade battalions, 21 April 1938, translated from Spanish.

34 ALBA (Moscow), 545/3/429, memorandum from Hans Klaus to the commanders of all units, 22 April 1938, translated from Spanish. The original document is dated 1937, clearly a typo.

Chapter 7: Back to the Ebro

1 See, for example, Antony Beevor, *The Battle for Spain: The Spanish Civil War 1936-1939* (London: Penguin Books, 2006), 345.

2 LAC, Mackenzie-Papineau Battalion collection, R2609-0-0-E, vol. 2, file 6, Walter E. Dent papers, letter from Charles Bartolotta home, 12 June 1938.

3 LAC, George Watt, interview with Mac Reynolds, c. 1965.

4 CBC RA, Walter Gawrycki, interview with Mac Reynolds, c. 1965.

5 LAC (Moscow), MG10-K2, 545/3/507, letter from Rogers to War Commissariat of the 15th Brigade, 11 May 1938.

6 LAC (Moscow), MG10-K2, 545/1/3, reports by Luigi Gallo.

7 LAC (Moscow), MG10-K2, 545/3/435, written declaration by René Landais, 25 June 1938, translated from Spanish. Landais received Bourne at the commissariat and said he was unaware that the money had been sent.

8 LAC (Moscow), MG10-K2, 545/3/435, report to party officials in the 35th Division, 27 June 1938, translated from Spanish.

9 CBC RA, Milt Cohen, interview with Mac Reynolds, c. 1965.

10 CBC RA, Walter Dent, interview with Mac Reynolds, c. 1965.

11 LAC (Moscow), MG10-K2, 545/1/3, report by Luigi Gallo, July 1938.

12 LAC (Moscow), MG10-K2, 545/1/3, report by Luigi Gallo, 4 August 1938, translated from Spanish.

13 Manuel Alvarez, *The Tall Soldier: My 40-Year Search for the Man Who Saved My Life* (Vancouver: New Star Books, 1983), 43.

14 LAC (Moscow), MG10-K2, 545/1/4, report by Luigi Gallo, 11 August 1938, translated from Spanish.

15 LAC (Moscow), MG10-K2, 545/3/435, unsigned report, 20 August 1938. Hoar, however, locates the 24th Battalion to the right of the Lincolns. He presumably based this position on interviews with veterans.

16 LAC (Moscow), MG10-K2, 545/3/435, 20 August 1938 report by John Gates; LAC (Moscow), MG10-K2, 545/3/435, report from John Gates to War Commissariat of the 35th Division, 23 August 1938.

17 LAC (Moscow), MG10-K2, 545/3/435, report from John Gates to War Commissariat of the 35th Division, 21 August 1938.

18 CBC RA, Joe Schoen, interview with Mac Reynolds, c. 1965.

19 Fred Kostyk, interview with author, Montreal, 10 September 2002.

20 CBC RA, Joe Schoen interview with Mac Reynolds, c. 1965.

21 LAC (Moscow), MG10-K2, 545/3/435, report from John Gates to War Commissariat of the 35th Division, 19 September 1938.

22 LAC (Moscow), MG10-K2, 545/3/435, minutes of 6 September 1938 meeting of political commissars, translated from Spanish.

23 LAC (Moscow), MG10-K2, 545/3/435, report by John Gates to War Commissariat of the 35th Division, 7 September 1938, translated from Spanish.

24 LAC, Mackenzie-Papineau Battalion collection, R2609-0-0-E, vol. 2, file 6, Walter E. Dent papers, Bartolotta to Florence, 12 June 1938.

25 LAC (Moscow), MG10-K2, 545/6/541, Charles Bartolotta's personnel file, letter from W. Bartolotta to Taylor.

26 CBC RA, Gerald Cook, interview with Mac Reynolds, c. 1965.

27 The description of this final battle draws heavily on Victor Hoar, *The Mackenzie-Papineau Battalion* (Toronto: Copp Clark, 1969), 222-23. He in turn had interviewed men who were there. The figure of thirty-five Mac-Paps still able to walk at the end of day is the consensus of several American veterans interviewed by Victor Hoar. Tapes of these interviews are at the CBC RA. It is also the estimate of Lawrence Cane, expressed in a letter to Victor Hoar, date unknown: LAC, Mackenzie-Papineau Battalion collection, R2609-0-0-E, vol. 1, file 3, Victor Howard (Hoar) papers.

Chapter 8: Leaving Spain

1 LAC, RG 146, vol. 4948, CSIS files B1-71, vol. 1, Spanish Civil War, International Brigade, personal diary of Frank Hadesbeck, who served with an anti-aircraft battery near Valencia, was not relieved until 22 October.

2 Dolores Ibárruri, quoted in a pamphlet printed in Barcelona, 1938.

3 LAC (Moscow), MG10-K2, 545/6/537. Several evaluations for individual volunteers report that the volunteer "turned in his Party book rather than defend Barcelona."

4 Fred Kostyk, interview with the author, Montreal, 10 September 2002.

5 LAC, RG 146, vol. 4183, CSIS files 95-A-00088, Recruiting for the Spanish Army Canada, part 1, supplement 4, box 58. Document is from the RCMP's Toronto special section, dated 31 January 1948. The Ukrainians in question were certainly Ukrainian Canadians.

6 LAC (Moscow), MG10-K2, 545/6/537, evaluations of individual volunteers prepared for district party committees in Canada.

7 CBC RA, Ron Liversedge, interview with Mac Reynolds, c. 1965.

8 CBC RA and LAC, Ron Liversedge, interview with Mac Reynolds, c. 1965.

9 CBC RA, Ron Liversedge, interview with Mac Reynolds, c. 1965.

10 William Brennan fonds, F5636-0-3, Irving Weissman, interview with Alex Cramer, c. 1975.

11 CBC RA, Tim Buck, interview with Mac Reynolds, c. 1965.

12 Ibid.

13 Matthew Halton, *Ten Years to Alamein* (Toronto: S.J. Reginald Saunders and Company, 1944), 52-53.

14 LAC (Moscow), MG10-K2, 545/3/438, "Report given by comrade MCLEOD from the Committee of the Friends of the Mackenzie-Papineau Battalion," 19 January 1939, translated from Spanish. The report is signed by A.M. Elliott.

15 LAC, RG 146, vol. 4183, CSIS files 95-A-00088, Recruiting for Spanish Army Canada, part 1, supplement 4, box 58.

16 LAC (Moscow), MG10-K2, 545/3/438, letter from Lamont to Taylor, 1 February 1939.

17 Victor Hoar with Mac Reynolds, *The Mackenzie-Papineau Battalion* (Toronto: Copp Clark, 1969), 228.

18 CBC RA, Frank Hadesbeck, interview with Mac Reynolds, c. 1965.

19 Maurice Constant, interview with the author, Kitchener-Waterloo, ON, August 2002.

20 LAC, William Brennan fonds, R5636-0-3, William Beeching, interview with Alex Cramer, c. 1975.

21 CSIS files from access to information request 86-A-57, RCMP Nova Scotia Preventive Service Squad, 4 February 1939.

22 CBC RA, Ron Liversedge, interview with Mac Reynolds, c. 1965.

23 CBC RA and LAC, Ron Liversedge, interview with Mac Reynolds, c. 1965.

24 CBC RA, Konstantin Olynyk, interview with Mac Reynolds, c. 1965.

25 A few Canadian prisoners were released earlier. Bert "Yank" Levy, captured with the British at Jarama, was released in June 1937. Two other Canadians, Percival Dagesse and Joseph Przedwojewski, were released with a British contingent in October 1938.

26 See Carl Geiser, *Prisoners of the Good Fight: The Spanish Civil War 1936-1939* (Westport, CT: Lawrence Hill and Company, 1986), 217, 236. See also LAC, Mackenzie-Papineau Battalion collection, R2609-0-0-E, vol. 1, file 20, in Friends of the Mackenzie-Papineau Battalion series. It is noted on biographical file cards kept by the Friends of the Mackenzie-Papineau Battalion that Cameron, Bukovi, Szucsko, and Zdanauskas were prisoners as of May 1939. The cards also contain Robert Dickie's observations and a report that Cameron was held on civil charges. Geiser, *Prisoners of the Good Fight*, 236, confirms that Cameron was held to be court-martialled.

Chapter 9: Crimes

1 The story of "K.O." reciting Robert Service's poem comes from K.E. Heikkinnen, *Our Boys in Spain*, trans. Matti A. Mattson (Finnish Workers' Federation, 1939; reprint n.p.: n.p., 2002), 26-27. The town the internationals were soon to attack was Villanueva de la Cañada.

2 CBC RA, Irving Weissman, interview with Mac Reynolds, c. 1965.

3 Ibid.

4 Ibid.

5 ALBA (Moscow), 545/6/21, Abe Lewis, "Report on the Political Development of the International Brigades," Barcelona, 2 January 1939.

6 ALBA (Moscow), 545/6/21, Abe Lewis, "Report on the Work of the North Americans in the XV Brigade," [January 1939].

7 LAC (Moscow), MG10-K2, 545/6/569, Cecil-Smith's personnel file. A note from the foreign cadres' commission of the Communist Party of Spain, dated 30 December 1938 and addressed to Jim Bourne, suggests that Cecil-Smith give a report explaining problems relating to the Canadian volunteers. A subsequent document, "Precis of statement made by myself during a meeting with comrade Lewis and Elliot of the Central Committee," consists of Cecil-Smith's summary of his presentation; this is the document quoted.

8 CBC RA, John "Paddy" McElligott, interview with Mac Reynolds, c. 1965; a copy of this interview exists at LAC, but the sound quality is not as good.

9 CBC RA, Helge Meyer, interview with Mac Reynolds, c. 1965.

10 CBC RA, John "Paddy" McElligott, interview with Mac Reynolds, c. 1965.

11 Ibid.

12 ALBA (Moscow), 545/6/11, letter from Taylor to the Commission of Work among Internationals, Communist Party of Spain's Central Committee, 20 February 1938.

13 Imperial War Museum Sound Archive (IWM SA) interviews, accession numbers 12385, recorded in 1990; accession number 1425, date recorded unknown. The interview on accession number 12385 spans eighteen reels of tape. The interview on accession number 1425 spans three reels of tape and is somewhat repetitive.

14 LAC (Moscow), MG10-K2, 545/3/435, minutes of 16 June 1937 meeting of political commissars, translated from Spanish. Mikhail Tukhachevsky was a Soviet general executed in 1937 during a Stalinist purge. His name was spelled incorrectly in the document quoted here.

15 Thomas Fisher Rare Book Library, University of Toronto (TFRBL), William Krehm uncatalogued private papers, League for a Revolutionary Workers' Party (LRWP) pamphlet, 10 September 1937.

16 LAC, RG 146, vol. 4183, CSIS files 95-A-00088, Recruiting for Spanish Army Canada, part 3, box 58, article clipping, *Daily Clarion*, 14 September 1937.

17 LAC (Moscow), MG10-K2, 545/6/537, letter from Ewen to Marty, 8 September 1939.

18 LAC, Mackenzie-Papineau Battalion collection, R2609-0-0-E, vol. 1, file 2, Victor Howard (Hoar) papers, Robert Bell memoirs. The author of the memoir is listed in the archives as Robert Bell, but I have been able to confirm that his true name was Robert Hamilton.

19 D.P. (Pat) Stephens, *A Memoir of the Spanish Civil War: An Armenian Canadian in the Lincoln Battalion*, ed. Rick Rennie (St. John's, NF: Canadian Committee on Labour History, 2000), 54.

20 See Antony Beevor, *The Battle for Spain: The Spanish Civil War 1936-1939* (London: Penguin Books, 2006), 304-7.

21 Peter N. Carroll, *The Odyssey of the Abraham Lincoln Brigade: Americans in the Spanish Civil War* (Stanford, CA: Stanford University Press, 1994), 196.

22 Stephens, *A Memoir of the Spanish Civil War*, 93-94.

23 Ibid., 94-96.

24 LAC (Moscow), MG10-K2, 545/6/548, Fromberg's personnel file, February 1938.

25 Carroll, *The Odyssey of the Abraham Lincoln Brigade*, 196.

26 LAC (Moscow), MG10-K2, 545/6/565, Rayfield's personnel file, report by "5th Comp. cell committee," 25 February 1938, translated from Spanish.

27 Carroll, *The Odyssey of the Abraham Lincoln Brigade*, 193.

28 LAC (Moscow), MG10-K2, 545/6/549, Grainger's personnel file, evaluation, 21 October 1938.

29 LAC (Moscow), MG10-K2, 545/6/539, evaluation, 19 November 1938.

30 LAC (Moscow), MG10-K2, 545/6/537, report on Greysdale by Edward Cecil-Smith, 15 December 1938.

31 LAC (Moscow) MG10-K2, 545/6/549, Grainger's personnel file, report by Helge Meyer, 12 December 1938.

32 LAC (Moscow), MG10-K2, 545/6/534, Edward Cecil-Smith, "Activities of Group of Disrupters among Canadian Volunteers in Ripoll," 15 December 1938.

33 Most of the evaluations completed in the autumn of 1938 were meant for the consumption of party officials in Canada who were considering which veterans might have a future with the party – hence the desire to weed out anyone not sufficiently loyal to the party line.

34 LAC (Moscow), MG10-K2, 545/6/559, McDowell's personnel file, questionnaire completed by McDowell between October and December 1938.

35 Ibid., note by A. Donaldson in McDowell's personnel file.

36 Ibid., note by R. Turner in McDowell's personnel file.

37 Ibid., note by A. Donaldson in McDowell's personnel file.

38 Ibid.

39 LAC (Moscow), MG10-K2, 545/6/537, evaluations of individual volunteers awaiting repatriation.

40 LAC (Moscow), MG10-K2, 545/6/541, Ashplant's personnel file, questionnaire complete between October and December 1938.

41 CBC RA, John "Paddy" McElligott, interview with Mac Reynolds, c. 1965.

42 LAC (Moscow), MG10-K2, 545/6/537, evaluations of volunteers from Vancouver, completed between October and December 1938.

43 LAC (Moscow), MG10-K2, 545/6/559, McElligott's personnel file.

44 Ibid., report by A. Donaldson.

45 LAC (Moscow), MG10-K2, 545/6/537. An evaluation of McElligott sent to party officials in Vancouver notes that the party district secretary should "have a serious talk with him before being readmitted to the Party"; LAC (Moscow), MG10-K2, 545/6/559. A 19 October 1938 report from the War Commissariat in McElligott's personnel file notes his incarceration.

46 LAC (Moscow), MG10-K2, 545/6/537, evaluation sent to party officials in Vancouver, completed between October and December 1938.

47 LAC (Moscow), MG10-K2, 545/6/559, McElligott's personnel file, evaluation, 20 October 1938.

48 LAC (Moscow), MG10-K2, 545/3/435, minutes of 6 September 1938, translated from Spanish.

49 Author's database.

50 LAC (Moscow), MG10-K2, 545/6/537, report on Canadian deserters in Paris, 4 June 1938.

51 This figure, accounting for differences in the total number of volunteers from both countries, is comparable to the figure of British volunteers who deserted: more than 270. James Hopkins, *Into the Heart of the Fire: The British in the Spanish Civil War* (Stanford, CA: Stanford University Press, 1998), 254, citing records from the Moscow archives, concludes that 271 deserted. He notes that Bill Alexander, a British veteran of the International Brigades, puts the figure even higher, at 298.

52 LAC (Moscow), MG10-K2, 545/6/560, Moffat's personnel file, letter to Jack Taylor or Bob Kerr, undated.

53 LAC (Moscow), MG10-K2, 545/6/559, MacLean's personnel file, letter to Bob Kerr, 17 January, 1938.

54 LAC (Moscow), MG10-K2, 545/6/559, MacLean's personnel file, letter to Jack Taylor, 21 June 1938.

55 LAC (Moscow), MG10-K2, 545/6/549, Garner's personnel file, letter asking for repatriation.

56 Ibid. Arthur Moffat, the wounded man Garner writes of, survived the war.

57 Hopkins, *Into the Heart of the Fire*, 254.

58 LAC (Moscow), MG10-K2, 545/6/537, Edward Cecil-Smith, "Activities of Group of Disrupters among Canadian Volunteers in Ripoll," 15 December 1938.

59 LAC (Moscow), MG10-K2, SYS/6/569, Cecil-Smith's personnel file, report from the commissariat of the 5th Corps, 30 January 1938.

60 LAC (Moscow), MG10-K2, 545/6/569, Cecil-Smith's personnel file, report by Irving Weissman for the War Commissariat, 15 September 1938.

61 Several reports refer to Cecil-Smith's attempted desertion, including a 15 September 1938 report by Irving Weissman. LAC (Moscow), MG10-K2, 545/6/569, Cecil-Smith's personnel file.

62 LAC (Moscow), MG10-K2, 545/6/569, Cecil-Smith's personnel file, report by Jim Bourne, translated from Spanish.

63 ALBA (Moscow), 545/3/425, "Brigade Order No. 5," from Vladimir Copic and Hans Klaus, 15 March 1937.

64 LAC (Moscow), MG10-K2, 545/6/569, Cecil-Smith's personnel file, evaluation, 20 October 1938.

Chapter 10: Punishments

1 ALBA (Moscow), 545/2/142, letter from unnamed member of the International Brigades Judicial Commission to Copic, 5 April 1937, translated from French.

2 Ibid.

3 Ibid.

4 LAC (Moscow), MG10-K2, 545/2/1, Luigi Gallo, "Decision on the Reorganization of the Base," 12 April 1938, translated from Spanish.

5 ALBA (Moscow), 545/2/150, Moreno testimony, 31 August 1938, translated from Spanish. Moreno might have actually been a Yugoslav communist with a Spanish *nom de guerre*. See Antony Beevor, *The Battle for Spain: The Spanish Civil War 1936-1939* (London: Penguin Books, 2006), 305.

6 ALBA (Moscow), 545/2/150. Toscano's initial testimony, quoted here, translated from Spanish, is not dated, but he made a subsequent declaration on 14 September 1938.

7 ALBA (Moscow), 545/2/150, Courson testimony, 14 September 1938, translated from Spanish.

8 ALBA (Moscow), 545/2/150, Lantez testimony, 14 September 1938, translated from Spanish.

9 ALBA (Moscow), 545/2/150, report by Alfredo Vinet. The undated document is co-signed, but the second signature cannot be deciphered; translated from Spanish.

10 Ibid.

11 Author's database. At least two Canadians were interned in the Carlos Marx prison, and two at Camp Lukacs. At least nineteen were interned elsewhere, though there is significant overlap – a soldier might have been held in more than one location. I have tried not to include those who appeared to have been jailed or held in a guardhouse for a day or two because of petty offences such as drunkenness, but the records are not always clear.

12 See Peter N. Carroll, *The Odyssey of the Abraham Lincoln Brigade: Americans in the Spanish Civil War* (Stanford, CA: Stanford University Press, 1994), 183-86, for a discussion of Wallach's death. Carroll describes allegations that Wallach was murdered as "dubious," a conclusion I dispute. A former American prisoner at Castillo de Fels asserted that Wallach was murdered by Anthony DeMaio, an American agent of the SIM. DeMaio denied ever knowing or even hearing of Wallach, which was revealed as a lie when the Moscow archives were opened and reports in which DeMaio accuses Wallach of being a spy were uncovered. See Harvey Klehr, John Earl Haynes, and Fridrikh Igorevich Firsov, *Secret World of American Communism* (New Haven, CT: Yale University Press, 1995), 155-60.

13 ALBA (Moscow), 545/3/451, letter from Judicial Commission official to Weissman, 23 March 1937, translated from French. "Arbeitskolonne" is German for "a group of workers."

14 ALBA (Moscow), 545/2/142, letter from "M" at Judicial Commission to Marty and Vidal, undated, translated from French.

15 LAC, Mackenzie-Papineau Battalion collection, R2609-0-0-E, vol. 1, file 7, Victor Howard (Hoar) papers, Robert Bell memoirs.

16 LAC (Moscow), MG10-K2, 545/1/56, letter from international volunteer to the inspector of the War Commissariat of the International Brigades, 3 July 1937. The signature on this document is unclear; the prisoner's name could be M.E. Woodfield, or perhaps M. Ellodfield.

17 LAC (Moscow), MG10-K2, 545/1/57, letter from international volunteer to the military judge of Segovia. A copy of the letter was forwarded to party officials, c. February 1938. The signature on the letter appears to be "R. Lamiguu," translated from French.

18 ALBA (Moscow), 545/3/450, Pike to George Wattis, a British commander in the 15th International Brigade, "Examination of Francis North," 18 April 1937.

19 ALBA (Moscow), 545/3/449, directive from Vladimir Copic and Jean Barthol to 15th Brigade commanders and commissars, undated, translated from French. Based on the dates of surrounding documents in the file, I surmise that the document was issued in March 1937.

20 LAC (Moscow), MG10-K2, 545/3/435, minutes of 10 May 1937 meeting of political commissars.

21 CBC RA, "Arts in Review" special, 6 July 1974; the program consisted of conversations between Garner and Ted Allan.

22 ALBA (Moscow), 545/3/451, Judicial Commission to Weissman, 23 March 1937, translated from French.

23 LAC (Moscow), MG10-K2, 545/1/60, letter from Mirco Marcovichi to "El Capitan Mayor de las B/I/ Al Capitan Jelesov," 20 April 1938, translated from Spanish. The signature reads "Mirco Marcovichi." It is possible that another prominent International Brigade commander, perhaps in the Djakovic Battalion, had a name similar to the Yugoslav-American described here.

24 LAC (Moscow), MG10-K2, 545/3/435, report by Gates to the commissariat of the 35th Division, "Summary of the Experience Obtained in the Belchite-Caspe Sector," translated from Spanish.

25 ALBA (Moscow), 545/3/429, "Special Order for the Brigade for Today," 26 April 1938, signed by Gates, translated from Spanish.

26 Carroll, *The Odyssey of the Abraham Lincoln Brigade*, 183. Carroll says that the Spaniard executed with White was an anarchist. The rest of the information presented here is derived from the leaflet.

27 ALBA (Moscow), 545/3/429, "Special Order for the Brigade for Today," 26 April 1938, signed by Gates, translated from Spanish.

28 Carroll, *The Odyssey of the Abraham Lincoln Brigade*, 183.

29 LAC, William Brennan fonds, R5636-0-3-E, Gerald Cook, interview with Alex Cramer, c. 1975.

30 LAC, Mackenzie-Papineau Battalion collection, R2609-0-0-E, vol. 5, file 2, Walter E. Dent papers, Bill Matthews' recollections.

31 Marx Memorial Library, London, International Brigade archive and library, box A 12, Joe Fuhr's file, "My Experience in Spain."

32 LAC, Mackenzie-Papineau Battalion collection, R2609-0-0-E, vol. 2, file 9, Walter E. Dent papers, letter from William Beeching to Walter Dent, 15 July 1983.

33 LAC (Moscow), MG10-K2, 545/2/199, Sandor Voros notebook.

34 LAC (Moscow), MG10-K2, 545/3/435, from War Commissariat of the 15th Brigade to political commissars, "Report on the Trials of 12 Deserters," 9 October 1937.

35 Carroll, *The Odyssey of the Abraham Lincoln Brigade*, 165, says that none of the deserters tried at this time faced a firing squad. Cecil Eby, *Between the Bullet and the Lie: American Volunteers in the Spanish Civil War* (New York: Holt, Rinehart and Winston, 1969), 272, says that Eisenberg died under suspicious circumstances but does not elaborate or provide any evidence to indicate he might have been executed.

36 Jules Paivio and Fred Kostyk, interviews with the author, 2002-4. Paivio had already been captured by Franco forces by the time of Nieminen's execution. However, as a Finnish Canadian, he might have obtained further details from other Finnish veterans after the war. Harvey Hall, in an interview with Mac Reynolds, said two men were shot for a "particularly nasty" rape, but he did not give details; CBC RA, interview with Mac Reynolds, c. 1965. Nick Elendiuk, CBC RA, interview with Mac Reynolds, c. 1965, said, "Our own guys were shot, by our own personnel," and seemed to confirm that this was for rape. Carroll, in *The Odyssey of the Abraham Lincoln Brigade*, 184, also describes the execution, though the victims are not named. The names of the executed men given here may not be 100 percent accurate; records are scarce and spellings vary.

37 Anonymous, email to the author, 7 October 2004. The medic in question could be "Lamont," discussed in the text below. That this man was caught with a large amount of money suggests that he might also have been the executed man described by veteran Len Norris.

38 Carroll, *The Odyssey of the Abraham Lincoln Brigade*, 187.

39 LAC, RG 146, vol. 4183, CSIS files 95-A-00088, Recruiting for Spanish Army Canada, part 8, box 58. The relevant information is contained in a 17 August 1938 informer's report. In LAC, Mackenzie-Papineau Battalion collection, R2609-0-0-E, vol. 1, file 13, Edward Cecil-Smith papers, there is a list of volunteers in the Mackenzie-Papineau Battalion, compiled by the battalion's clerk Frank Rogers in 1938. It appears that the author Victor Hoar mailed a copy of this list to American volunteer Lawrence Cane, whom he consulted while writing his book *The Mackenzie-Papineau Battalion*. Cane added comments and biographical information beside the names of several of the men. Beside Vincent Usera's name Cane wrote that Usera deserted from the Lincolns during the retreats and was a "suspected agent [of the] U.S. military intelligence."

40 D.P. (Pat) Stephens, *A Memoir of the Spanish Civil War: An Armenian Canadian in the Lincoln Battalion*, ed. Rick Rennie (St. John's, NF: Canadian Committee on Labour History, 2000), 47.

41 Robert Rosenstone, *Crusade of the Left: The Lincoln Battalion in the Spanish Civil War* (New York: Pegasus, 1969), 309-10.

42 LAC, Mackenzie-Papineau Battalion collection, R2609-0-0-E, vol. 1, file 20, Friends of the Mackenzie-Papineau Battalion series, file card on Burton.

43 Arthur Landis, *The Abraham Lincoln Brigade* (New York: The Citadel Press, 1967), 262.

44 LAC, Mackenzie-Papineau Battalion collection, R2609-0-0-E, vol. 1, file 7, Victor Howard (Hoar) papers, Hamilton's written recollections.

45 Toronto Public Library, Baldwin Room, Mackenzie-Papineau collection, box 2, file 7, letter from Frederick Martin to Hamilton, 1970.

46 CBC RA, Ron Liversedge, interview with Mac Reynolds, c. 1965. Liversedge must have repeated this

story to William Beeching, who asked Walter Dent about it in a 1983 letter; LAC, Mackenzie-Papineau Battalion collection, R2609-0-0-E, vol. 2, file 9, Walter E. Dent papers, letter from Beeching to Dent, 15 August 1983.

47 Harry Fisher, *Comrades: Tales of a Brigadista in the Spanish Civil War* (Lincoln: University of Nebraska Press, 1998), 140-42 and 186-87.

48 LAC, Mackenzie-Papineau Battalion collection, R2609-0-0-E, vol. 2, file 9, Walter E. Dent papers, letter from Beeching to Walter Dent, 5 March 1984; the letter is dated 1983, but based on the surrounding letters in the collection, this appears to be a typo.

49 CBC RA, Lionel Edwards, interview with Mac Reynolds, c. 1965.

Chapter 11: The Photographer

1 Imperial War Museum Sound Archives (IWM SA), accession numbers 12385, recorded in 1990; accession number 1425, date recorded unknown. The interview on accession number 12385 spans eighteen reels of tape. The interview on accession number 1425 spans three reels of tape and is somewhat repetitive.

   Where I quote Williamson directly, I use an appropriate note. The broad outlines of his story, however, are not sourced at every detail in an effort to not clutter the text. My sources on Williamson are the IWM SA interviews and a series of letters and notes, parts of which are based on a diary he kept in Spain, and which are now housed at LAC, Mackenzie-Papineau Battalion collection, R2609-0-0-E, vol. 5, file 24, Walter E. Dent papers. Parts of his story are also confirmed in his personnel file from his time in the International Brigades; LAC (Moscow), MG10-K2, 545/6/575. Williamson's photos from Spain are at LAC, Mackenzie-Papineau Battalion collection, R2609-1-2-E. Williamson's first name was Edgar, but Bill was the name he more often used for himself.

2 IWM SA interviews.

3 Ibid.

4 Ibid.

5 Ibid.

6 LAC, Mackenzie-Papineau Battalion collection, R2609-0-0-E, vol. 5, file 24, Walter E. Dent papers, letter from Edgar "Bill" Williamson to Lee Burk and Walter Dent, fellow Canadian International Brigadiers, c. 1980.

7 IWM SA interviews.

8 Ibid.

9 Hugh Thomas, *The Spanish Civil War* (London: Penguin Books, 1977), 616.

10 Ibid.

11 IWM SA interviews.

12 Ibid.

13 Ibid.

14 LAC (Moscow), MG10-K2, 545/6/575, Williamson's personnel file.

Chapter 12: The Idealist

1 William Krehm, interview with the author, Toronto, 2004.

2 CBC RA and LAC, William Krehm, interview with Mac Reynolds, c. 1965.

3 Ibid.

4 Ibid.

5 Ibid.

6 Ibid.

7 William Krehm, interview with the author, Toronto, 28 November 2004.

8 Thomas Fisher Rare Book Library, University of Toronto (TFRBL), William Krehm uncatalogued private papers, letter from Krehm to "Aubrey," 18 February 1937.

9 William Krehm, interview with the author, Toronto, 2004.

10 Antony Beevor, *The Battle for Spain: The Spanish Civil War 1936-1939* (London: Penguin Books, 2006), 264.

11 See George Orwell, *Homage to Catalonia*, 1938 (reprint, New York: Harvest/HBJ Books, 1980).

12 CBC RA and LAC, William Krehm, interview with Mac Reynolds, 1965.

13 Tim Rees, "The Highpoint of Comintern Influence? The Communist Party and the Civil War in Spain," in *International Communism and the Communist International*, ed. Tim Rees and Andrew Thorpe (Manchester: Manchester University Press, 1999), 154.

14 ALBA (Moscow), 545/2/148, "Report on Confiscations/Poum Material," July 1937, translated from German.

15 Stanley G. Payne, *The Spanish Civil War, The Soviet Union, and Communism* (New Haven, CT: Yale University Press, 2004), 226. Orlov's real name was Nikolsky.

16 ALBA (Moscow), 545/2/148, "Report on Defence Work," 15 June 1937, translated from German. The quotation is from the report summary.

17 The exact date of his arrest is unclear. The anti-POUM sweep took place on 16-17 June 1937, and in interviews Krehm places his arrest on or around 15 June. But in a 1937 article in the *Workers' Voice*, he says he was arrested on 22 June, which is when Charles Orr claims he himself was arrested.

18 Helen Graham, *The Spanish Republic at War 1936 – 1939* (Cambridge: Cambridge University Press, 2002), 285. See also Rees, "The Highpoint of Comintern Influence?" 155; Payne, *The Spanish Civil War*, 228.

19 Graham, *The Spanish Republic at War*, 286.

20 ALBA (Moscow), 545/2/148, "Work Report," 26 July 1937, translated from German. "Special brigade" was the name later given to a particularly feared unit of the SIM responsible for interrogation. See Beevor, *The Battle for Spain*, 305.

21 TFRBL, William Krehm uncatalogued private papers, *Some Facts on the Persecution of Foreign Revolutionaries in "Republican" Spain,* League for a Revolutionary Workers' Party (LRWP) pamphlet. These "Russians" might also have been Slavic-speaking members of the SIM, perhaps recruited from the International Brigades.

22 CBC RA and LAC, William Krehm, interview with Mac Reynolds, 1965.

23 Beevor, *The Battle for Spain*, 304-7; Payne, *The Spanish Civil War*, 205. Helen Graham notes that in the latter weeks of June, the Spanish Communist Party, Comintern representatives, and Soviet police personnel set up private interrogation centres on republican state territory but beyond the control of its constitutional authorities. Here they "assaulted and assassinated anti-Stalinist dissidents with virtual impunity." See Graham, *The Spanish Republic at War*, 284-85.

24 ALBA (Moscow), 545/2/148, "Work Report," 26 July 1937, translated from German.

25 Ibid.

26 Ibid.

27 CBC RA and LAC, William Krehm, interview with Mac Reynolds, c. 1965; William Krehm, interview with the author, Toronto, 2004.

28 William Krehm's private archives, November 1937 edition of *Workers' Voice*. Krehm did not mention these imprisoned members of the International Brigades in later interviews.

29 TFRBL, William Krehm uncatalogued private papers, LRWP pamphlets. Orr, who belonged to an American group closely affiliated with the LRWP, returned to the United States and wrote of his arrest and of the imprisonment of William Krehm for booklets distributed by the LRWP.

30 William Krehm, interview with the author, Toronto, 28 November 2004.

31 ALBA (Moscow), 545/2/148, "Report on Confiscations/POUM Material," July 1937, translated from German.

32 LAC (Moscow), MG10-K2, 545/6/556, Krehm's personnel file, translated from Spanish. Often documents in a personnel file are copies of originals found elsewhere. This is the case with those in Krehm's file, and it is difficult to know the origins and authors of some of these documents and fragments of documents. Some reports are sufficiently similar to a German note on Krehm in the files of the SIM (ALBA [Moscow], 545/2/148) that we can assume they originate there.

33 William Krehm, interview with the author, Toronto, 28 November 2004.

34 LAC (Moscow), MG10-K2, 545/6/566, Krehm's personnel file, translated from Spanish.

35 TFRBL, William Krehm uncatalogued private papers, report on visit to Spain by Fenner Brockway.

36 Ibid.

37 TFRBL, William Krehm uncatalogued private papers, letter from Fenner Brockway to B.J. Field, 30 July 1937.

38 TFRBL, William Krehm uncatalogued private papers, Davis' report on 13 August 1937 telephone call.

39 TFRBL, William Krehm uncatalogued private papers, letter from Jim Martin to Ben Borsook, 9 August 1937.

40 LAC, RG25, External Affairs, vol. 1833, file 1937-291-C, "Safety in Spain of W. Krehm" and "Activities of W. Krehm"; letter from Skelton to H. Krehm, 14 August 1937.

41 Krehm's private archives, November 1937 issue of *Workers' Voice*.

42 TFRBL, William Krehm uncatalogued private papers, letter from Oscar Douglas Skelton to Hyman Krehm, 6 September 1937.

43 See Tom Buchanan, "The Death of Bob Smillie, the Spanish Civil War, and the Eclipse of the Independent Labour Party," *The History Journal* 40, 2 (1997): 435-61.

44 LAC, RG25, External Affairs, vol. 1833, file 1937-291-C, "Safety in Spain of W. Krehm" and "Activities of W. Krehm"; letter from Skelton to acting deputy minister of justice, seeking charges against Krehm, 17 December 1938; memorandum saying that Krehm's case should be considered closed, as it is too costly to pursue charges, 13 September 1939. The Canadian government reimbursed the British Foreign Office in 1938. Krehm reimbursed the Department of External Affairs in 1942. He had been refused a visa to enter British Honduras by the British minister in Guatemala City and feared this was because of his outstanding debt. See 9 March 1942 letter from Canada's secretary of state for external affairs to British minister in Guatemala.

45 LAC, RG25, External Affairs, vol. 1833, file 1937-291-C, "Safety in Spain of W. Krehm" and "Activities of W. Krehm"; letters from William Krehm to Gladys Cowan, 19 May 1942 and 7 June 1942.

46 William Krehm, interview with the author, Toronto, 28 November 2004.

Chapter 13: The Doctor

1 Roderick Stewart, *Bethune* (Hamden, CT: Archon Books, 1979), 89.

2 Larry Hannant, *The Politics of Passion: Norman Bethune's Writing and Art* (Toronto: University of Toronto Press, 1998), 119.

3 Stewart, *Bethune*, 89.

4 This version of the poem was found among Bethune's papers by Ted Allan and published in a biography he and Sydney Gordon wrote of the doctor: *The Scalpel, The Sword: The Story of Doctor Norman Bethune* (Toronto: McClelland and Stewart, 1952). A slightly modified version appeared in the July 1937 edition of *Canadian Forum*.

5 Stewart, *Bethune*, 90.

6 LAC, Mackenzie-Papineau Battalion collection, R2609-0-0-E, vol. 4, file 18, Walter E. Dent papers, Sorensen's personal memoir or notes from an interview, c. 1981.

7 LAC, Ted Allan fonds, R2931-0-4-E, vol. 30, file 33, handwritten notes recounting a timetable of events in Spain. The author is Sorensen and the notes were sent to Sise, who presumably was trying to piece together the details of their time in Spain. The notes appear to have been written in the 1940s. "Kléber" had travelled on a fake Canadian passport forged by the Soviet NKVD; this partially explains several erroneous reports that identify "Kléber" as a Canadian. See Antony Beevor, *The Battle for Spain: The Spanish Civil War 1936-1939* (London: Penguin Books, 2006), 161.

8 LAC, Mackenzie-Papineau Battalion collection, R2609-0-0-E, vol. 4, file 18, Walter E. Dent papers, Sorensen's personal memoir or notes from an interview, c. 1981.

9 Ibid.

10 Ibid.; LAC, Ted Allan fonds, R2931-0-4-E, vol. 30, file 33, Henning Sorensen's written recollections, c. 1940.

11 Hannant, *The Politics of Passion*, 118.

12 LAC, Mackenzie-Papineau Battalion collection, R2609-0-0-E, vol. 1, file 4, Victor Howard (Hoar) papers, text of Hazen Sise's speech at a Montreal Physiological Society meeting, 21 March 1963. Sise, among others, acknowledged the sophistication of Dr. Duran Jorda's blood transfusion work, which has gone largely unnoticed.

13 Ibid.

14 Ted Allan, *Canadian Magazine* (supplement to the *Toronto Star*), 6 July 1975.

15 Hannant, *The Politics of Passion*, 124.

16 LAC, Ted Allan fonds, R2931-0-4-E, vol. 30, file 32, Sise's handwritten notes, c. 1940s.

17 LAC, Hazen Edward Sise fonds, R4915-0-7-E, vol. 35, file 4, transcript of CBC Radio interview with Hazen Sise.

18 Stewart, *Bethune*, 106-7.

19 LAC, Hazen Edward Sise fonds, R4915-0-7-E, vol. 35, file 4, transcript of CBC Radio interview with Hazen Sise.

20 LAC, Ted Allan fonds, R2931-0-4-E, vol. 16, file 2, letter from Bethune to Jefe de Sanidad Militar, 9 April 1937.

21 LAC, Ted Allan fonds, R2931-0-4-E, vol. 16, file 3. The text of Bethune's telegram is quoted in a letter from Benjamin Spence to the remaining Canadians in Spain, 12 August 1937. Bethune's telegram is dated 13 April 1937.

22 LAC, Mackenzie-Papineau Battalion collection, R2609-0-0-E, vol. 3, file 19, Walter E. Dent's papers, William Kashtan's recollections.

23 LAC (Moscow), MG10-K2, 545/6/542, Bethune's personnel file, "Report on the Canadian Delegation in Spain," 3 April 1937; translated from Spanish. This report appears to have been written by someone in the Central Committee of the Communist Party of Spain. It notes that Sorensen and Allan are trustworthy and have already denounced Bethune's behaviour to the Communist Party of Canada and have requested that he be replaced.

24 LAC, Hazen Edward Sise fonds, R4915-0-7-E, vol. 35, file 4, transcript of CBC Radio interview with Hazen Sise.

25 LAC, Ted Allan fonds, R2931-0-4-E, vol. 30, file 26, Hazen Sise diary entry, 6 April 1937.

26 LAC, Hazen Edward Sise fonds, R4915-0-7-E, vol. 43, file 18, Sorensen's handwritten notes, c. 1940s.

27 LAC, Ted Allan fonds, R2931-0-4-E, vol. 16, file 3, letter from Ben Spence to Hazen Sise, Ted Allan, Allen May, and Henning Sorensen, 12 August 1937.

28 LAC, Ted Allan fonds, R2931-0-4-E, vol. 30, file 26, Hazen Sise diary entry, 29 May 1937; LAC, Hazen Edward Sise fonds, R4915-0-7-E, vol. 43, file 18, Sorensen's handwritten notes, c. 1940s. Both Hazen Sise's diary and Henning Sorensen's notes confirm that this took place. The telegram was sent to Allen May, who showed it to Sise and Sorensen.

29 LAC, Ted Allan fonds, R2931-0-4-E, vol. 16, file 3, letter from Ben Spence to Sise, Allan, May, and Sorensen, 12 August 37, referring to a 31 May 1937 telegram from Allen May in Spain.

30 LAC, Ted Allan fonds, R2931-0-4-E, vol. 30, file 26, Hazen Sise diary entry, 30 May 1937.

31 LAC (Moscow), MG10-K2, 545/6/542, Norman Bethune's personnel file, note from Juan Alcántara at the Madrid Provincial Committee to Central Committee of Spanish Communist Party, 17 August 1937, translated from Spanish. "TAJSA" is a misspelling of "Kajsa," who is discussed in the text below.

32 LAC (Moscow), MG10-K2, 545/6/542, Norman Bethune's personnel file, "Report on the Performance of the Canadian Delegation in Spain," 3 April 1937, translated from Spanish.

33 Lucy Viedma, "Allt det ni gör för oss spanska barn ska alltid stanna i vårt mine," http://www.arbarkiv.sc/pdf_wrd/viko6.pdf. Samuel Karlsson, an author in Sweden who is researching a book on Rothman, has also confirmed the outlines of Rothman's biography in a telephone conversation with me. There is a small file on Rothman at the Labour Movement Archives and Library in Stockholm, where Viedma is an archivist. Additional articles about her have been printed in the *Värmlands Folkblad* newspaper and can be found at www.vf.se using the newspaper's search engine, "sök."

34 Viedma writes that Rothman worked for the charity and wrote for a Swedish paper. Her work for the Red Cross is noted by Sven Johansson in a 27 November 2004 *Värmlands Folkblad* article and is confirmed elsewhere. That she broadcast for UGT, the General Union of Workers, is confirmed in LAC (Moscow), MG10-K2, 545/6/542, Norman Bethune's personnel file, "Report on the Performance of the Canadian Delegation in Spain," dated 3 April 1937, translated from Spanish.

35 LAC (Moscow), MG10-K2, 545/6/542, Norman Bethune's personnel file, "Report on the Performance of the Canadian Delegation in Spain," dated 3 April 1937, translated from Spanish.

36 Hannant, *The Politics of Passion*, 126. Hannant cites the unpublished memoirs of Kate Mangan, a British woman who worked in the republican press and censorship office, for this reference. Mangan says Kajsa's full name was Kajsa von Rothman.

37 Hannant, *The Politics of Passion*, 361; Ted Allan, *Canadian Magazine* (supplement to the *Toronto Star*), 6 July 1975.

38 ALBA (Moscow), 545/2/147, report on Kajsa Rothman, translated from German.

39 LAC (Moscow), MG10-K2, 545/6/542, Norman Bethune's personnel file, "Report on the Performance of the Canadian Delegation in Spain," 3 April 1937, translated from Spanish.

40 LAC (Moscow), MG10-K2, 545/6/548, Eugene Fogarty's personnel file, report from the International Brigades base to the control commission, 7 April 1937; letter from Oscar Telge, chief of the medical service, to Etat Major, 11 June 1937; and report on Fogarty for John Lawson, c. January 1938. Victor Hoar, citing a private conversation with the historian Cecil Eby, says that Fogarty disappeared from Villanueva de la Jara in 1940. His personnel file, however, reveals that he was no longer in Villanueva de la Jara as of July 1937. The last entry in his file, dated January 1938, records that no further information is available about him.

41 I am grateful to the staff at McGill University Archives who searched graduation records for any trace of Eugene Fogarty; they found none.

42 The rough draft of this letter, dated 21 July 1937, is at LAC, Ted Allan fonds, R2931-0-4-E, vol. 16, file 2. The actual letter, dated 21 July 1937, is in the archives of the Communist International at LAC (Moscow), MG10-K2, 545/6/534. The reference to Bethune having "made many mistakes" appears only in the rough draft. It appears that Sise, Sorensen, and May elected not to include this observation in their final version.

43 Viedma, "Allt det ni gör för oss spanska barn ska alltid stanna i vårt minne."

44 Hannant, *The Politics of Passion*, 164-65.

45 LAC, Ted Allan fonds, R2931-0-4-E, vol. 16, file 1, letter from Bethune to "Elizabeth," November 1937.

Chapter 14: Undesirables

MacBrien's comments appear on a memorandum from Stuart Taylor Wood to MacBrien; MacBrien added his handwritten comments to this memorandum; LAC RG 146, vol. 4183, CSIS files 95-A-00088, Recruiting for Spanish Army Canada, part 3, box 58.

1 CSIS files from access to information request 86-A-57, letter from MacBrien to Skelton, 8 July 1937.

2 CSIS files from access to information request 86-A-57, memorandum from Charles Rivett-Carnac to director of criminal investigation, 27 August 1937.

3 CSIS files from access to information request 86-A-57, letter from MacBrien to Lapointe, 25 August 1937.

4 LAC, RG 146, vol. 4183, CSIS files 95-A-00088, Recruiting for Spanish Army Canada, part 3, box 58, handwritten note attached to a memorandum from Stuart Taylor Wood to MacBrien, 28 August 1937.

5 LAC, RG 146, vol. 4183, CSIS files 95-A-00088, Recruiting for Spanish Army Canada, part 4, box 58, letter from Frederick J. Mead to Wood, 16 December 1937.

6 LAC, RG 146, vol. 4183, CSIS files 95-A-00088, Recruiting for Spanish Army Canada, part 5-A, box 58, François-Philippe Brais to Frederic J. Mead, 28 February 1938.

7 LAC, RG 146, vol. 4183, CSIS files 95-A-00088, Recruiting for Spanish Army Canada, part 5-B, box 58, letter from Frank W. Zaneth to Charles Rivett-Carnac, March 1938.

8 LAC, RG 146, vol. 4183, CSIS files 95-A-00088, Recruiting for Spanish Army Canada, part 5-B, box 58, letter from Frank W. Zaneth to Stuart Taylor Wood, 11 March 1938.

9 LAC, RG 146, vol. 4183, CSIS files 95-A-00088, Recruiting for Spanish Army Canada, part 6, box 58, letter from Cadiz to Stuart Taylor Wood, 25 March 1938.

10 LAC, RG 146, vol. 4183, CSIS files 95-A-00088, Recruiting for Spanish Army Canada, part 6, box 58, letter from Hancock to Stuart Taylor Wood, 22 March 1938.

11 LAC, RG 146, vol. 4183, CSIS files 95-A-00088, Recruiting for Spanish Army Canada, part 6, box 58, letter from Stuart Taylor Wood to Ernest Lapointe, 29 March 1938.

12 LAC, RG 146, vol. 4183, CSIS files 95-A-00088, Recruiting for Spanish Army Canada, part 7, box 58, letter from Stuart Taylor Wood to Deputy Minister of Justice William Stuart Edwards, 12 April 1938. Wood refers to Lapointe's instructions that no further actions be taken regarding prosecutions relating to conspiracy to infringe the provisions of the Foreign Enlistment Act.

13 LAC, RG 146, vol. 4183, CSIS files 95-A-00088, Recruiting for Spanish Army Canada, part 7-A, box 58, letter from Stuart Taylor Wood to Frederick J. Mead, 1 June 1938.

14 LAC, RG 146, vol. 1830, CSIS files 95-A-00088, Edward Cecil-Smith, part 1, box 58, newspaper clipping, *Toronto Daily Star*, 26 December 1939.

15 CBC RA, Harvey Hall, interview with Mac Reynolds, c. 1965.

16 Anonymous, interview with the author, October 2002.

17 Arne Knudsen, telephone interview with the author, 2002.

18 Ibid.

19 CBC RA, Terrence Cunningham, interview with Mac Reynolds, c. 1965.

20 Jules Paivio, interview with the author, Sudbury, September 2002.

21 CBC RA, William Krysa, Mike Storgoff, and Milt Cohen, interviews with Mac Reynolds, c. 1965.

22 LAC, RG 146, vol. 1830, CSIS files 95-A-00088, Edward Cecil-Smith, part 1, box 58, letter from Robert Rose Tait, assistant commissioner, director of criminal investigation, to the "director of organization" at the Department of National Defence; the letter is not dated but appears to date from December 1939, based on surrounding documents in the file.

23 LAC, RG 146, vol. 1880, CSIS files 95-A-00088, Friends of the Mackenzie-Papineau Battalion of

Canada, part 4, box 59, letter from a lieutenant-colonel in army intelligence to Charles Batch, 27 February 1941.

24 LAC, RG 146, vol. 1830, CSIS files 95-A-00088, Edward Cecil-Smith, part 1, box 58, report by Vernon Alfred Miller Kemp, officer commanding at O Division in Toronto, to Stuart Taylor Wood, 30 September 1939.

25 LAC, RG 146, vol. 1830, CSIS files 95-A-00088, Edward Cecil-Smith, part 1, box 58, report by R.J. Smith at the RCMP Toronto branch.

26 CSIS files from access to information request 86-A-57, Wood to Major J.R. Bowler, general secretary of the Canadian Legion, 27 January 1939.

27 LAC, RG 146, vol. 4183, CSIS files 95-A-00088, Recruiting for Spanish Army Canada, part 10, box 58, letter from Bowler to Wood, 27 January 1939.

28 LAC, RG 146, vol. 1881, CSIS files 95-A-00088, Mackenzie-Papineau Battalion (Veterans of), part 1, report by RCMP Toronto branch, 22 November 1946.

29 LAC, RG 146, vol. 4183, CSIS files 95-A-00088, Recruiting for Spanish Army Canada, part 1, supplement 4, box 58, RCMP memorandum to Inspector John Leopold, 19 December 1947.

30 CSIS files from access to information request 86-A-57, RCMP memorandum to officers commanding F, D, A, H, and C divisions, 15 December 1947.

31 LAC, RG 146, vol. 4183, CSIS files 95-A-00088, Recruiting for Spanish Army Canada, part 10, supplement 4, box 58, dispatch from the RCMP Vancouver's special branch, 4 January 1949.

32 LAC, RG 146, vol. 4183, CSIS files 95-A-00088, Recruiting for Spanish Army Canada, part 10, supplement 4, box 58, application by veterans John George Johnson, Niels Madsen, and John McElligott.

33 LAC, RG 146, vol. 4183, CSIS files 95-A-00088, Recruiting for Spanish Army Canada, part 10, supplement 4, box 58, report from Legal Advisor, Corporations Branch, Department of Consumer and Corporate Affairs, 26 January 1971.

34 LAC, RG 146, vol. 4183, CSIS files 95-A-00088, Recruiting for Spanish Army Canada, part 10, supplement 4, box 58, letter from Parent to Rettie, 23 December 1970.

35 LAC, RG 146, vol. 4183, CSIS files 95-A-00088, Recruiting for Spanish Army Canada, part 10, supplement 4, box 58, Department of External Affairs, 15 December 1970.

36 LAC, RG 146, vol. 1880, CSIS files 95-A-00088, Friends of the Mackenzie-Papineau Battalion of Canada, part 6, box 59. The most recent document I could find in this file is a July 1984 Mackenzie-Papineau Battalion veterans' newsletter.

37 LAC, RG 146, vol. 1880, CSIS files 95-A-00088, Friends of the Mackenzie-Papineau Battalion of Canada, part 6, box 59, RCMP report, 25 June 1980.

Conclusion

1 LAC, Victor Himmelfarb, interview with Mac Reynolds, c. 1965.

2 Fred Kostyk, interview with the author, Montreal, 10 September 2002.

3 LAC, Mackenzie-Papineau Battalion collection, MG30-E173, vol. 4, file 17, Walter E. Dent papers. This statement, taken from a short memoir, was written in the 1970s or 1980s, but the speaker later asked not to be identified.

4 LAC, Mackenzie-Papineau Battalion collection, MG30-E173, vol. 2, file 24, Walter E. Dent papers, Walter Dent, interview with Charles G. Roland, 21 May 1980.

5 CBC RA, John "Paddy" McElligott, interview with Mac Reynolds, c. 1965.

6 Manuel Alvarez, *The Tall Soldier: My 40-Year Search for the Man Who Saved My Life* (Vancouver: New Star Books, 1983), 226.

7 LAC, RG 146, vol. 1880, CSIS files 95-00088, Friends of the Mackenzie-Papineau Battalion of Canada, part 6, box 59, newspaper clipping, Communist Party of Canada, *Pacific Tribune*, c. October 1979.

8 LAC, RG 146, vol. 1880, CSIS files 95-00088, Friends of the Mackenzie-Papineau Battalion of Canada, part 6, box 59, newspaper clipping, Peter Krawchuk, *Canadian Tribune*, 15 October 1979, published by the Communist Party of Canada.

9 LAC, Ron Liversedge, interview with Mac Reynolds, c. 1965.

10 Fred Kostyk, interview with the author, Montreal, 10 September 2002.

Postscript

1 Jules Paivio, interview with the author, Sudbury, September 2002.
2 Carl Geiser, telephone interview with the author, 2 October 2002.
3 Fred Kostyk, interview with the author, Montreal, 10 September 2004.
4 William Krehm, interview with the author, Toronto, 28 November 2004.

Select Bibliography

Alexander, Bill. *British Volunteers for Liberty: Spain – 1936-39*. London: Lawrence and Wishart, 1986.

Allan, Ted, and Sydney Gordon. *The Scalpel, The Sword: The Story of Dr. Norman Bethune*. Toronto: McClelland and Stewart, 1952.

Alpert, Michael. *A New International History of the Spanish Civil War*. London: Palgrave Macmillan, 2004.

Alvarez, Manuel. *The Tall Soldier: My 40-Year Search for the Man Who Saved My Life*. Vancouver: New Star Books, 1983.

Alvarez, Santiago. *Historia politica y militar de las Brigadas Internacionales*. Madrid: Compañía Literaria, 1996.

Andrew, Christopher, and Vasili Mitrokhin. *The Sword and the Shield: The Mitrokhin Archive and the Secret History of the KGB*. New York: Basic Books, 1999.

Angus, Ian. *Canadian Bolsheviks: The Early Years of the Communist Party of Canada*. Montreal: Vanguard Publications, 1981.

Avakumovic, Ivan. *The Communist Party in Canada: A History*. Toronto: McClelland and Stewart, 1975.

Balfour, Sebastian, and Paul Preston, eds. *Spain and the Great Powers in the Twentieth Century*. London: Routledge, 1999.

Baxell, Richard. *British Volunteers in the Spanish Civil War: The British Battalion in the International Brigades, 1936-1939*. London: Routledge, 2004.

Beeching, William C. *Canadian Volunteers: Spain 1936-1939*. Regina: Canadian Plains Research Center, 1989.

Beeching, William C., and Phyllis Clarke, eds. *Yours in the Struggle: Reminiscences of Tim Buck*. Toronto: NC Press, 1977.

Beevor, Antony. *The Battle for Spain: The Spanish Civil War 1936-1939*. London: Penguin Books, 2006.

—. *The Spanish Civil War*. London: Orbis Publishing, 1982.

Bessie, Alvah. *Alvah Bessie's Spanish Civil War Notebooks*. Edited by Dan Bessie. Lexington: University Press of Kentucky, 2001.

—. *Men in Battle*. New York: Veterans of the Abraham Lincoln Brigade, 1954.

Borkenau, Franz. *The Spanish Cockpit: An Eye-witness Account of the Political and Social Conflicts of the Spanish Civil War*. London: Faber and Faber, 1937.

Brenan, Gerald. *The Spanish Labyrinth: An Account of the Social and Political Background of the Civil War*. Cambridge: Cambridge University Press, 1943.

Brome, Vincent. *The International Brigades*. London: Heinemann, 1965.

Buchanan, Tom. "Anti-Fascism and Democracy in the 1930s." *European History Quarterly* 32, 1 (2002): 39-57.

—. "'A Far Away Country of Which We Know Nothing'?: Perceptions of Spain and Its Civil War in Britain, 1931-1939." *Twentieth Century British History* 4, 1 (1993): 1-24.

—. *Britain and the Spanish Civil War*. Cambridge: Cambridge University Press, 1997.

—. "Britain's Popular Front? Aid Spain and the British Labour Movement." *History Workshop* 31 (Spring 1991): 60-73.

—. "The Death of Bob Smillie, the Spanish Civil War, and the Eclipse of the Independent Labour Party." *The Historical Journal* 40, 2 (June 1997): 435-61.

Carr, E.H. *The Comintern and the Spanish Civil War*. New York: Pantheon Books, 1984.

Carr, Raymond. *The Spanish Tragedy: The Civil War in Perspective*. London: Weidenfeld and Nicolson, 1987.

Carroll, Peter N. *The Odyssey of the Abraham Lincoln Brigade: Americans in the Spanish Civil War*. Stanford, CA: Stanford University Press, 1994.

Cunningham, Valentine, ed. *The Penguin Book of Spanish Civil War Verse*. Harmondsworth, UK: Penguin Books, 1980.

—, ed. *Spanish Front: Writers on the Civil War*. New York: Oxford University Press, 1986.

Dallet, Joe. *Letters from Spain: An American Volunteer to His Wife*. New York: Workers Library Publishers, 1938.

Delisle, Esther. *The Traitor and the Jew: Anti-Semitism and the Delirium of Extremist Right-Wing Nationalism in French Canada from 1929 to 1939*. Translated by Madeleine Hébert, with Claire Rothman and Käthe Roth. 2nd ed., rev. Montreal: R. Davies Publishing, 1993.

Eby, Cecil. *Between the Bullet and the Lie: American Volunteers in the Spanish Civil War*. New York: Holt, Rinehart, and Winston, 1969.

Esenwein, George, and Adrian Shubert. *Spain at War: The Spanish Civil War in Context 1931-1939*. London: Longman, 1995.

Felsen, Milt. *The Anti-Warrior: A Memoir*. Iowa City: University of Iowa, 1989.

Heikkinen, K.E., ed. *Our Boys in Spain*. Translated by Matti A. Mattson. Finnish Workers Federation, 1939. Reprint. N.p.: n.p., 2002.

Fisher, Harry. *Comrades: Tales of a Brigidista in the Spanish Civil War*. Lincoln: University of Nebraska Press, 1998.

Francis, Hywel. *Miners against Fascism*. London: Lawrence and Wishart, 1984.

—. "'Say Nothing and Leave in the Middle of the Night': The Spanish Civil War Revisited." *History Workshop Journal* 32 (Autumn 1991): 69-76.

Fraser, Ronald. *Blood of Spain: An Oral History of the Spanish Civil War*. New York: Penguin Books, 1981.

Garner, Hugh. *One Damn Thing after Another: The Life Story of a Canadian Writer, an Autobiography*. Toronto: McGraw-Hill Ryerson, 1973.

Geiser, Carl. *Prisoners of the Good Fight: The Spanish Civil War 1936-1939*. Westport, CT: Lawrence Hill and Company, 1986.

Gerassi, John. *The Premature Antifascists: North American Volunteers in the Spanish Civil War, 1936-39, an Oral History*. New York: Praeger, 1986.

Gibbs Ervin, Randy. "The Men of the Mackenzie-Papineau Battalion: A Case Study of the Involvement of the International Communist Movement in the Spanish Civil War." MA thesis, Carleton University, 1972.

Graham, Helen. *The Spanish Civil War: A Very Short Introduction*. Oxford: Oxford University Press, 2005.

—. *The Spanish Republic at War, 1936-1939*. New York: Cambridge, MA: Cambridge University Press, 2002.

Gurney, Jason. *Crusade in Spain*. Newton Abbot: Readers Union, 1974.

Halton, Matthew. *Ten Years to Alamein*. Toronto: S.J. Reginald Saunders and Company, 1944.

Hannant, Larry, ed. *The Politics of Passion: Norman Bethune's Writing and Art*. Toronto: University of Toronto Press, 1998.

Harrison, Stanley. *Good to Be Alive: The Story of Jack Brent*. London: Lawrence and Wishart, 1954.

Haynes, John Earl, and Harvey Klehr. *Venona: Decoding Soviet Espionage in America*. New Haven, CT: Yale University Press, 1999.

Heney, Chris. *The Ebro 1938: Death Knell of the Republic*. Oxford: Osprey, 1999.

Hoar, Victor, with Mac Reynolds. *The Mackenzie-Papineau Battalion*. Toronto: Copp Clark, 1969.

Hopkins, James K. *Into the Heart of the Fire: The British in the Spanish Civil War*. Stanford, CA: Stanford University Press, 1998.

Horne, Harold. *All the Trees Were Bread and Cheese: The Making of a Rebel*. Luton: Owen Hardisty, 1998.

Howson, Gerald. *Arms for Spain: The Untold Story of the Spanish Civil War*. London: John Murray, 1998.

Inglis, Amirah. *Australians in the Spanish Civil War*. London: Allen and Unwin, 1987.

Jackson, Angela. *At the Margins of Mayhem: Prologue and Epilogue to the Last Great Battle of the Spanish Civil War*. Torfaen: Warren and Pell Publishing, 2007.

Jackson, Gabriel. *The Spanish Republic and the Civil War, 1931-1939.* Princeton, NJ: Princeton University Press, 1965.

Jackson, Michael. *Fallen Sparrows: The International Brigades in the Spanish Civil War.* Philadelphia: American Philosophical Society, 1994.

Johnston, Verle B. *Legions of Babel: The International Brigades in the Spanish Civil War.* University Park and London: Pennsylvania State University Press, 1967.

Kealey, Gregory S., and Reg Whitaker, eds. *R.C.M.P. Security Bulletins: The Depression Years, Part III, 1936.* St. John's, NF: Canadian Committee on Labour History, 1996.

—, eds. *R.C.M.P. Security Bulletins: The Depression Years, Part IV, 1937.* St. John's, NF: Canadian Committee on Labour History, 1997.

—, eds. *R.C.M.P. Security Bulletins: The Depression Years, Part V, 1938-1939.* St. John's, NF: Canadian Committee on Labour History, 1997.

Keene, Judith. *Fighting for Franco: International Volunteers in Nationalist Spain during the Spanish Civil War, 1936-39.* London: Leicester University Press, 2001.

Kemp, Peter. *Mine Were of Trouble.* London: Cassell, 1957.

Klehr, Harvey, John Earl Haynes, and Fridrikh Igorevich Firsov. *Secret World of American Communism.* New Haven, CT: Yale University Press, 1995.

Knight, Amy. *How the Cold War Began: The Gouzenko Affair and the Hunt for Soviet Spies.* Toronto: McClelland and Stewart, 2005.

Komodowski, John "Ed," and Fred Kostyk, eds. "With the Mackenzie-Papineau Battalion in Spain." Scrapbook ms. Winnipeg, 1980.

Kraljic, John Peter. "The Croatian Community in North American and the Spanish Civil War." MA thesis, City University of New York, 2002.

Landis, Arthur. *The Abraham Lincoln Brigade.* New York: The Citadel Press, 1967.

Lannon, Frances. *The Spanish Civil War, 1936-1939.* Oxford: Osprey, 2003.

Lee, Laurie. *A Moment of War.* London: Penguin Books, 1991.

—. *As I Walked Out One Midsummer Morning.* London: W.W. Norton and Company, 1969.

Lethbridge, David, ed. *Bethune: The Secret Police File.* Salmon Arm, BC: Undercurrent Press, 2003.

Lewis, Greg. *A Bullet Saved My Life: The Remarkable Adventures of Bob Peters. An Untold Story of the Spanish Civil War.* Torfaen: Warren and Pell Publishing, 2006.

Lobigs, Martin H.P. "Canadian Responses to the Mackenzie-Papineau Battalion, 1936 to 1939." MA thesis, University of New Brunswick, 1992.

Los Canadienses. 58 mins. Directed by Albert Kish. Ottawa: National Film Board of Canada, 1975.

Lunan, Gordon. *The Making of a Spy: A Political Odyssey.* Montreal: R. Davies Publishing, 1995.

Malraux, André. *Man's Hope.* Translated by Stuart Gilbert and Alastair Macdonald. 1938. Reprint, New York: Modern Library, 1983.

Markotich, Stanley. "International Communism and the Communist Party of Canada." PhD diss., Indiana University, 1992.

Matthews, Herbert. *Two Wars and More to Come.* New York: Carrick and Evans, 1938.

McLellan, Josie. *Antifascism and Memory in East Germany: Remembering the International Brigades 1945-1989.* Oxford: Oxford University Press, 2004.

Momryk, Myron. "The Fighting Canucks: A Biographical Dictionary of Canadians in the Spanish Civil War." Unpublished copy in possession of author.

—. "'For Your Freedom and for Ours': Konstantin (Mike) Olynyk, a Ukrainian Volunteer from Canada in the International Brigades." *Canadian Ethnic Studies/Etudes Ethniques au Canada* 10, 2 (1988): 124-34.

—. "Hungarian Volunteers from Canada in the Spanish Civil War, 1936-39." *Hungarian Studies Review* 24, 1-2 (1997): 3-14.

—. "Jewish Volunteers from Canada in the Spanish Civil War." *Outlook* 34, 5 (July/August 1996): 13-15, 30.

—. "Ukrainian Volunteers from Canada in the International Brigades, Spain, 1936-39: A Profile." *Journal of Ukrainian Studies* 16, 1-2 (Summer-Winter 1991): 181-94.

Neila, Jesús Majada, ed. *Norman Bethune: El crimen de la carretera Málaga – Almería (febrero de 1937).* Granada: N.p., 2004.

Orlov, Alexander. *The March of Time: Reminiscences.* London: St. Ermin's Press, 2004.

Orwell, George. *Homage to Catalonia.* 1938. Reprint, New York: Harvest/HBJ Books, 1980.

Page, Gregory. "Ideology and the Canadians in the Spanish Civil War, 1936-9." MA thesis, University of New Brunswick, 1998.

Parenteau, Ian. "The Anti-Fascism of the Canadian Volunteers in the Spanish Civil War, 1936-1939." MA thesis, University of New Brunswick, 1999.

Payne, Stanley G. *The Spanish Civil War, the Soviet Union, and Communism.* New Haven, CT: Yale University Press, 2004.

Peck, Mary Biggar. *Red Moon Over Spain: Canadian Media Reaction to the Spanish Civil War, 1936-1939.* Ottawa: Steel Rail, 1988.

Preston, Paul. *A Concise History of the Spanish Civil War.* London: Fontana Press, 1996.

—, ed. *Revolution and War in Spain 1931-1939.* New York: Methuen, 1984.

Preston, Paul, and Ann L. Mackenzie, eds. *The Republic Besieged: Civil War in Spain 1936-1939.* Edinburgh: Edinburgh University Press, 1996.

Radosh, Ronald, Mary R. Habeck, and Grigory Sevostianov, eds. *Spain Betrayed: The Soviet Union and the Spanish Civil War.* New Haven, CT: Yale University Press, 2001.

Rankin, Nicholas. *Telegram from Guernica.* London: Faber and Faber, 2003.

Regler, Gustav. *The Owl of Minerva: The Autobiography of Gustav Regler.* Translated by Norman Denny. London: Rupert Hart-Davis, 1959.

Rees, Tim, and Andrew Thorpe, eds. *International Communism and the Communist International, 1919-43.* Manchester: Manchester University Press, 1999.

Richardson, R. Dan. *Comintern Army.* Lexington: University Press of Kentucky, 1982.

Rolfe, Edwin. *The Lincoln Battalion: The Story of the Americans Who Fought in the International Brigades.* New York: Random House, 1939.

Rosenstone, Robert. *Crusade of the Left: The Lincoln Battalion in the Spanish Civil War.* New York: Pegasus, 1969.

Rubin, Hank. *Spain's Cause Was Mine: A Memoir of an American Medic in the Spanish Civil War.* Carbondale and Edwardsville: Southern Illinois University Press, 1997.

Rust, William. *Britons in Spain: The History of the British Battalion of the XVth International Brigade.* London: Lawrence and Wishart, 1939.

Ryan, Frank, ed. *The Book of the XV Brigade.* Madrid: Commissariat of War, XV Brigade, 1938.

Skoutelsky, Rémi. *L'espoir guidait leurs pas: Les volontaires français dans les Brigades Internationales, 1936-1939.* Paris: B. Grasset, 1998.

Sloan, Pat, ed. *John Cornford: A Memoir.* London: Jonathan Cape, 1938.

Stephens, D.P. (Pat). *A Memoir of the Spanish Civil War: An Armenian-Canadian in the Lincoln Battalion.* Edited by Rick Rennie. St. John's, NF: Canadian Committee on Labour History, 2000.

Stewart, Roderick. *Bethune.* Hamden, CT: Archon Books, 1979.

Stradling, Robert. *History and Legend: Writing the International Brigades.* Cardiff: University of Wales Press, 2003.

—. *The Irish and the Spanish Civil War, 1936-1939: Crusades in Conflict.* Manchester: Manchester University Press, 1999.

—. *Wales and the Spanish Civil War: The Dragon's Dearest Cause?* Cardiff: University of Wales Press, 2004.

Thomas, Frank. *Brother against Brother: Experiences of a British Volunteer in the Spanish Civil War.* Edited by Robert Stradling. Thrupp: Alan Sutton Publishing, 1998.

Thomas, Fred. *To Tilt at Windmills: A Memoir of the Spanish Civil War.* East Lansing: Michigan State University Press, 1996.

Thomas, Hugh. *The Spanish Civil War.* London: Penguin Books, 1977.

Voros, Sandor. *American Commissar.* Philadelphia: Chilton, 1961.

Vulpe, Nicola, ed., with Maha Albari. *Sealed in Struggle: Canadian Poetry and the Spanish Civil War.* Tenerife: El Centro de Estudios Canadienses de la Universidad de la Laguna, 1995.

Waiser, Bill. *All Hell Can't Stop Us: The On-to-Ottawa Trek and Regina Riot.* Calgary: Fifth House, 2003.

Wheeler, George. *To Make the People Smile Again: A Memoir of the Spanish Civil War.* Edited by David Leach. Newcastle upon Tyne: Zymurgy, 2003.

Wolff, Milton. *Another Hill.* Urbana and Chicago: University of Illinois Press, 1994.

Wyden, Peter. *The Passionate War: The Narrative History of the Spanish Civil War, 1936-1939.* New York: Simon and Schuster, 1983.

Zuehlke, Mark. *The Gallant Cause: Canadians in the Spanish Civil War 1936-1939*. Vancouver: Whitecap Books, 1996.

Index

Gandesa, 91, 96

Garner, Hugh: assignment to labour company, 130; on Brunete battle, 68; on difficulties being recruited for Spain, 53-54; on *esprit de corps* of Canadian volunteers, 48; on Jarama battle, 62, 64; on physical examination for recruits, 56; request for repatriation, 121-23

Garrow, Clifford Gordon, 123

Gates, John: on desertion of volunteers, 97, 98, 119-20, 131-32; evaluation of James McDowell, 118; evaluation of John Grainger, 116; evaluation of John McElligott, 119; on execution of deserters, 132; photograph, Plate 11 *following p. 74*

Gawrycki, Walter: departure for Spain, 53; difficulty of Depression for immigrant, 33; familiarity with cause of Spanish Republic, 37; lack of equipment in Spain, 94

Geiser, Carl: on death of Beckett, 11; on escape from execution (Mar. 1938), 88, 185; on executing prisoners, 72, 73; on illness in battalion (Mar. 1938), 87; on life in nationalist prison, 90; on roughness of Canadians, 25

George Washington Battalion: amalgamation into Lincoln Battalion, 65, 69; in Brunete offensive, 68, 69; Canadians in, 65; reason for name, 23

Germany: air support at Teruel, 80; attacks on Durango and Guernica, 145; captured airman, Plate 18 *following p. 74*; military assistance to nationalists, xiv-xv, 5

Gillis, Roderick, 77

Goldenberg, Israel, 12

Gould, Max, 155

Gouzenko, Igor, 41

Grainger, John, 116-17

Granollers, Plate 17 *following p. 74*

Greysdale, Fred, 116

Grupo de Información, 153

Guernica massacre, 66, 145

Hadesbeck, Frank: on esprit de corps, 48; on forced surrender of passport, 59; on motivation for fighting in Spain, 31; screening and repatriation, 103

Hall, Harvey, 31, 42, 174

Halton, Matthew, 102

Hamilton, Robert, 114, 128, 134-35

Hamilton, William, 53

Hancock, William, 172

Hellund, Walter, Plate 1 *following p. 74*

Hemingway, Ernest, 69

Higgins, Jim, 96, 182

Hill 609, Sierra de Pàndols, 96-97

Hill 666, Sierra de Pàndols, 96

Hilton, Percy: on commitment to Communist

Party, 44; on feeding the battalion at Teruel, 81; repatriation to Canada, 105; retreat in Aragón (Mar. 1938), 85; on town of Figueras, 59; on treatment as nationalist prisoner, 90

Himmelfarb, Victor, 181

Historical Commission of the International Brigades, 12

Hitler, Adolf, xiv-xv, 5. *See also* Germany

Hoar, Victor, 6

Hrvatski glas (newspaper), 35

Huesca offensive, 66

Huhtala, Sulo, 87

Hungarian-Canadian volunteers, 22-23

Hunter, Peter, 52-53

Hyduk, Mike, 90

Ibárruri, Dolores (La Pasionaria), 100

immigrants to Canada: difficulties during Depression, 27; familiarity of cause of Spanish Republic, 37-38; politically radicalized in Europe, 33-36, 38; repatriation of foreign-born volunteers, 103, 105, 174; volunteers for Spanish Civil War, 21-23, 48-49

Imperial War Museum, 7

Industrial Workers of the World (Wobblies), 24, 141

International Brigades: accomplishment in Spanish Civil War, 183-84; contempt of Spanish nationalists, 89; defence of Madrid (1936), xvii; definition of appropriate punishments, 130-31; discipline (*see* punishment and discipline); executions, 131-34; global support for anti-fascist cause, xvii, 6; Historical Commission, 12; lack of equipment in Spain, 66-67, 94, Plate 35 *following p. 138*; obscurity of many volunteers, 11-12; overview, xvi-xviii; record-keeping, 11-12; recruitment of international volunteers, xvi-xvii; relaxation, Plate 9 and 10 *following p. 74*; run by Soviet-trained Europeans, 135; training, 62, 73, 76, 87, 95, Plate 32 *following p. 138*; view of Trotskyism, 112-19. *See also* 15th International Brigade

Irish-Canadian volunteers, 35-36

Irish Republican Army, 35, 36

Irish volunteers, 25, 35, 36

Italy: Aragón offensive, 84, 86, 88; defeat at Guadalajara, 79; destruction of Durango, 145; ending resistance in northern Spain, 69; forced Italianization of Istria, 34; military assistance to nationalists, xiv-xv

Jarama, battle of (February 1937), 61-64, Plate 42 *following p. 138*

Jardas, Ed, 39, 65

Jewish volunteers in Spanish Civil War: